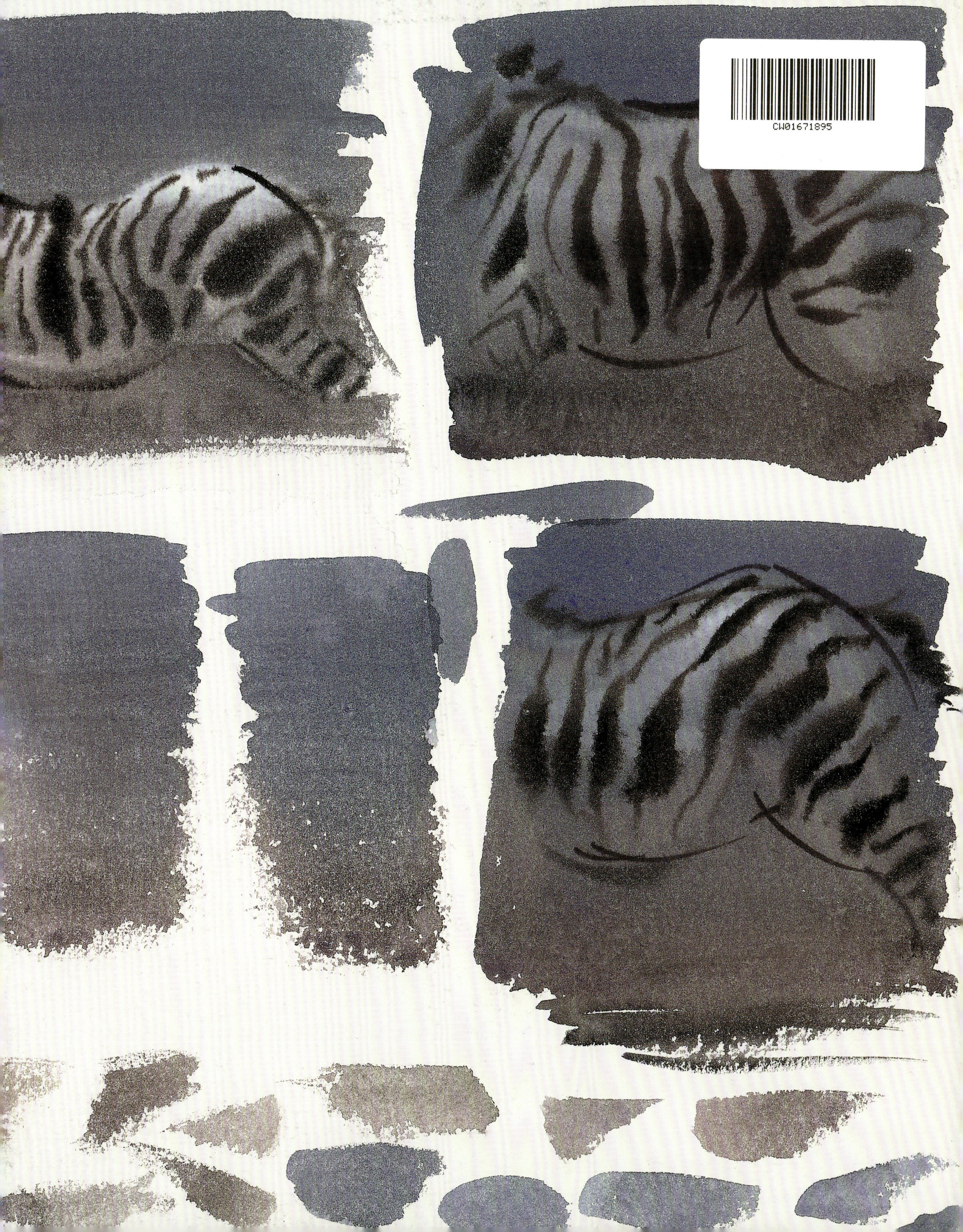

LANGFORD PRESS 2006

in association with THE WILDLIFE ART GALLERY

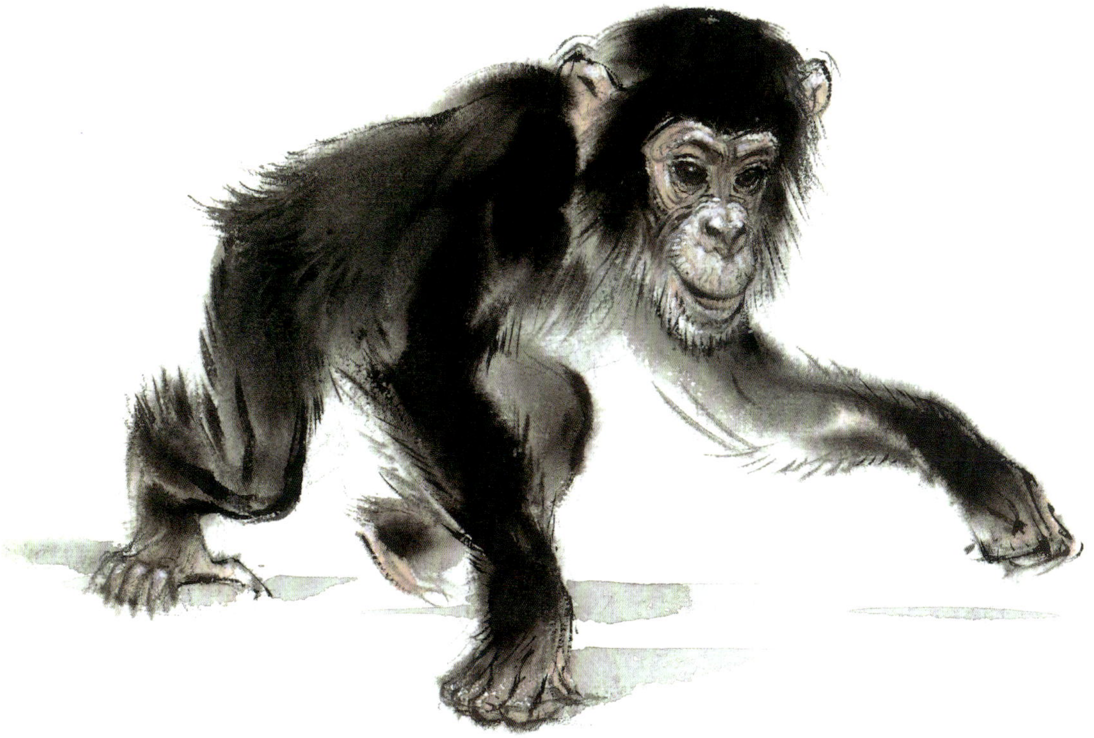

Dance of the Brush

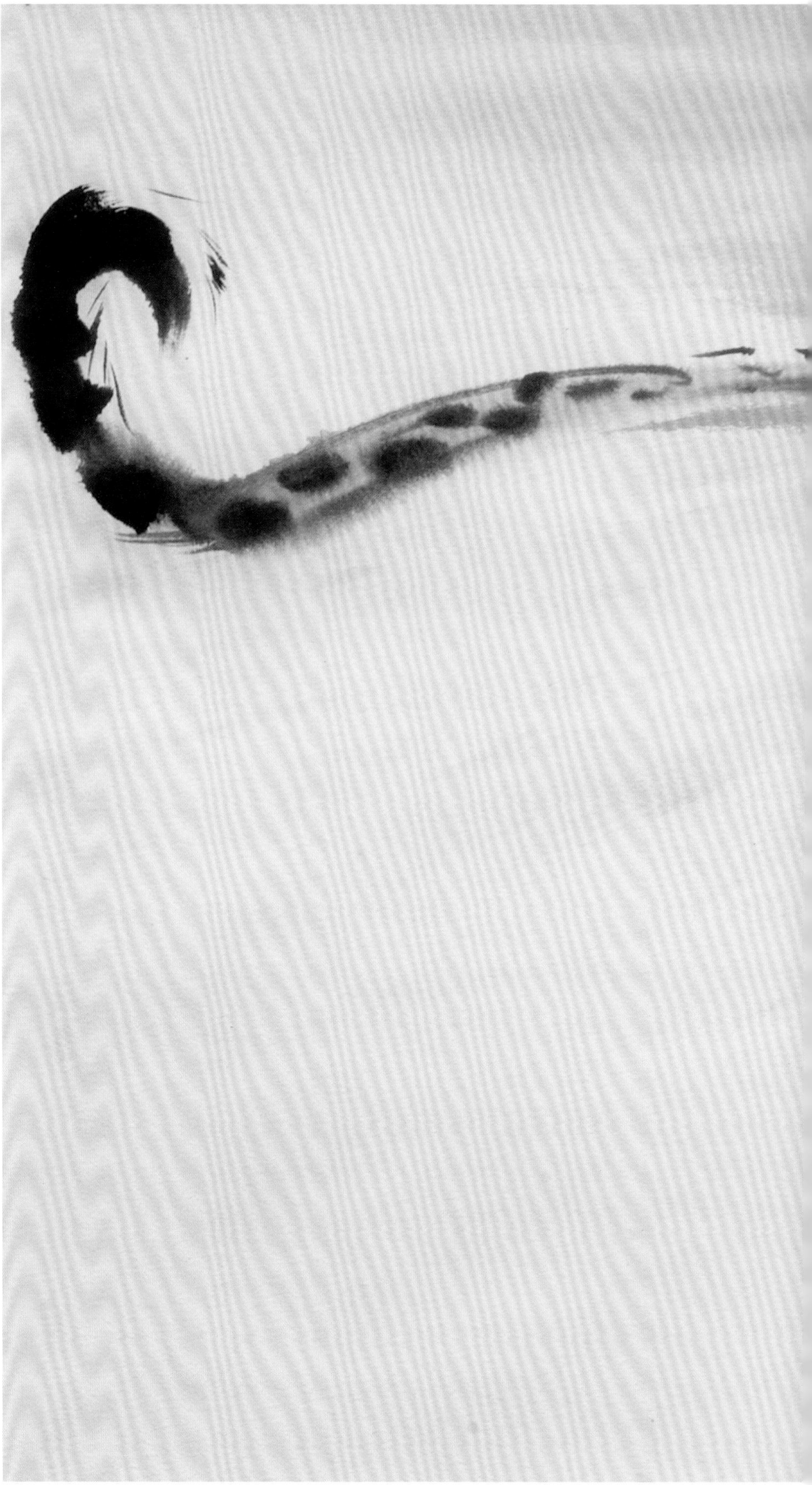

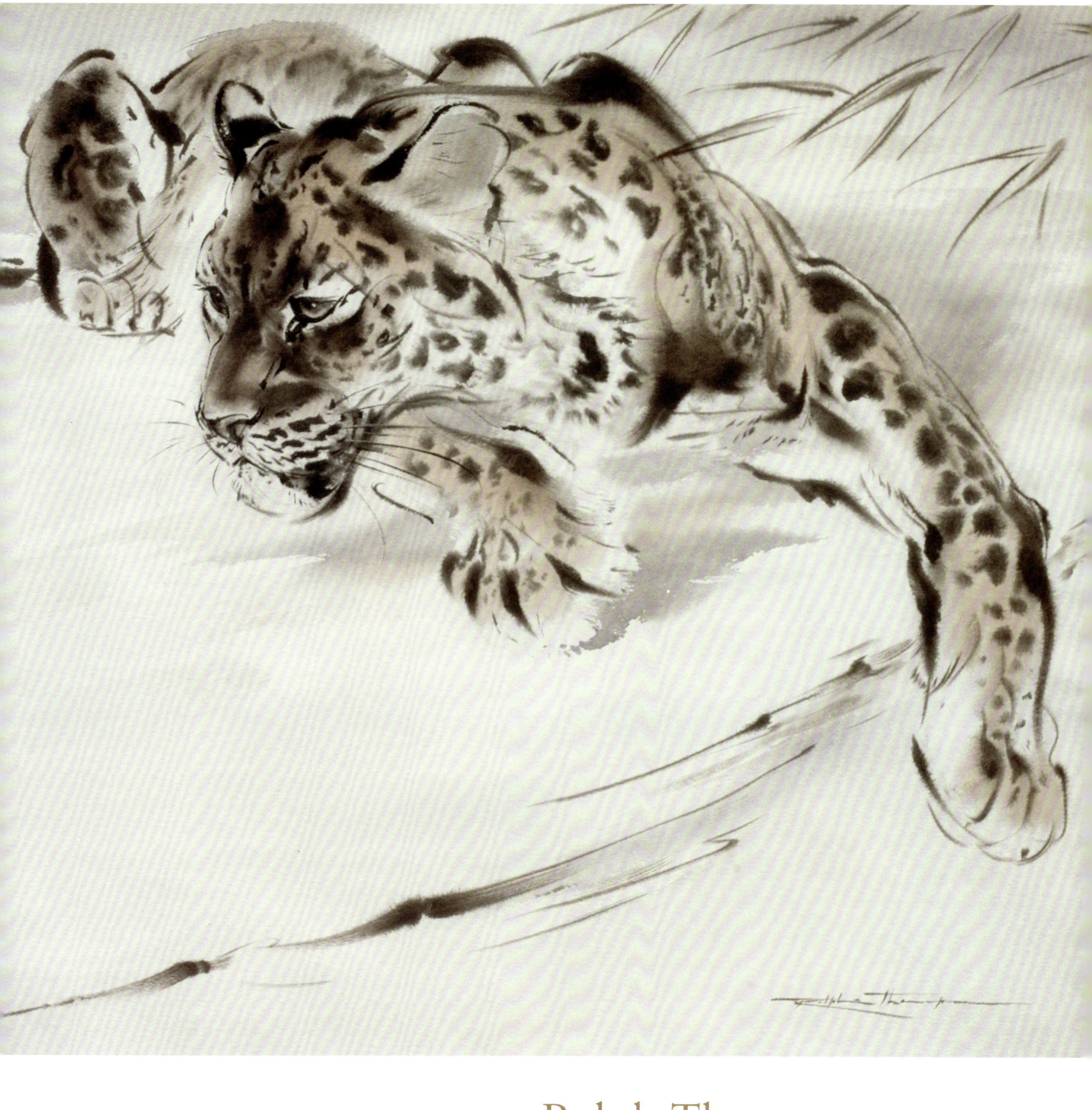

Ralph Thompson MBE

Sometimes the work comes effortlessly as intended. Sometimes it must be torn up. Sometimes the steps of the ***dance of the brush*** *become very complicated indeed. Often there is quite a battle. With the pressures of everyday life it is so easy to lose the trail. I need one or two trusted friends who will say exactly what they think. The work needs to have a lot of love and luck – and laughter – to help cope with the flops.*

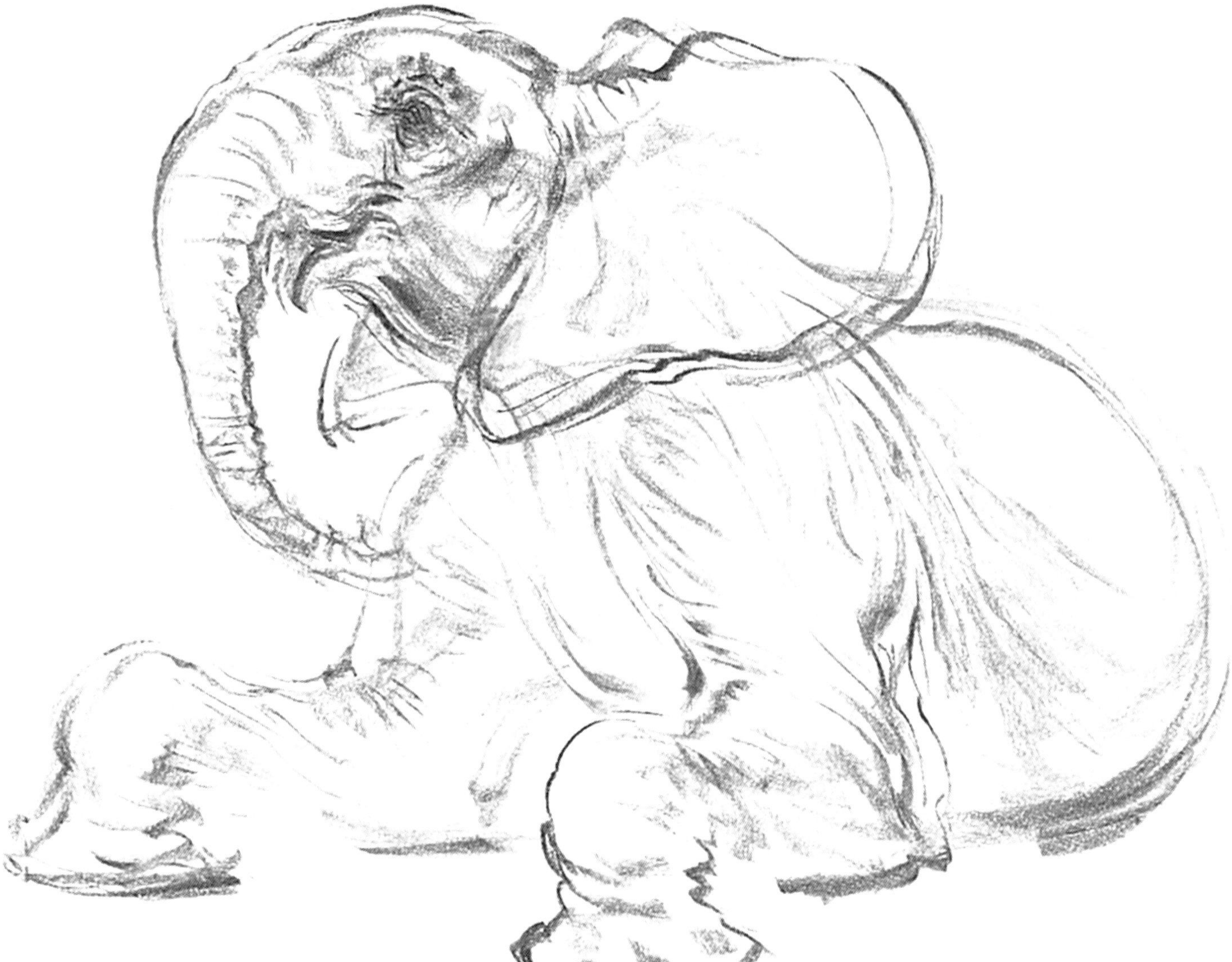

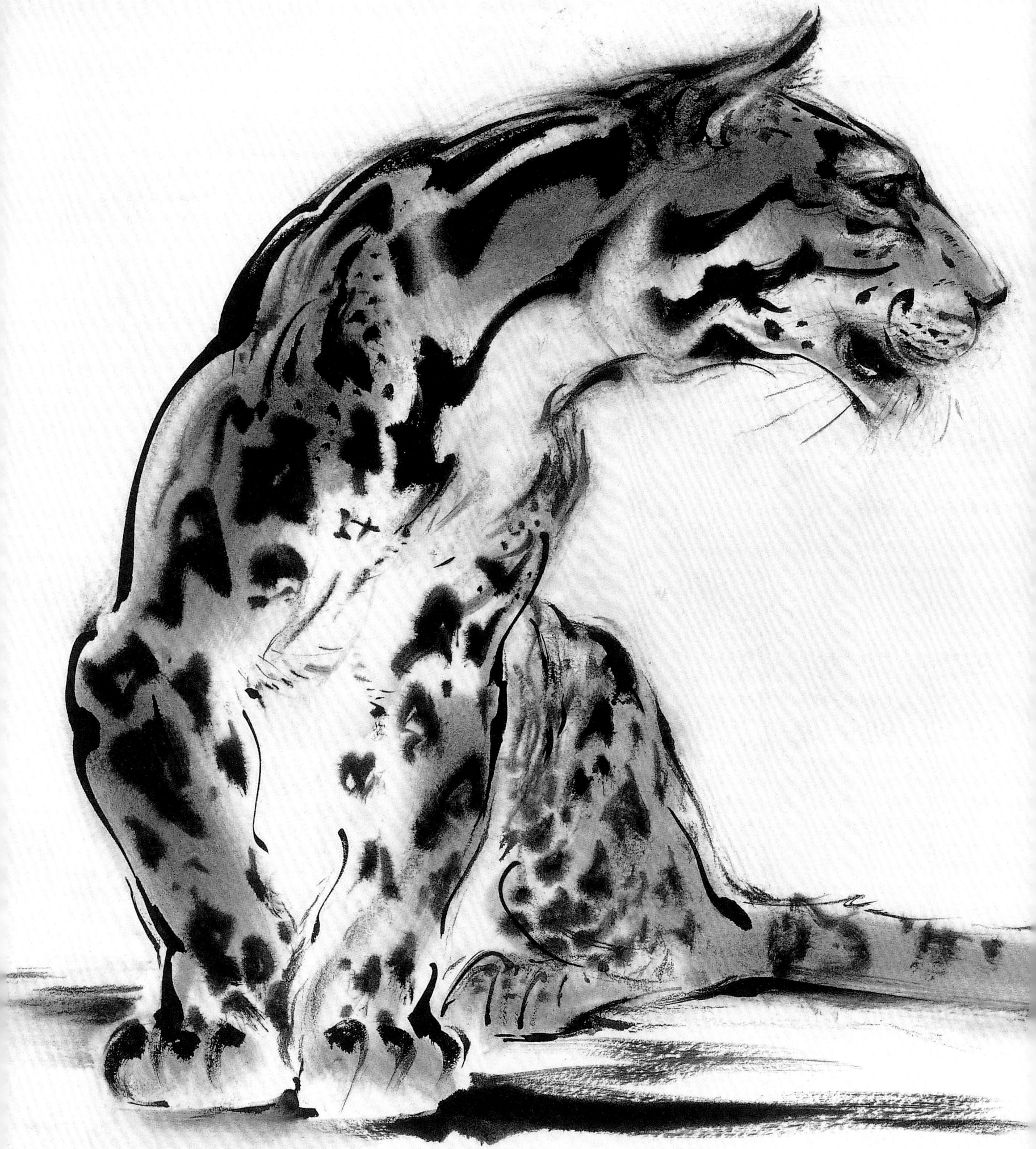

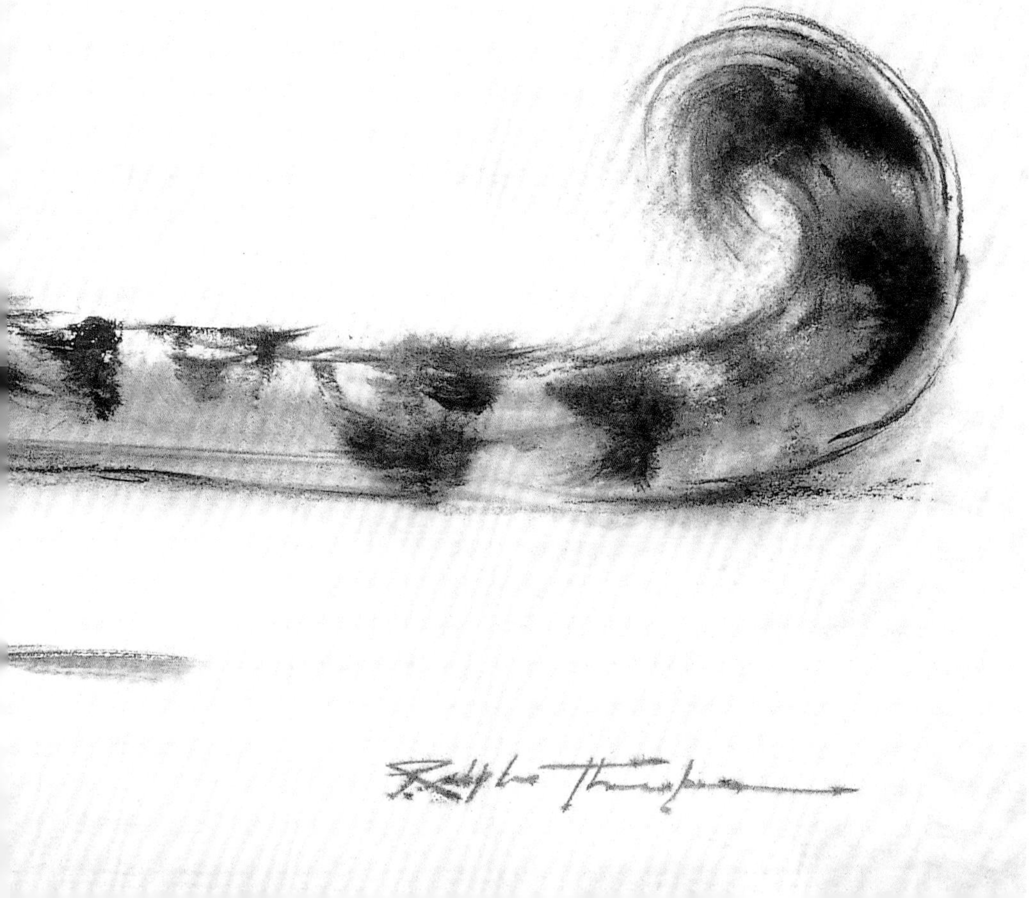

Clouded leopard
watercolour
470 × 650mm

Page 3
Young chimpanzee
watercolour
160 × 270mm

page 5
Leopard
watercolour
500 × 810mm

page 7
Baby elephant
charcoal drawing
300 × 410mm

Acknowledgments

Once you start on 'thank you's', where do you stop? However, I do wish to thank, my stepson Wyn Reilly, who has done so much to keep my life and work going over recent years; for helping with this book, sorting out my scribbles and producing a typewritten script. I am also indebted to my friend Nola Edgar for her ability to decipher and type some of my first attempts.

There is no way of thanking all the animals that have played such an important part in my life but I do wish to thank all those who have made it possible for their lives to continue in their own natural world. May I take this opportunity to thank David Attenborough and his skilled photographers for bringing the ways of wild animals so vividly into our homes.

I am truly grateful to the first rate sculptor and draughtsman, Jonathan Kenworthy, for his companionship and constructive criticism, especially over several formative years. I am indebted to Robert Gillmor for his generous introduction. Coming from such a good artist and skilled craftsman, I find his praise most gratifying. Thanks are also due to Lee Durrell for kindly allowing us to reproduce her late husband's hilarious, if exaggerated, introduction to 'A Brush with Animals'.

There are so many other people who have helped me in a multitude of ways to keep going and to focus on my work. Those who immediately spring to mind include, Greg Speller, Chris Tyrell, Philip Corbet, Barbara Dent, Mary Fallon and indeed many others whose names, I fear, have slipped my mind.

I would also like to thank Ian Langford of Langford Press for publishing this book. Last, but my no means least, I offer a particularly warm "thank you" to Andrew Haslen and Graham Barker of the Wildlife Art Gallery for their hard work and boundless patience in producing this book.

First published 2006

Langford Press, 10 New Road, Langtoft,
Peterborough PE 6 9 LE
Tel / Fax: 01778 341132
www.langford-press.co.uk
Email: sales@langford-press.co.uk

Designed & Edited by The Wildlife Art Gallery, Lavenham, Suffolk.
www.wildlifeartgallery.com

Printed & Bound by Healeys Printers, Ipswich, Suffolk.
Origination by Dean Hearn.

A cip Record for this book is available from the British Library.

ISBN 1-904078-21-4
978-1-904078-21-0

opposite
White-handed gibbon
watercolour
380 × 310mm

following page
Study of eagle owl stretching wings forward
charcoal drawing
730 × 540mm

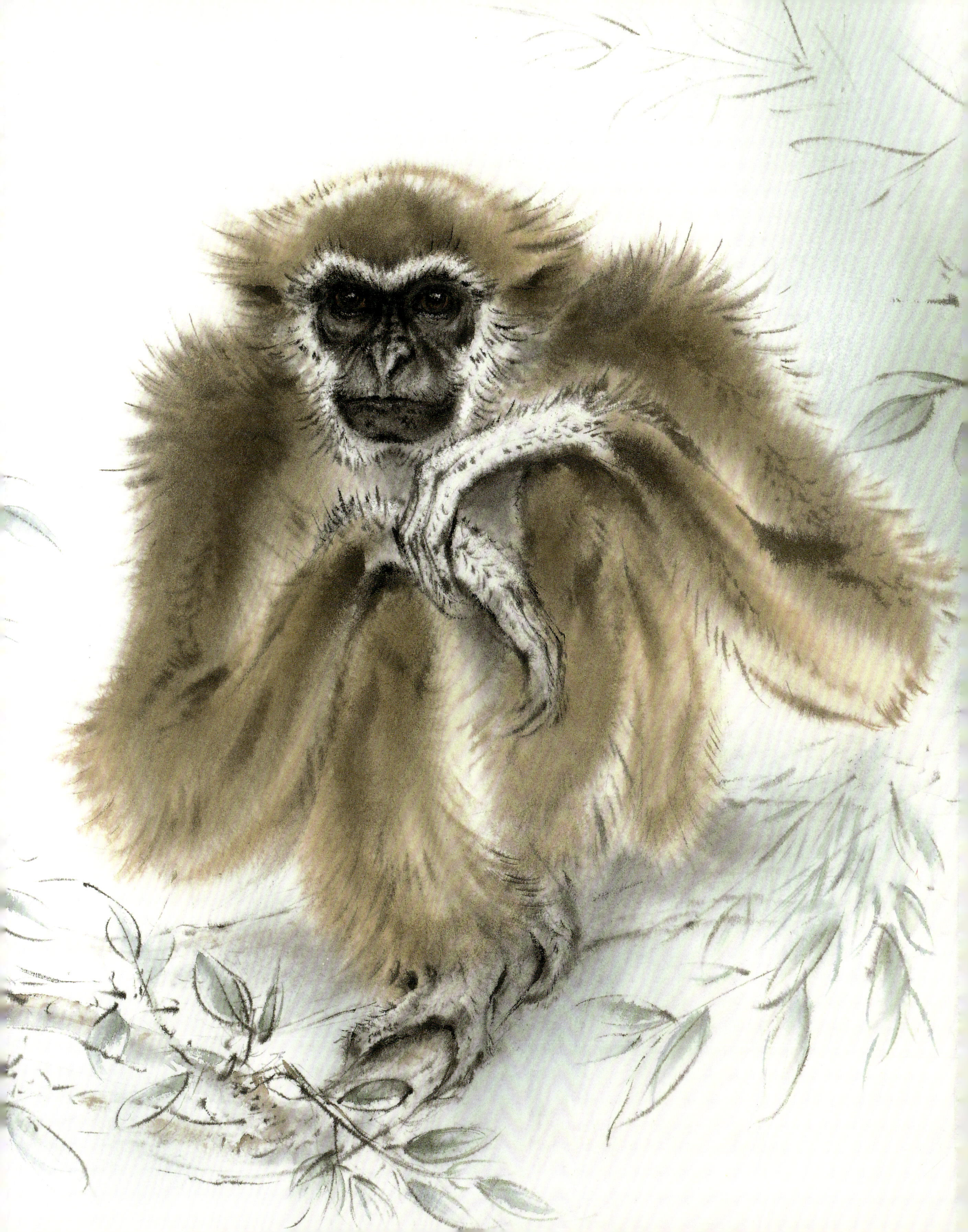

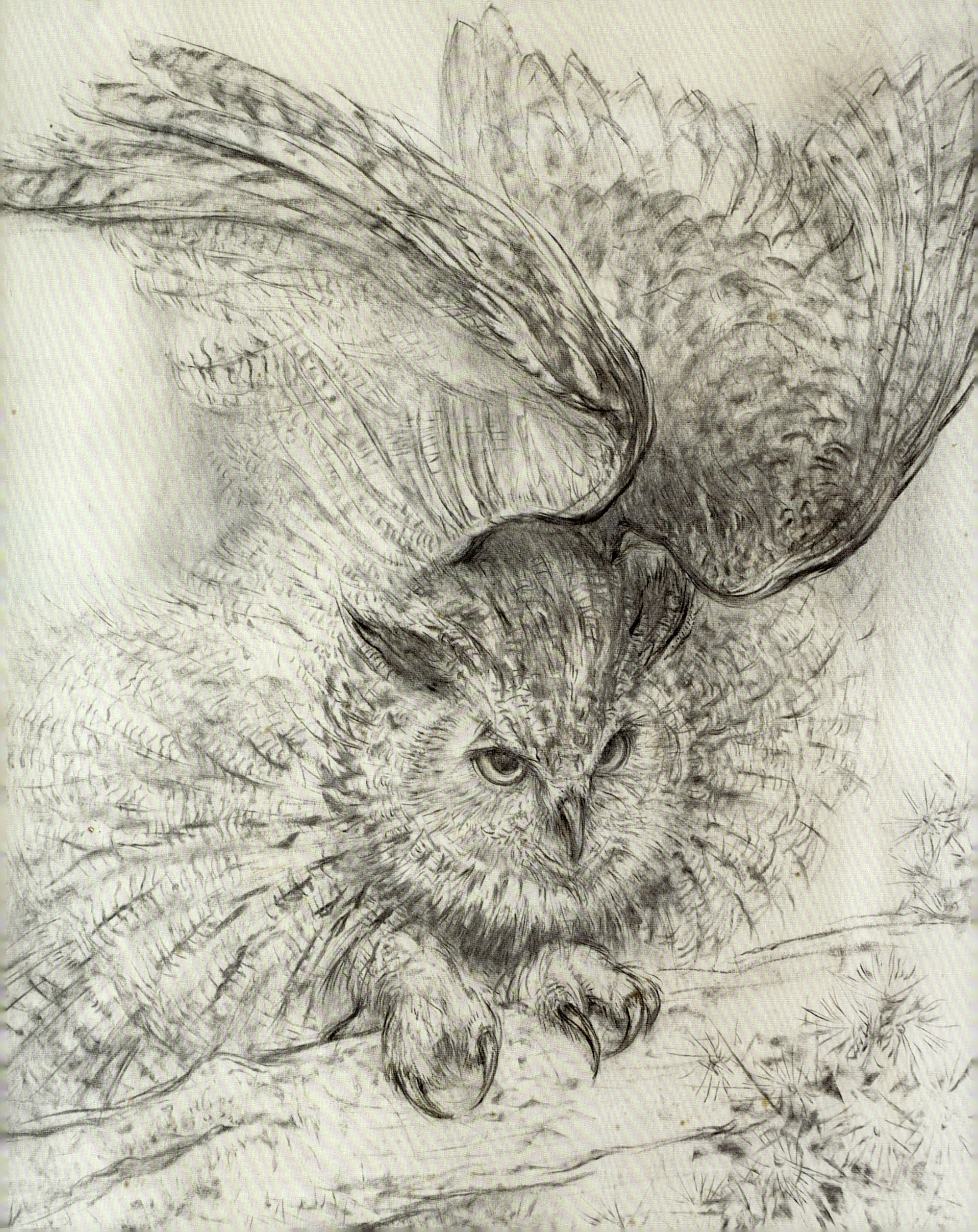

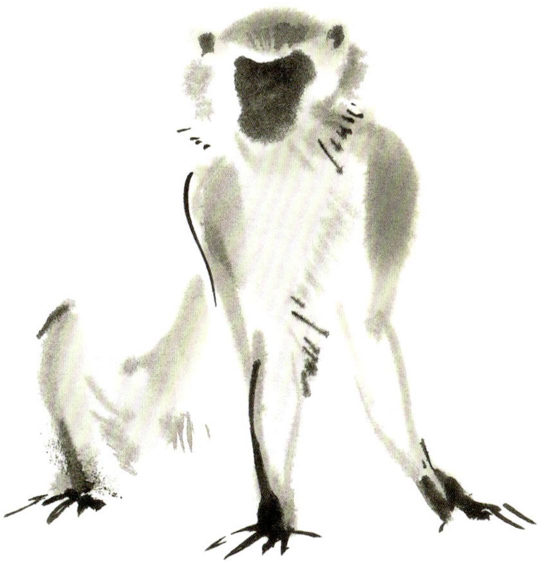

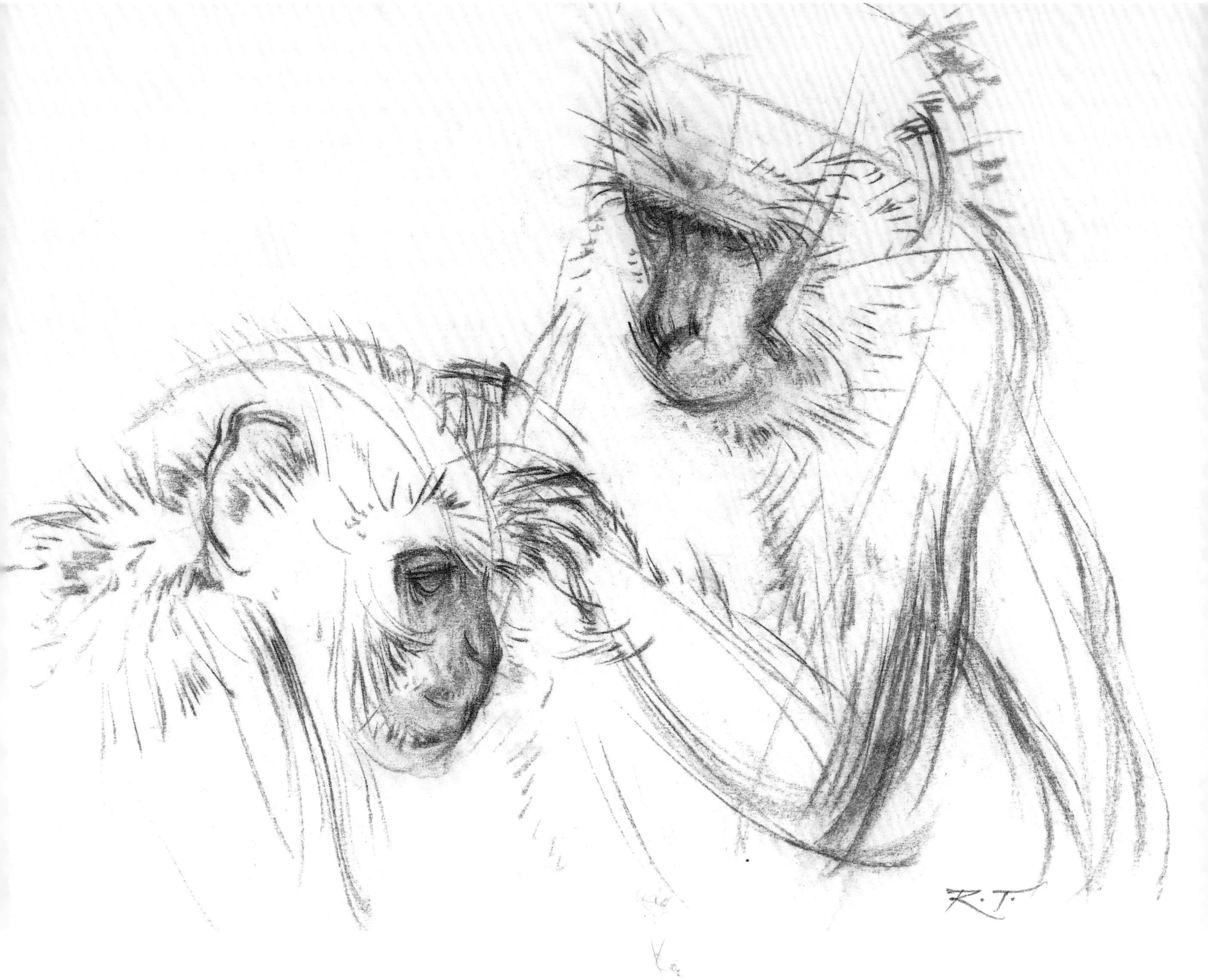
R. T.

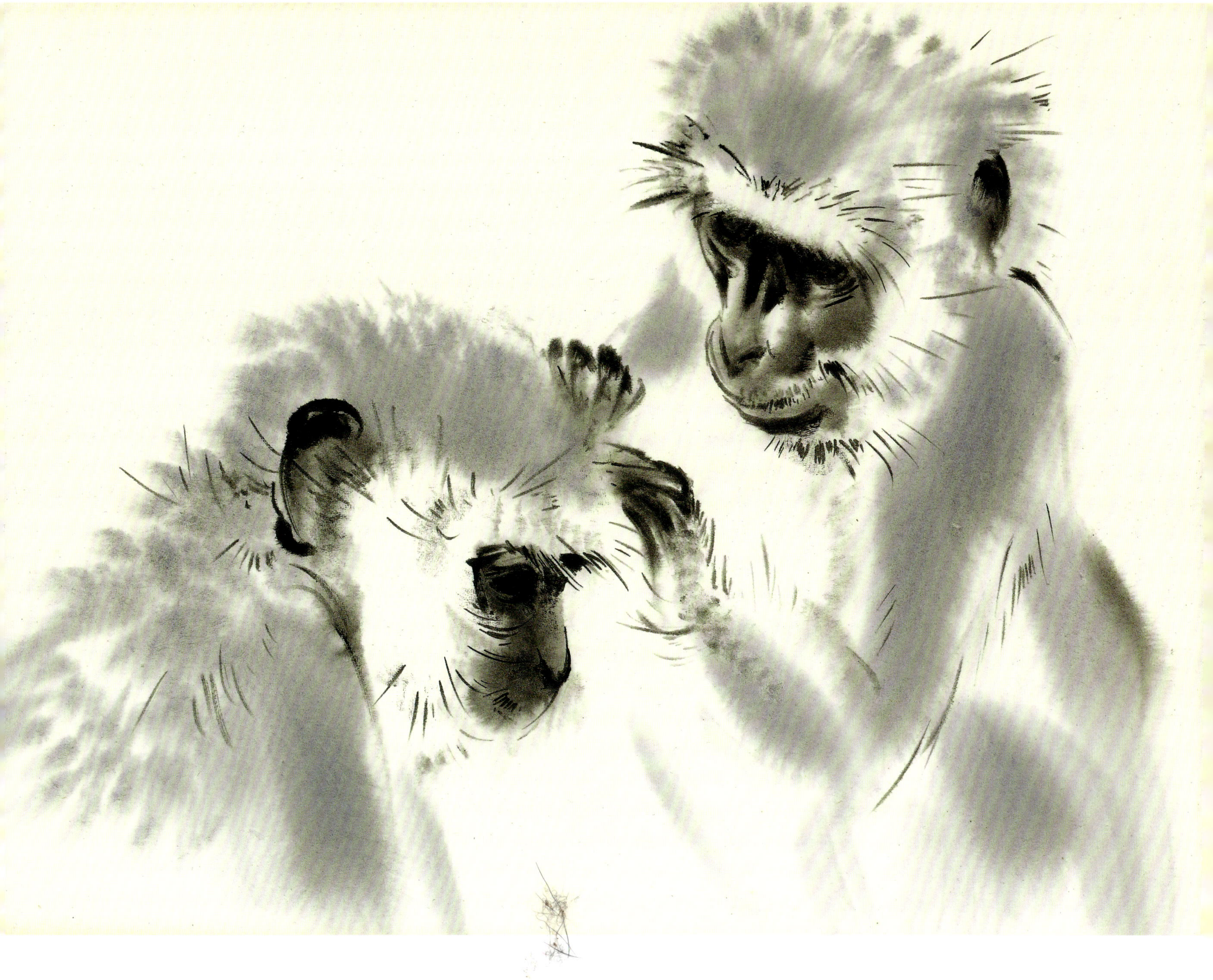

Vervet monkeys grooming
watercolour and charcoal drawing
each 280 × 380mm

following page
Colobus monkey with baby
watercolour
380 × 290mm

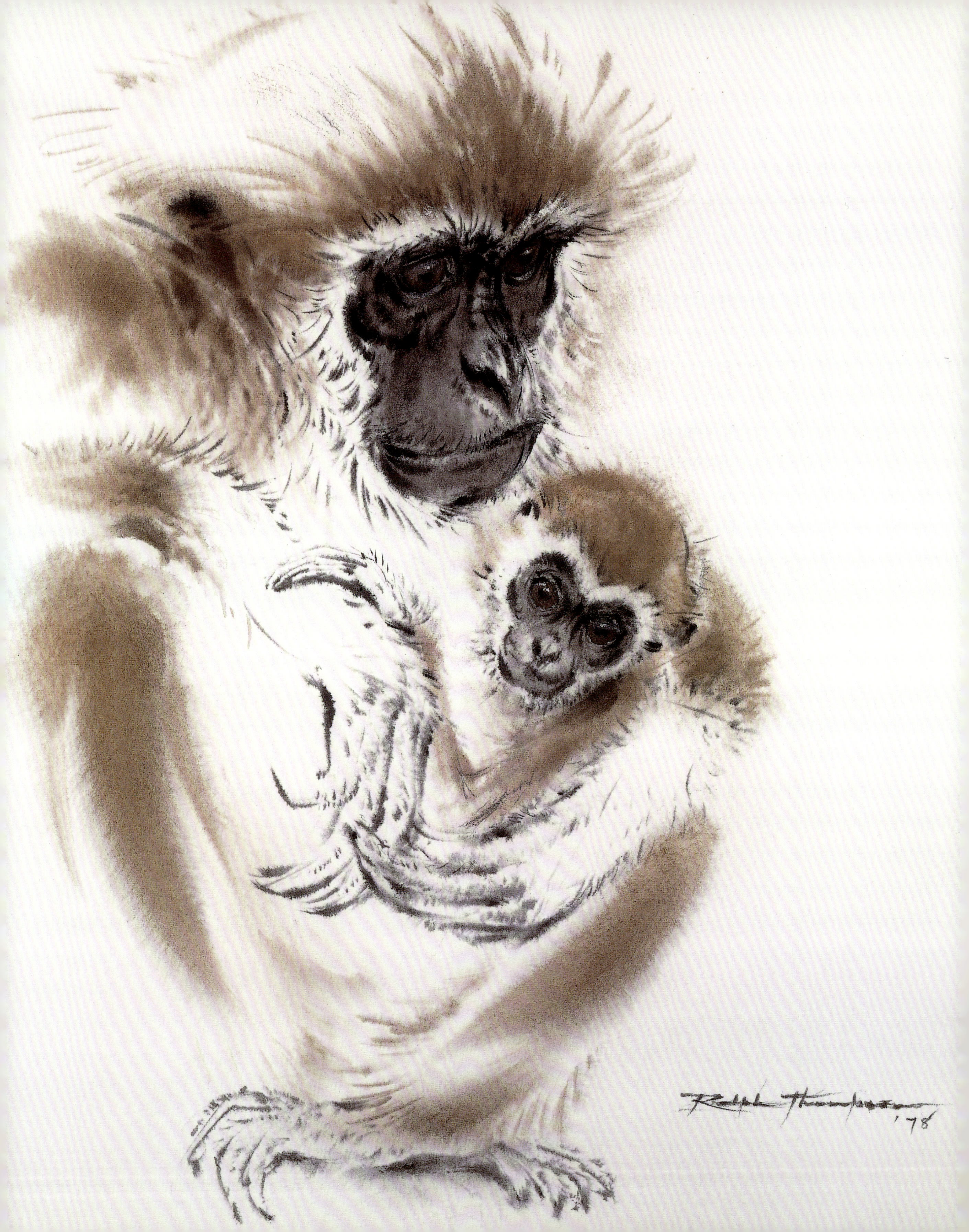
Ralph Thompson
'78

Foreword

Fifty years ago, television was black and white and just BBC. Colour, all day telly and ITV may have been dreams in the minds of some, but to others with sets, what we saw was amazing enough. Between programmes there were often short, filmed 'Interludes'. The most memorable was the Potter's Wheel, where we watched anonymous hands raise a pot from a whirling lump of clay. Among others was one which fascinated me when I chanced to see it on a friend's little set. The camera was looking down over a large drawing board. A hand holding a fat brush appeared and a mark was made across the paper. Further marks and lines were added and it was still not clear what was coming. A few more deft touches and suddenly, almost miraculously, there was an animal, full of life, about to spring from the board. 'Ralph Thompson Draws an Animal' was the simple title. Who was this Ralph Thompson who could conjure animals from apparently random strokes of his brush? Here was superb drawing allied to a deep knowledge of the subject. Later I discovered the illustrations which so enhanced Gerald Durrell's texts, and, later still, I came to know and admire the brilliant draughtsman behind so many illustrations and the glorious paintings in his one-man exhibitions at the Tryon Gallery, and in recent years at the Wildlife Art Gallery.

Ralph's wet-on-wet method of painting, of which he is the acknowledged master, is a technique which perfectly captures the hairy or furry texture of mammals, the animal group he understands so well. That understanding comes from endless observing and drawing. His sketchbooks are full of drawings, from the briefest lines, which pin down the character of the animal. These urgent pen lines brilliantly record the movement of animals, and back in the studio they are translated, through brush strokes, into paintings which retain Ralph's initial impression and excitement of whatever he was watching in the wild.

In this book we are presented with the full range of Ralph's work, sketches, studies and finished paintings which show him to be a true original, a master draughtsman with a rare ability to show us the nature of the animal and it's relation to the habitat in which it lives.

Age has not diminished Ralph's enthusiasm and passion for animals and art. Through his art he has made a huge contribution to the conservation of animals worldwide, recognised by the award of the MBE in 2004. We are deeply grateful for the pleasure and insight he has given us over the years and for an enduring legacy of wonderful images which will continue to delight and inspire future generations.

Robert Gillmor
Cley-next-the-Sea
July 2006

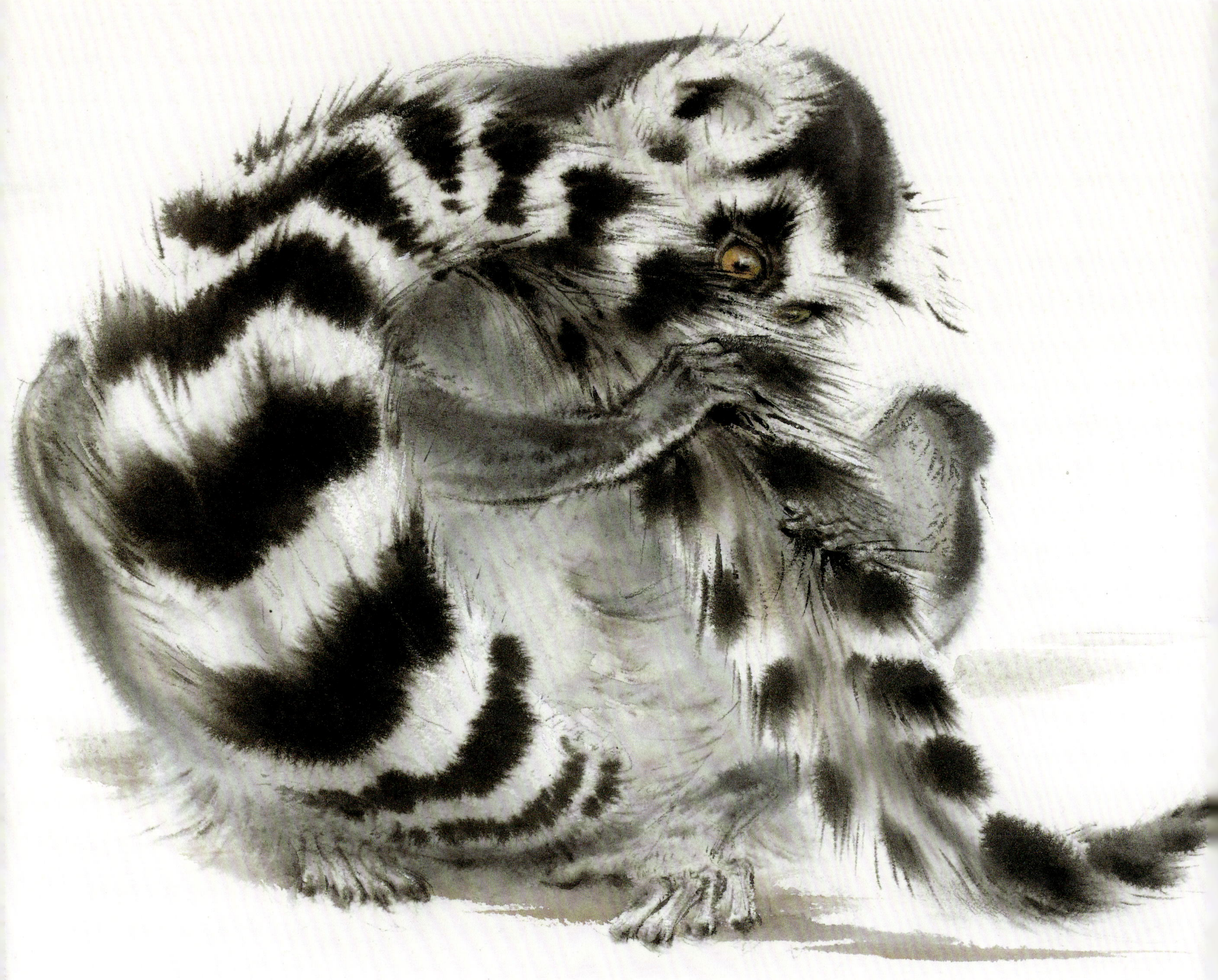

A Brush with Animals

I think I am right in saying that a good artist is a reasonably common creature which can be found in flocks or bevies in a suitable habitat, such as Chelsea or the civilised bits of Cornwall and Devon. The good *animal* artist is, however, an extremely rare creature, and should you – after years of careful stalking – finally catch up with one, then it must be treated with the deference and respect an ornithologist would bestow upon a live specimen of a dodo. So I am extremely flattered to have been asked to write this introduction.

My first contact with Ralph was when he agreed to illustrate one of my books. I was a bit doubtful about the idea of illustrating an animal-travel book with line drawings, but everyone else thought it was a splendid idea. I was out of the country when he started work, and he had no photographs to go on. He had to rely entirely on the text. When I returned to England and saw the finished illustrations I got the shock of my life. Not only were they beautiful, sensitive and accurate, but many of the things he had drawn were *so* accurate that he might as well been with me in Africa, peering over my shoulder at the things I saw. It was quite uncanny, and I began to suspect that Ralph had indulged in some curious form of witchcraft to obtain these startling results. Even now that I have seen him at work I still strongly suspect him of using magic to get his results. I have not actually *seen* him sacrificing black and white cocks, or making up a brew of hemlock and toad's eyes, but he must, I am convinced, indulge in something of the sort. Those who have seen him drawing on Television will, I am sure, know what I mean. He sits there in front of a large sheet of paper, dips his brush into the ink, and then tells you – in a rather hesitant manner – that he is going to draw you a tiger's head. He says this with such modesty that you begin to wonder if he is sure of the outcome himself. Then he waves his brush about in a vague manner over the surface of the paper, as though brushing away a small colony of ants that has taken up residence there. Some dark lines appear on the surface of the paper which bear no relation whatsoever to anything in your experience. Least of all do they resemble a tiger's head. Doubts begin to assail you. Is this, perhaps, *not* Ralph Thompson, but some lunatic who has crept into the studio when no one was looking? Or maybe it *is* Ralph Thompson but the strain has deranged him ? Or – worst of all – perhaps this is Modern Art? Meanwhile Ralph has recharged his brush. He leans forward and continues what appears to be an unequal struggle with the ant colony. You watch, more in pity than in anger. Then suddenly, to your astonishment, there on the paper is a tiger's head, a beautiful tiger's head, where only a moment ago there had been nothing but vague lines. And a tiger's head, moreover, that is so realistic that you know beyond doubt, that if you leant forward to touch it, it would bite you – hard. If this is not Black Magic, then what is?

But however Ralph achieves his results, let us be grateful for them, for it is not often that one can enjoy drawings such as his. Over the years his drawings have greatly enhanced my books, and have, I know, added incalculably to their popularity. So with this, his first book, I wish him all the luck he deserves and will surely get. May we have many more brushes with animals like this one.

Gerald Durrell

Introduction from 'A Brush with Animals'

Published 1963 Rupert Hart-Davis

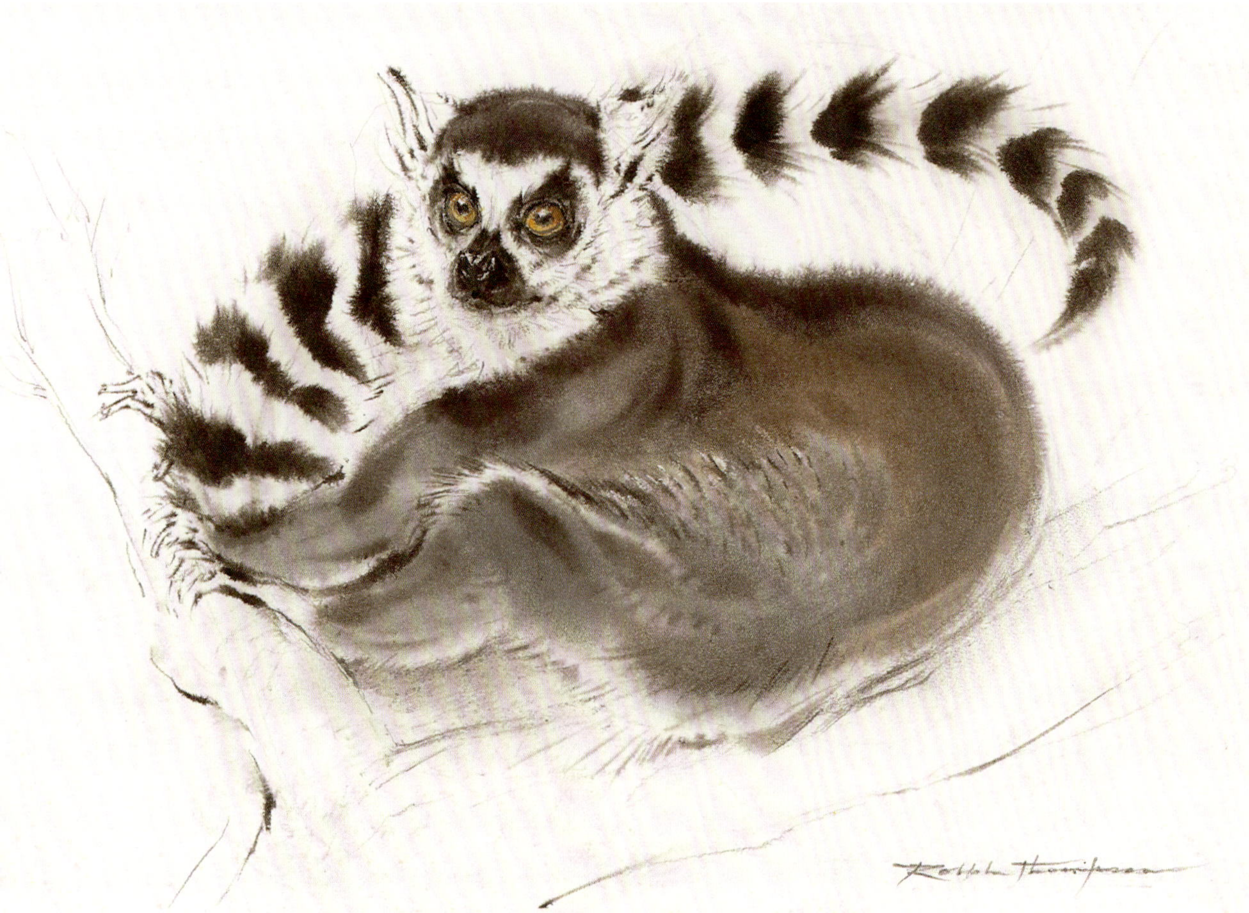

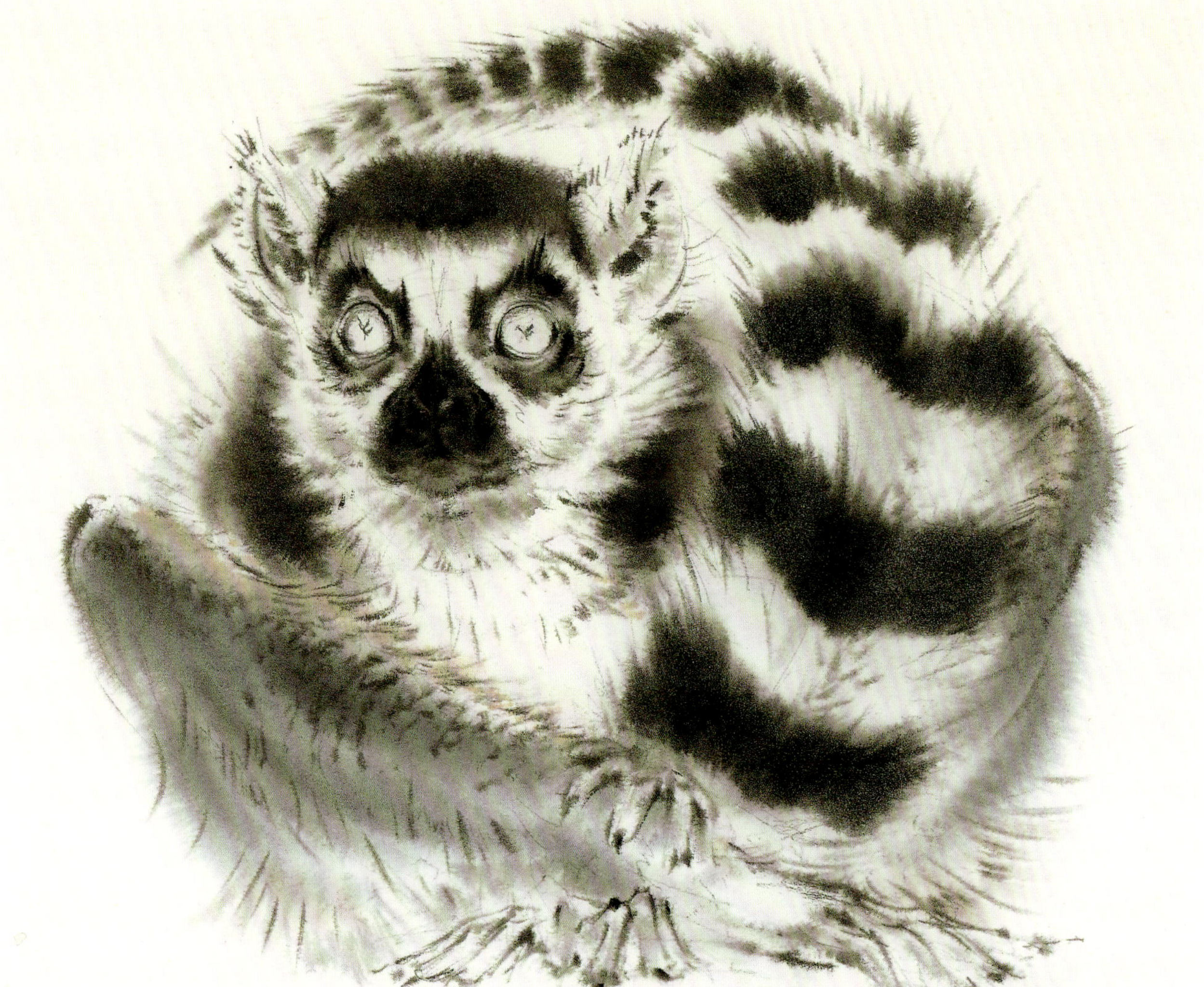

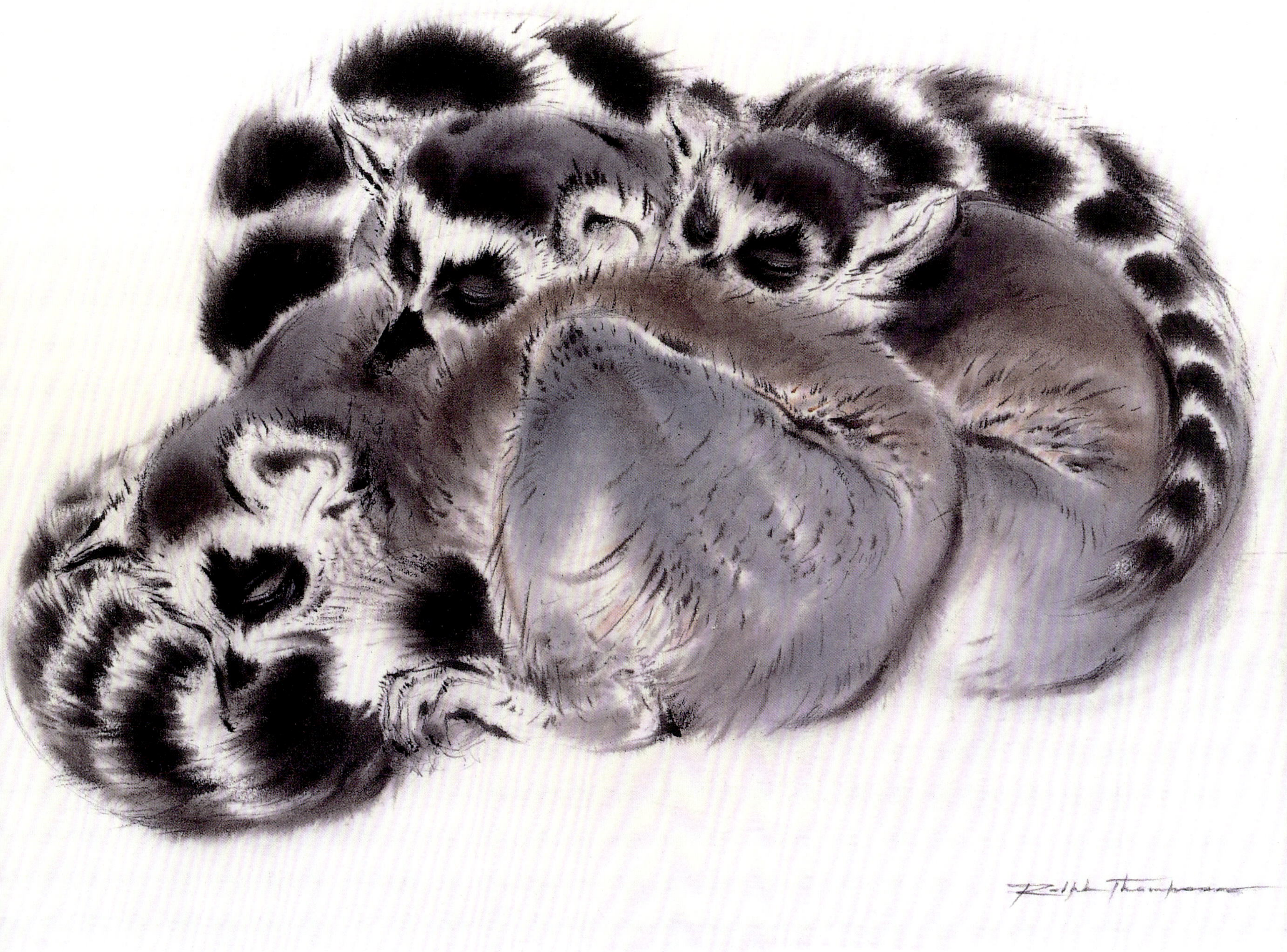

opposite
Ring-tailed lemur studies
watercolour
255 × 350mm *top*
270 × 380mm *bottom*

previous page
Ring-tailed lemur grooming its tail
watercolour
280 × 380mm

Ring-tailed lemurs sleeping
watercolour
330 × 510mm

Face to Face

The old London Zoological Gardens were bad for the animals, but often good for artists. This was years before television programmes made animals in the wild so familiar to us. We were dependant on picture books for their appearance and ways of life. I was a student at the Royal College of Art in the late thirties and, on what may well have been my first visit to the Zoo, after making some sketches, I went off to explore one of the mammal houses.

Suddenly I found myself face to face with a most astonishing head. It seemed to be that of a creamy white pony, but it was covered with elegantly tapering black stripes and a very striking black and white crest, which stood high above it. I pictured a Roman soldier's helmet. It could have come straight out of a fairy tale. But there it was, a zebra, kicking noisily around its stall.

So unexpected and at such close quarters, the impact was electric. It was an experience of greatest delight, a revelation.

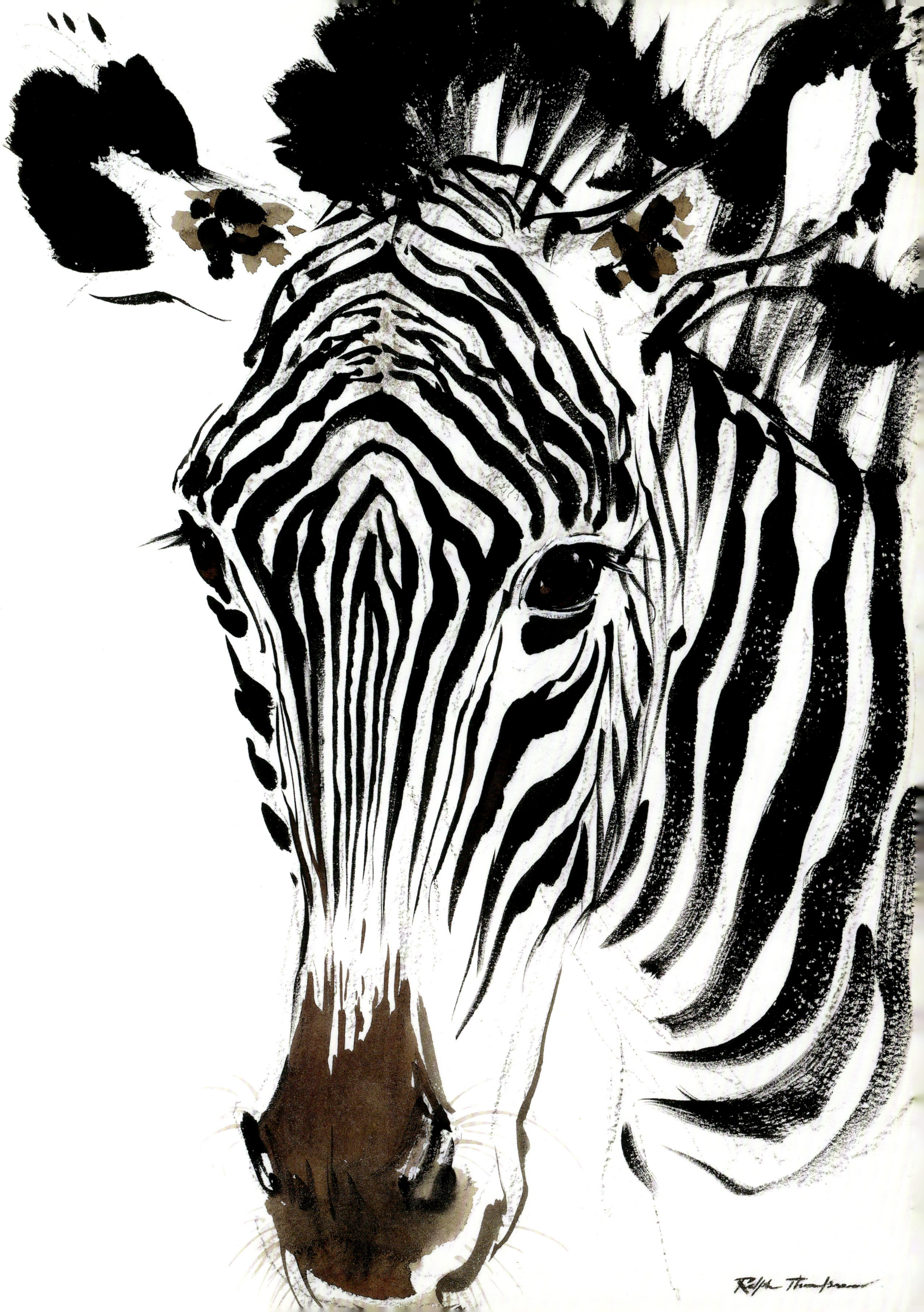

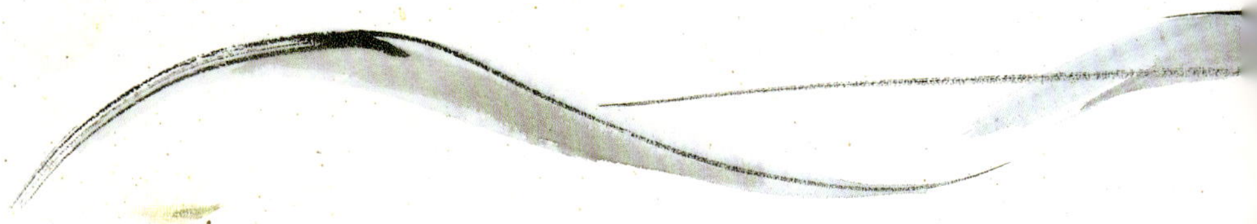

Red-capped mangabey
watercolour
400 × 550mm

previous page
Zebra portrait
watercolour
390 × 280mm

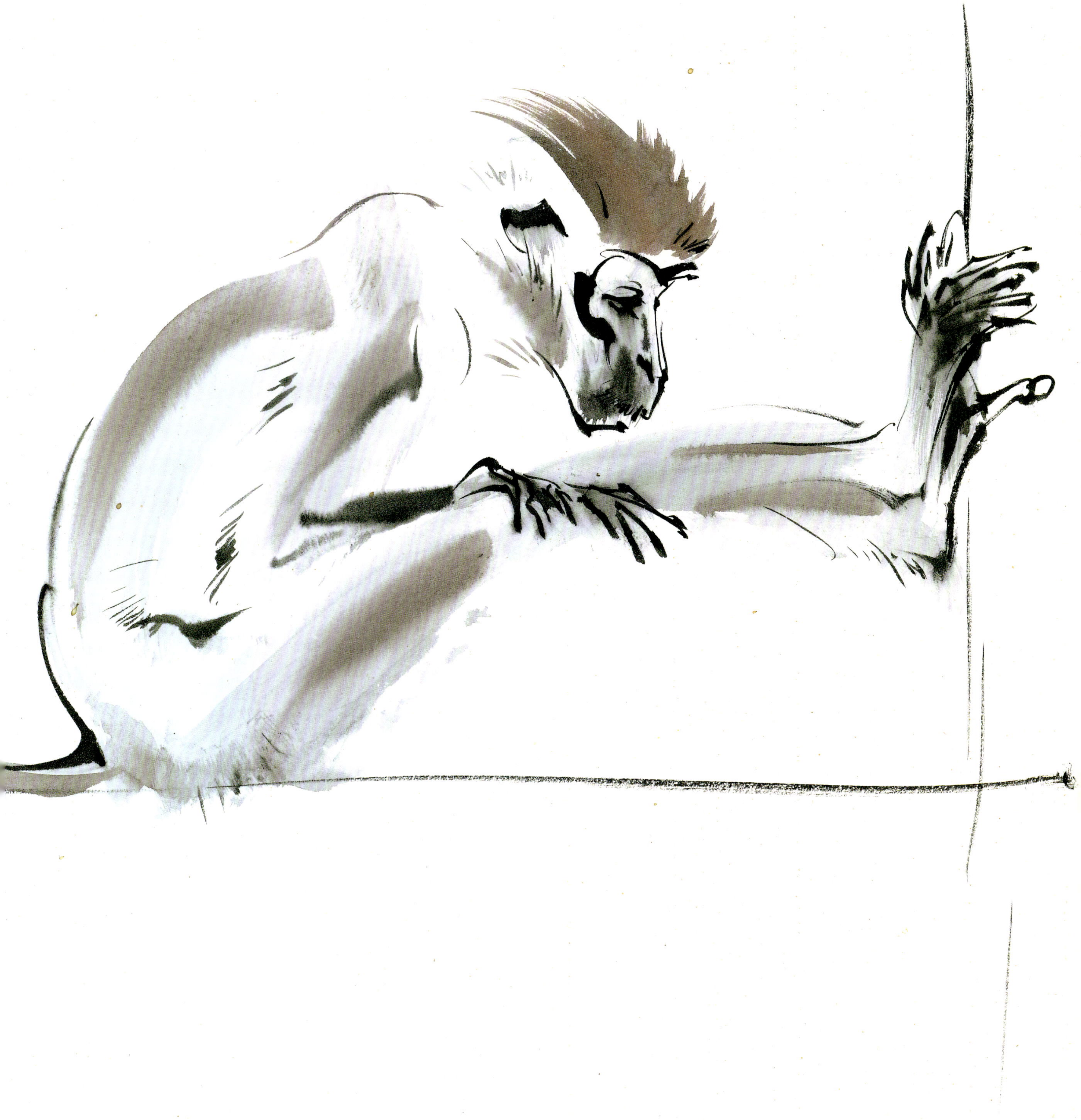

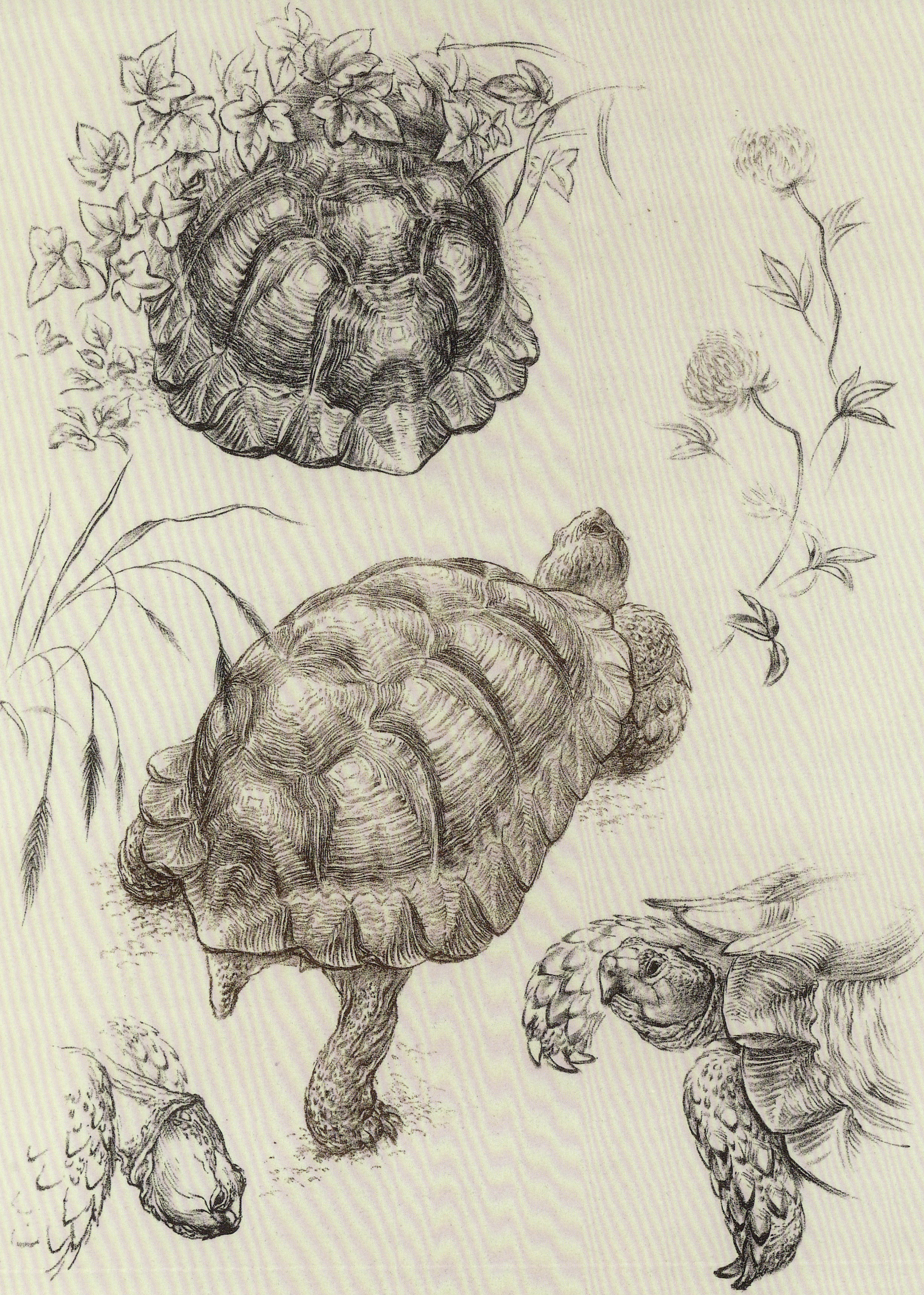

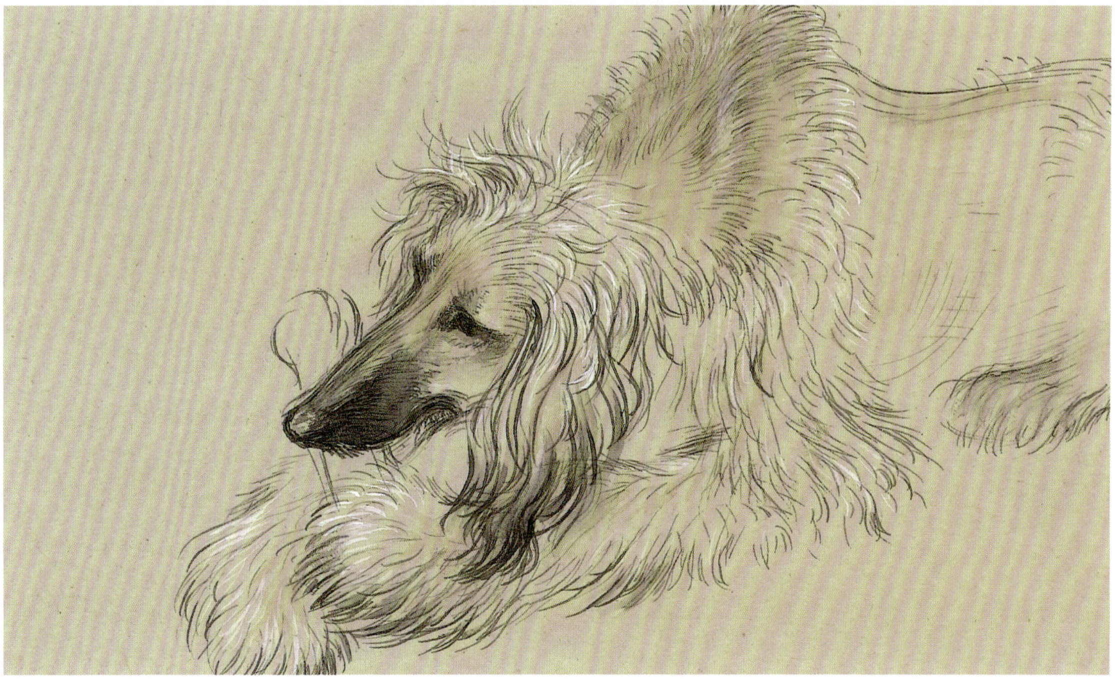

The Sniffer Dog

I was born in 1913 into a happy, supportive family in a Yorkshire village called Thorner. From an early age I wanted to draw and paint, but in a family with no background in the Arts and giving little encouragement, I had to struggle on my own. My father was adamant that learning to be an artist was a waste of time, as was drawing instead of working for my exams. The northern work ethic was deeply engrained and my brothers and I all did well when it came to matriculation. With his matriculation over, Frank, fourteen months my senior, went off on a scholarship to build the empire. Alan, eight years older than me, went on to study gas engineering at Leeds University. While all I wanted to do was to learn drawing.

To cut a long story short, I managed to get Dad to have a change of heart and with his help I applied to Leeds College of Art. To be accepted I was to do a portrait drawing, an object in use around the house, (in fact, I drew Mother's sewing machine) and a landscape from the window. On the strength of these drawings, I was accepted. Later I was able to do some credible 'plant drawings' which secured me a scholarship. In my third year, I gained high marks for 'drawing', did quite well in 'life painting', but did poorly in 'composition', in which current ideas about Art were involved.

Having failed to gain a scholarship to the Royal College of Art in painting, my father insisted that I spend a year taking a teaching diploma, for which, I was told, I obtained the highest marks in the UK. This was followed by a year doing illustration as opposed to painting, the most memorable reminders of which

Afghan
coloured pencil
120 × 200mm

opposite
Mr McGinty (tortoise studies)
lithograph
310 × 240mm

were an etching, drawn straight onto the plate, of beech trees at Temple Museum and a line engraving of a carthorse led by a farmhand, at my uncles farm at East Rigton, a few miles from home at Thorner. Both of these were shown at the Yorkshire Artists Exhibition and, I think helped me to gain the scholarship to the Royal College on this my second attempt. The scholarship paid for my fees and materials but not maintenance, which I had to cover with a loan from Dad.

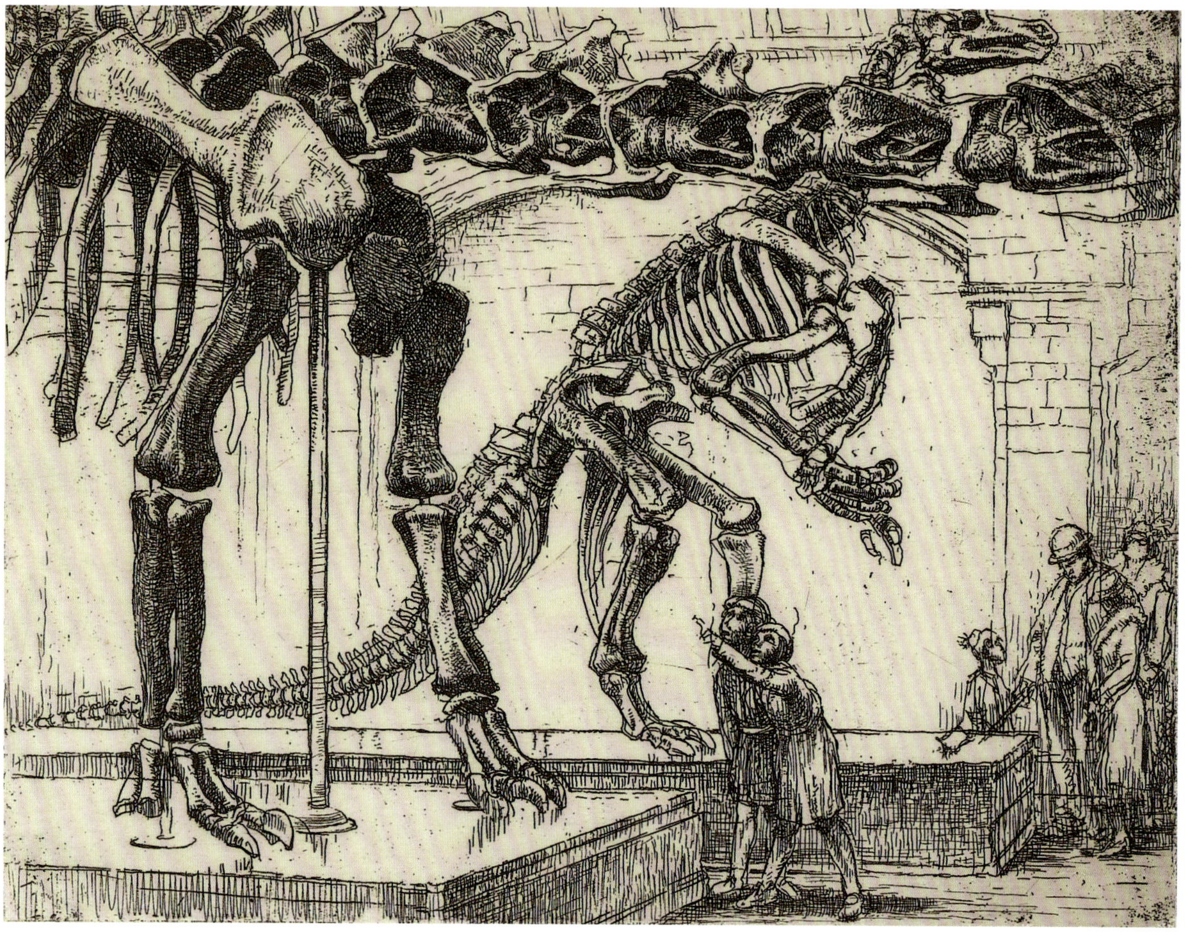

Thinking back over the years, the Royal College did not make a big impact. Like some peculiar breed of *sniffer dog*, I spent all of my time exploring this exciting new world of art I had discovered and trying to make sense of it. I loved drawing, but never seemed to get the hang of art with a capital 'A'. It was this preoccupation with drawing that kept me on the scent for ten long but enjoyable years as an art student.

I opted for the Painting School, the Head of which was Gilbert Spencer, Sir Stanley Spencer's younger brother. Frankly, he was pretty useless. Because Stanley was now famous as an artist rebel, Gilbert was in demand in the art

The Natural History Museum
etching
120 × 160mm

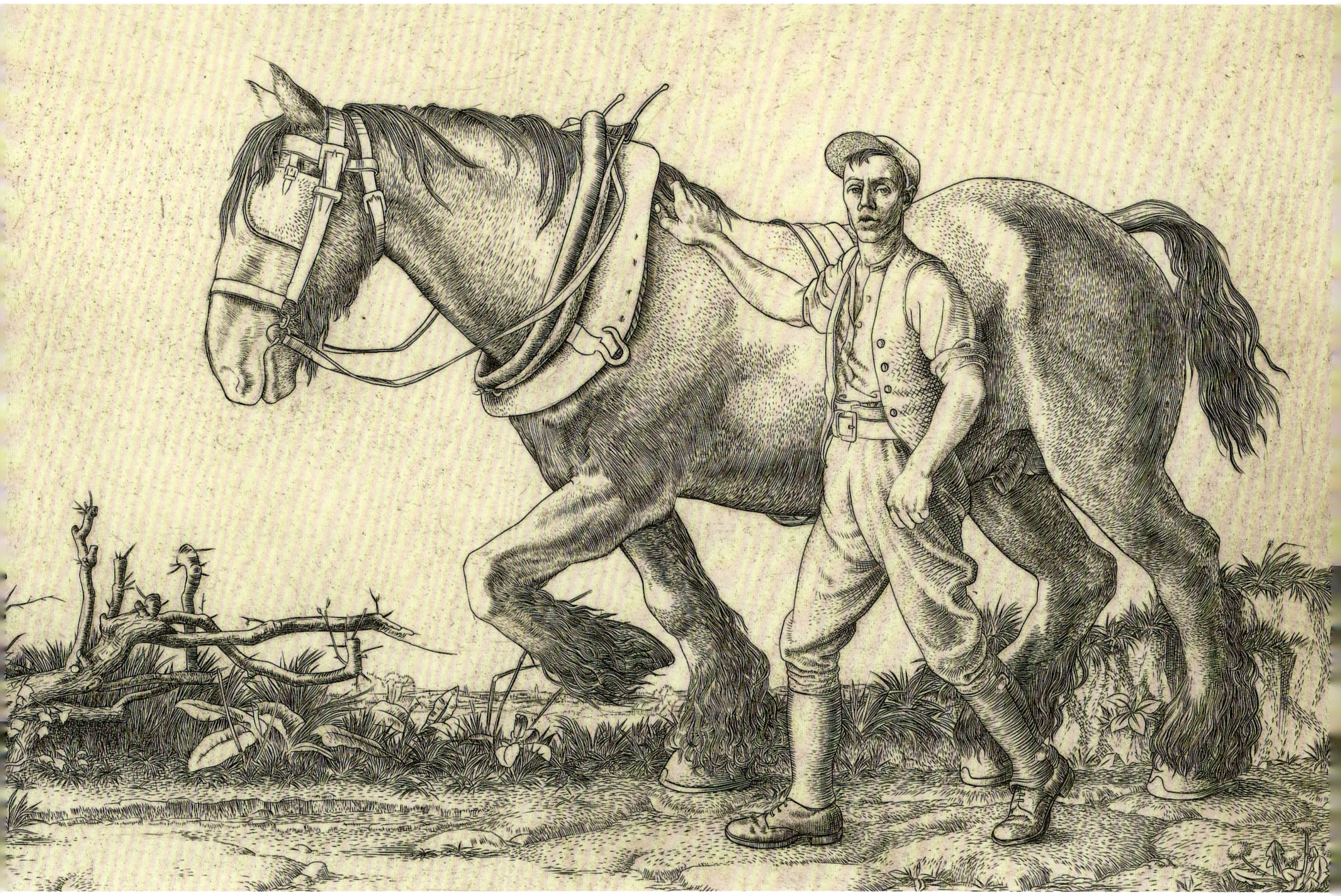

world and knew everyone worth knowing. Thus, Gilbert's only value to us students was to tell racy stories about them. There were one or two interesting men teaching life drawing, but none who really commanded my attention.

The war began during my last year at the Royal College and I was spray-painting camouflage on buildings and open spaces while waiting for my 'call up'. Through a pianist friend of some repute, Dorothy Manley, I was invited to live at and to care-take a house at 10 Chepstow Place in Bayswater, owned by the Reilly family, who were close friends of Dorothy's brother. It was full of little paintings, watercolours and pastels, mostly done by Nell Reilly. One of her

Cart horse and farmhand
line engraving
200 × 300mm

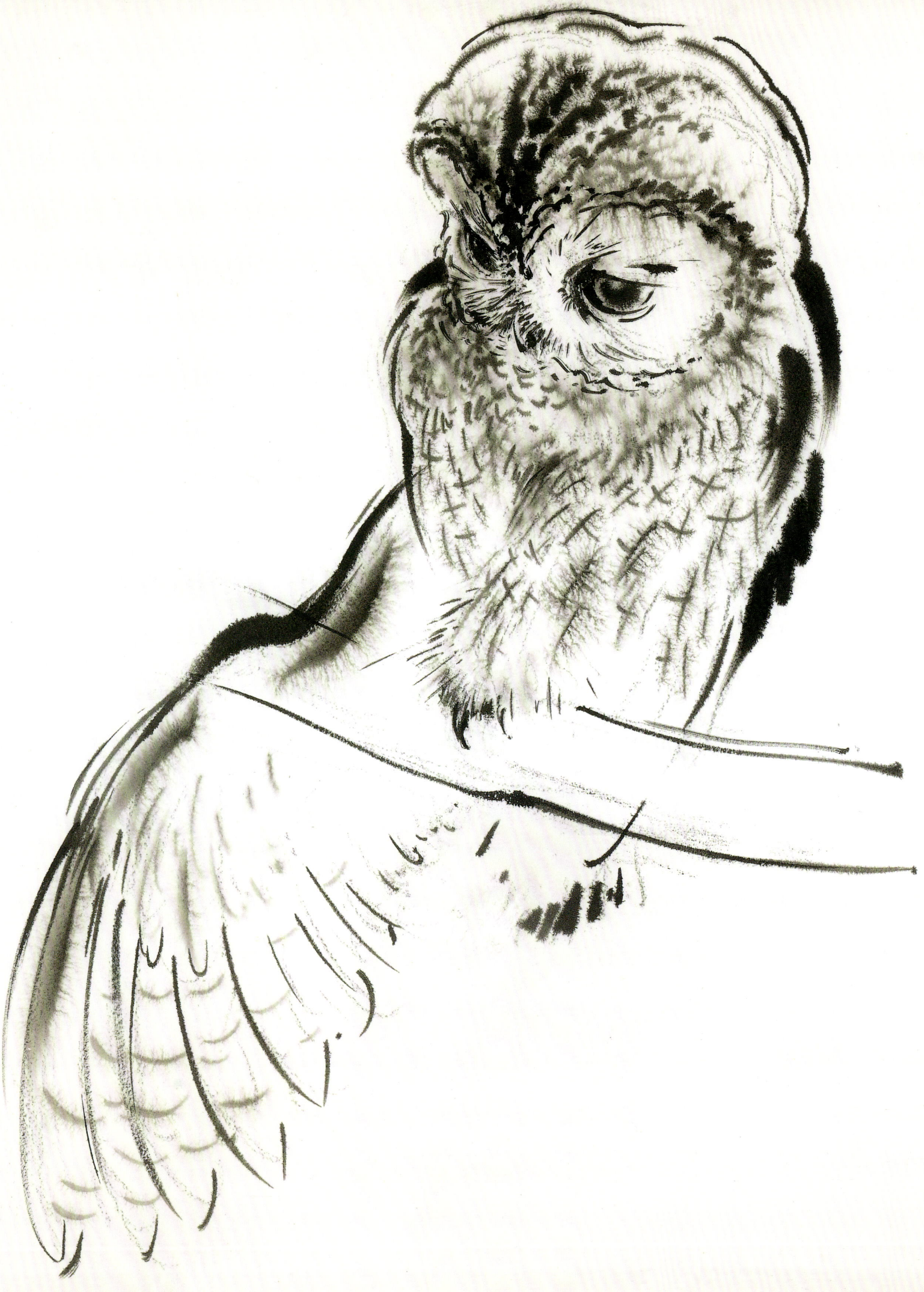

sons, Peter Reilly, who was a Civil Servant based in London, would sometimes call and stay the night. On one of his visits in September 1940, Peter warned me that the German bombing of London, the 'blitz', had started in earnest. He said that he had to work all over the country, leaving his wife and young children unprotected. So, would I come and live at his place, Bigfrith End in Cookham Dean? He had heard that I was a conscientious objector and was going to appeal to work on the land as a farm labourer. He thought it might impress the tribunal if I made a start in the large orchard and vegetable garden at his home. Thus, I went to Cookham Dean just a fortnight before 10 Chepstow Place received a direct hit. I have lived there ever since!

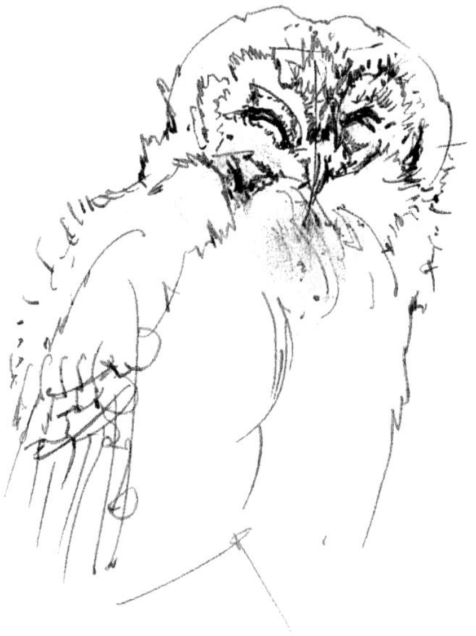

Mrs Reilly, who was later to become my wife, was known as 'Bill' and her two children were June, then aged nine, and Wyn, aged ten. For the duration of the war I worked as a farm labourer, working six days a week pretty much from dawn to dusk, which left very little time or energy for painting and drawing.

When the war was over, I was discharged from farm work. I was simply grateful still to be alive and living among friends in this lovely Berkshire village. A local artist and one of the founders of the Cookham Arts Club recommended me for the job of teaching Life Drawing at Camberwell School of Art. As an Associate of the Royal College of Art I was qualified but maybe I got the job largely because there was a lack of artists due to losses during the war. Certainly, the other instructors were well over the call up age. The work included two whole days and two evening classes a week.

My training at the Royal College under Gilbert Spencer seemed inappropriate as a basis for teaching, so I clung to my favourite draughtsmen, Michelangelo, Rembrandt and Wattau, and to Goya's drawings, etchings and aquatints for inspiration.

I went round the students giving them what advice and help that I could, but became very conscious of the influence at Camberwell of the 'London Group'. This was a group that was inspired by the artist Richard Sickert and his followers, the chief amongst whom was William Coldstream, who was the Head of Camberwell before becoming the Head of the Slade. He was influential in the world of contemporary art and, in his early work, produced some very sensitive portraits. At Camberwell, he developed a technique of carefully measuring the appearance of a figure that seemed to be based on measuring the accurate position of key features with dots or marks, rather than reacting to the flow of forms with lines and, to my mind, laboriously and slowly building an image. I found this very confusing at the time.

In Coldstream's own hands, this technique became an art form – a way of distancing himself emotionally from his subject, or becoming more objective, timeless and detached. There may well have been a link with Cezanne's method of drawing and painting and of faithfully recording his 'sensations', his actual

opposite
Tawny owl stretching wing
ink
520 × 380mm

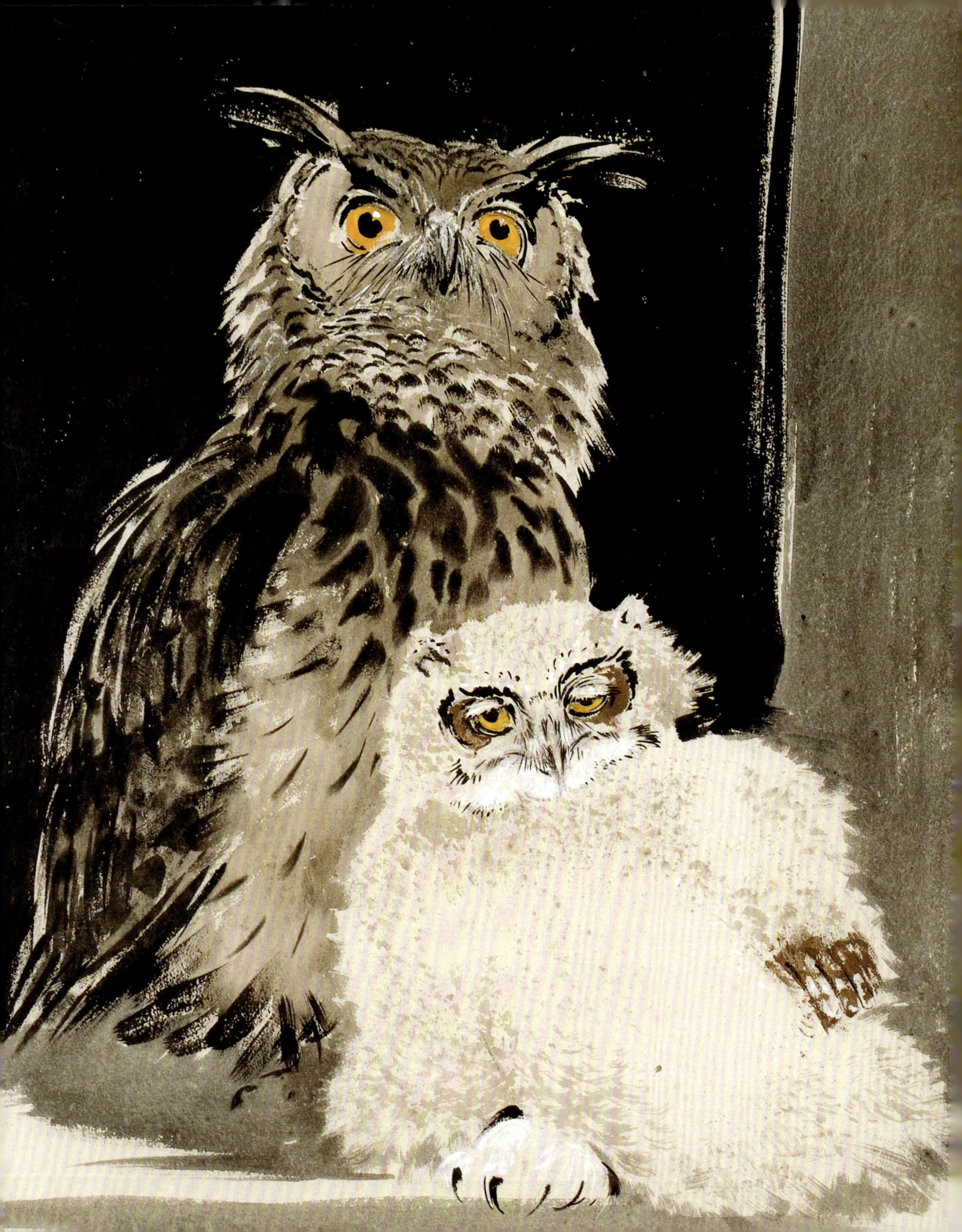

visual experience and so, rediscovering appearances of nature for himself. The fashion did not last long and was, for most artists, just an unimportant part of a big change in outlook of the Avant-Garde approach of the London Group.

The London Group consisted of a large number of forward-looking artists who were rebelling against the influence of the Royal Academy and its traditional, academic vision. It encompassed artists who were trying to come to terms with modern art. They were influenced by artists such as Picasso, Braque and Matisse and were themselves experimenting with the new way of looking at nature. The Group became quite influential. For the beginnings of the London Group, my mind goes back to the paintings and drawings of Richard Sickert, who exhibited in the early years of the Group. He visited Paris where he saw the new works of Toulouse Lautrec and Degas and one can see the influence of both.

I came to know the artist, Ivon Hitchens and his wife, Molly. She was a buxom and homely woman who had been at school with Mary Bingham, who was then living at Bigfrith End Cottage. Ivon had created a new form of landscape painting, which used daringly simplified oils with a unique feeling for colour. He had found a new vision in his paintings that was more than just acceptable. His work became popular and was seen outside the London Group in a series of one-man shows. Another artist who was part of the Group and who became a friend was John Dodgson. His work seemed deliberately unpretentious, with the paint overlaid by very thick changes, but always with hidden surprises. He had a family link with Lewis Carol, the author of Alice in Wonderland. I spent many enjoyable evenings in his Chelsea home. He owned a wonderful Bonnard coast scene, which I thought was the essence of painting and which became a great source of enjoyment on my visits.

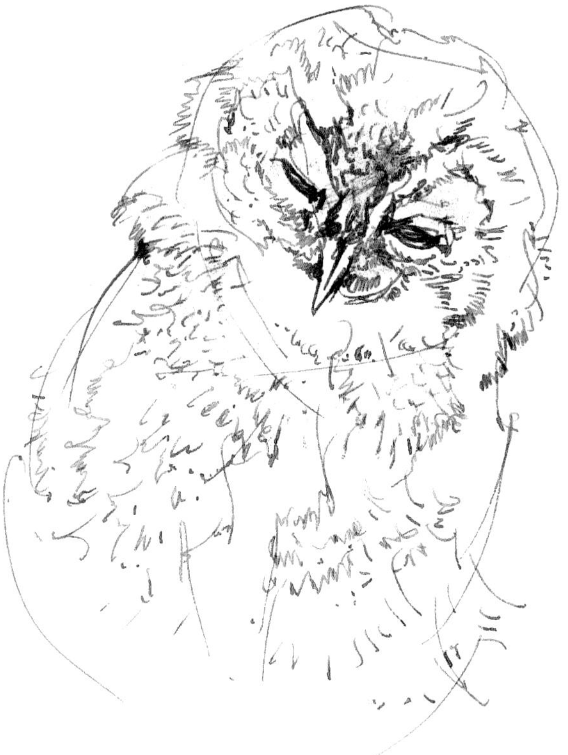

At this time my colleague at the Royal College, John Ward, who became a member of the Royal Academy in 1956, (resigning in 1957), was illustrating 'Vogue' with wonderful, apparently effortless, line drawings of flowers and plant forms as well as models. He ignored the London Group and was able in, his portraits of eminent people, to give a fresh life to the academic vision. In my view, he really excelled himself in his unselfconscious self-portrait. His published sketches of Rome and Venice are quite superb.

Stanley Spencer was a frequent visitor to Bigfrith End and delighted in the pleasure of eating Bill's dripping toast and playing Bach on her piano. He was by far the most unique, and now the most famous artist that I was to know personally. I also got to meet his two daughters, Unity and Sherin, and his grandson, John, who much later came to live in Bigfrith End Cottage. So much has been written about Stanley and his work and his Memorial Chapel at Burghclere that I shall only mention a few of the more memorable things about him.

opposite
Eagle owl and chick
watercolour
770 × 570mm

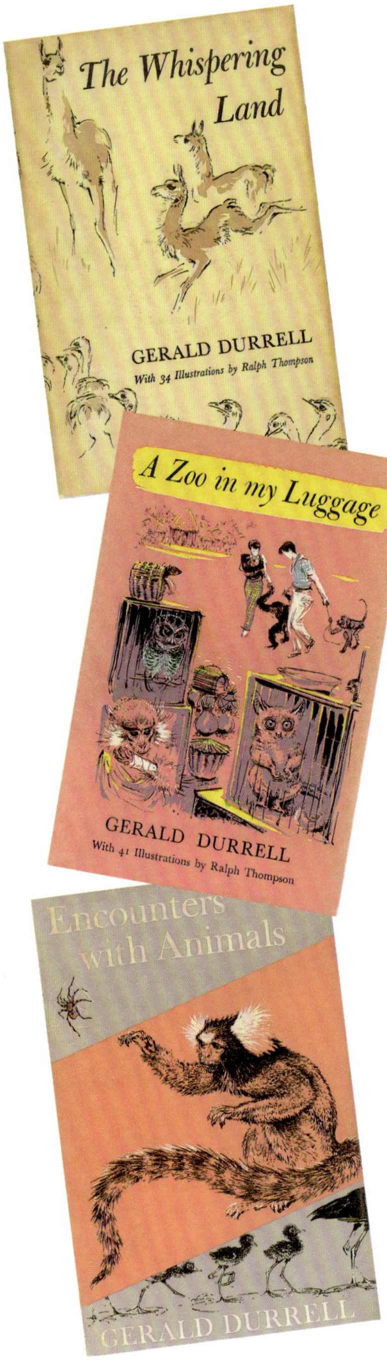

Stanley never exhibited with the London Group. He did not appear to notice it and it certainly did not influence his own work, which was the only thing that had any meaning for him. I can understand that. He was the nearest to an artistic genius I have ever met. He gave the impression of being self-centred because he kept talking about 'me', but by 'me' he meant the 'inner me', his genius me rather than an egotistic me. No doubt he was a flawed genius, but looking again, recently, at the murals in the Burghclere Memorial Chapel, I felt the stamp of his genius.

He was thrown out of the Royal Academy when he included the painting, 'St. Francis and the birds' in 1935. The hunchback, St. Francis, was very provocative. I could never come to terms with its distortions. I felt that he was asking for the fuss and furore that it raised. He probably enjoyed the scandal.

I was in his studio at the bottom of his garden when he was just back from Glasgow where he had been sketching shipbuilding on the Clyde. I was able to watch him drawing and painting the 'shipbuilding murals' from his sketches, which were drawn on what seemed to me, to be wartime lavatory paper. Under his influence, I too made drawings for the 'Betrayal of Christ' at the bottom of Quarry Woods with sketches of our evacuees, the Webbs, all floating like saints or angels over the roof of their new home, the garden room at Bigfrith End.

I saw, and very much admired Stanley's pencil portrait drawings, drawn with an HB pencil and no rubber, often finishing an eye completely and going on continuously until the drawing was completed. This was all against the advice of the time which was to develop the whole of the head as the artist went along, letting the artist's eye move over the whole head and relating all the features together as the drawing progressed. He was kind enough to praise my own drawings and particularly liked a lithograph I made of our tortoise, 'Mr McGinty'.

But for the *sniffer dog* it was a confusing time. Teaching at Camberwell brought a welcome addition to my finances, which were otherwise dependant on uncertain commissions, initially to design book jackets for the first books coming out about the War. However I needed to illustrate everything that came my way to try and make ends meet. Book tokens were then in vogue and I drew a series of wild animals for Rupert Hart-Davis as children's tokens. It also happened to be the time that Rupert was discovering the talent of Gerald Durrell. His books were then being illustrated without an appreciation of the racy style of Durrell's writing, so Rupert was looking for a new illustrator. The first book I was asked to illustrate was the 'Bafut Beagles'. Gerald Durrell was delighted! This proved extremely stimulating and increasingly led to a wider study of animals for the whole series of books that followed.

opposite
Watercolours from
'Winkie the Grey Squirrel'

Also at that time, Bill's children, June and Wyn, were very taken by a baby squirrel that they had found abandoned at Bigfrith End and had adopted. It

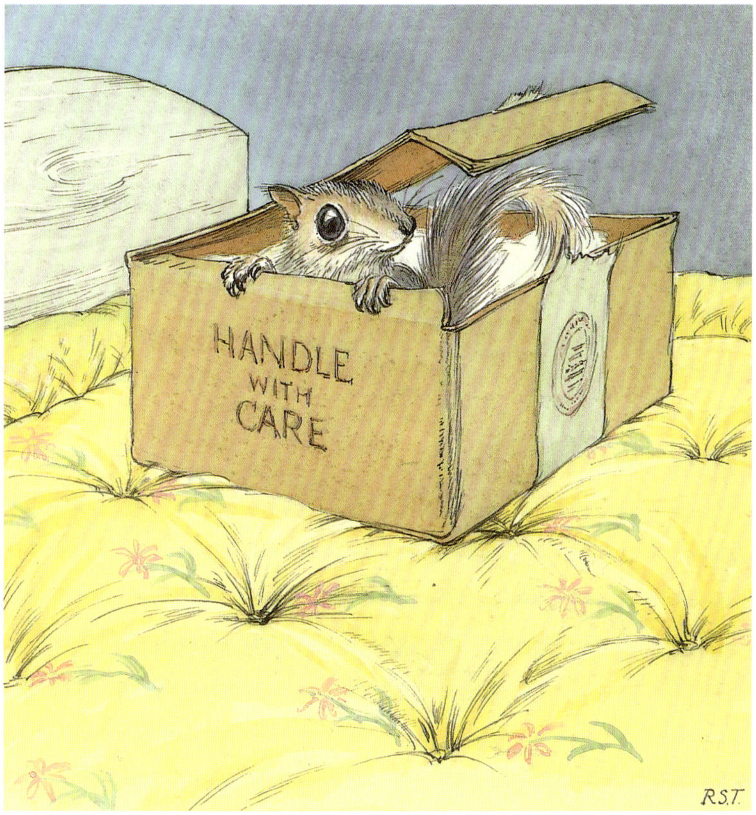
HANDLE
WITH
CARE
R.S.T.

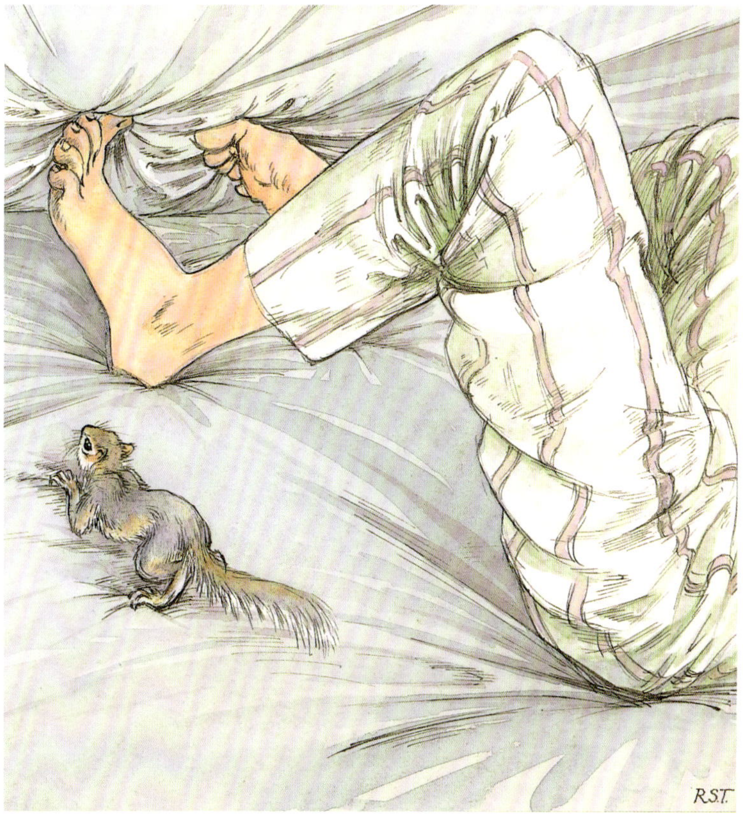
R.S.T.

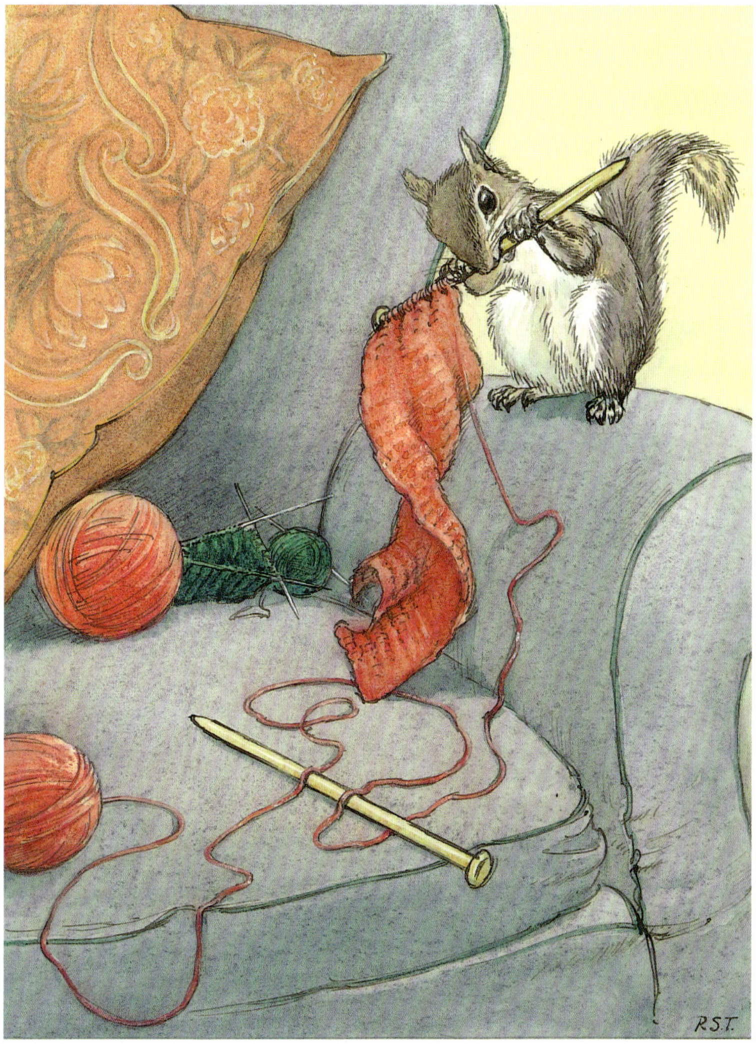
R.S.T.

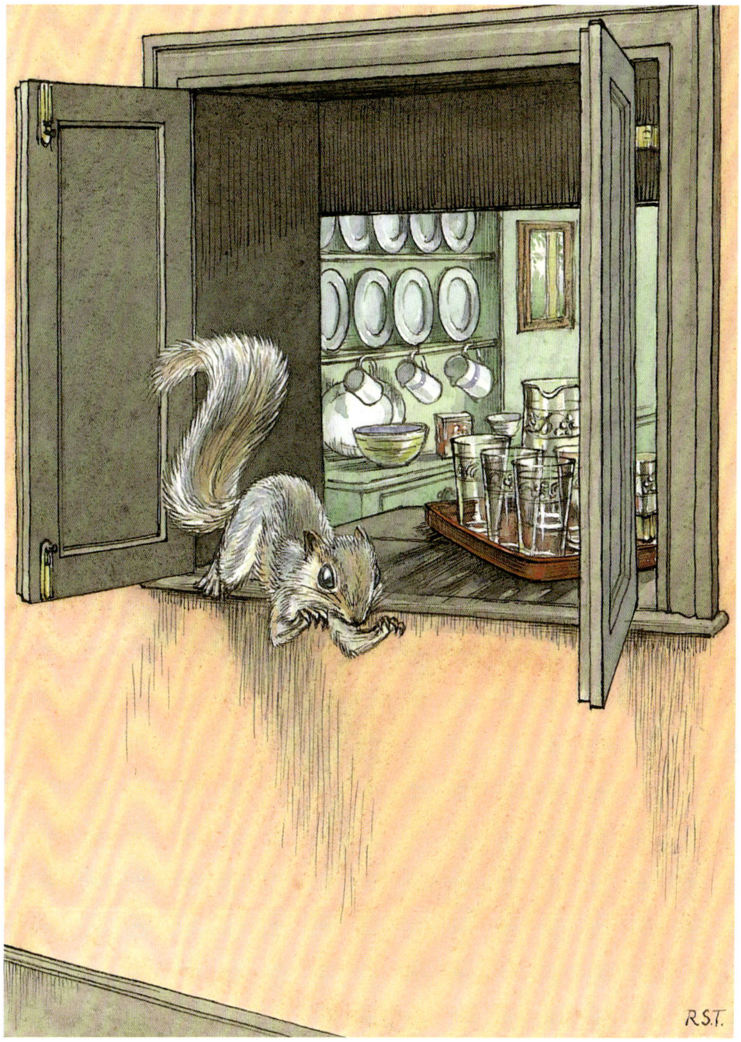
R.S.T.

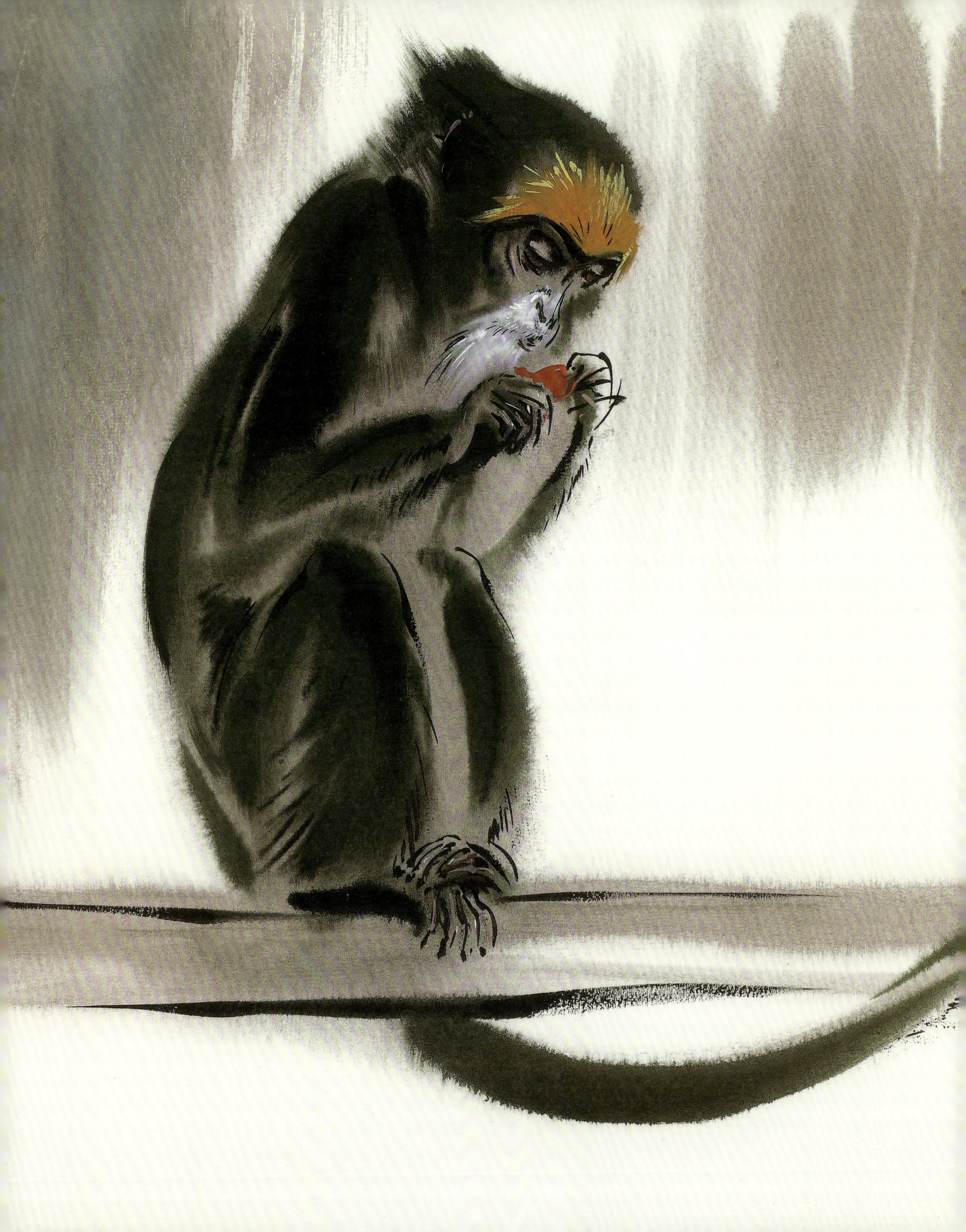

Red-capped mangabey eating fruit
watercolour
380 × 490mm

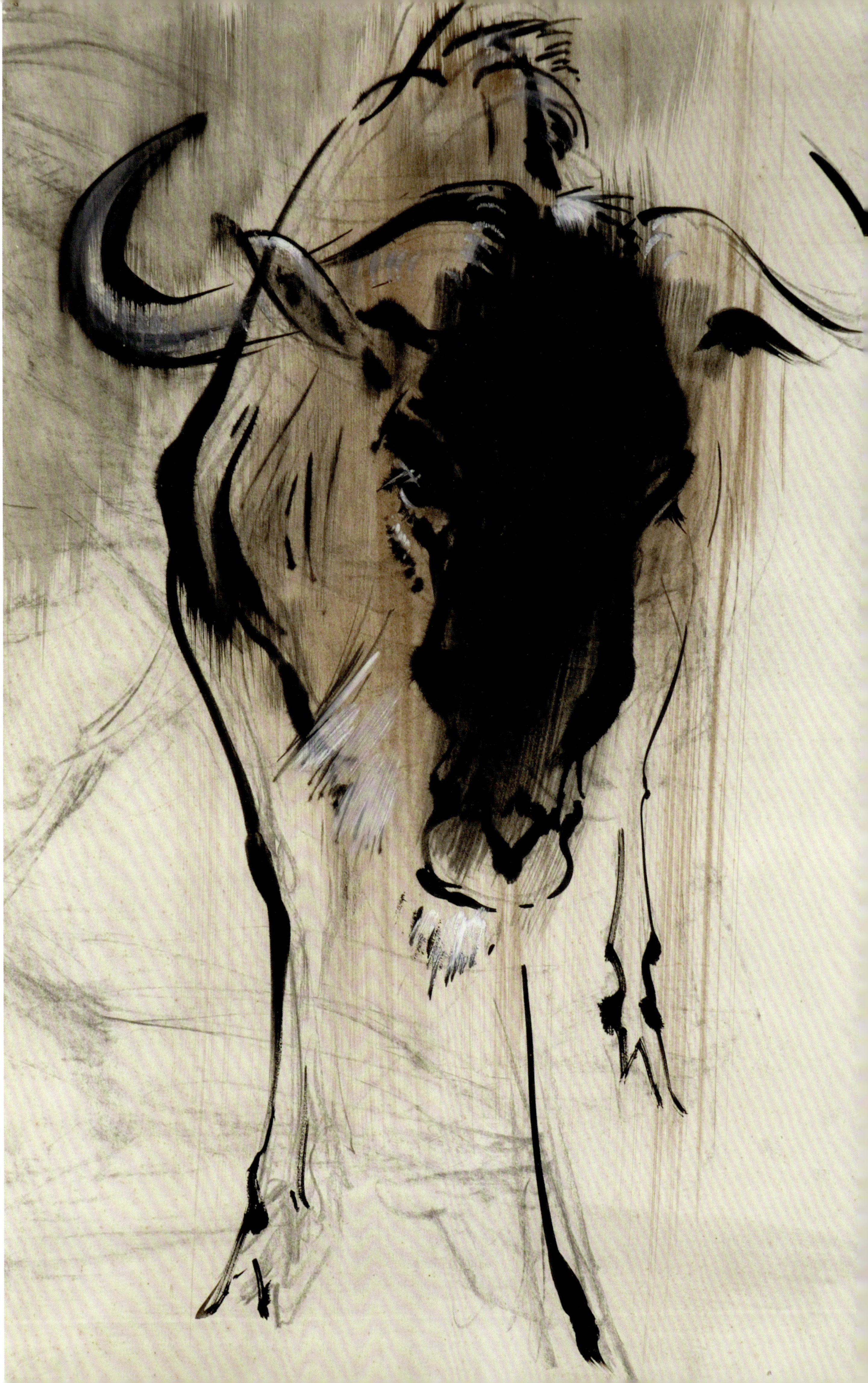

lived in a cardboard box and had the run of the house. Bill wrote a story about the squirrel, called Winkie, which I illustrated and which was then published by Oxford University Press.

Working on so many book illustrations, I began to tire of having to work on a small scale and with the constraints of such limited technique. The idea of drawing for television using a variety of brushes came to mind and this was taken up by the BBC and used as a 'fill up' just before the Six o'clock News under the title 'Ralph Thompson draws an Animal'. The subject would dictate the size and the character of the drawing. For example, a woolly caterpillar could be laid with dabs of a shaving brush and completed with a few touches of an ordinary brush in just a few seconds whereas a tiger's head required quite different brushes and several minutes. These drawings appeared on the black and white screen to the accompaniment of a guitar. Realising the drawing would be seen for a few moments only, the sequence and pattern of the brushwork was all important.

From television, which also had its constraints, my interest shifted to the finished drawing – the development of the picture in its own right. Stimulating new works by British artists were again showing in London and from abroad there came fine exhibitions of the Post-Impressionists, soon to be followed by Cubism. I was puzzled yet fascinated by such revolutionary ways of looking at the world and experiments in modern art began to appear in my studio alongside the illustrative work.

Several factors were now coming together. The experience of simplifying the subject into a couple of brush strokes was one. Another was the purchase of a lavishly illustrated book on the Lascoux cave paintings which became one of my 'bibles' – other influences included Tashism in France and 'action' painting in America which were giving primary importance to the significance of the brush stroke based on the beauty of calligraphy – a vital element of Chinese art. This brought back memories of the 1935 exhibition of Chinese art at Burlington House, which had made such an impression on me during my student days. I particularly remembered the long scroll paintings, 'A Myriad Miles of the Yangtze' and 'The Hundred Geese'. These were the superb paintings from the 11th to 13th centuries – brush drawings in Chinese ink of animals, birds, insects and humans. They were so full of movement, which I loved, and there was a visual poetry, cherishing our relationship with nature. At last I had found my own trail to follow and realised that my previous work had been but an apprenticeship.

opposite
Wildebeest
watercolour
570 × 380 mm

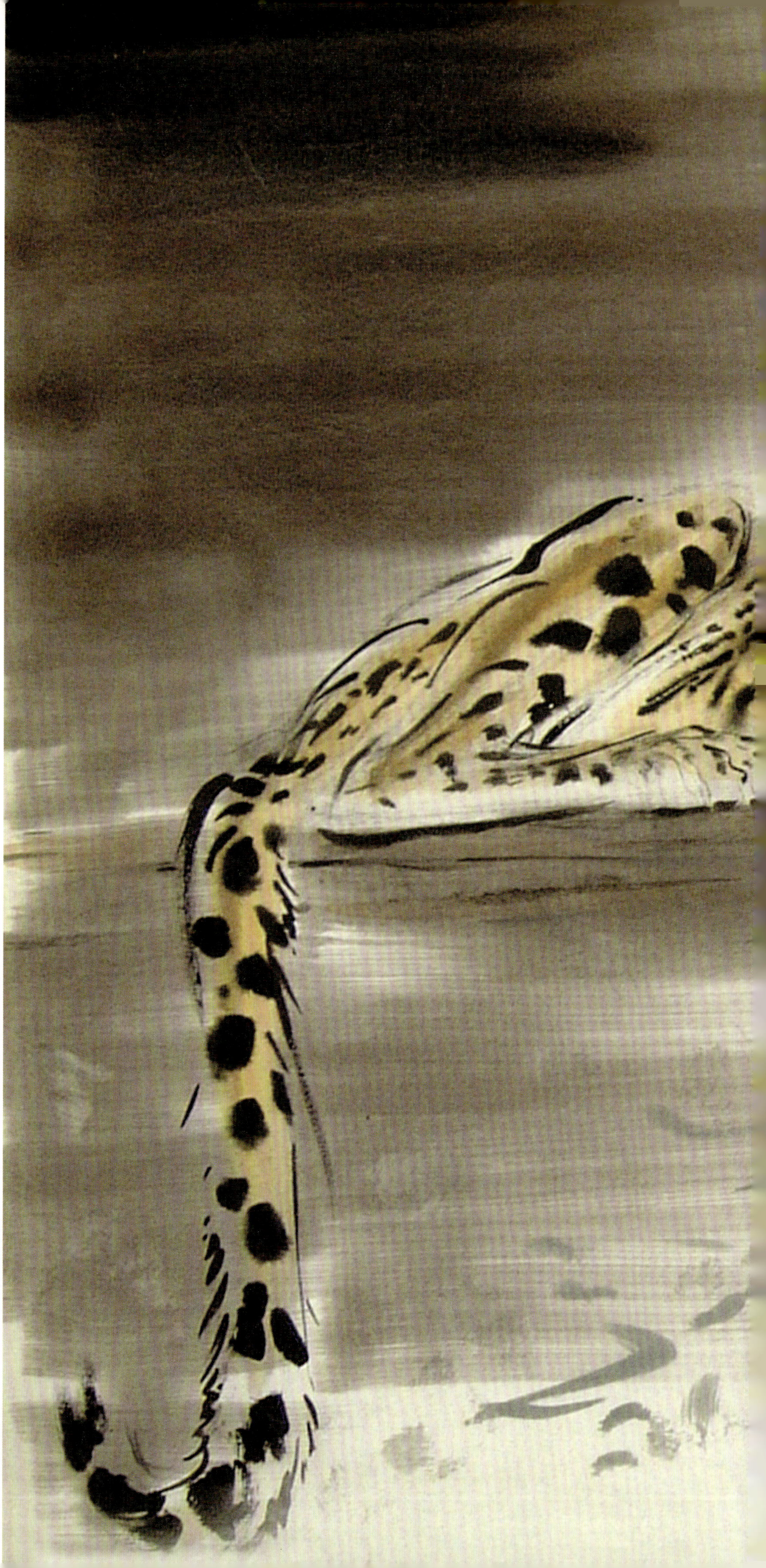

Resting leopard on flat rock
watercolour
700 × 950mm

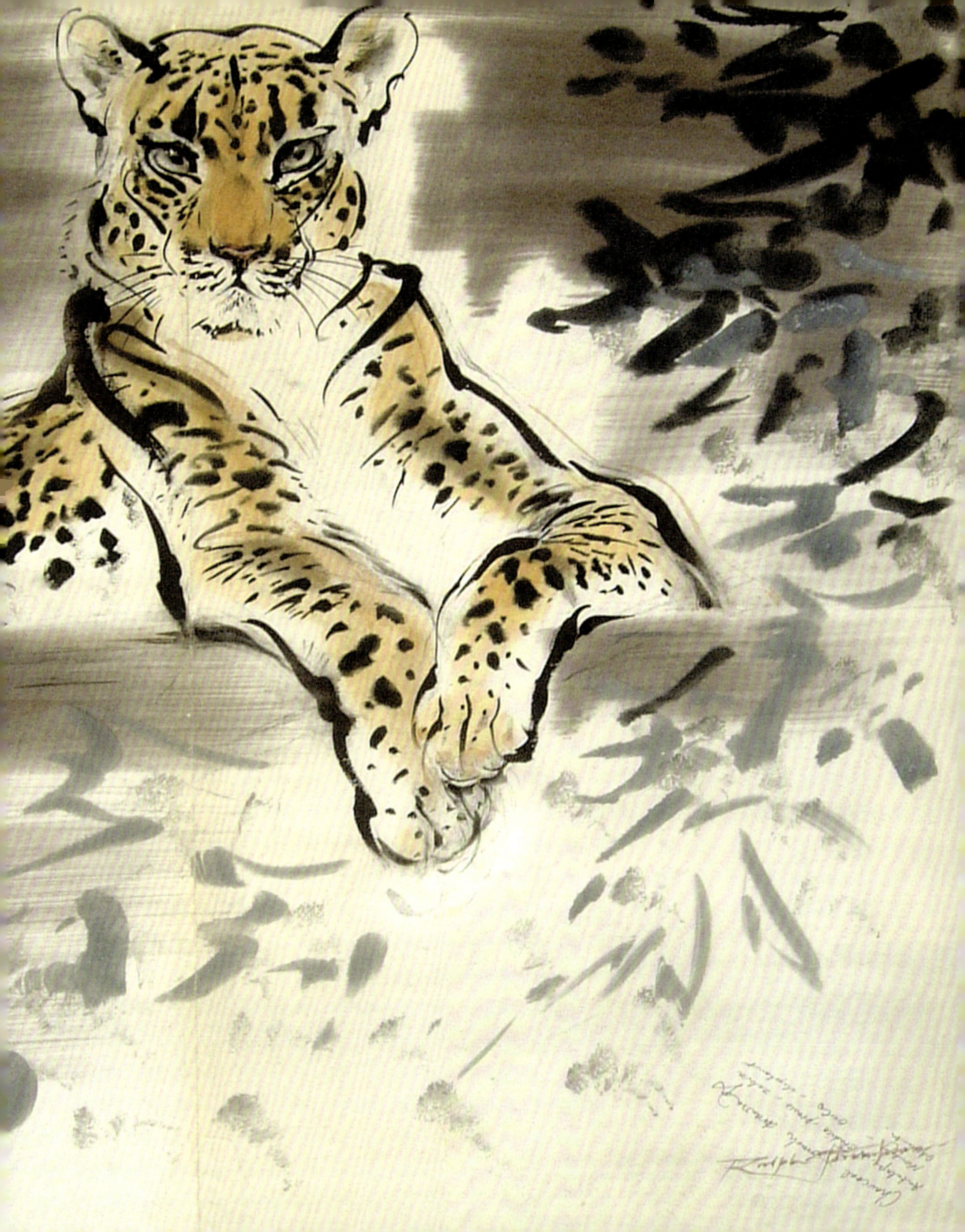

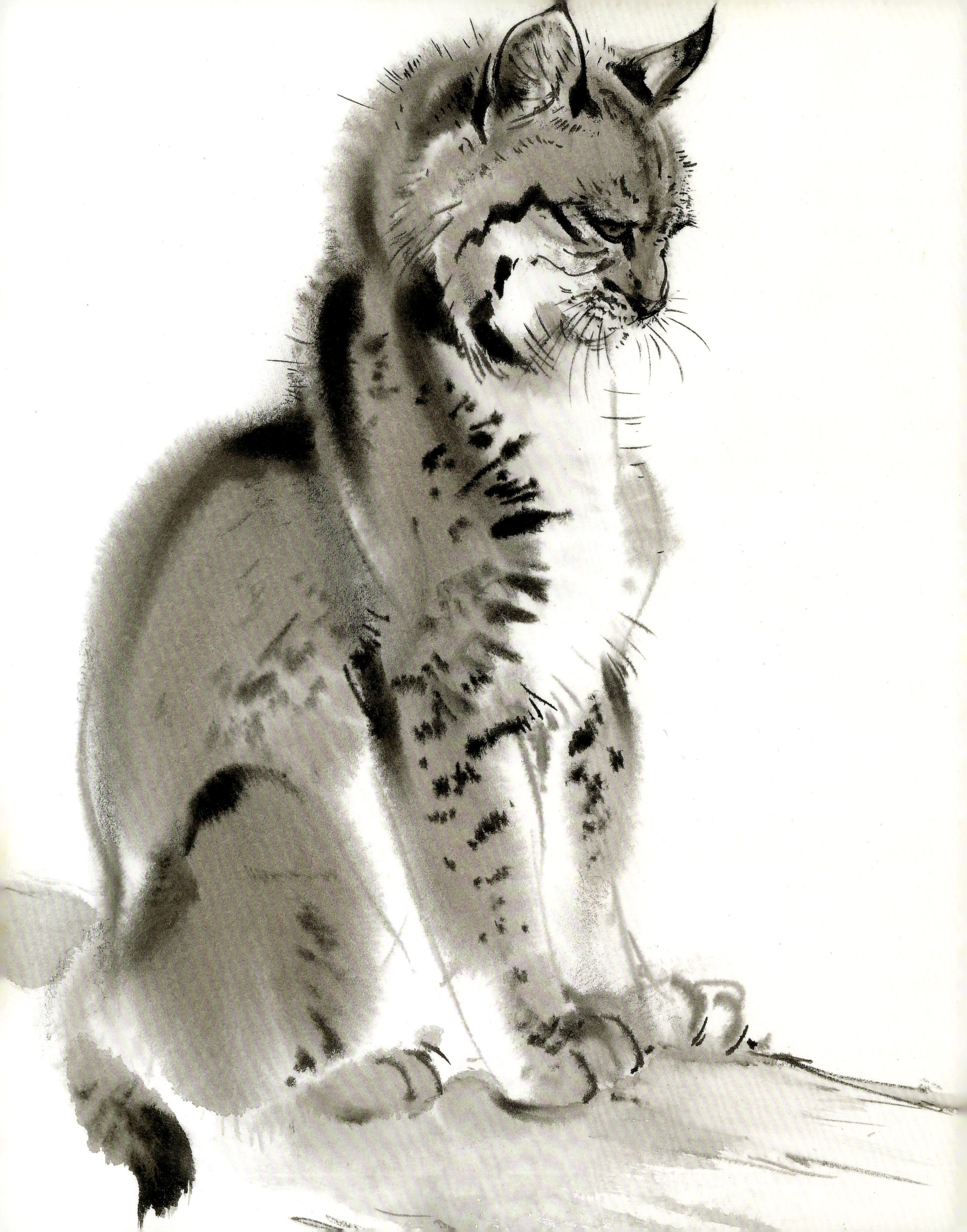

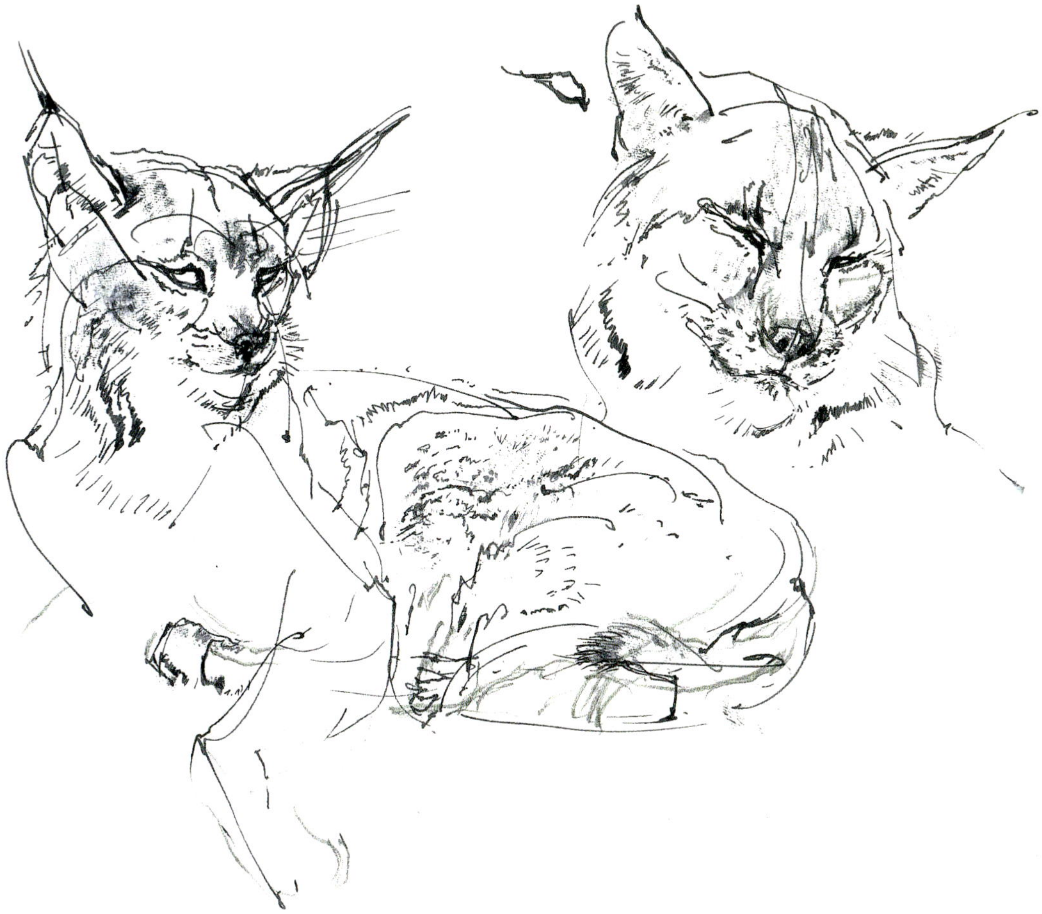

The Steps of the Dance

Catching the movement of an animal has always been a challenge. When making zoo studies I like to use a lot of paper, snatching at positions which take my eye as best as I can. There is a barrier of self-consciousness to break through before reaching the necessary level of concentration: I need to draw and draw regardless of results. Sometimes just a line or two can catch the essence. For me, the camera must be kept as a valuable tool, but as a servant – never a master.

Parallel to my fascination with the movement of animals is the continuing attempt to confront the mysteries, which lie behind the eyes of the animals – the big cats or some of the apes. Also of course, I have never been able to resist the charm of young animals. There comes a 'moment of truth', of success or failure. And this has a link with the first moment of seeing the animal and trying to get it down in a few lines. On a good day, with a lot of luck, a 'lay-in' goes down. Modifying tints and touches can be added later.

On safari, concentration is no longer a problem. Deep-seated hunter instincts give a heightened awareness – but I am hunting with a sketchbook. The sketchbook must be ready and open, with the camera at hand, in case there is time to use it after tackling the subject with my pen. It is the effort to draw at a key moment, which seems to imprint the memory and stir the imagination. At times one can be so caught up in 'happening' that it feels as if the animals themselves are pushing the pen around.

opposite
Northern lynx
watercolour
340 × 250mm

following page right
Northern lynx
oil
610 × 460mm

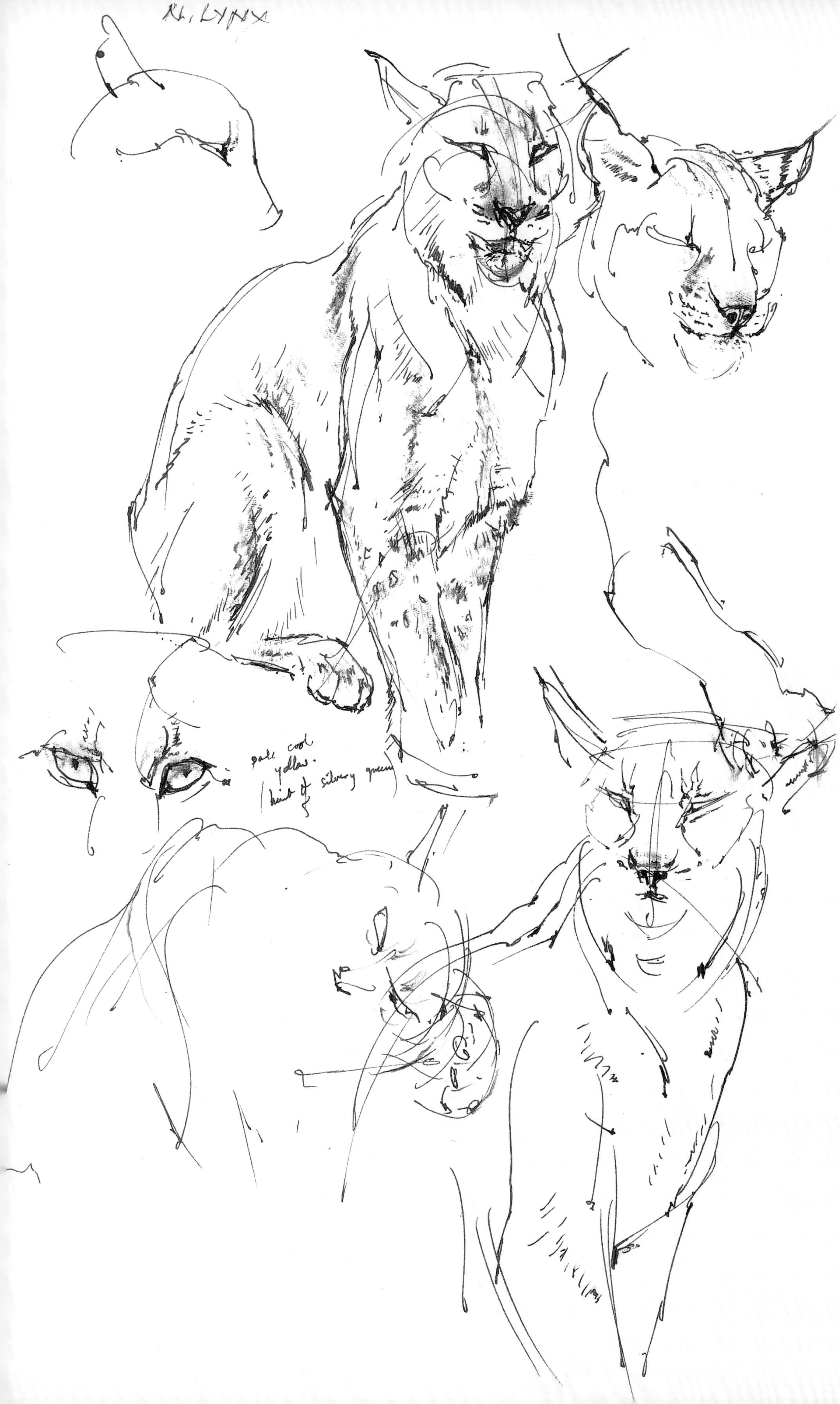
LYNX
pale cool yellow.
hint of silvery green

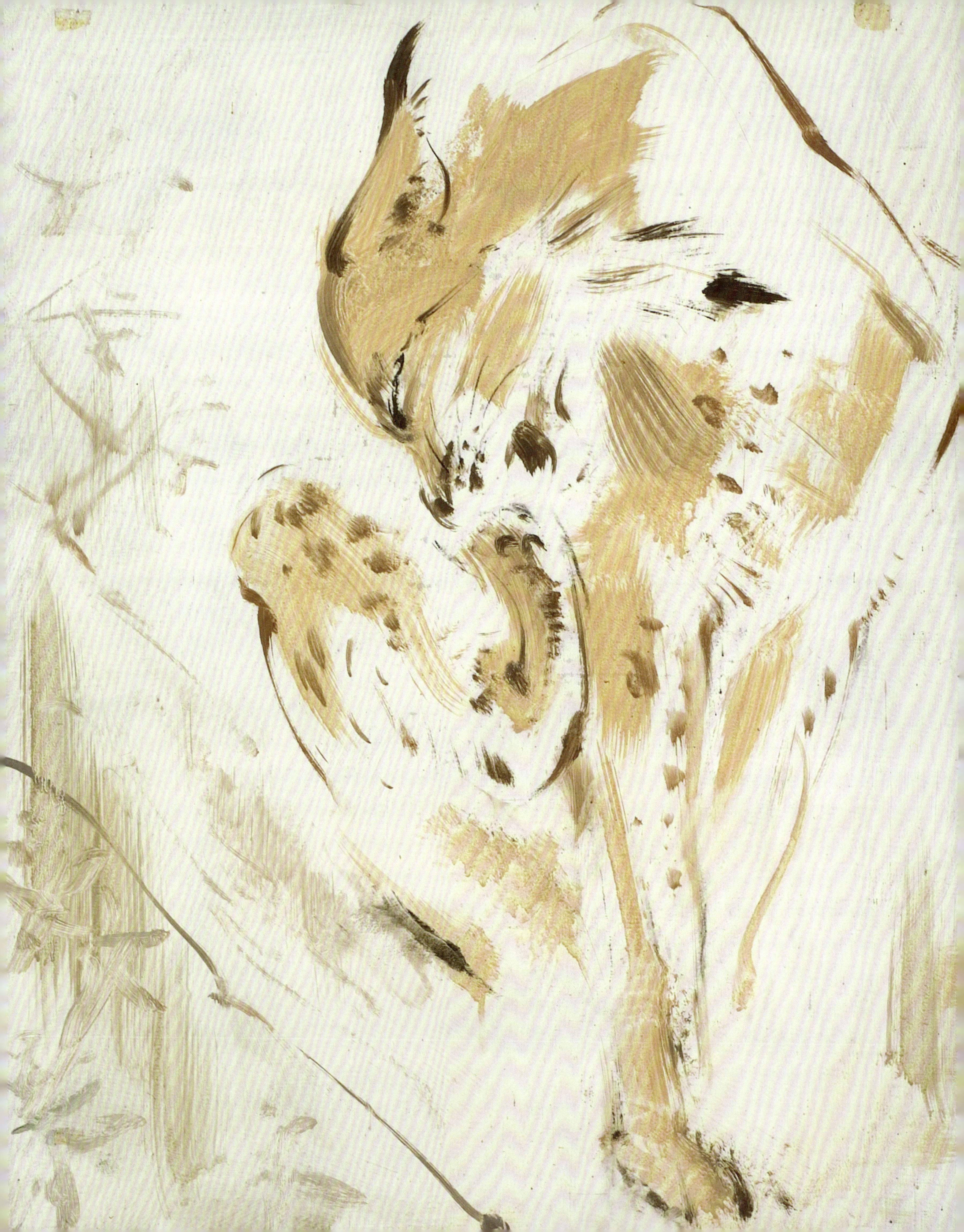

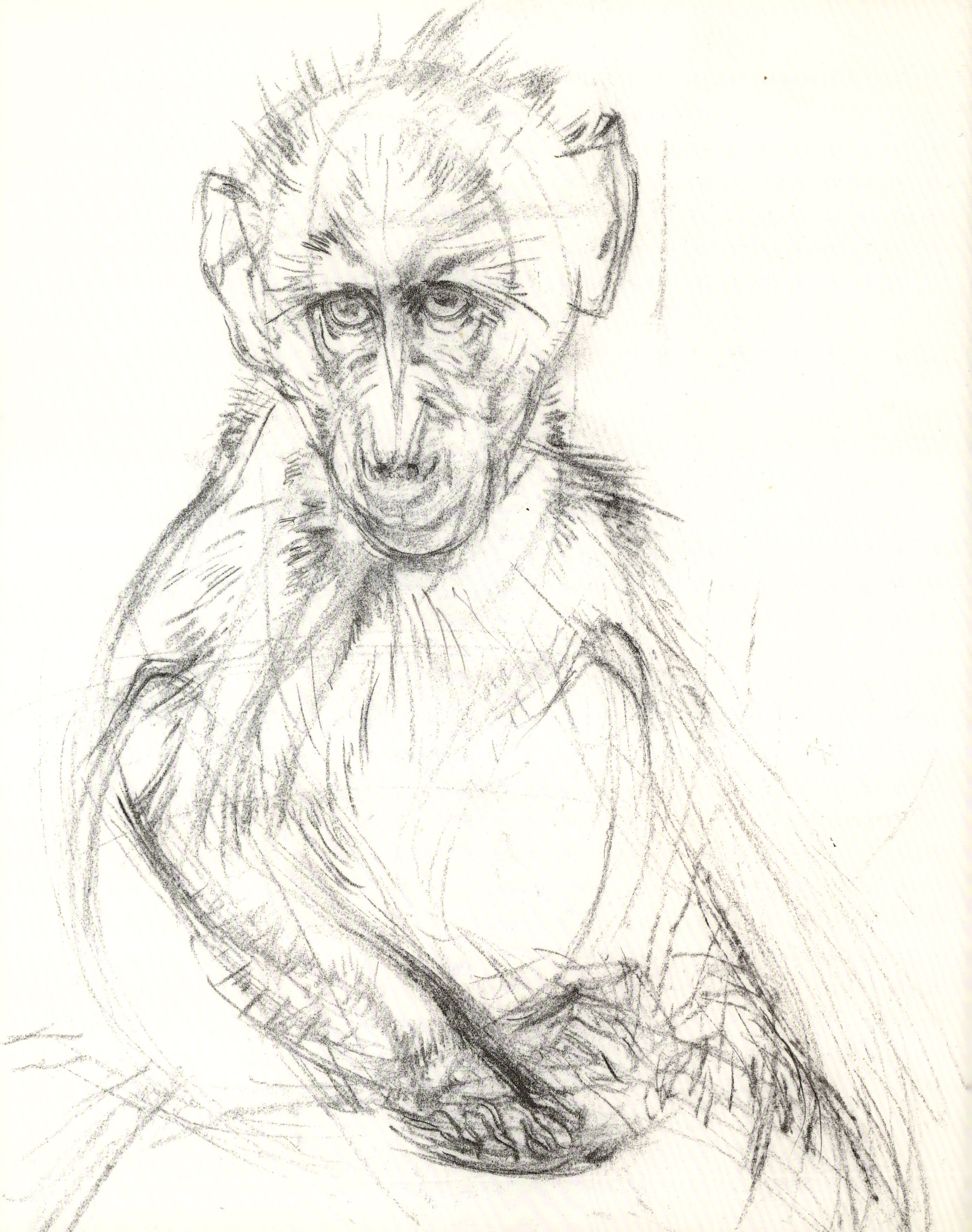

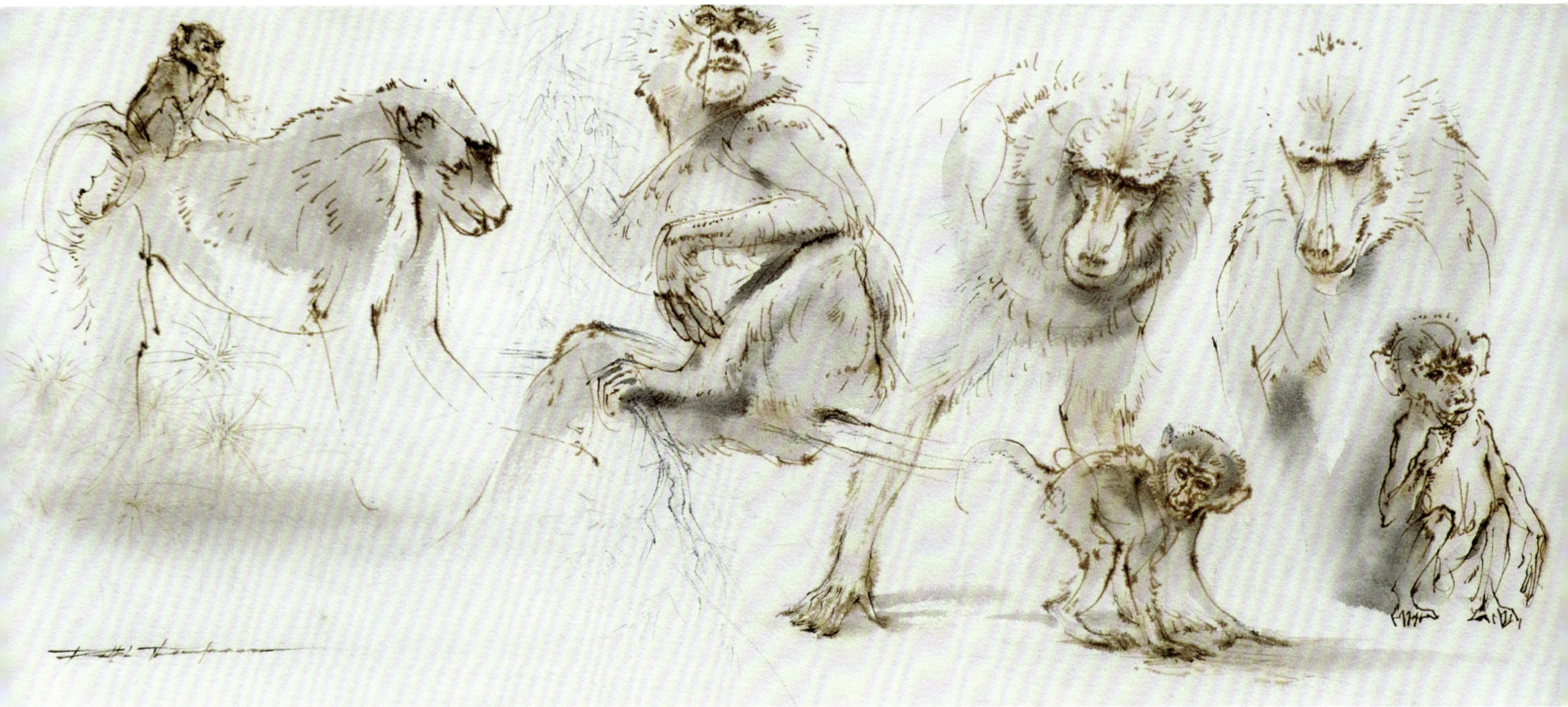

Working from my studies back in the studio, my technique could be labelled 'wet on wet' in artists' jargon. Briefly, on wet paper a line or wash will spread, the spread varying with the 'stiffness' of colour and moistness of the paper, a technique I call 'brush drawing' which I discovered partly by accident. Looking at Turner's watercolours, I saw that he sometimes used a stronger colour in areas already wet with colour. For me drawing with watercolour proved too weak, but with thick gouache on wet drawing paper this produced a spreading line that promised well for depicting animals. By using broad oil paint brushes for large areas and more pointed ones for line drawing, I found it was possible to produce what I called a 'lay-in' for the final painting. Wetting both sides of thick watercolour paper and sponging the top surface to remove surplus water prolonged the period for producing a 'lay-in'.

The colours must be mixed ready and tried. I usually started with a 'whisper' of very pale colour. If the 'lay-in' was not satisfactory, I sponged it out at once, leaving a stain that could be invaluable in producing a second, or with more sponging, a third 'lay-in'. To this end, I made charcoal drawings the same size as the intended painting to put up in front of me as I worked. Charcoal, because it is so strong and flexible can be pushed around, partly removed with a thumb or finger or smudged to a pale grey, if the drawing needs a correction as it often does. After all, drawing is what it's all about and, for me it usually

Baboon studies
ink and watercolour
560 × 240mm

opposite
Young baboon
charcoal drawing
370 × 280mm

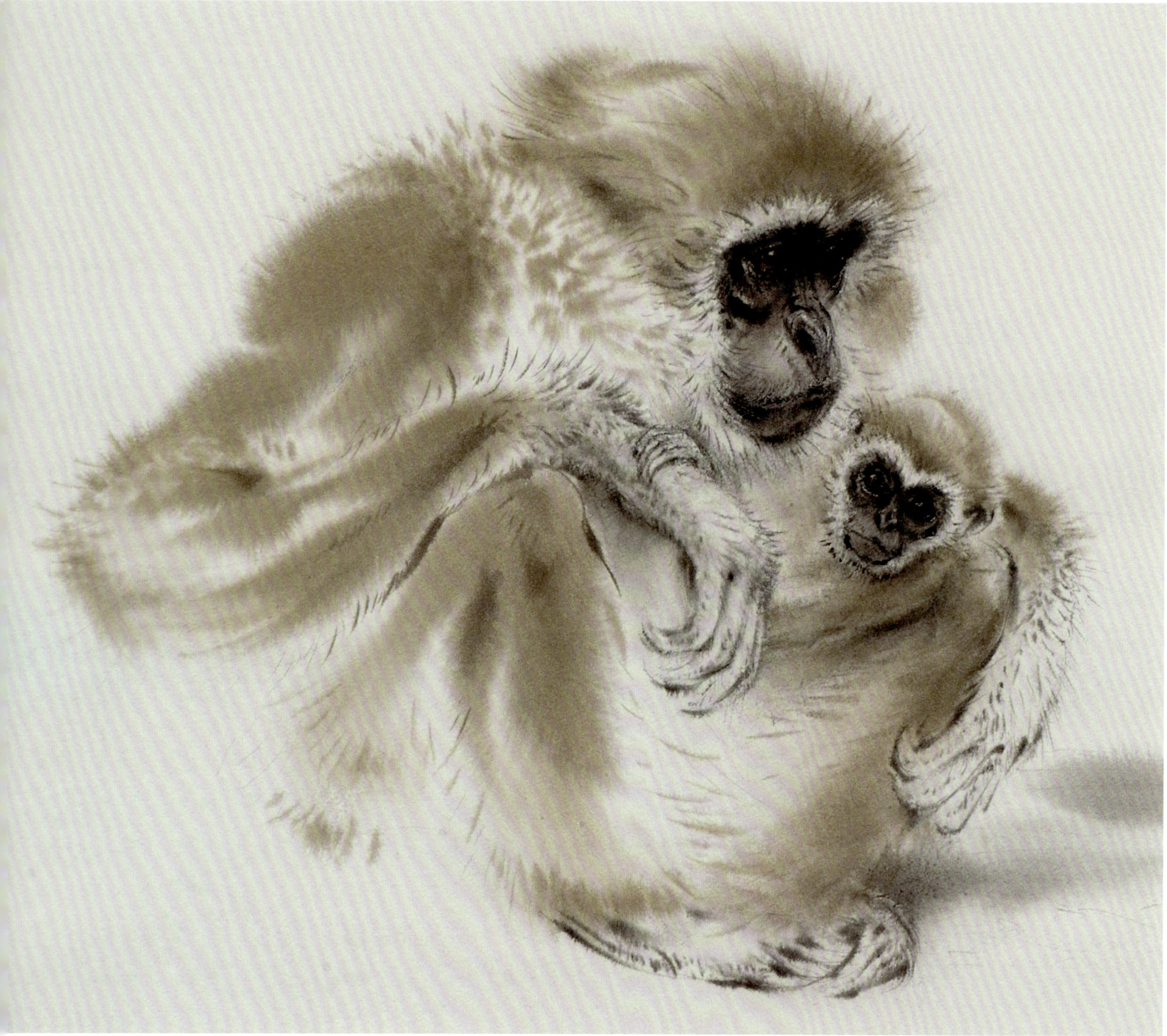

White-handed gibbon and baby
watercolour
380 × 560mm

opposite
White-handed gibbon
charcoal drawing
460 × 390mm

following pages
Nyala study sheet
ink and watercolour
actual size

starts with the drawing of live animals on the move. With practice and good fortune just a few lines can convey the essentials. This in itself is problematical and varies with each artist. I sometimes feel my line going round the forms enjoying and defining them, but sometimes the lines go through the forms, simplifying them if the drawing is to work and to give the essence of the particular idea of the subject created in my mind. I make several attempts and they each contribute to the character of the final brush drawing.

'The privilege and delight, if not, sometimes the distress of watching an ancient, timeless wilderness world had begun.'

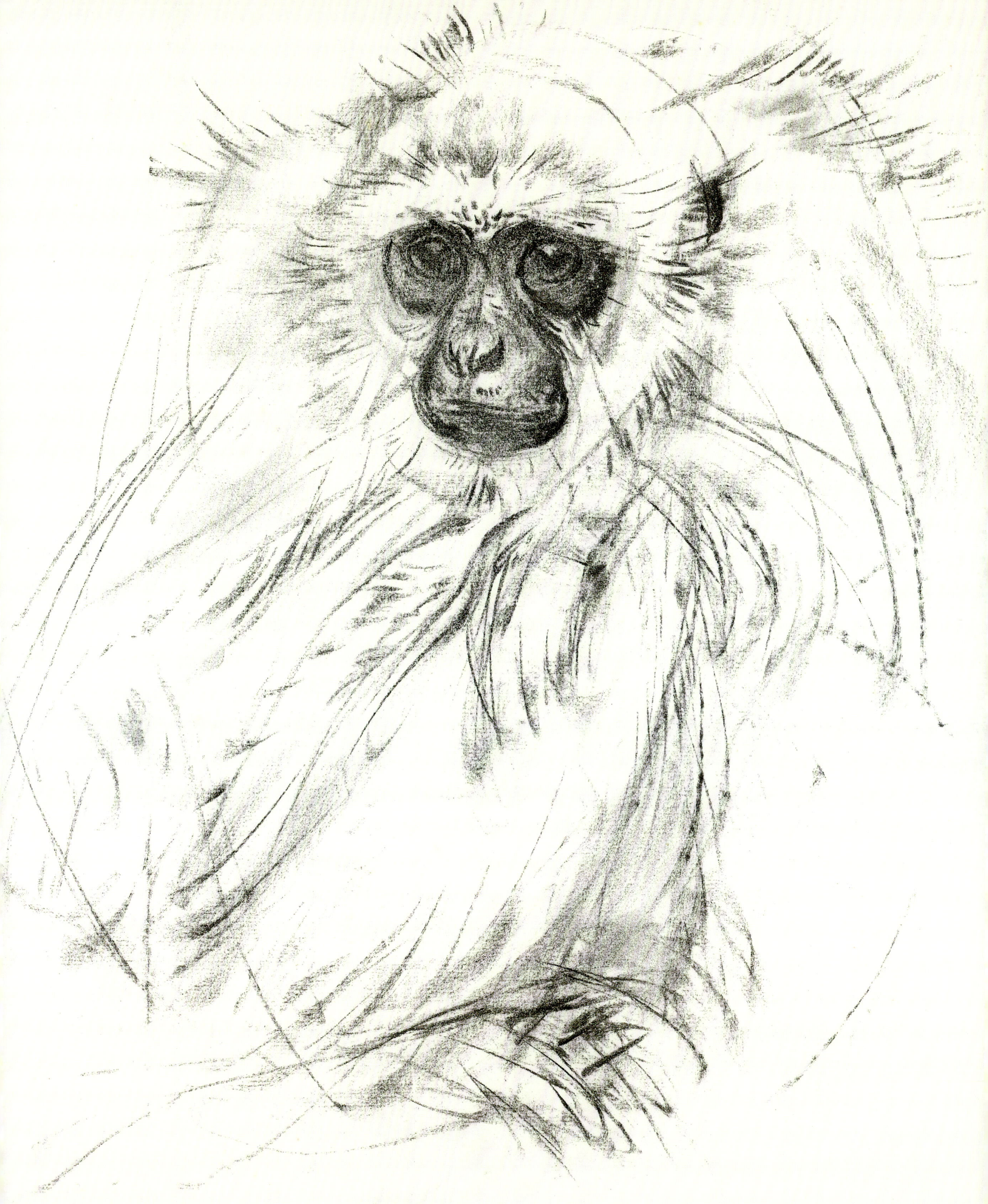

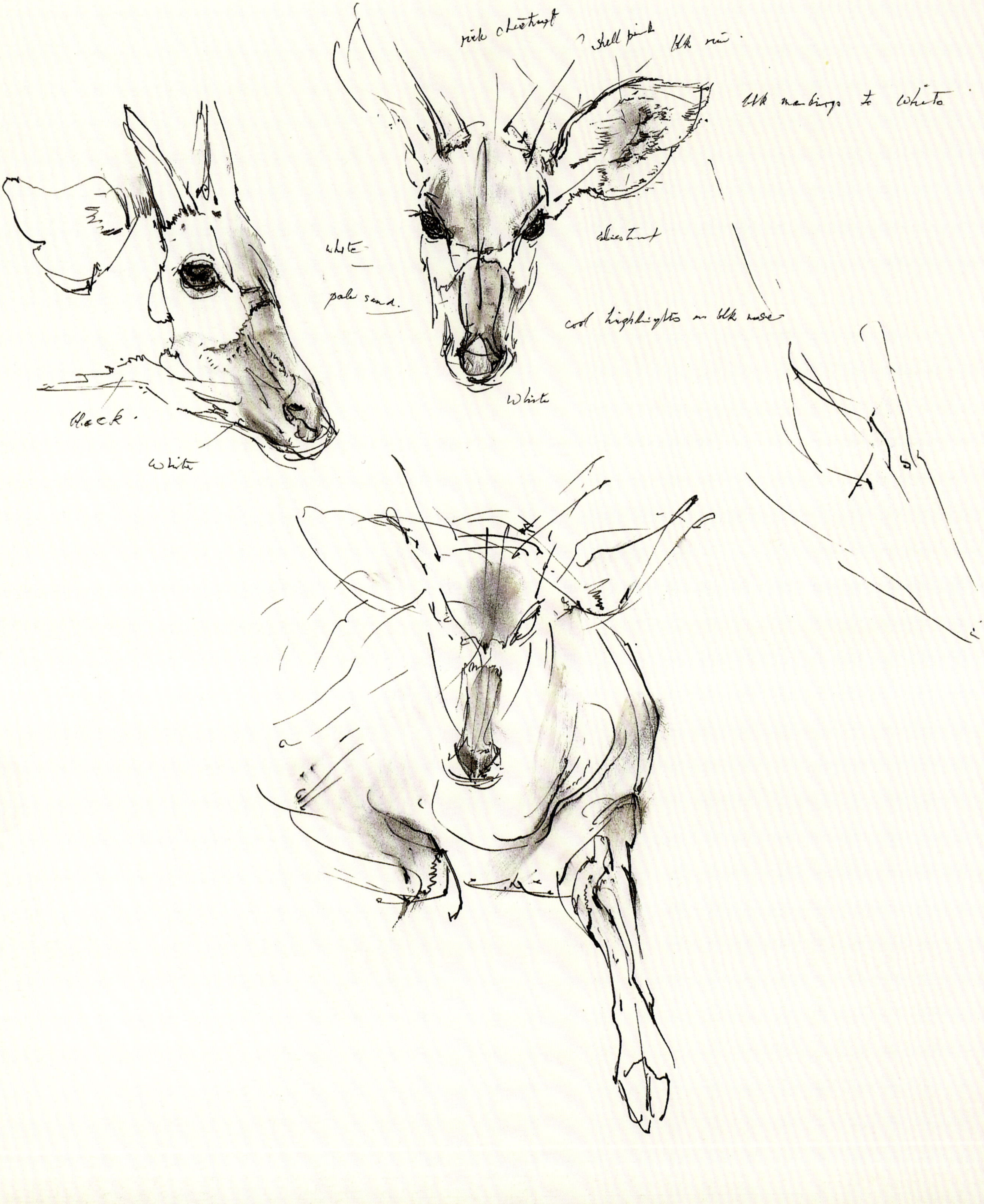
rich chestnut
shell pink
blk rim
blk markings to white
white
pale sand.
chestnut
cool highlights on blk nose
White
black.
White

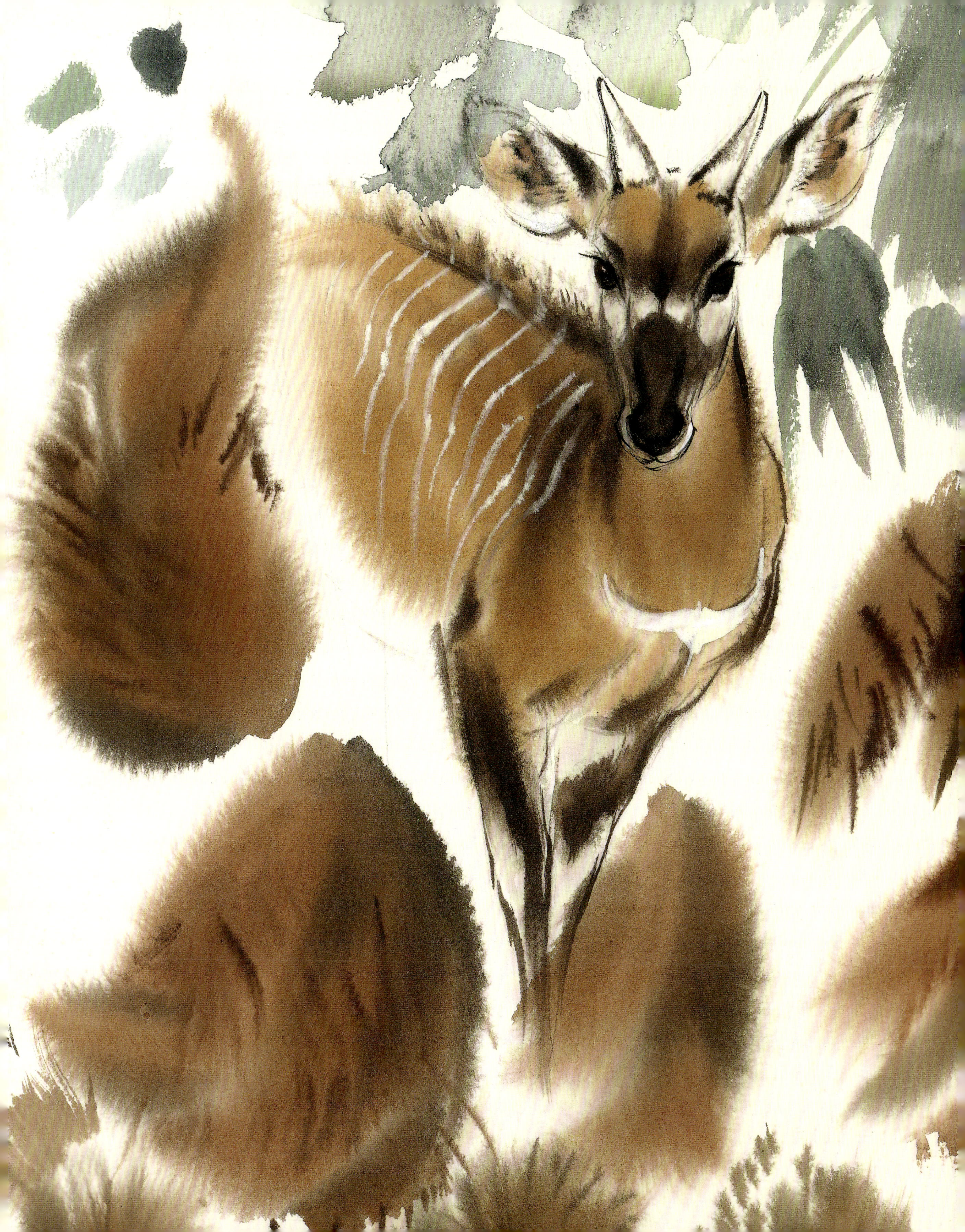

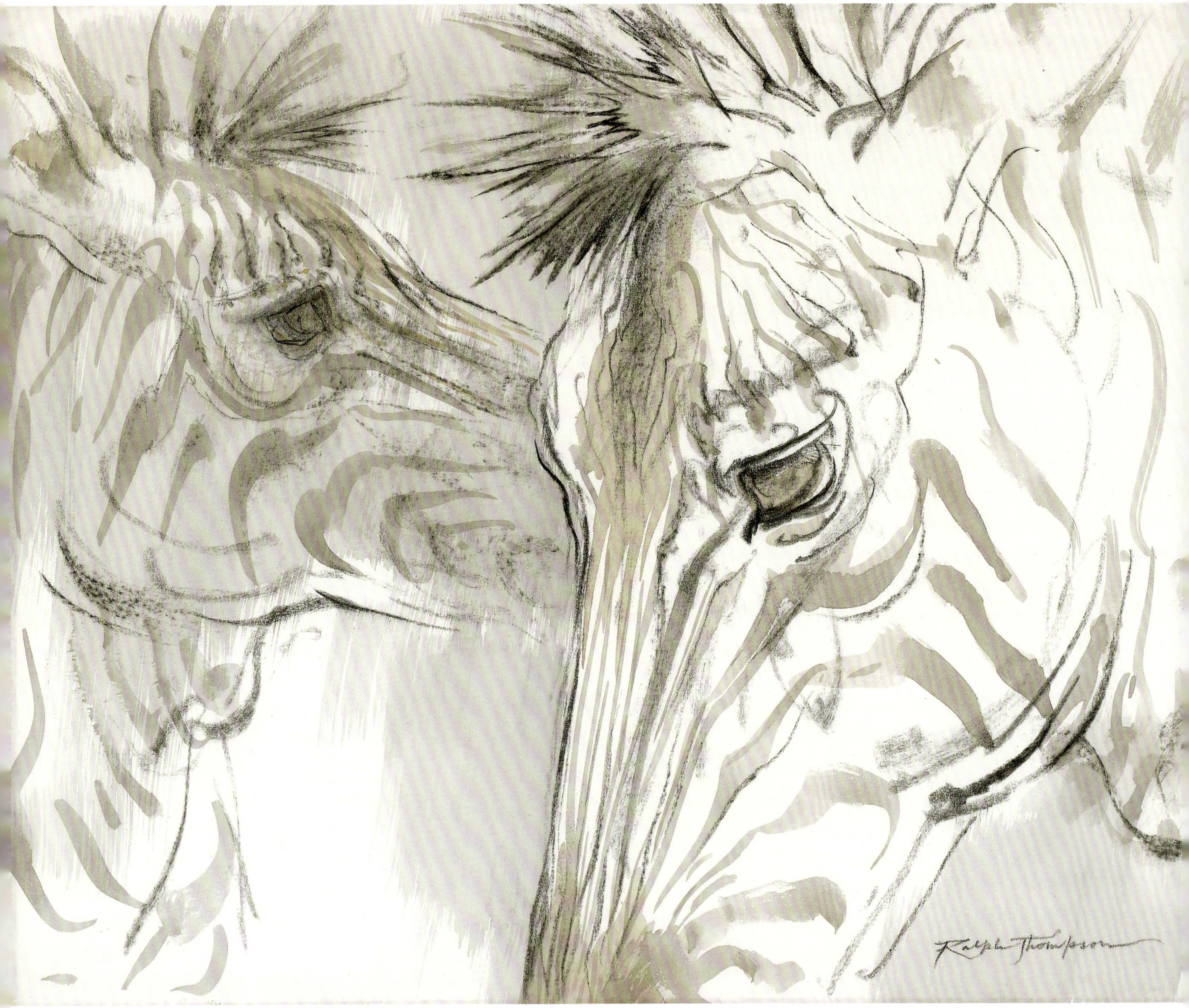
Ralph Thompson

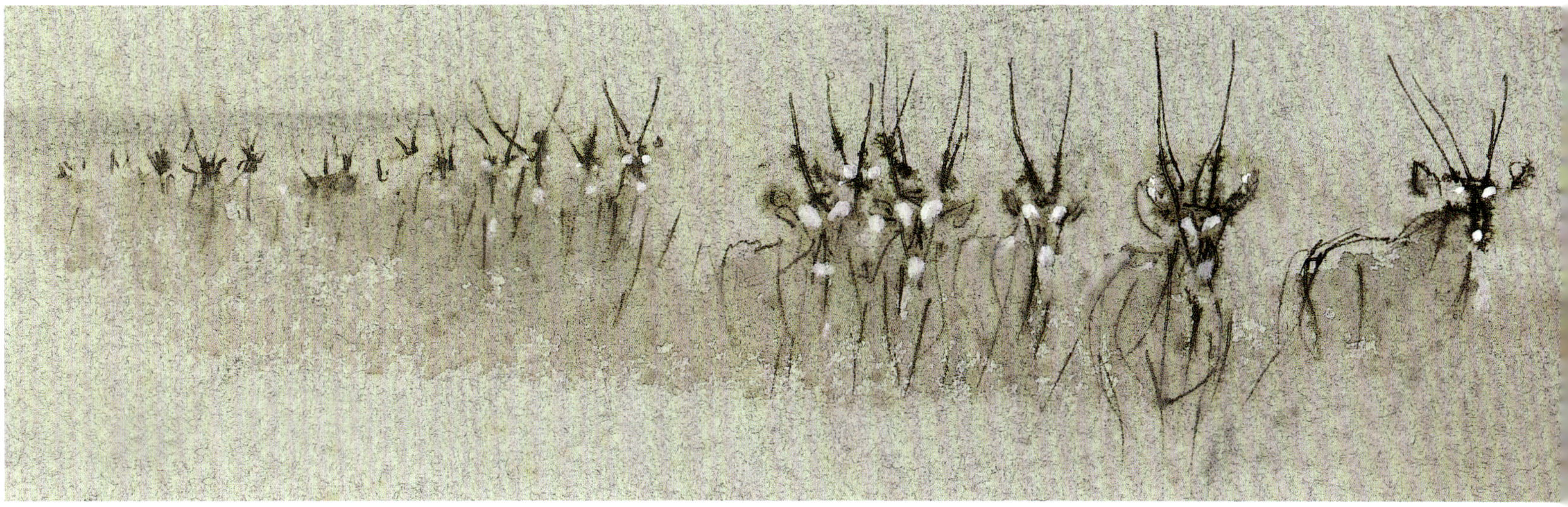

South Africa – Kruger National Park

At my first exhibition at the Tryon Gallery in London I met Everard Read, the director of a gallery in Johannesburg. He suggested I come out to South Africa bringing about twenty paintings, enough for a small exhibition. He would pay my airfare and would personally act as my guide around the Kruger National Park and pay my car hire so that I could see other important reserves.

As we approached the northern entrance to the Kruger National Park, there were many tiny colourful birds, their iridescent colours suddenly gleaming rich and lustrous. Everard identified them as Sunbirds and pointed to a double collard sunbird and a black sunbird. They were in and out among the poinsettias at the entrance.

It seemed right that the first animals for me to see in the wild should be zebra, about a dozen of them, like plump little striped ponies taking little or no notice of our car and looking so much a part of the landscape. For me it was a thrilling new experience.

But new experiences were waiting for me around every bend. Very soon Everard was able to show me, my first Malachite kingfisher. It was tiny, no larger than our native one but even more eye-catching, brilliant in colour, perched on a branch above a stream by the road side – all that remained, according to Everard, of the dried up Limpopo River - a stretch of sand lying beyond.

Oryx herd on the move
watercolour
80 × 240mm

opposite
Zebra
charcoal and watercolour
320 × 400mm

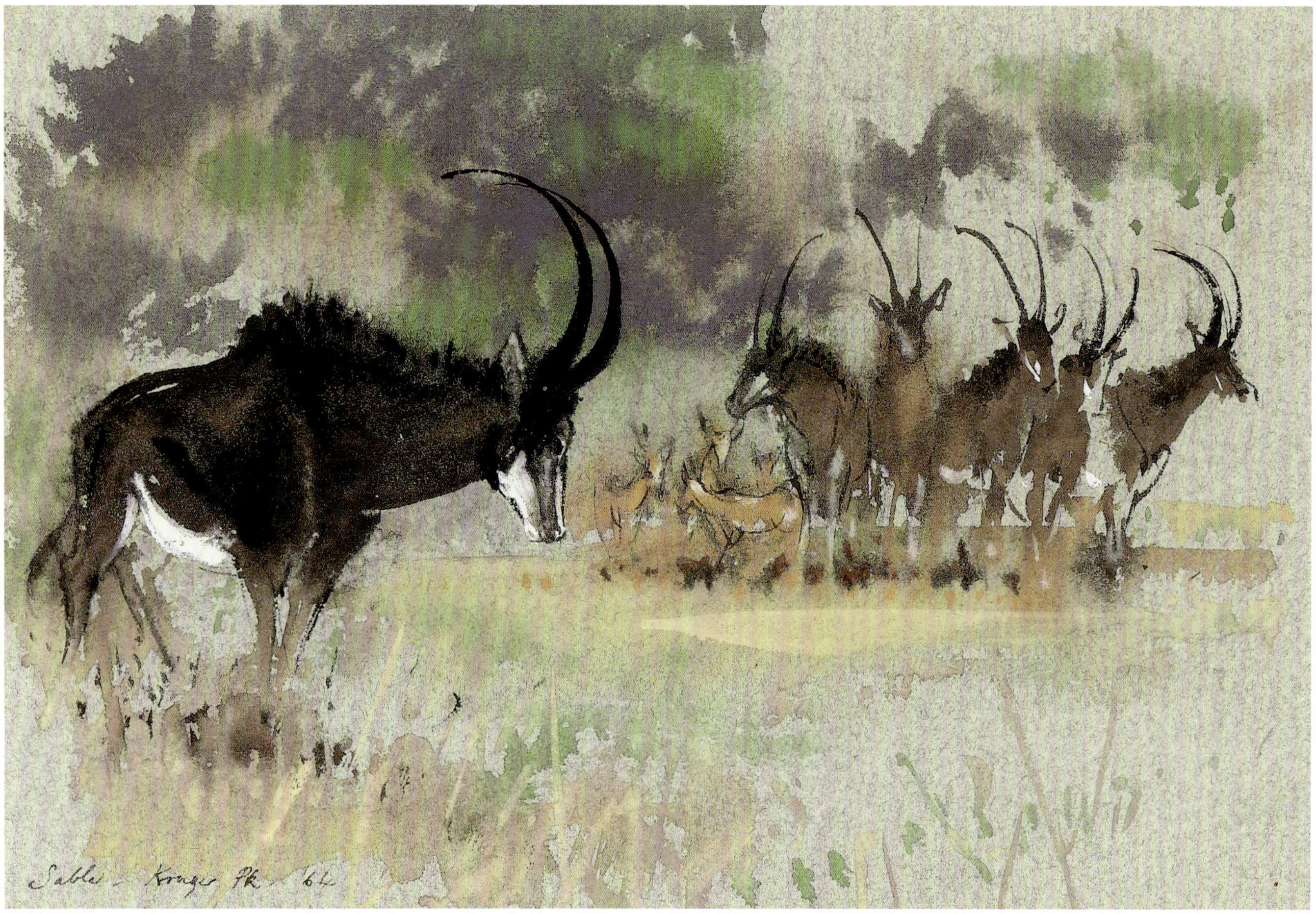
Sable – Kruger Pk. '64

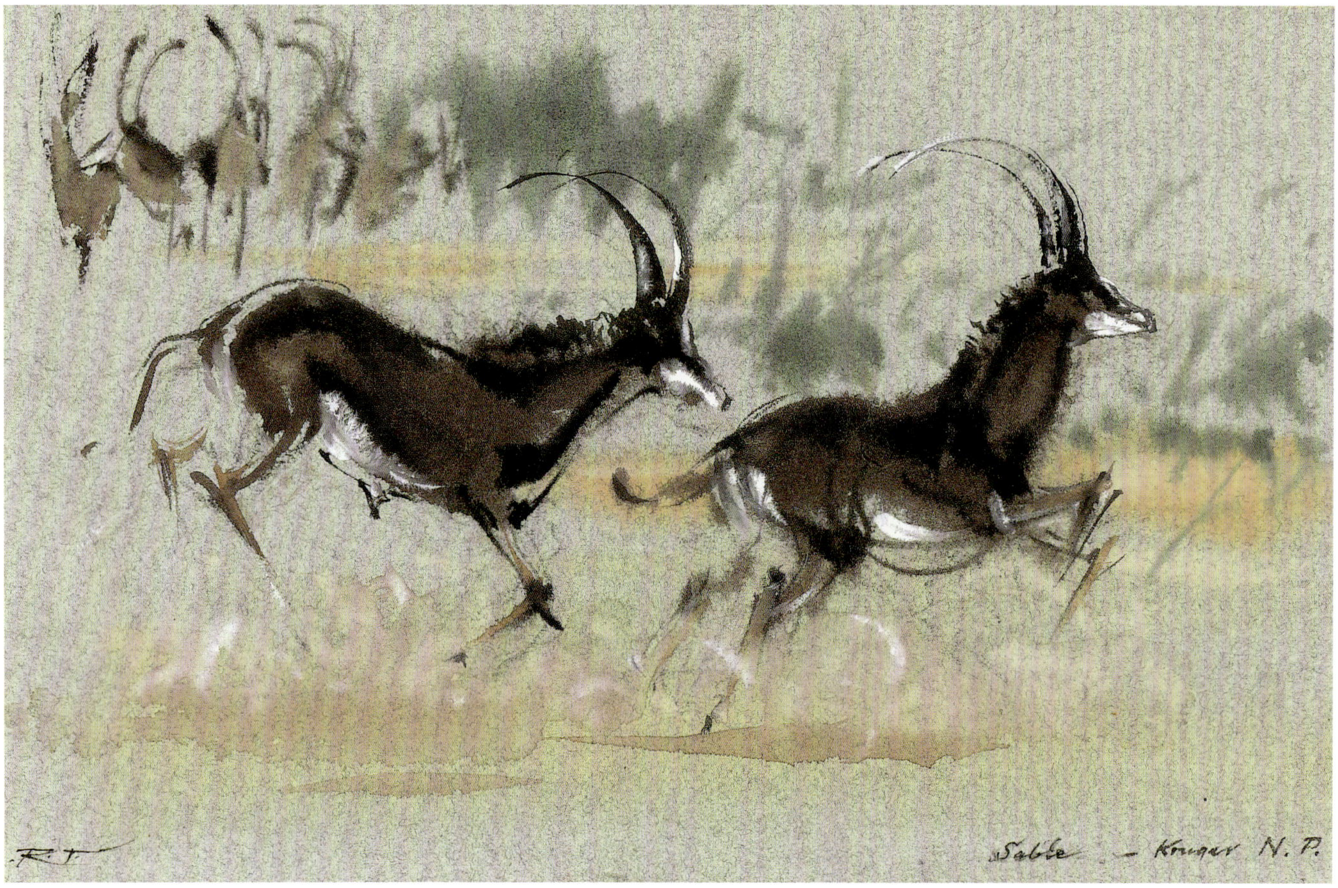
R.T.
Sable – Kruger N.P.

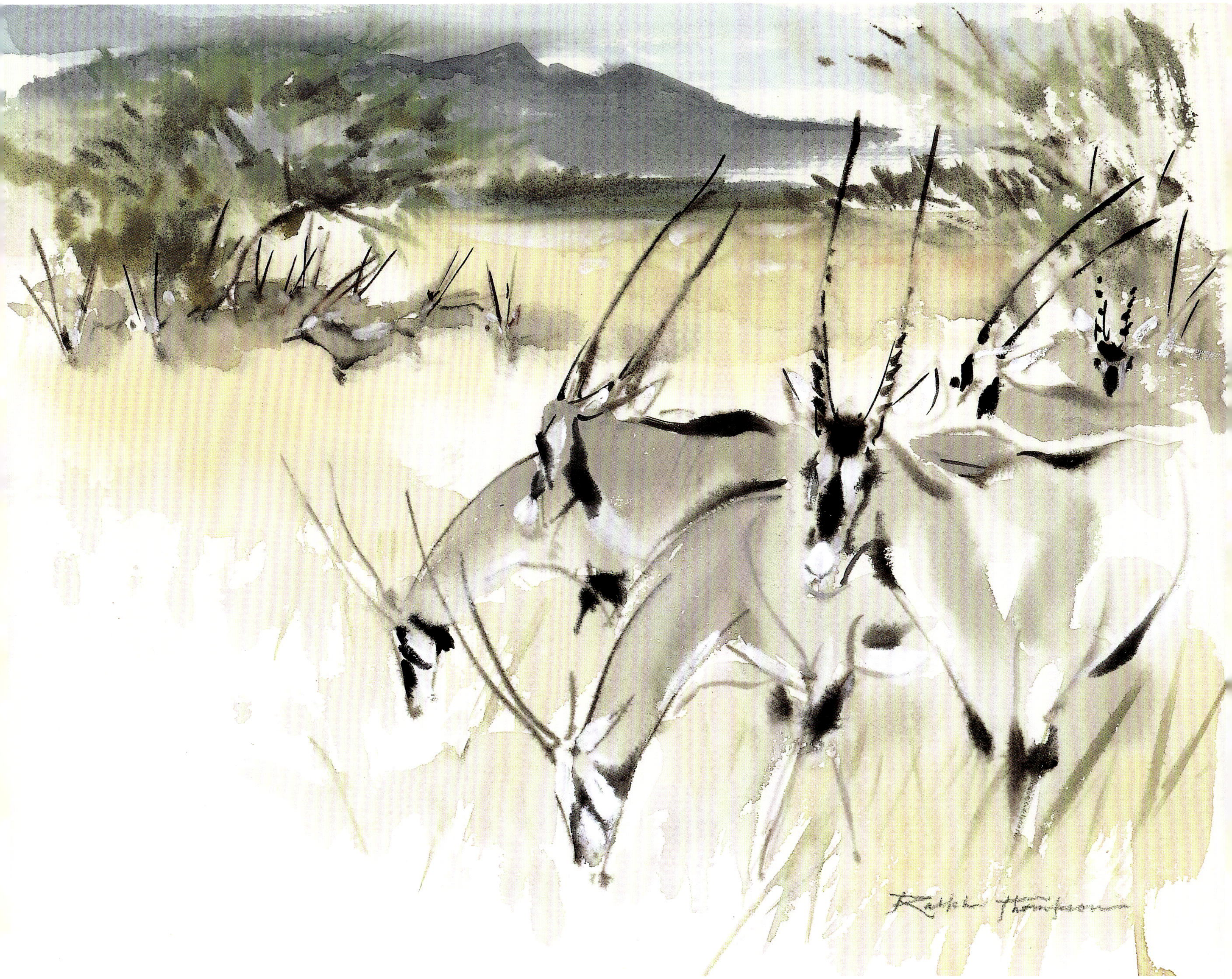

Oryx
watercolour
260 × 340mm

opposite
Sable antelope studies
gouache
each 137 × 205mm

following page
Grant's gazelles
pencil and watercolour
320 × 480mm

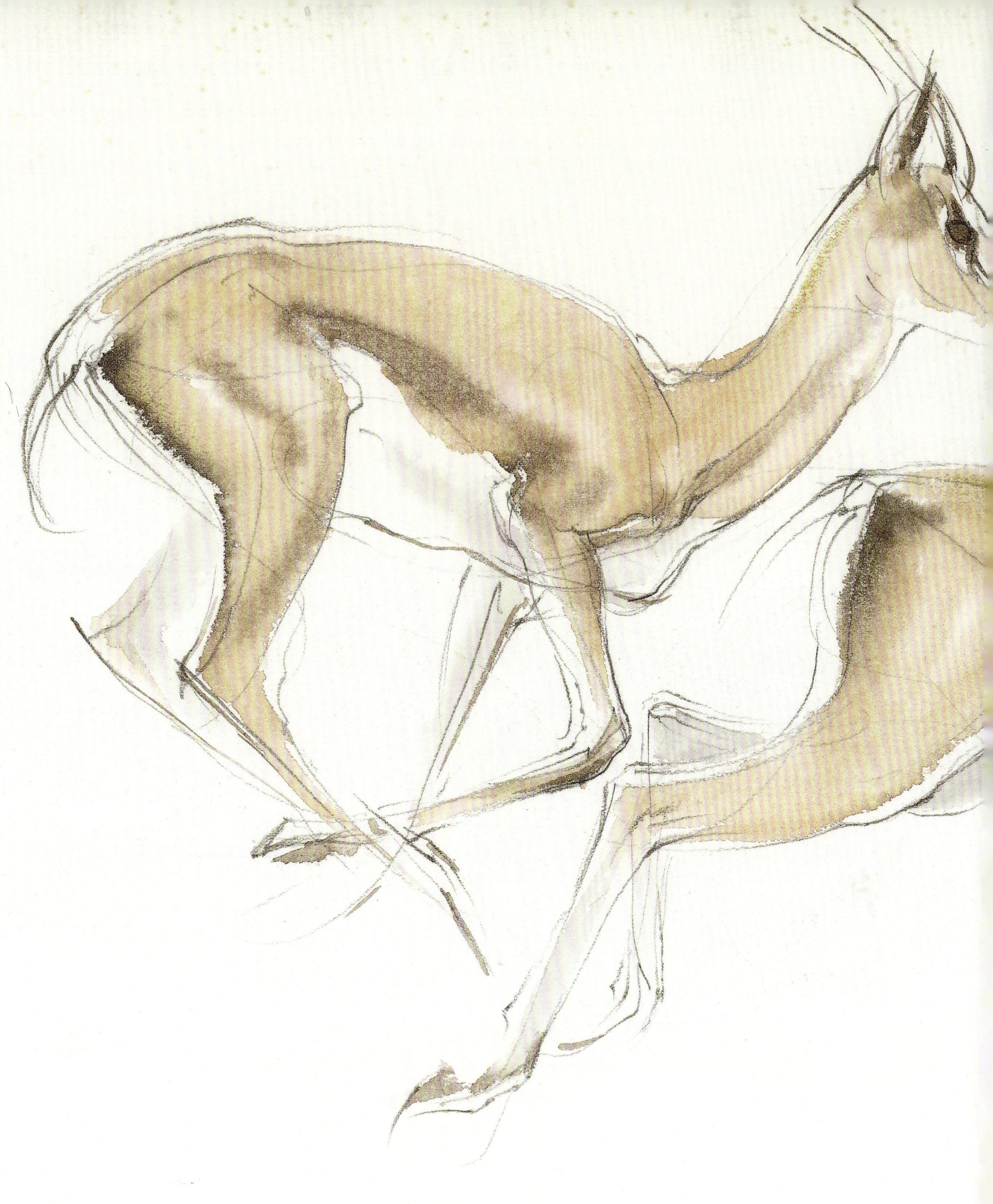

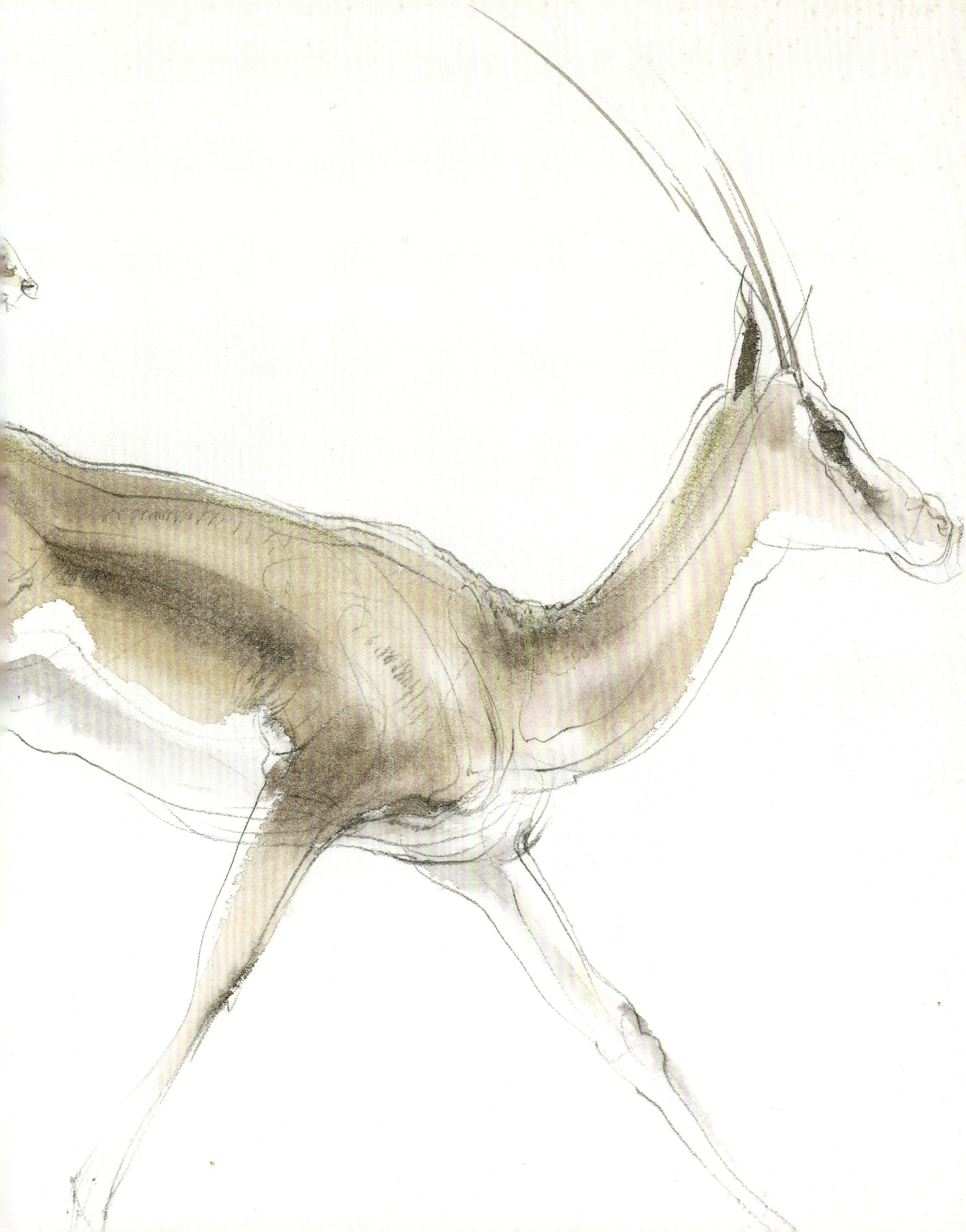

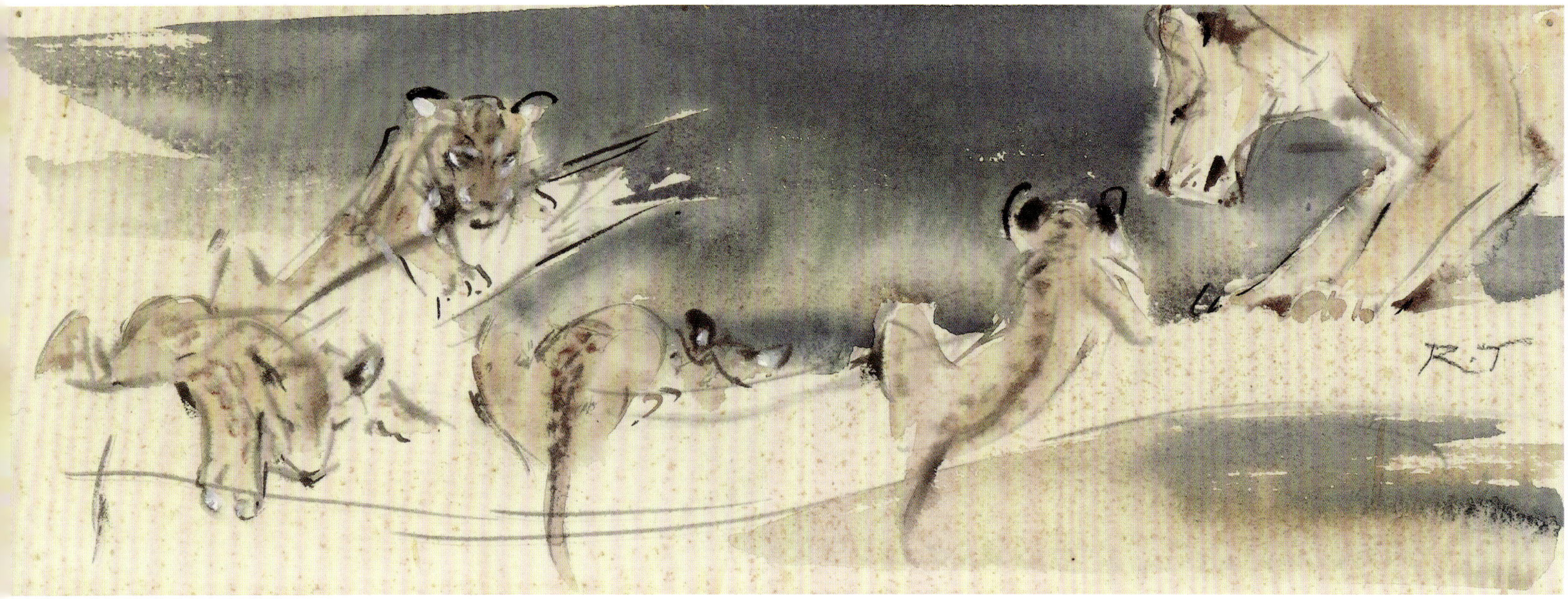

Lioness and cubs
watercolour
130 × 350mm

opposite and following pages
Sketchbook studies
actual size

One day I was taken so completely by surprise I was quite unable to draw. On a narrow road, with cover each side, a lioness stepped out from the left side, glanced towards our oncoming car, probably checked that it had halted, then, one after another, ten cubs followed her. Then a second 'an aunty' brought up the rear.

Having looked through two hundred pages or so of my sketchbook (a 'publisher's dummy') with rapid sketches of the many different scenes, which caught my eye each day, as I drove slowly from the north to the south of the Kruger National Park, I found myself faced with the difficult task of choosing the very few which the available space in this book would allow. As I leafed through one scene after another, although some were too confused to use, I found it almost impossible to make the choice. In the end I called upon Andrew and Graham, my publishers, to make it for me.

Incidentally, a publisher's dummy is now largely a thing of the past. To give the artist designing a book jacket, the exact size of the book, the publisher made a 'dummy' of the blank pages. These made excellent sketchbooks. The title of this particular dummy book, written freehand on a hard cloth cover happened to be 'The problem of method'!

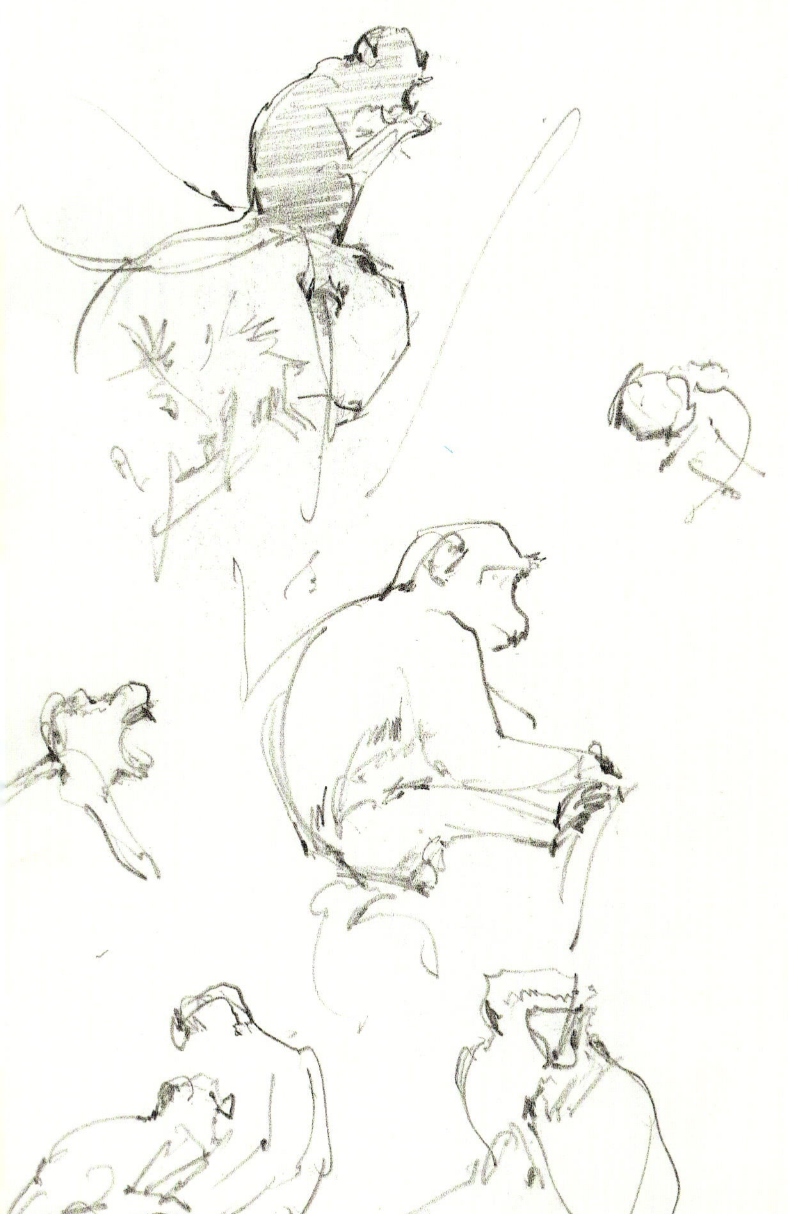

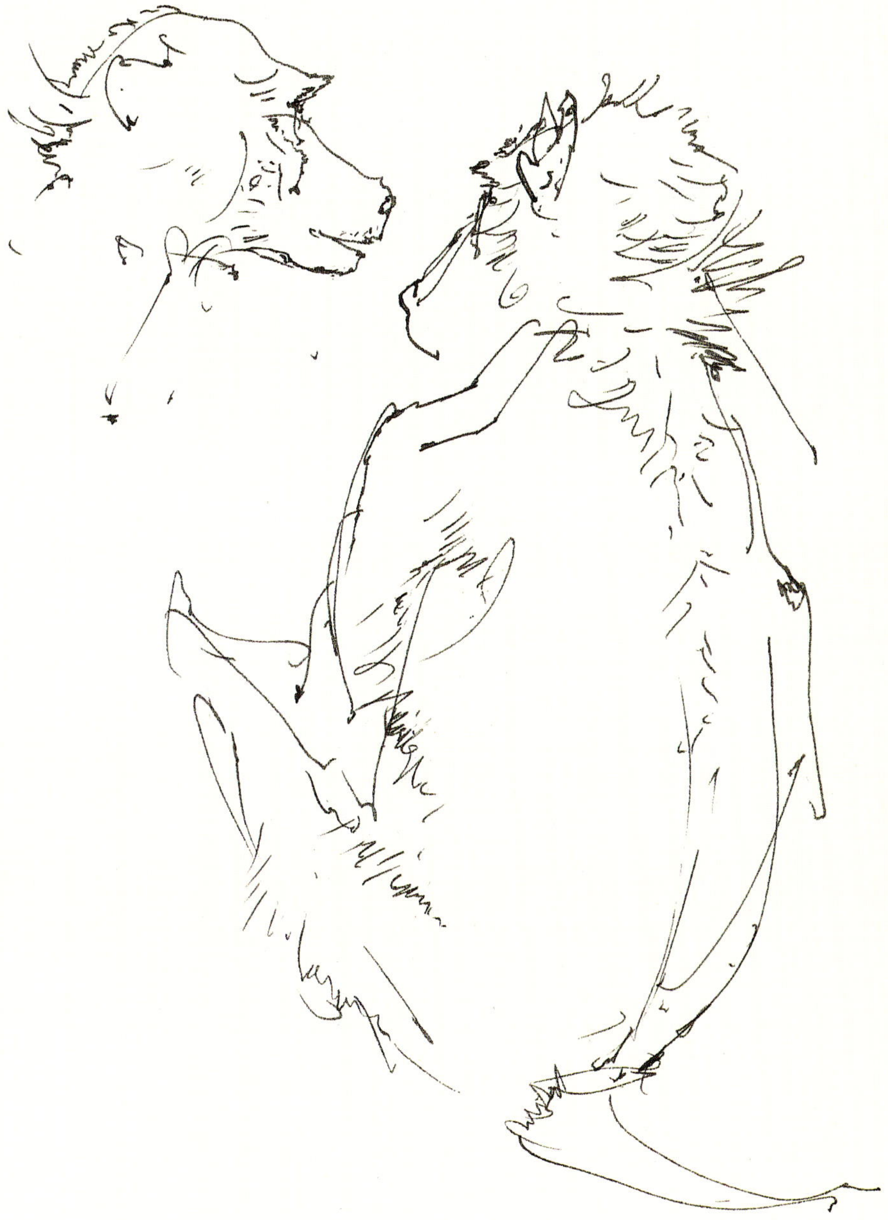

Babboons

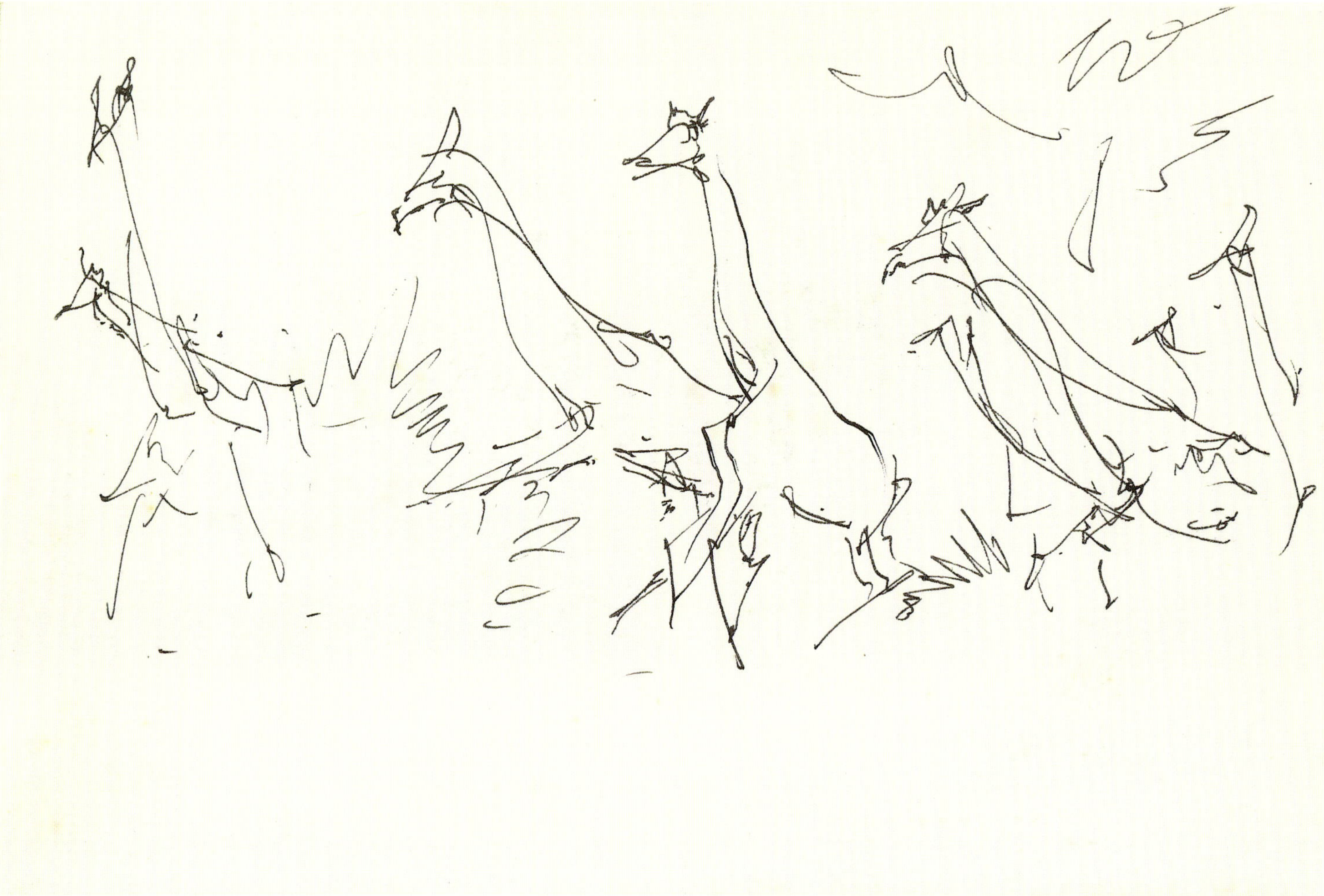

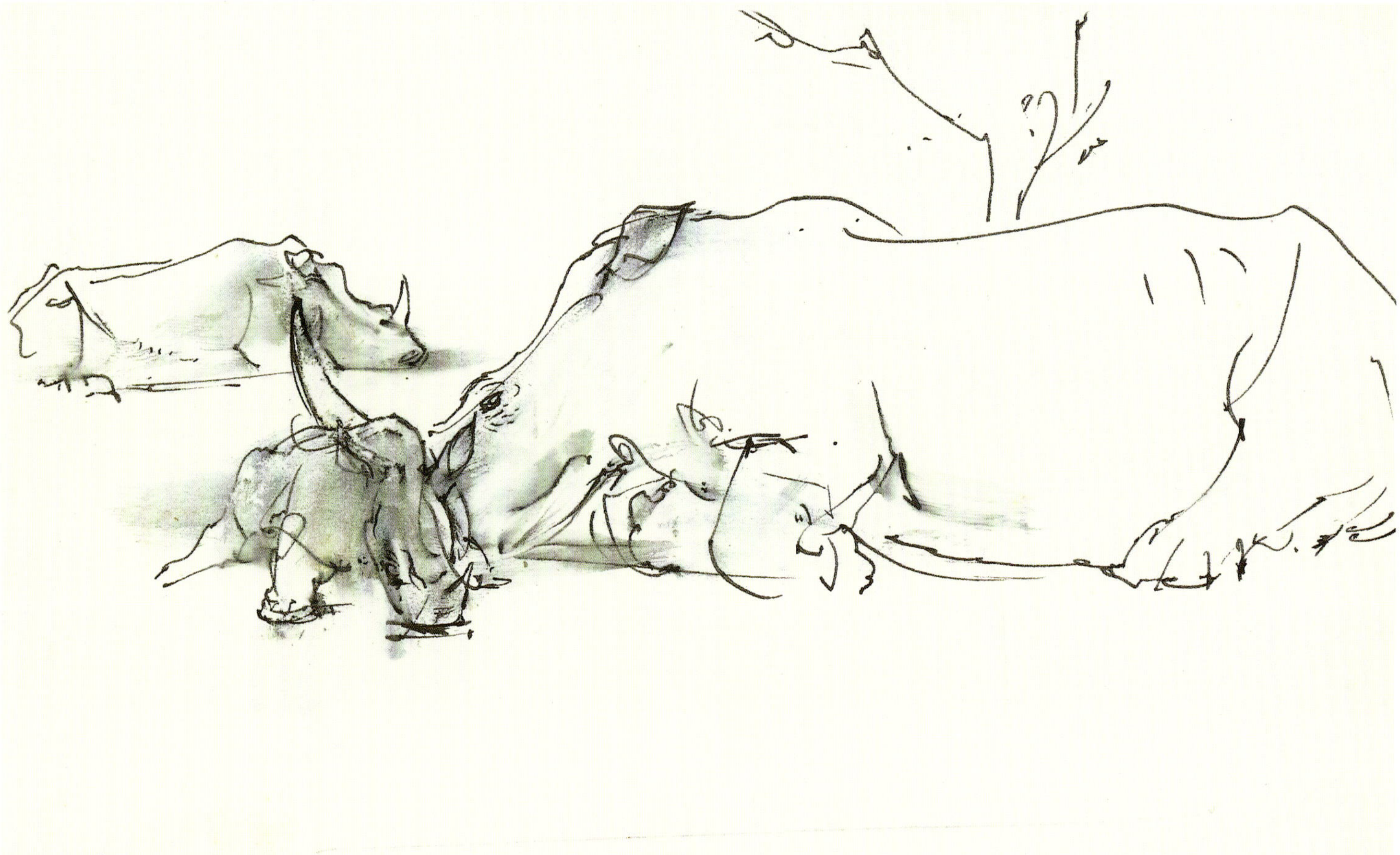

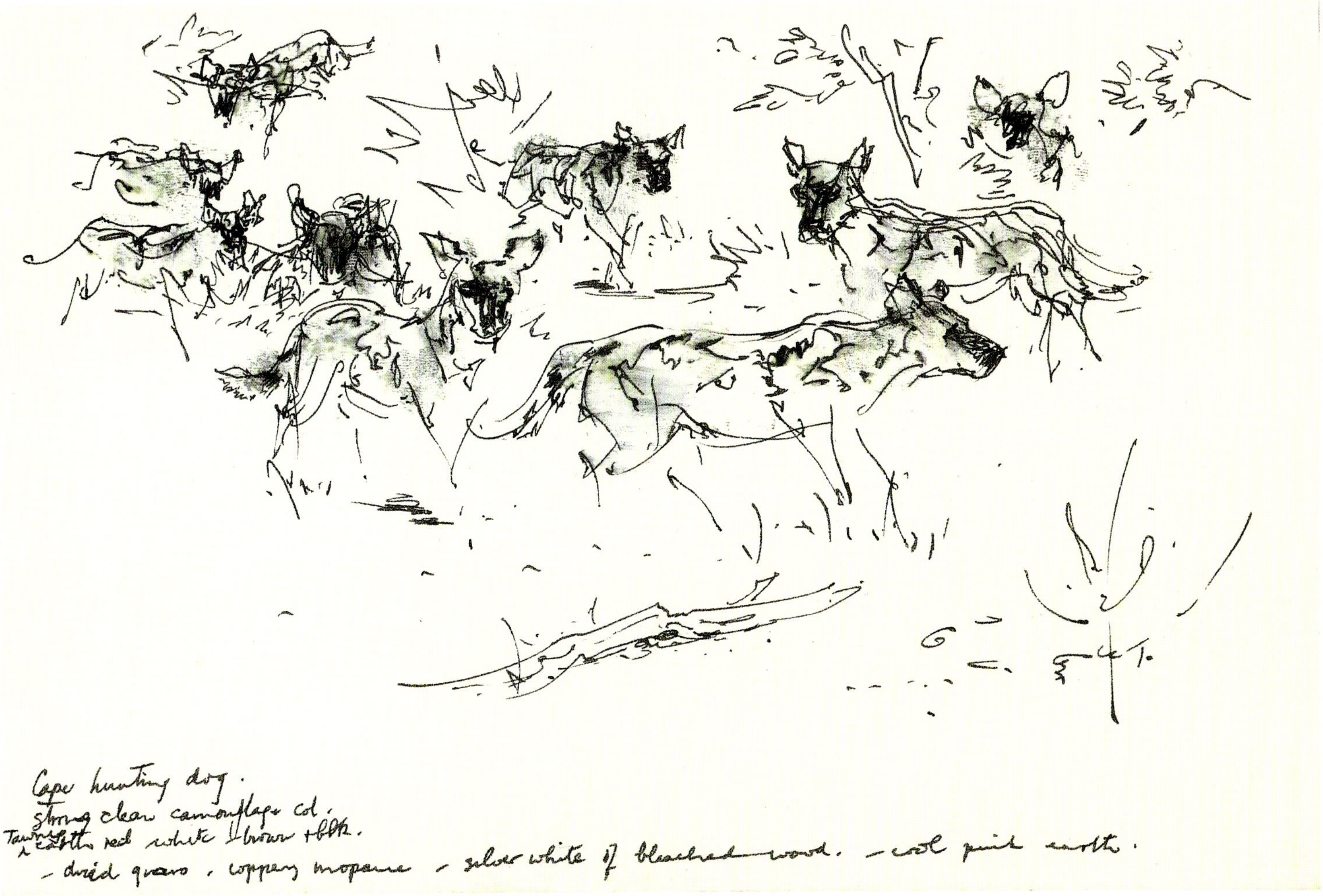
Cape hunting dog.
strong clean camouflage col.
Tawny earth red white & brown + blk.
- dried grass, coppery mopane - silver white of bleached wood. - cool pink earth.

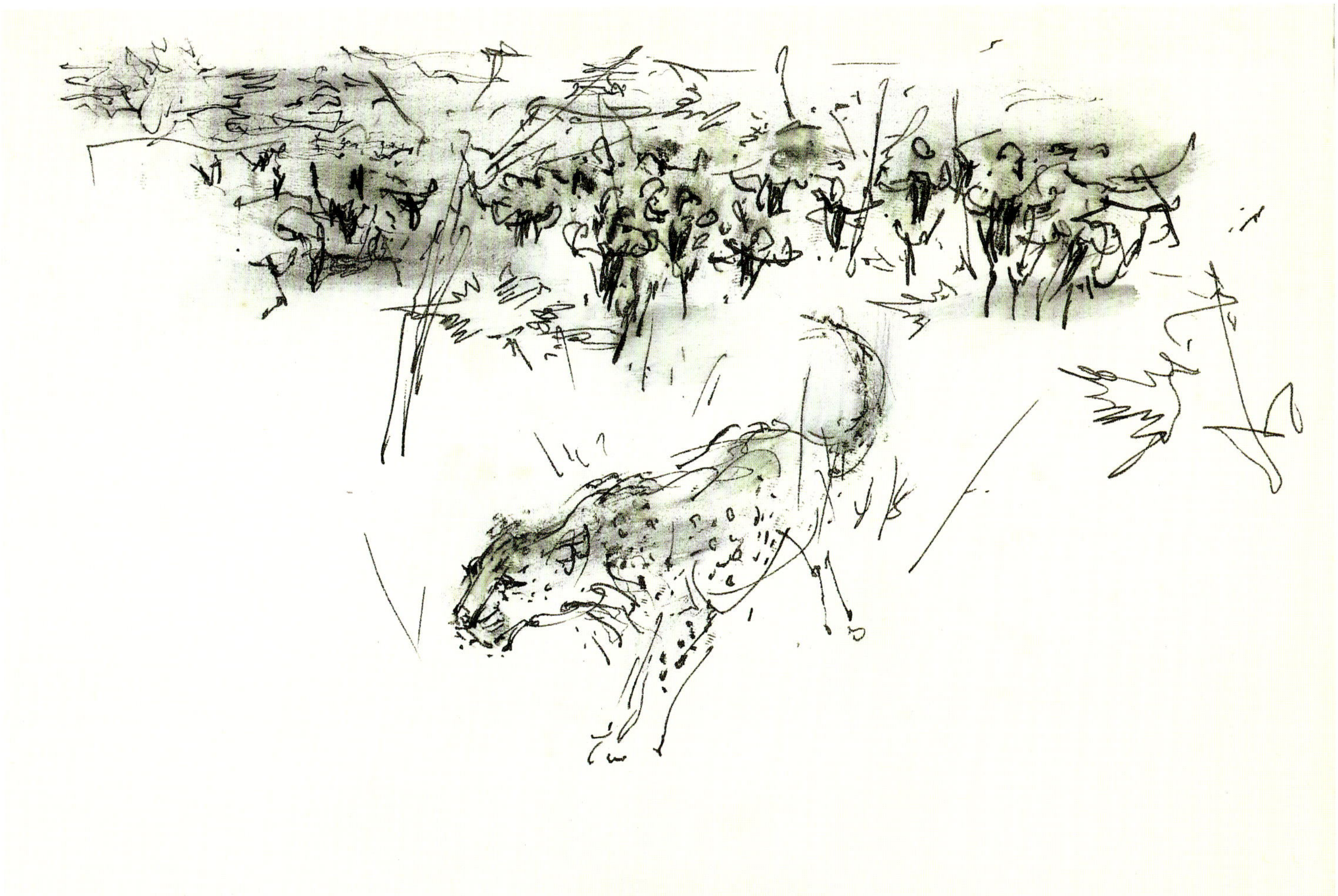

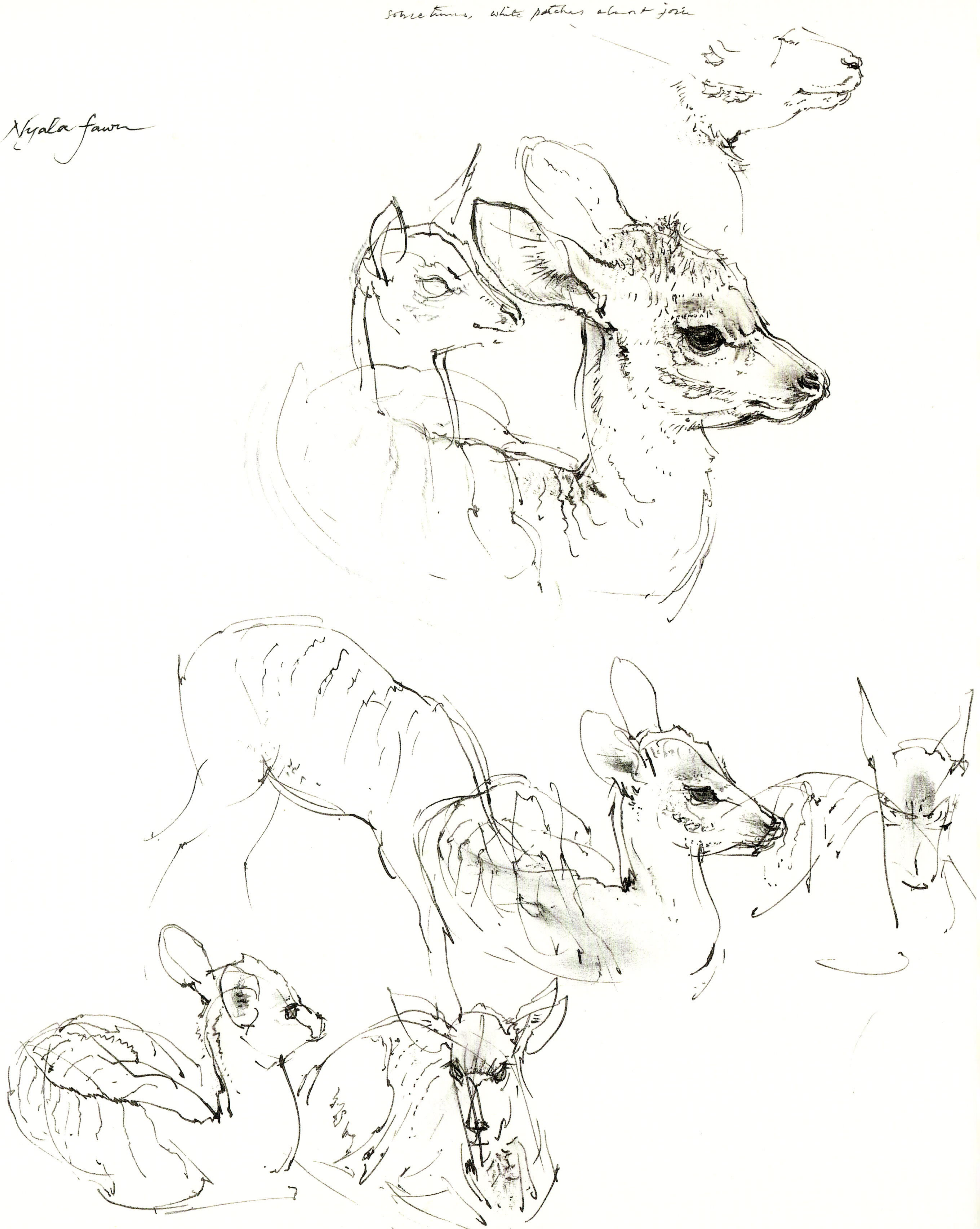
sometimes, white patches almost gone
Nyala fawn

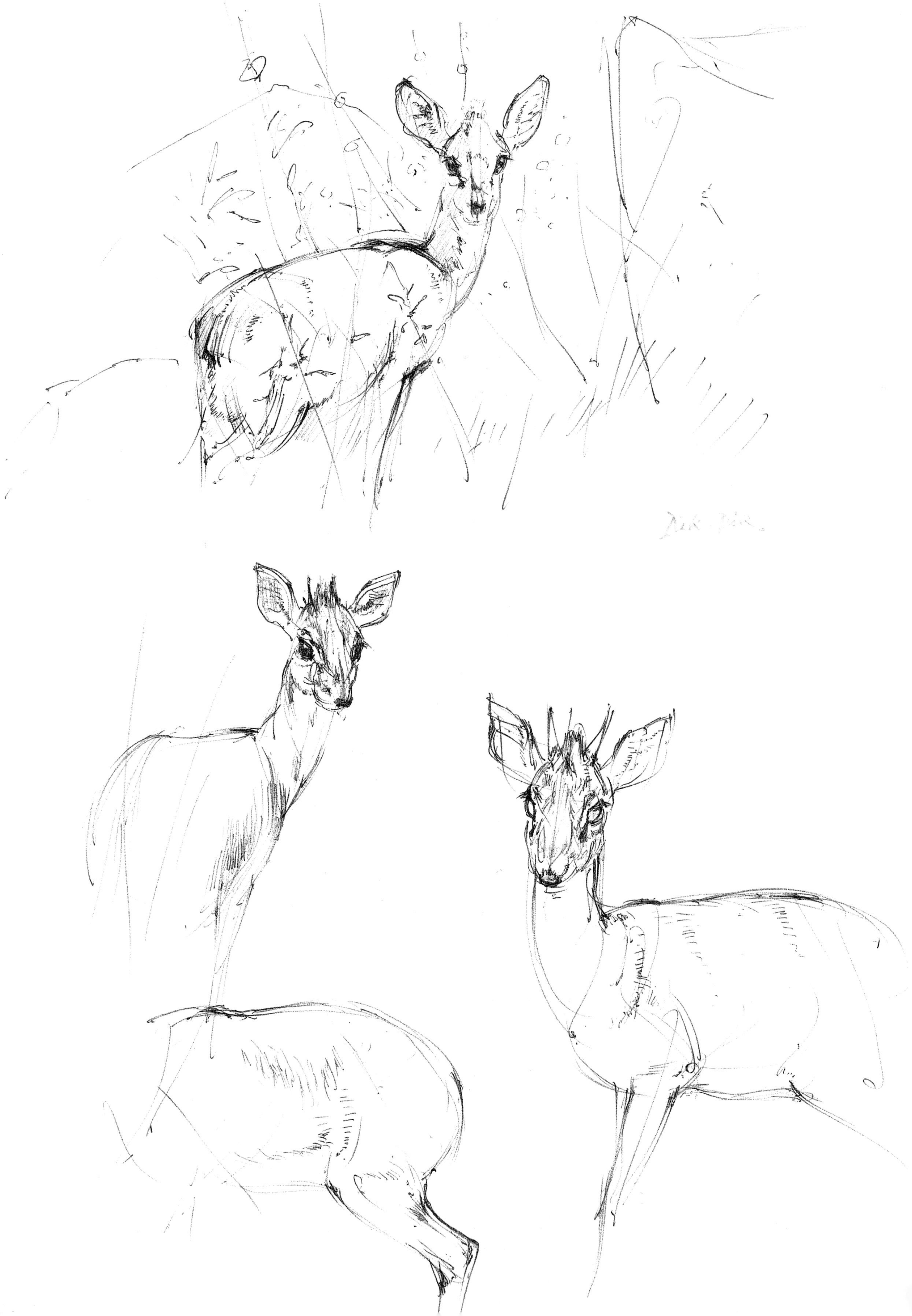
Dik-Dik

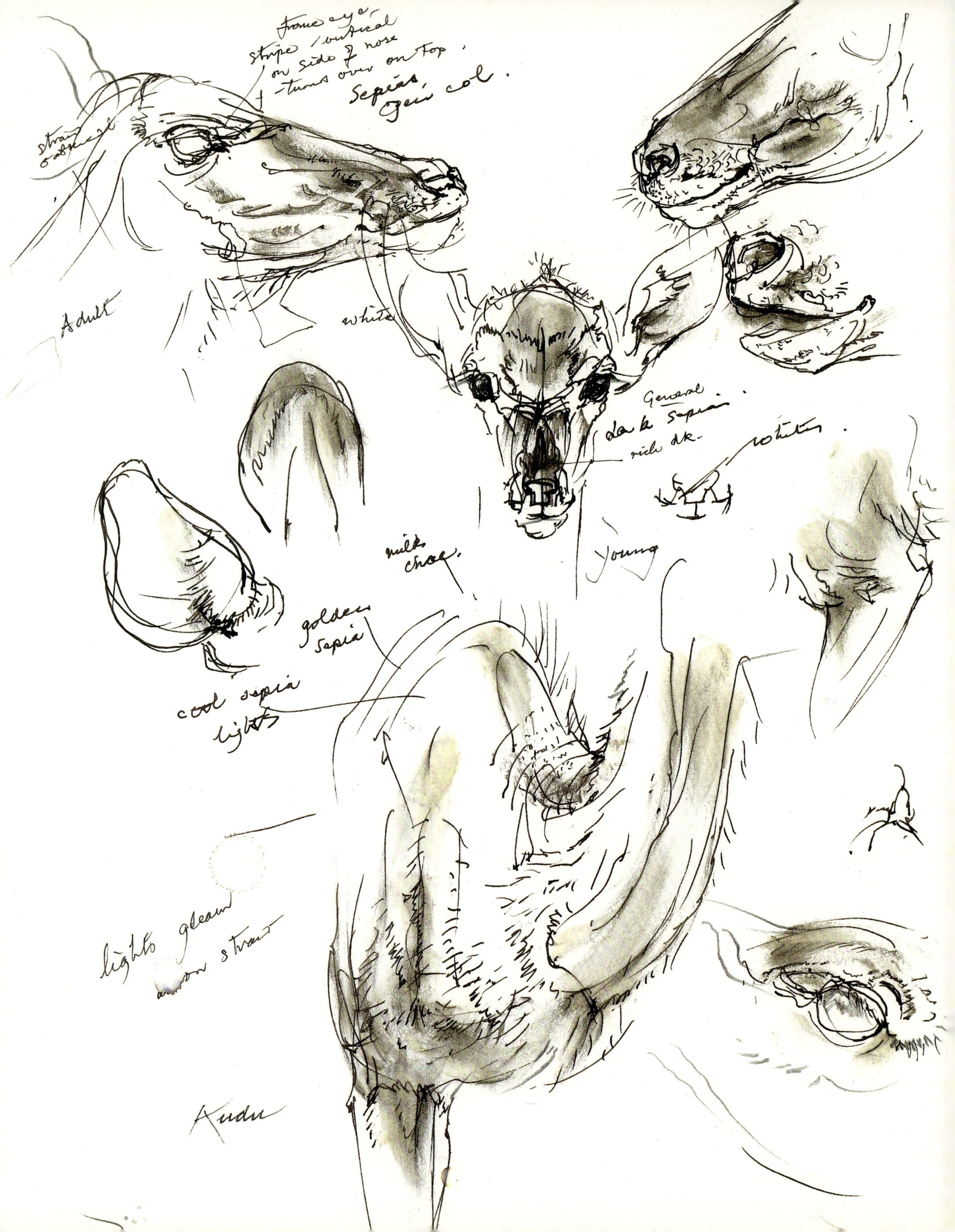
Adult
white
dark sepia
rich dk.
whites
milk choc.
Young
golden sepia
cool sepia lights
Kudu

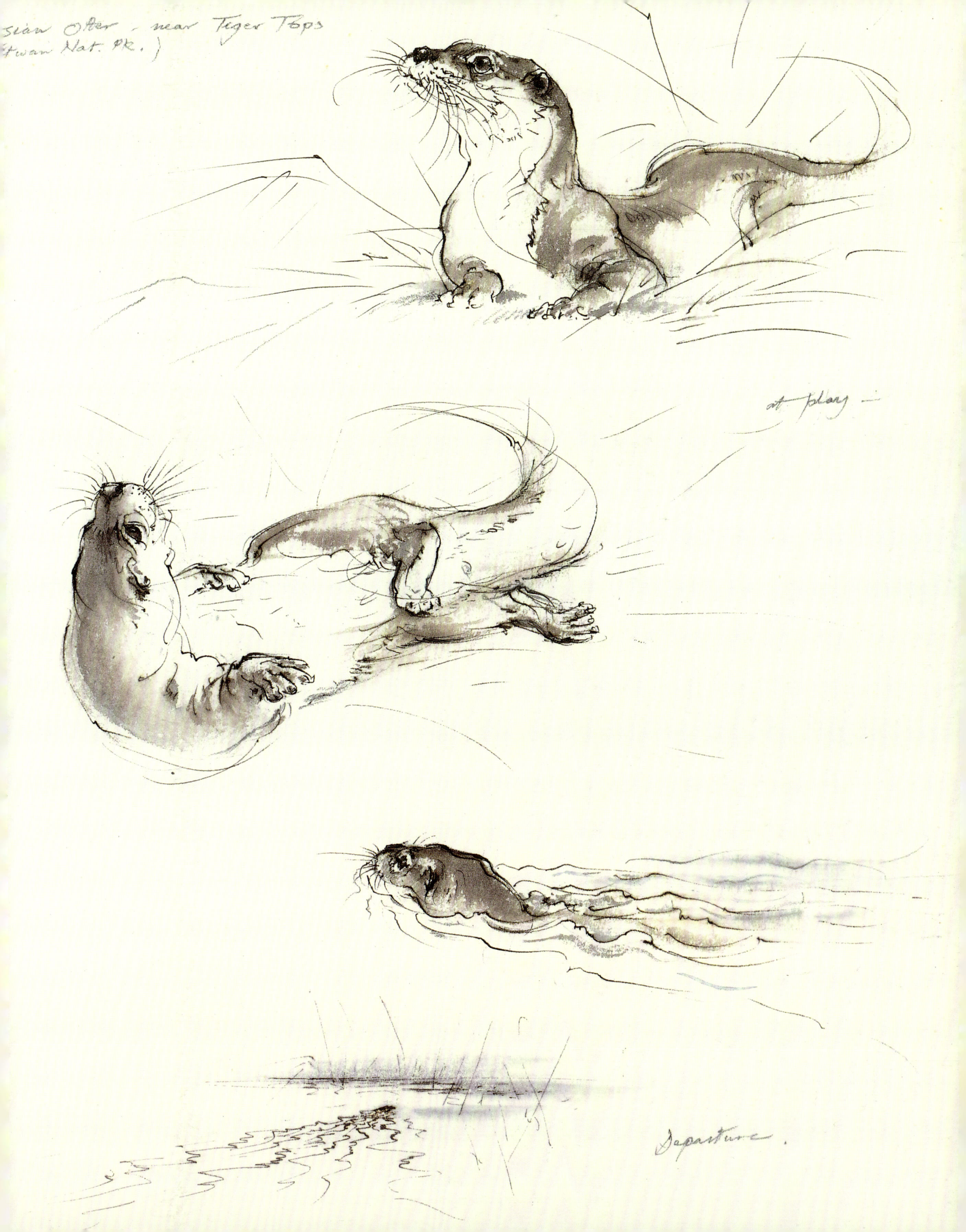
sian Otter - near Tiger Tops
twan Nat. Pk.)
at play -
Departure.

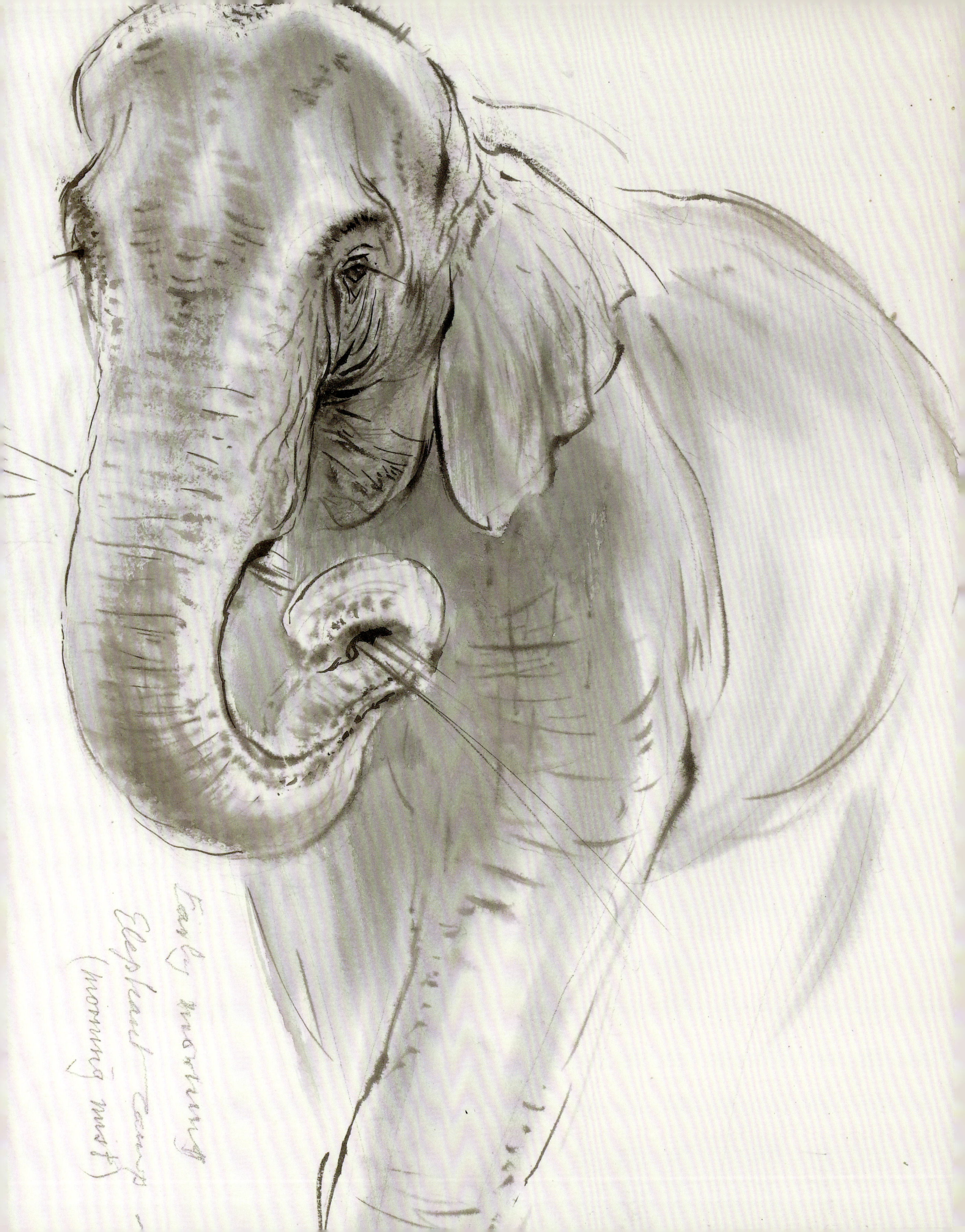
Early morning
Elephant Camp
(morning mist)

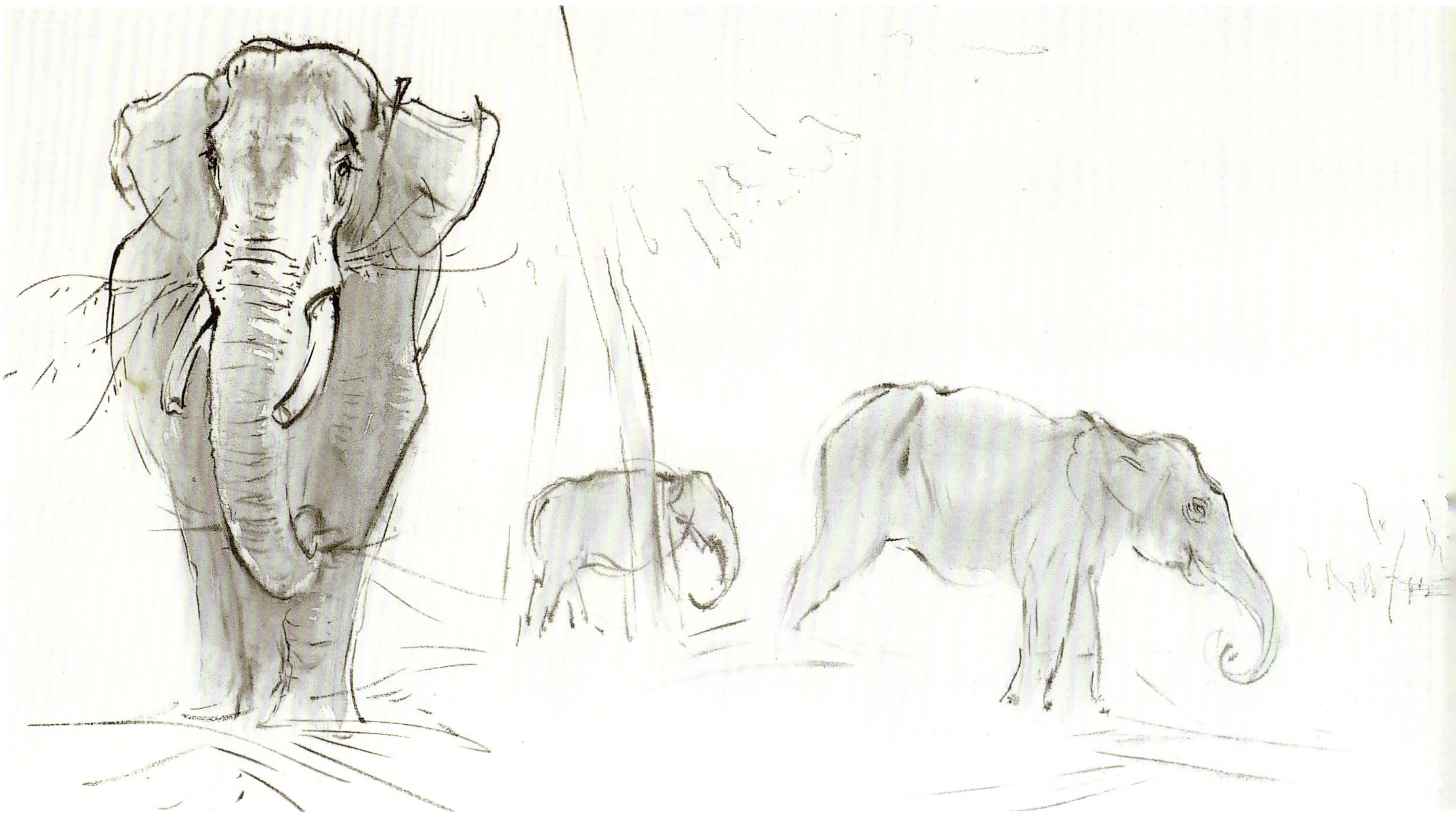

Another day we were told that an elephant was going to collect grass, so we took a second elephant to see for ourselves what happened, following on the typical narrow elephant trails by which elephants can place their feet in almost the same place as the one in front, creating what seems like an impossibly narrow trail through tall reeds and grasses. We presently reached an area of rich tall grass. The men ahead slipped off their elephant, sickles in hand. They wasted no time and were soon loading their elephant with a huge amount of grass. I never learned how they managed to keep it there, but they returned to camp with a giant load.

I was then to watch several men making special tit-bits for the elephants. They took one big handful of grass, deftly folded it over and, reaching out with the other for a handful of cooked rice from a basket already to hand, skilfully produced a packet of rice to toss into a tall wooden container nearby. If a harnessed elephant being led away for the day's work passed near one of these tubs, out would go the trunk to seize one - a game apparently accepted by the Nepalese staff.

At Tiger Tops one could take a small boat and visit the tented camp to look for more tigers. I had hoped to find the fishing cat there, but I think a hide and more time would have been needed. It is the world of the strongly flowing river itself, which, for some reason, haunts my memory – full of birds and coming from the Himalayas two hundred miles away.

opposite, above and following pages
Studies from the elephant camp
ink and wash
actual size

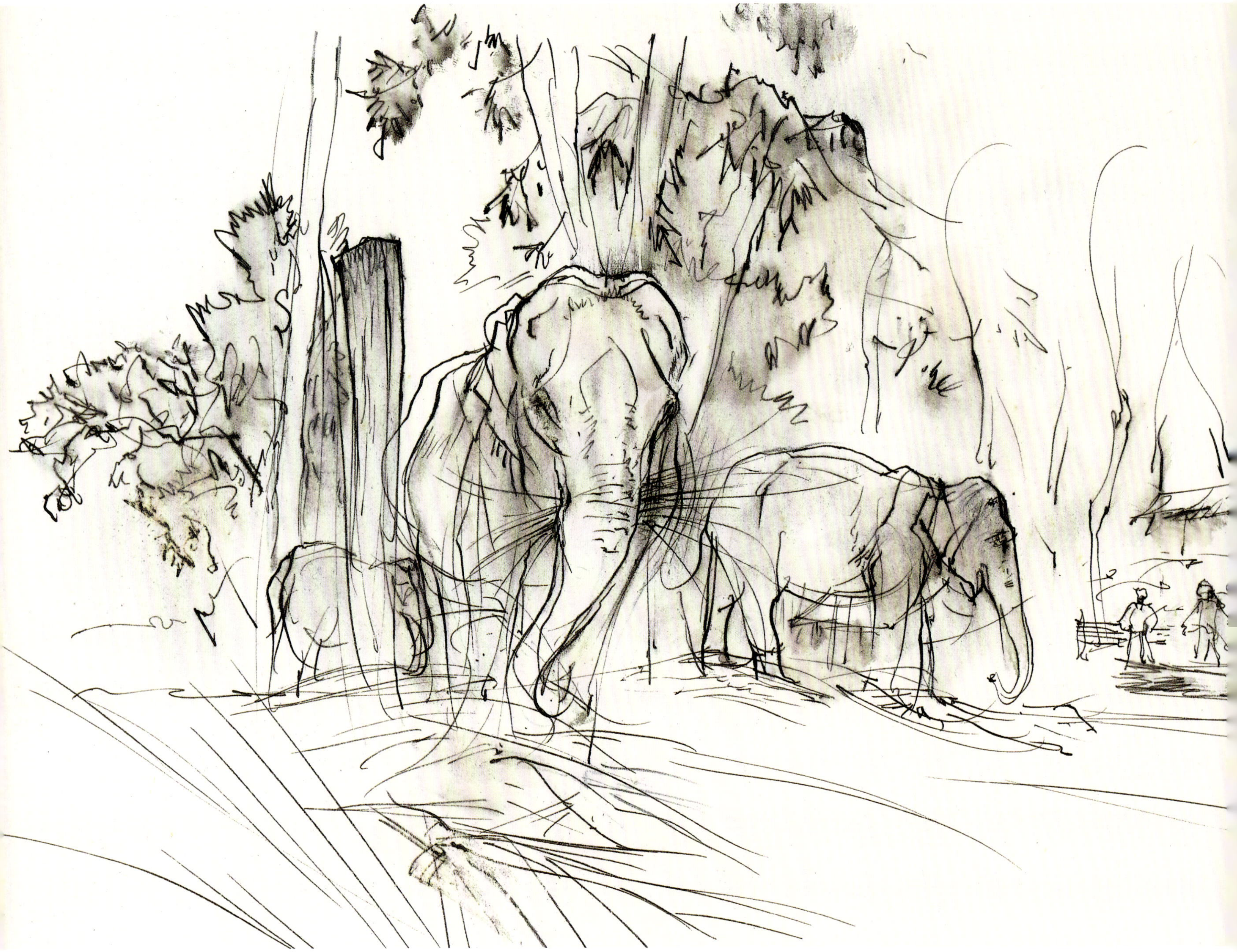

Oliver having left with Janet for a few days in the foothills of the Himalayas, I had opted to stay with the ample material at Tiger Tops. One day I took an elephant and its driver, said to be 'the best tracker in India' to look for the sloth bear and axis deer. We found their droppings only but no memorable sightings, though my tracker did find a nest of a grass owl with half grown chicks. We inched slowly forward but the owl flew away. I made a quick sketch of both the chicks and withdrew.

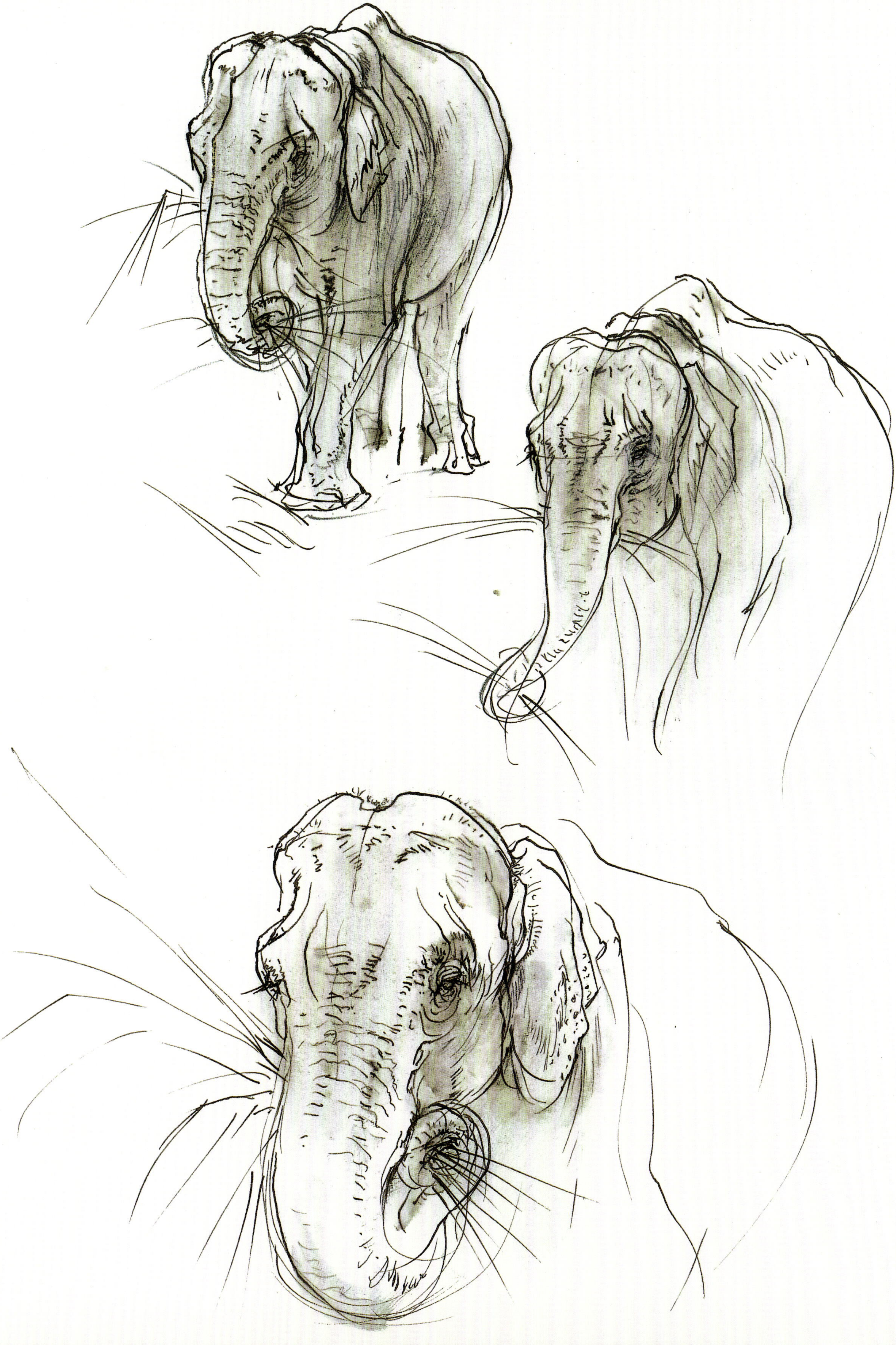

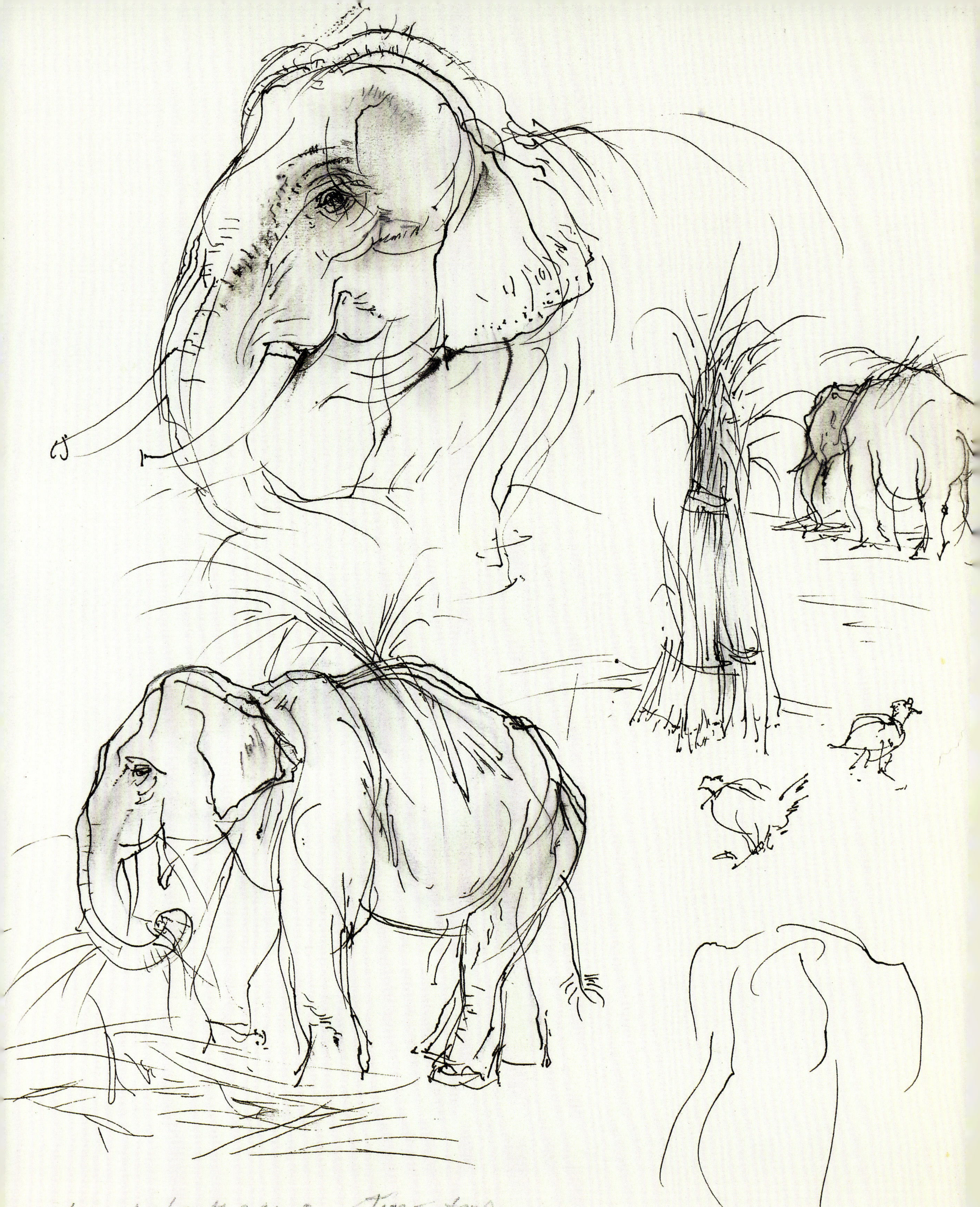

the elephant camp – Tiger tops.

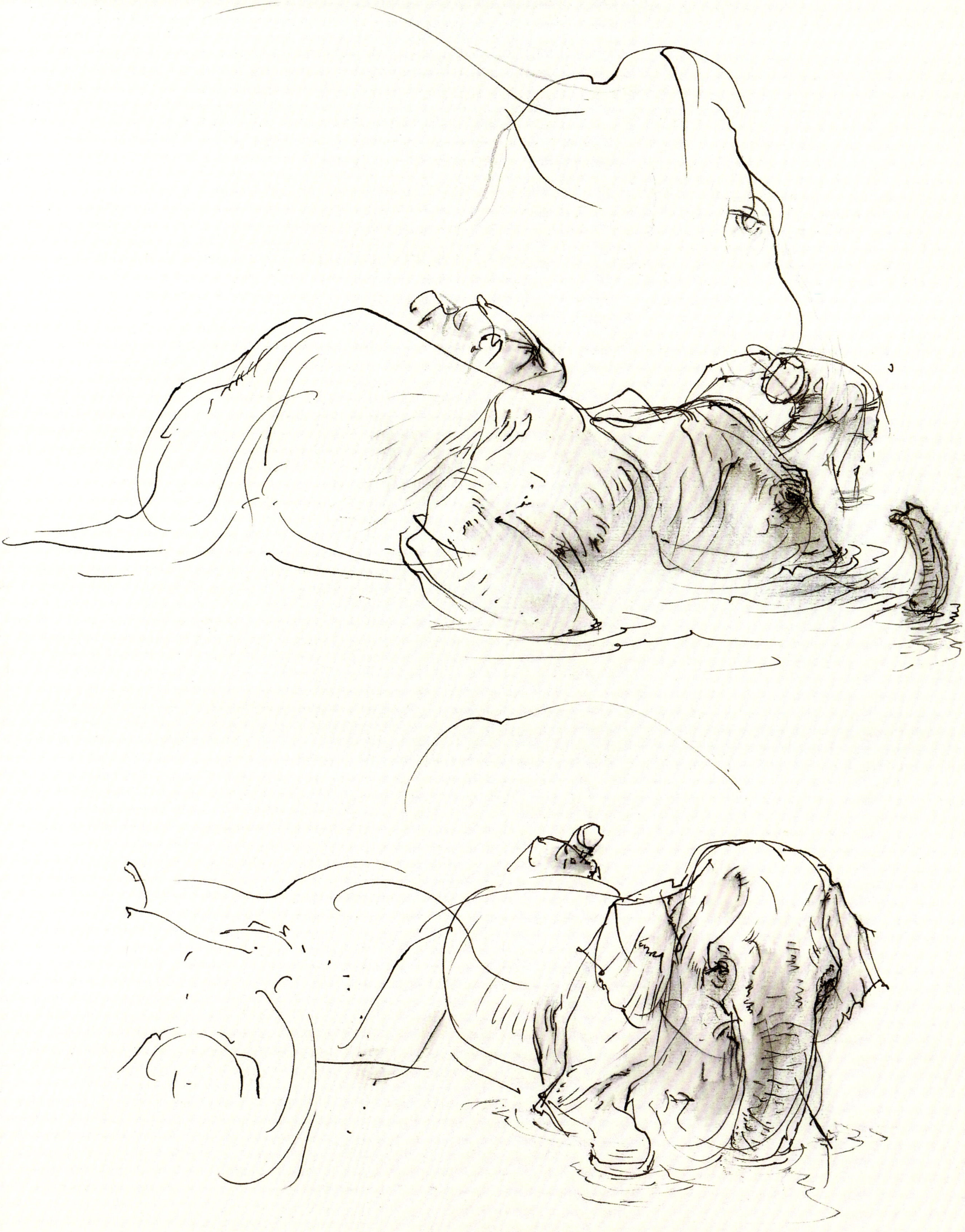

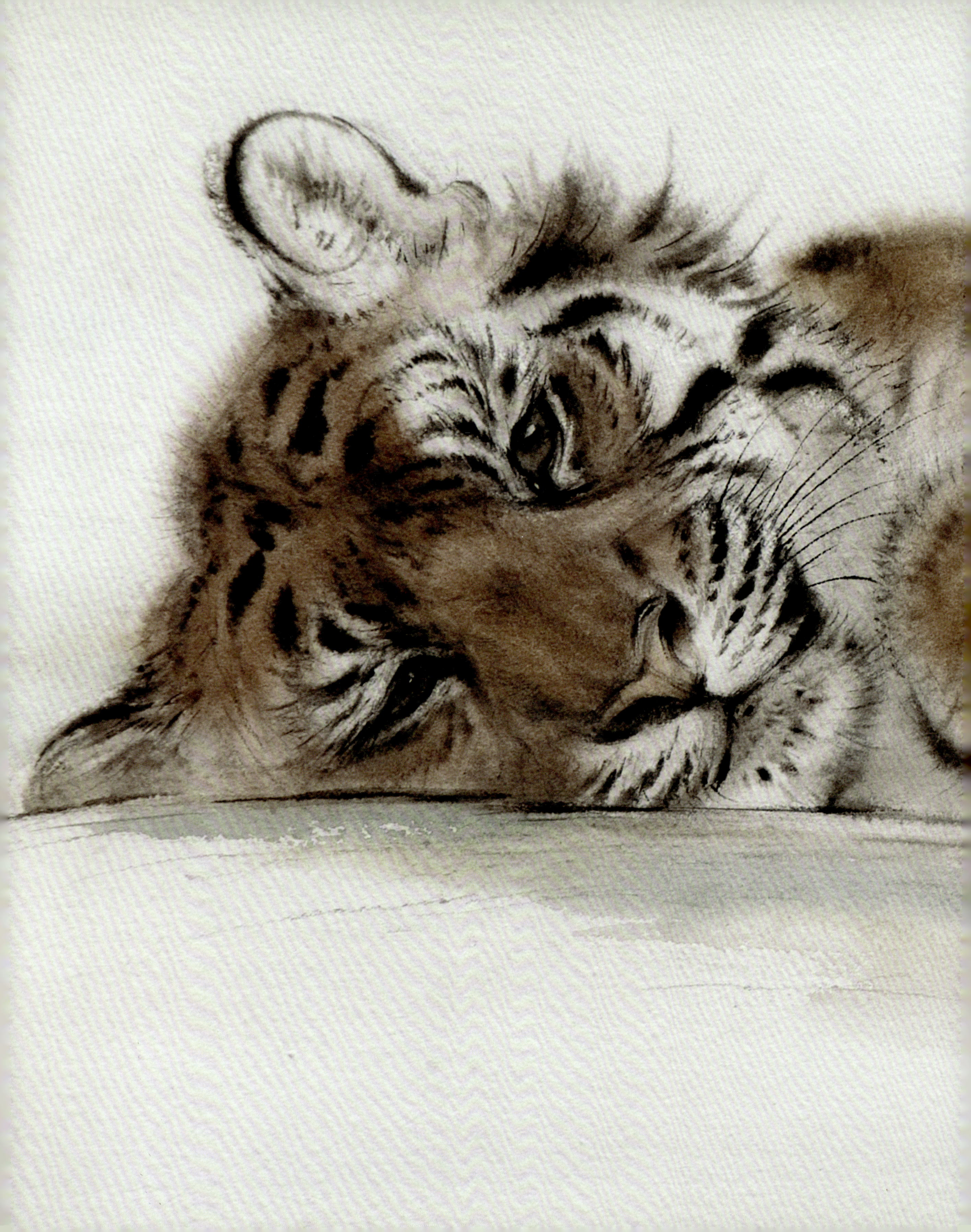

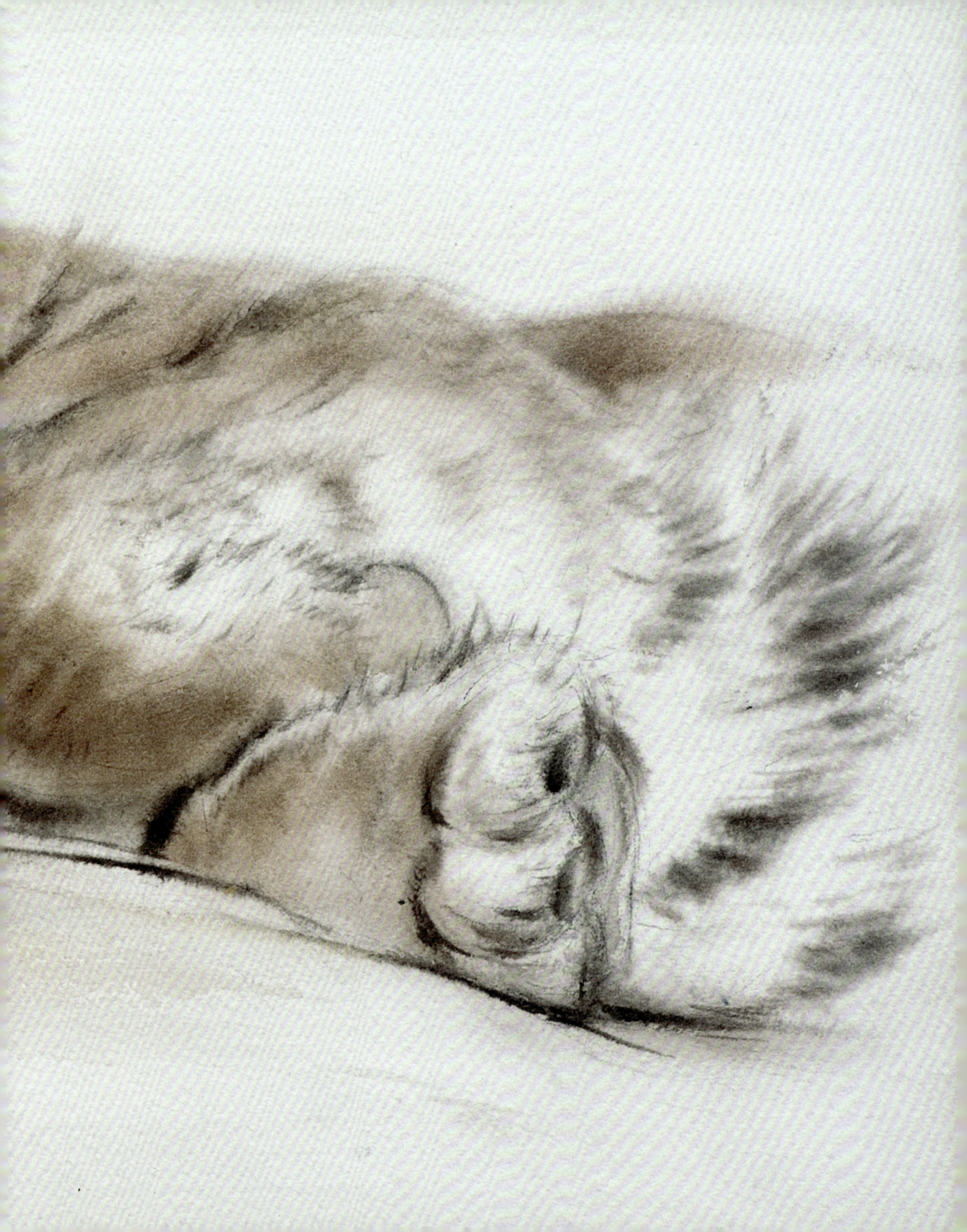

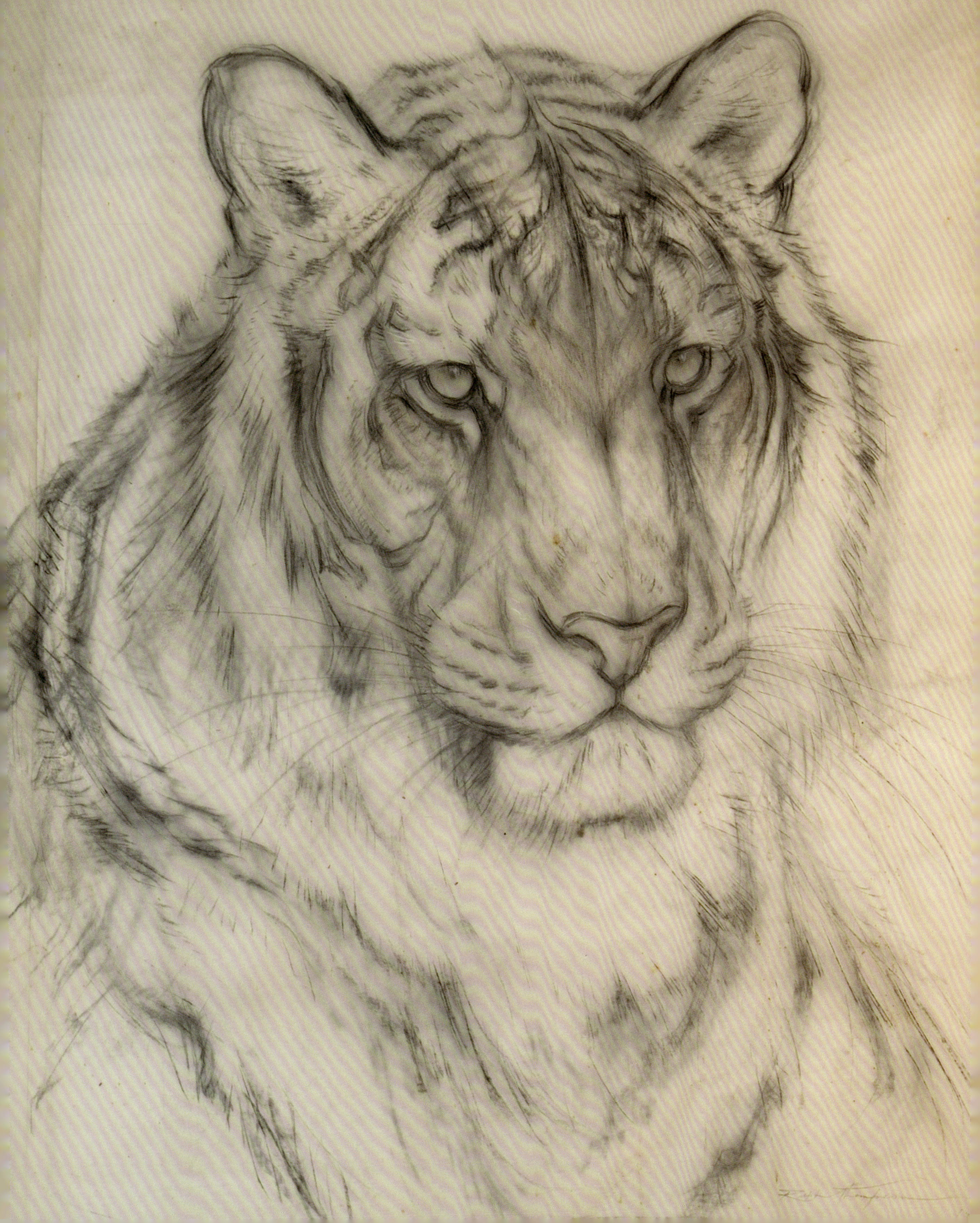

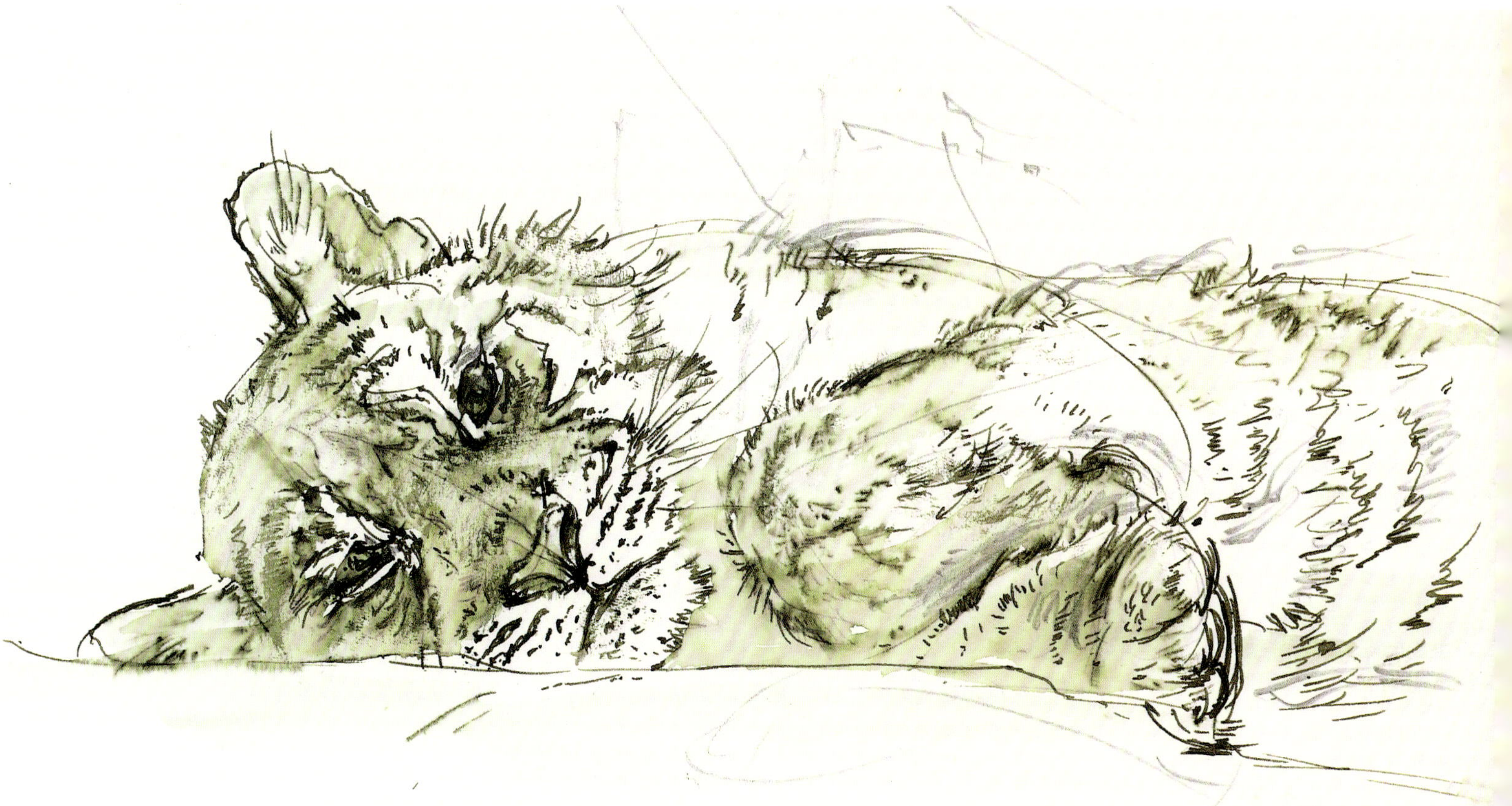

On the map, the game reserve named Kanha looks to be exactly in the middle of India. My driver and I were on our way back from the Taj Mahal and Agra to look for tigers at Kanha and to call en route at the age-old ruins of a famous palace. All I remember now of the ruins are some well-preserved mural paintings of elephants. Driving to Kanha was a bone shattering experience, but interesting because the villages through which we passed had their own particular beauty, a timeless, natural beauty. It was as if they had just happened quite naturally and individually to make interesting shapes. The oxen ploughing the fields looked so serene and beautiful. I was foolishly too excited by the thought of the tigers at Kanha to stop long enough to take photographs and make sketches, something I shall always regret.

So, on we bumped to the forest reserve of Kanha. It had a well-built centre for study and was able to house a limited number of guests. We were to stay for several days searching for tigers in particular. On the following day, several elephants appeared with howdahs on their backs and drivers apparently sitting on their heads. Actually, the drivers were astride their necks. I was placed, with my sketchbook, at the back of the howdah while a group of Americans, bristling with impressive cameras, were poised at the front.

above and following page
Sleepy tiger cub
ink and wash
actual size

opposite
Tiger portrait
charcoal
740 × 600mm

previous page
Sleepy tiger cub
watercolour
370 × 570mm

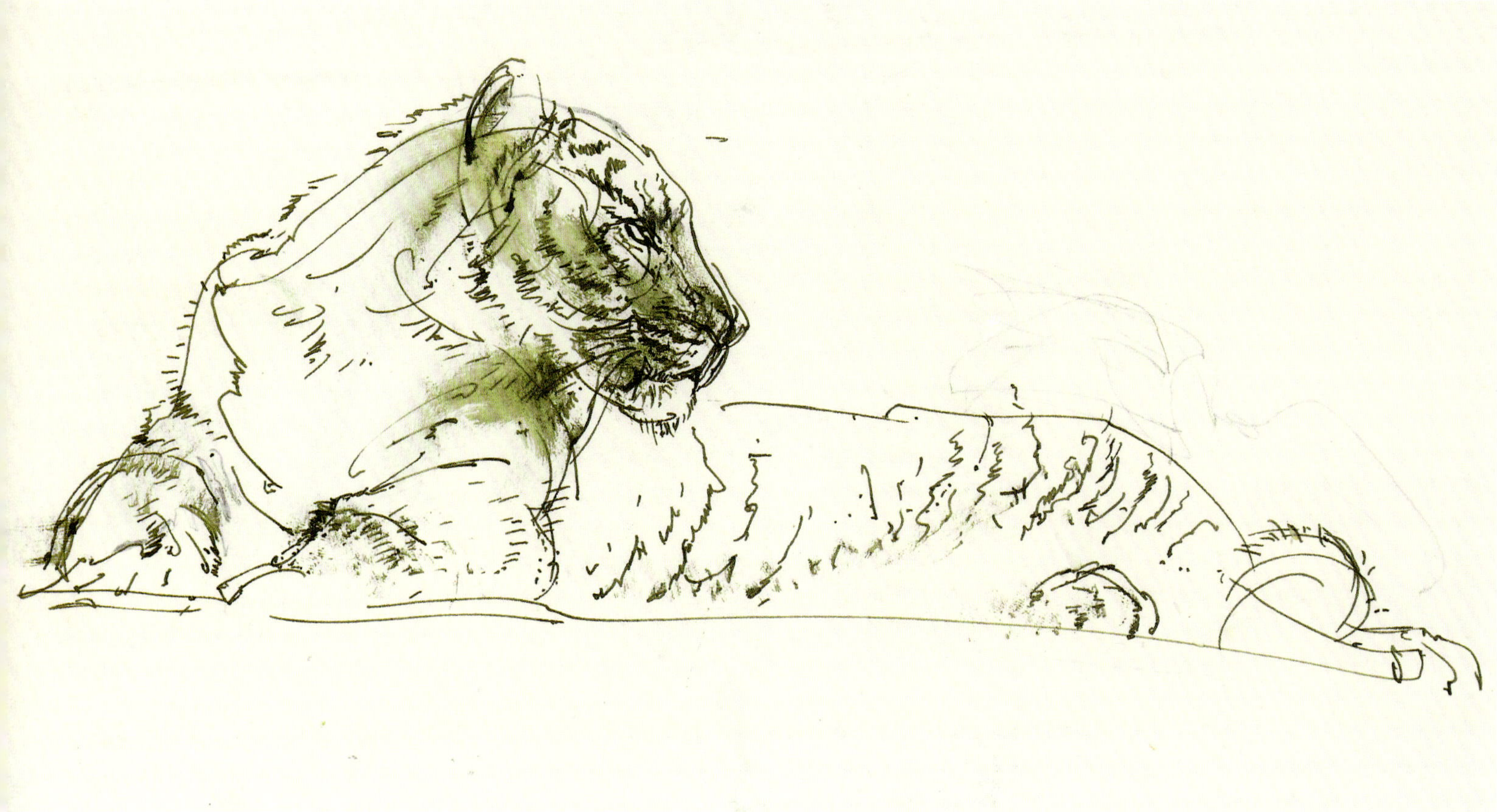

The forest trails along which we were making our way were festooned with huge spider-webs, complete with outsized spiders. It soon became clear that there were drivers of several other elephants combing the area, calling to each other. The forest was dense and the ground rather hilly. I was alarmed at first when our elephant began to traverse a steep slope, but I soon gained confidence in her ability to move up, down or across quite steep slopes at will. The sound signals gradually became frequent and more elephants appeared. After about an hour, we came to a stand still. Our driver pointed to some dense cover directly ahead of us. At first I could not see anything, but gradually I made out the tawny colour visible within the cover. It was my first tiger.

As all the cameras clicked, I managed to draw what I could of the tiger, adding more sketches as it changed position. The tiger seemed from experience to know that this was only a 'camera hunt'. Eventually, it made off into the jungle. We tried to follow it but soon lost sight.

Two more tiger hunts followed with one more sighting. Meanwhile, I was invited to go for a walk with two young leopards. The two young Indians with us were completely unarmed, each carrying no more than a bamboo cane. The leopards must have done this often before. They took no notice of me whatsoever and made no attempt to escape up the forest trees. They obviously enjoyed romping with each other through the forest before returning to their enclosure. For me, this proved to be an extremely valuable experience.

opposite
Tiger in bamboo
charcoal and coloured pencil
585 × 460mm

following page left
Sleeping tiger cubs
ink
actual size

following page right
Tiger cub
watercolour
320 × 255mm

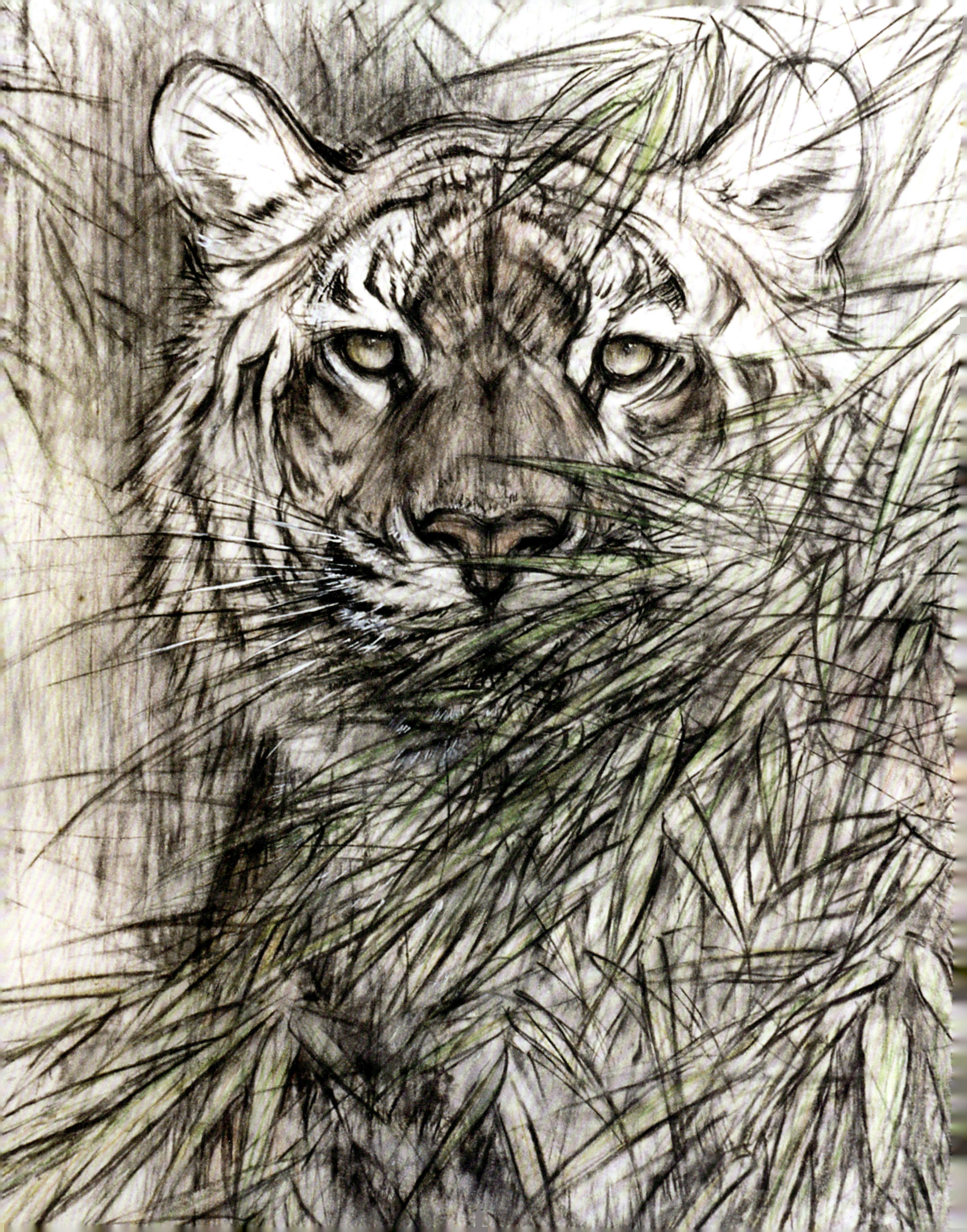

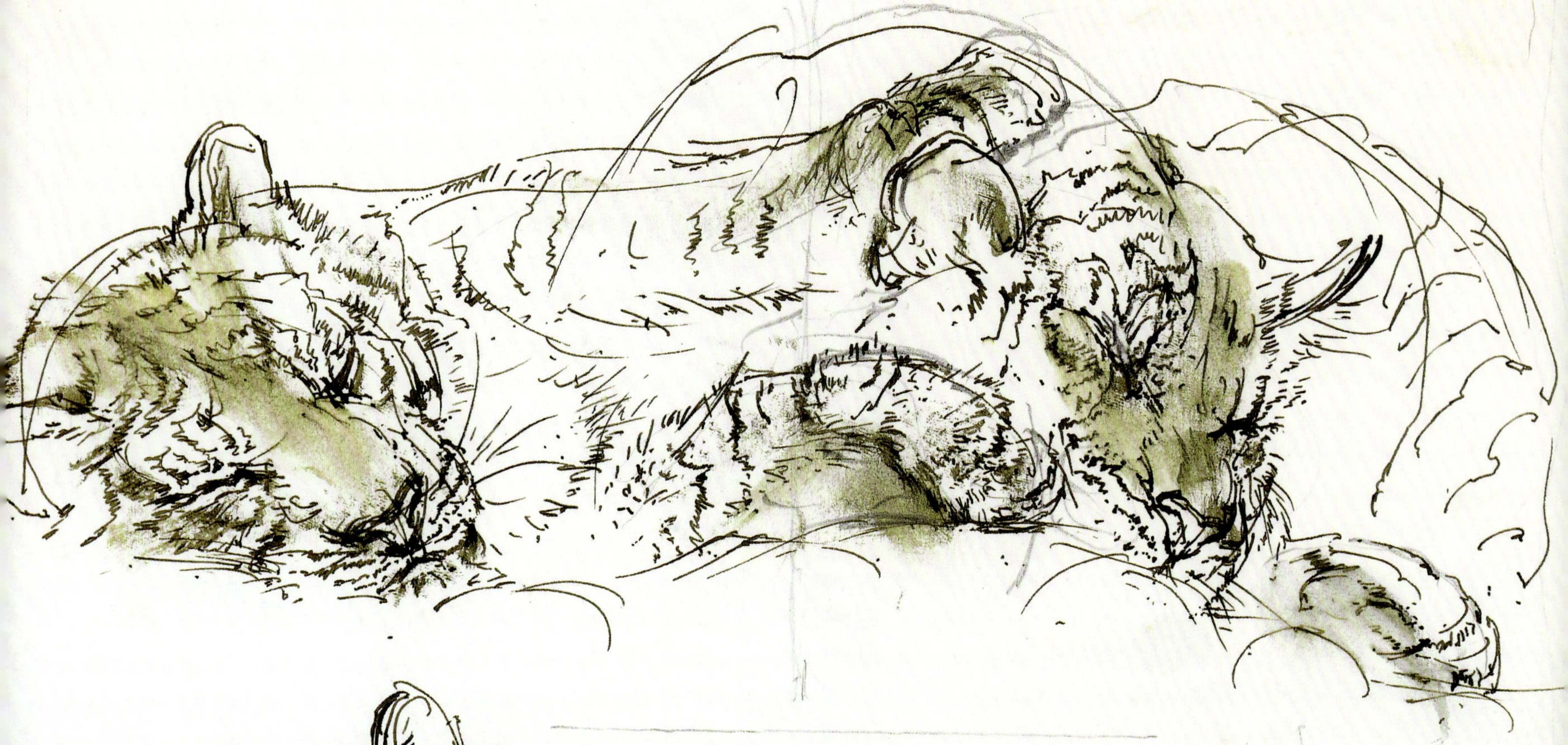

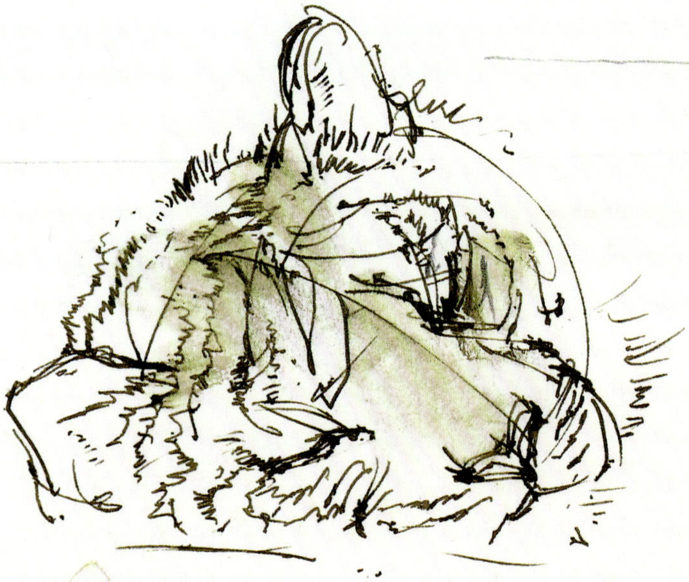

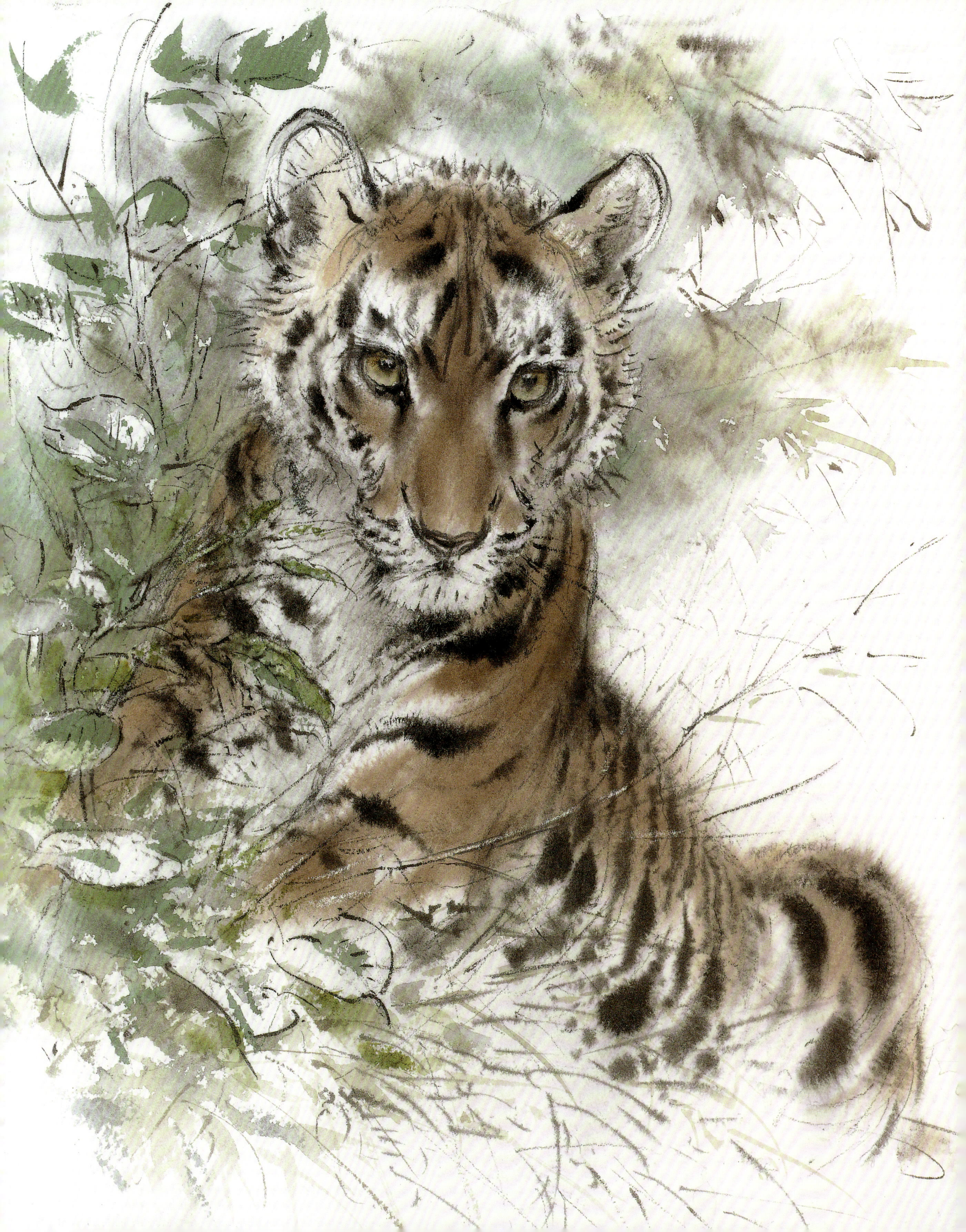

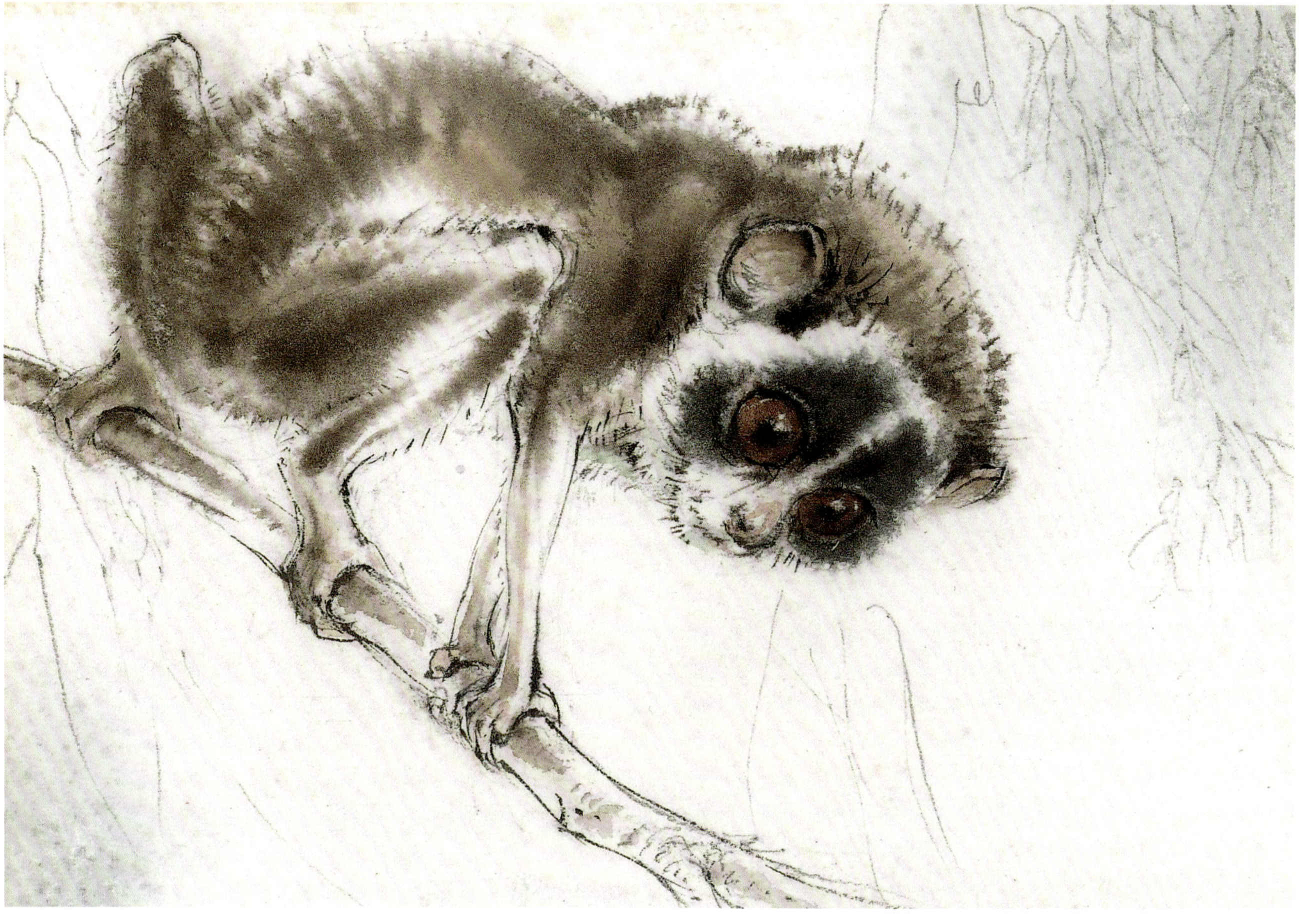

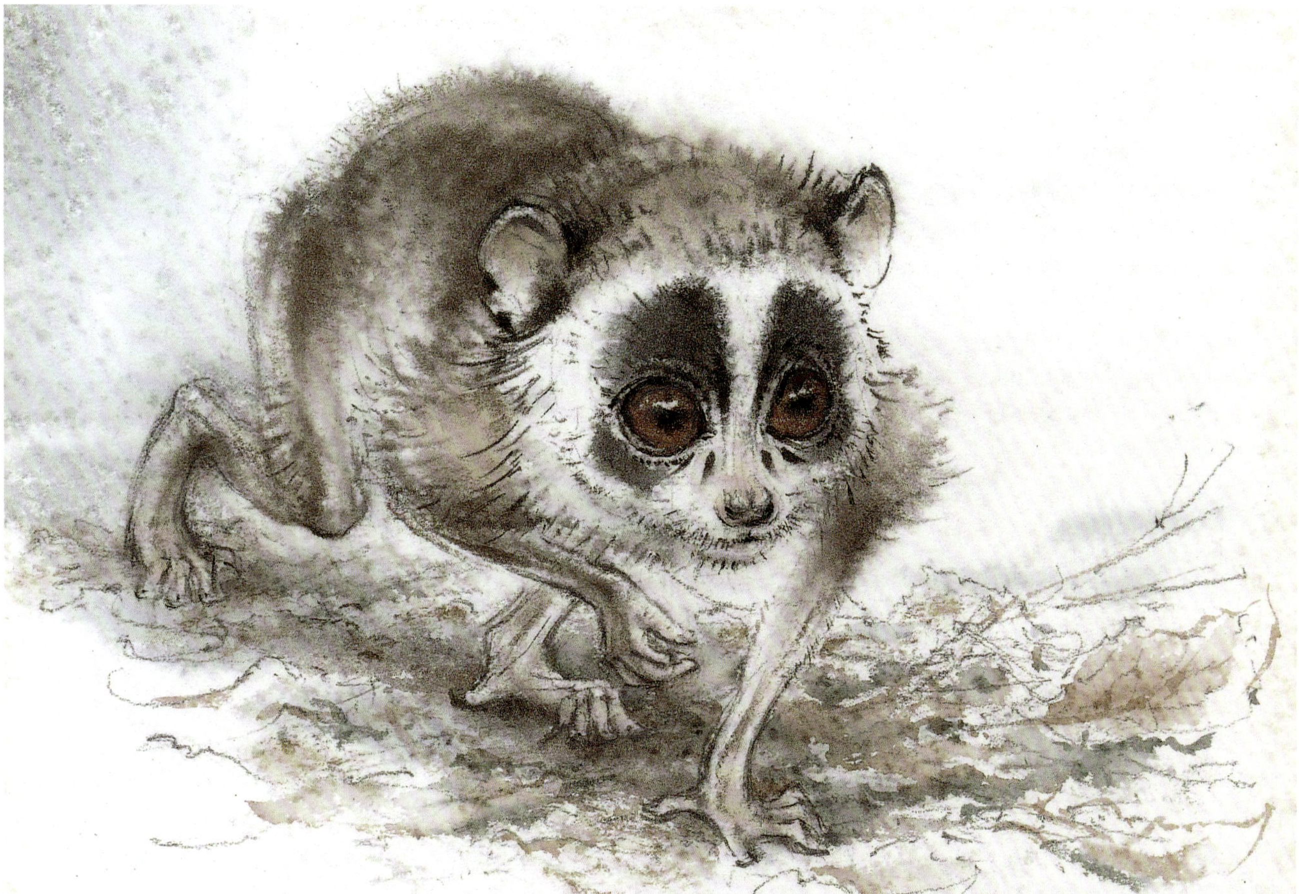

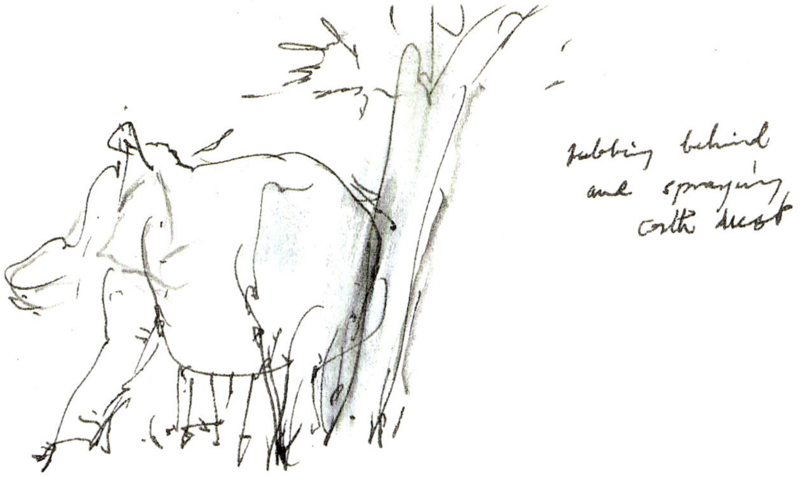
rubbing behind
and spraying
earth dust

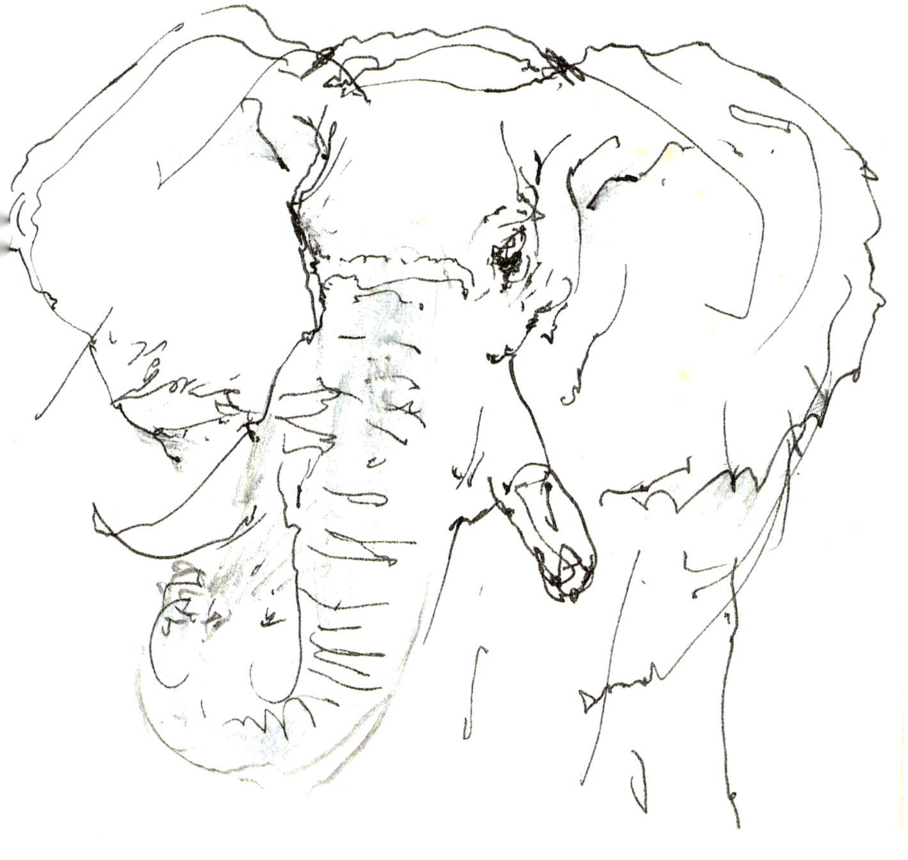

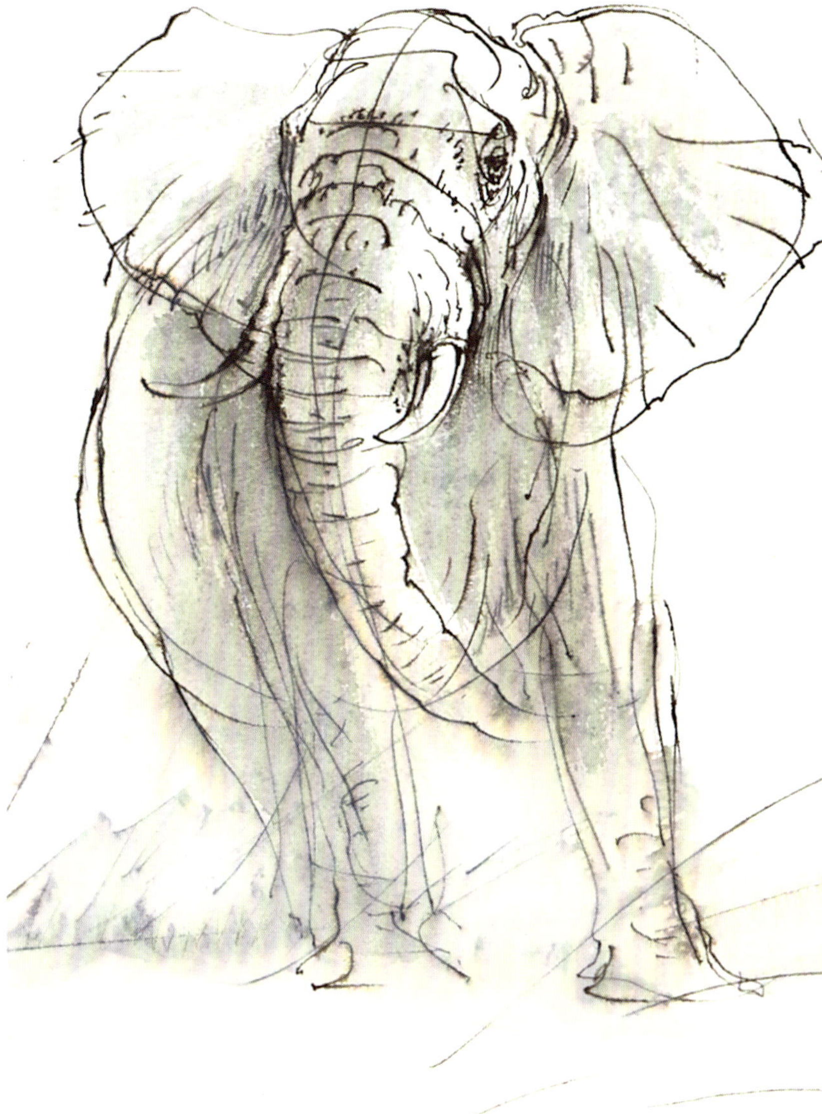

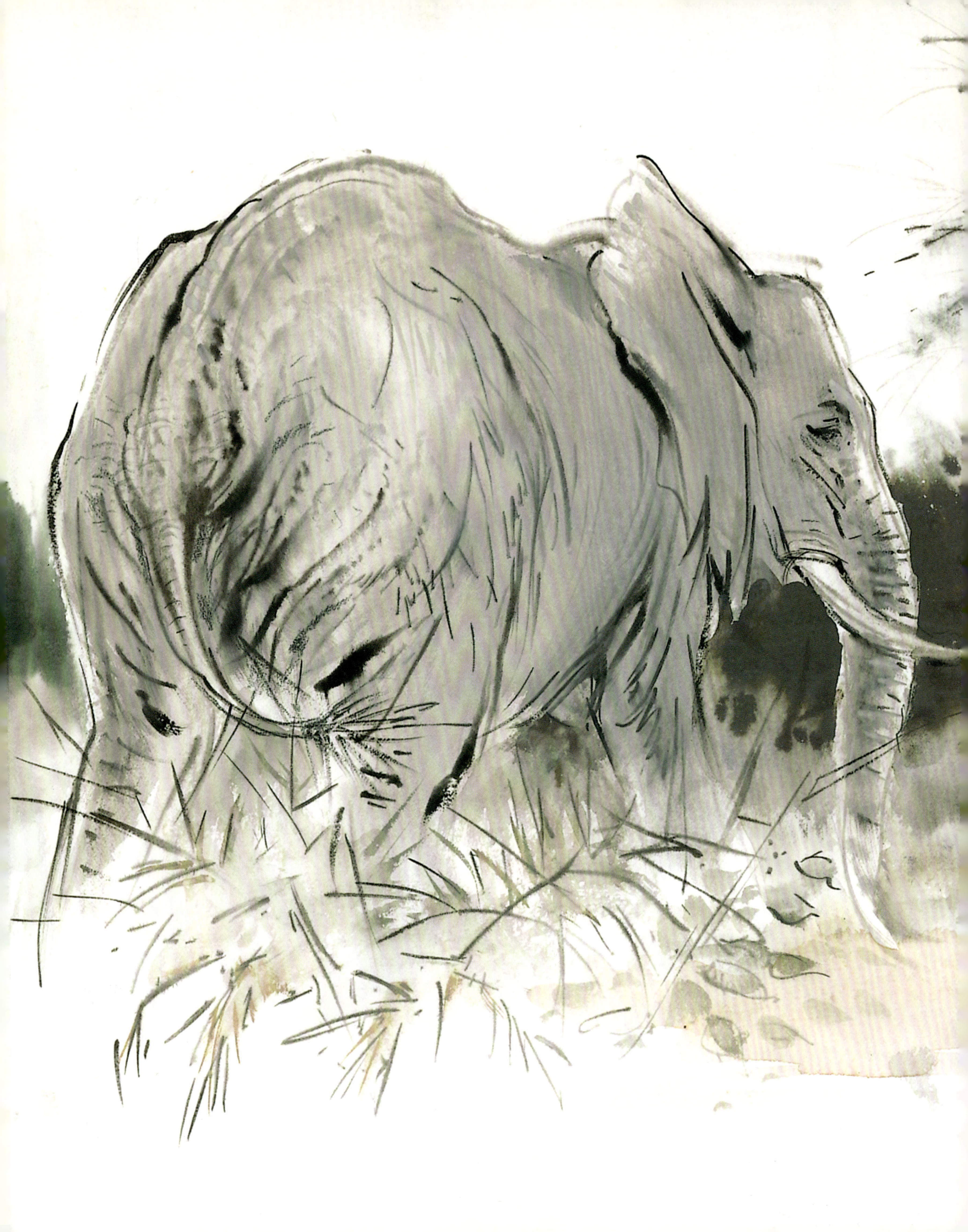

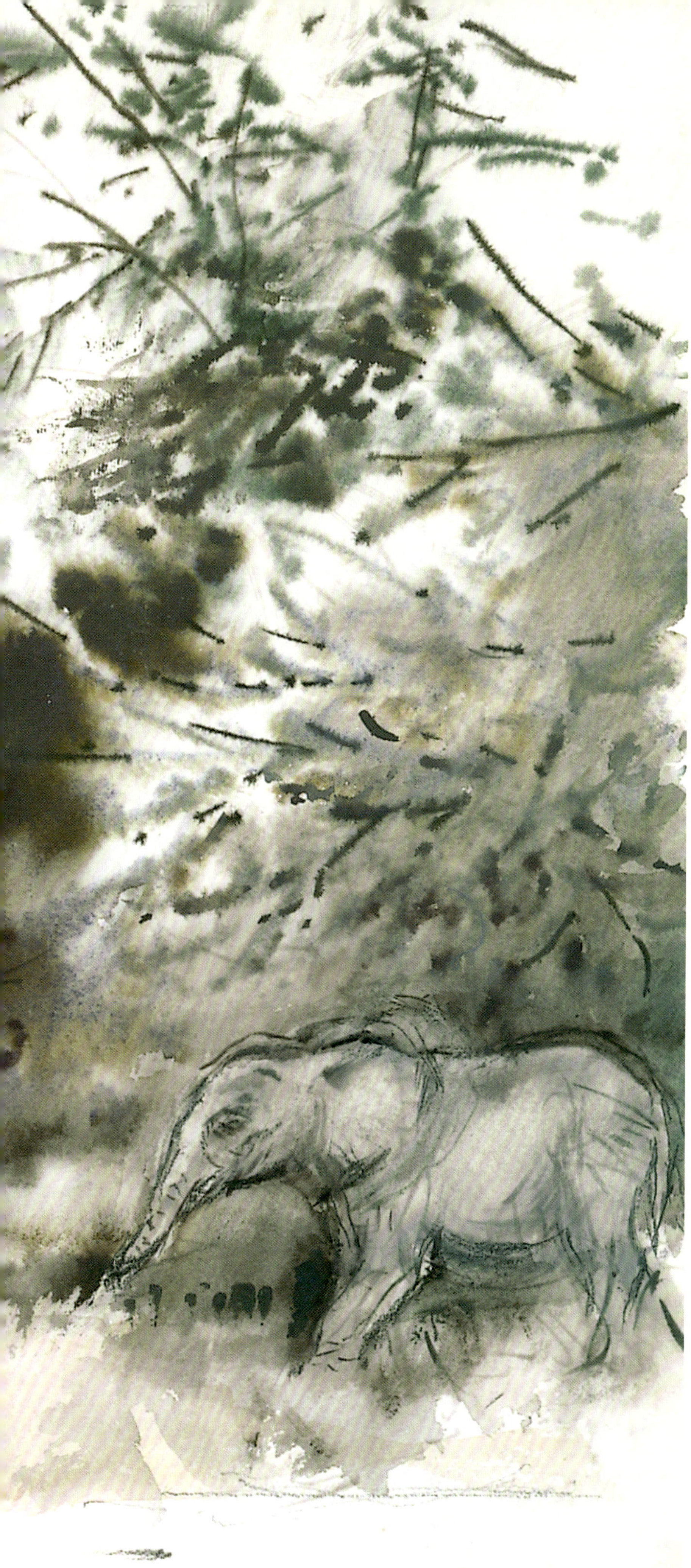

Elephant mother and calf
watercolour
270 × 380mm

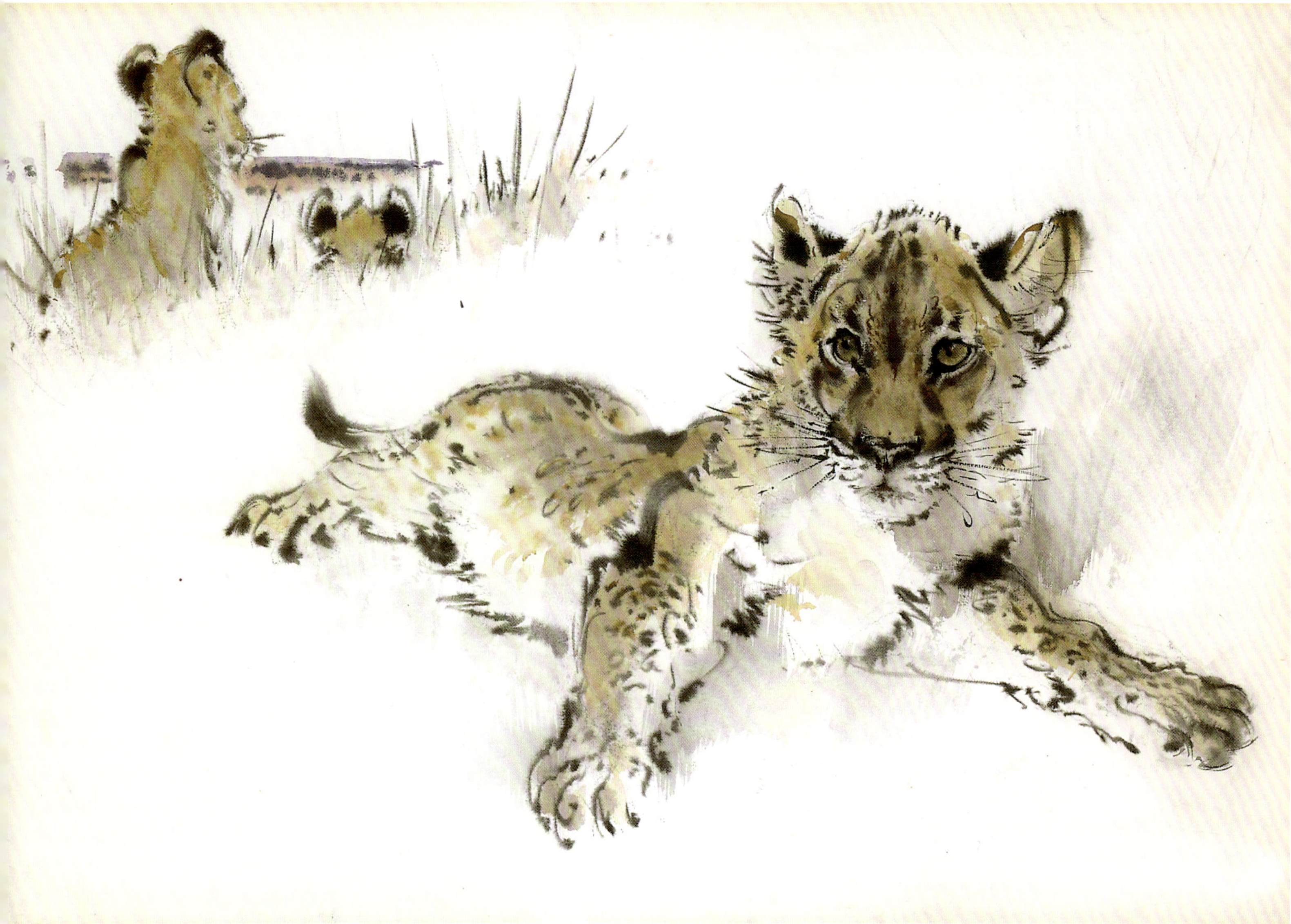

Waiting for mother
watercolour
400 × 600mm

opposite
Lions in a tree
watercolour
480 × 360mm

following page top left
Lioness and cubs
watercolour
130 × 340mm

Lions are classed as one of the big cats, but I don't think they quite belong as leopards and tigers do. I see something doggy about them compared to leopards and tigers. They climb trees when they want to and they are always much too conspicuous. Their big advantage is that they can (while leopards and tigers are lone hunters) hunt together as a pride. This means that they can openly drive their prey to a position where a part of the pride is hidden, and are sure of a kill. As a pride they can often succeed in skilfully creeping forwards until they have almost surrounded their prey before making their last dash to their successful kill. Lion cubs are always an attraction but leopard and tiger cubs are rarely seen.

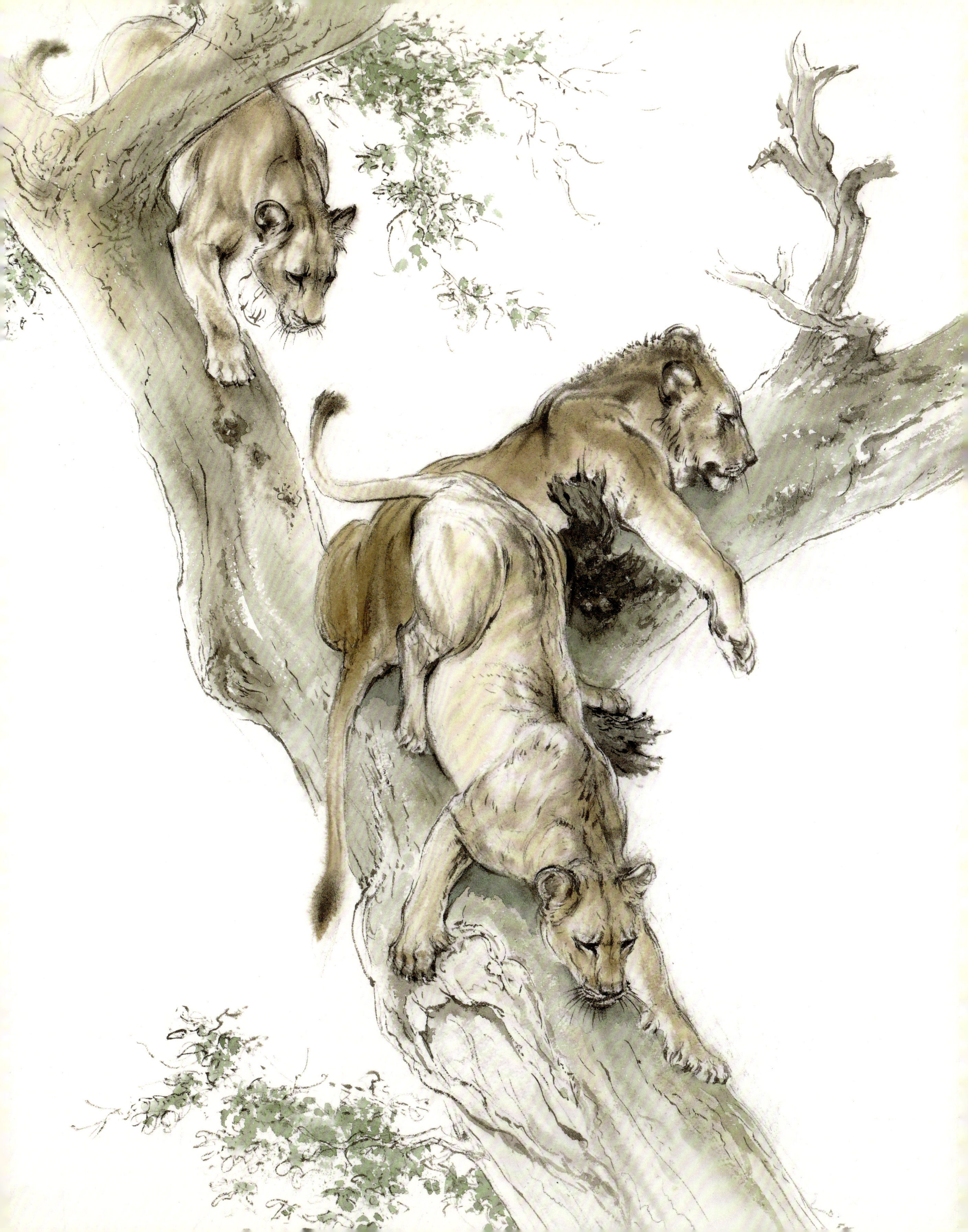

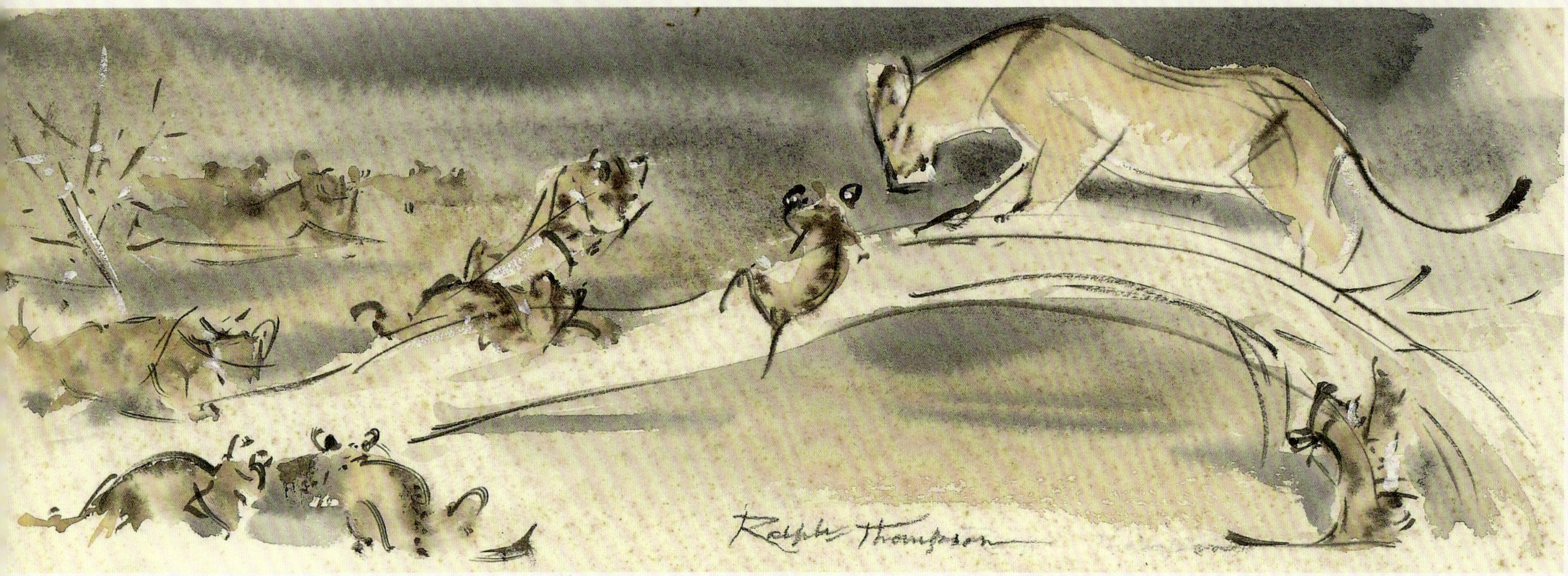
Ralph Thompson

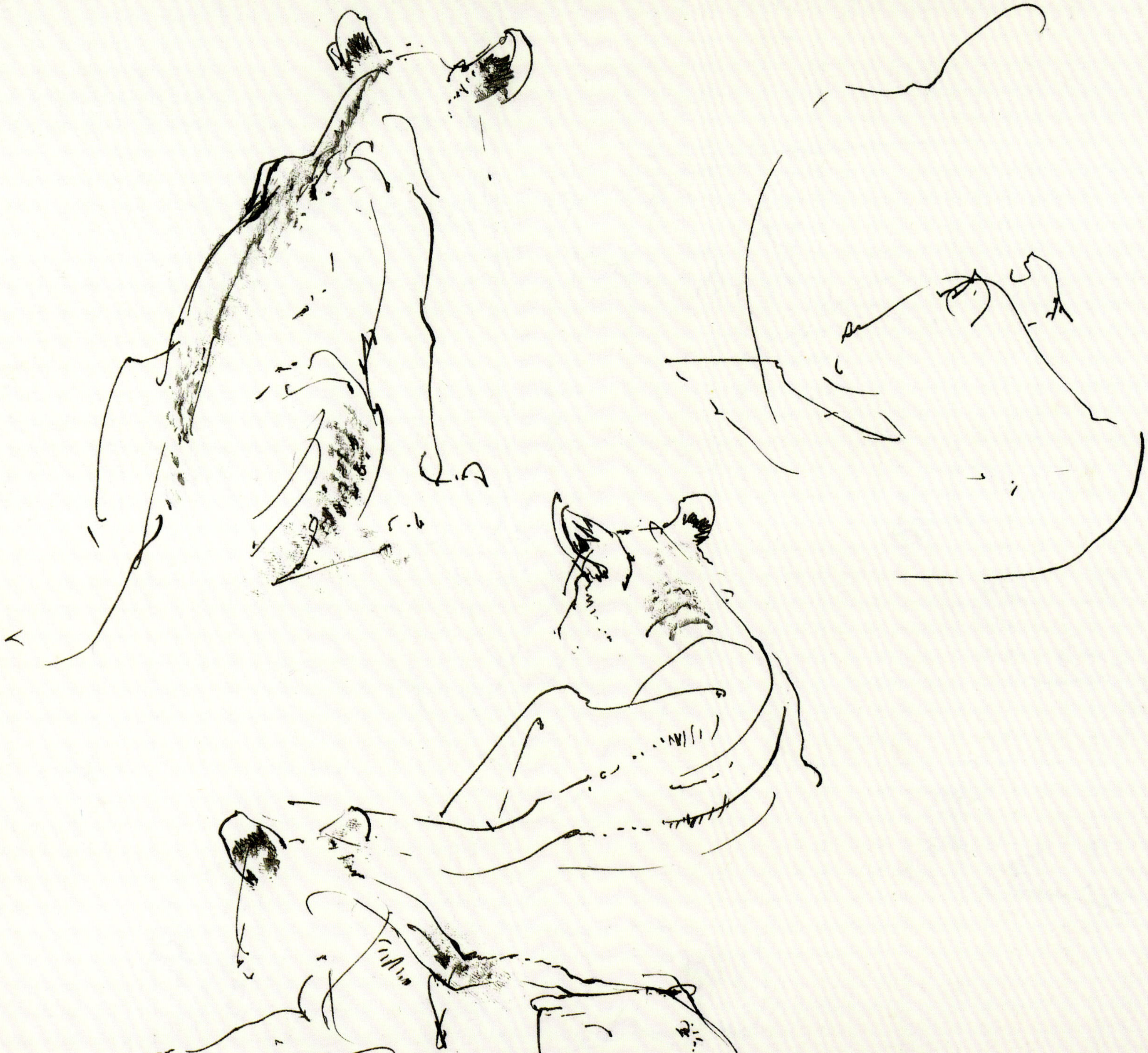

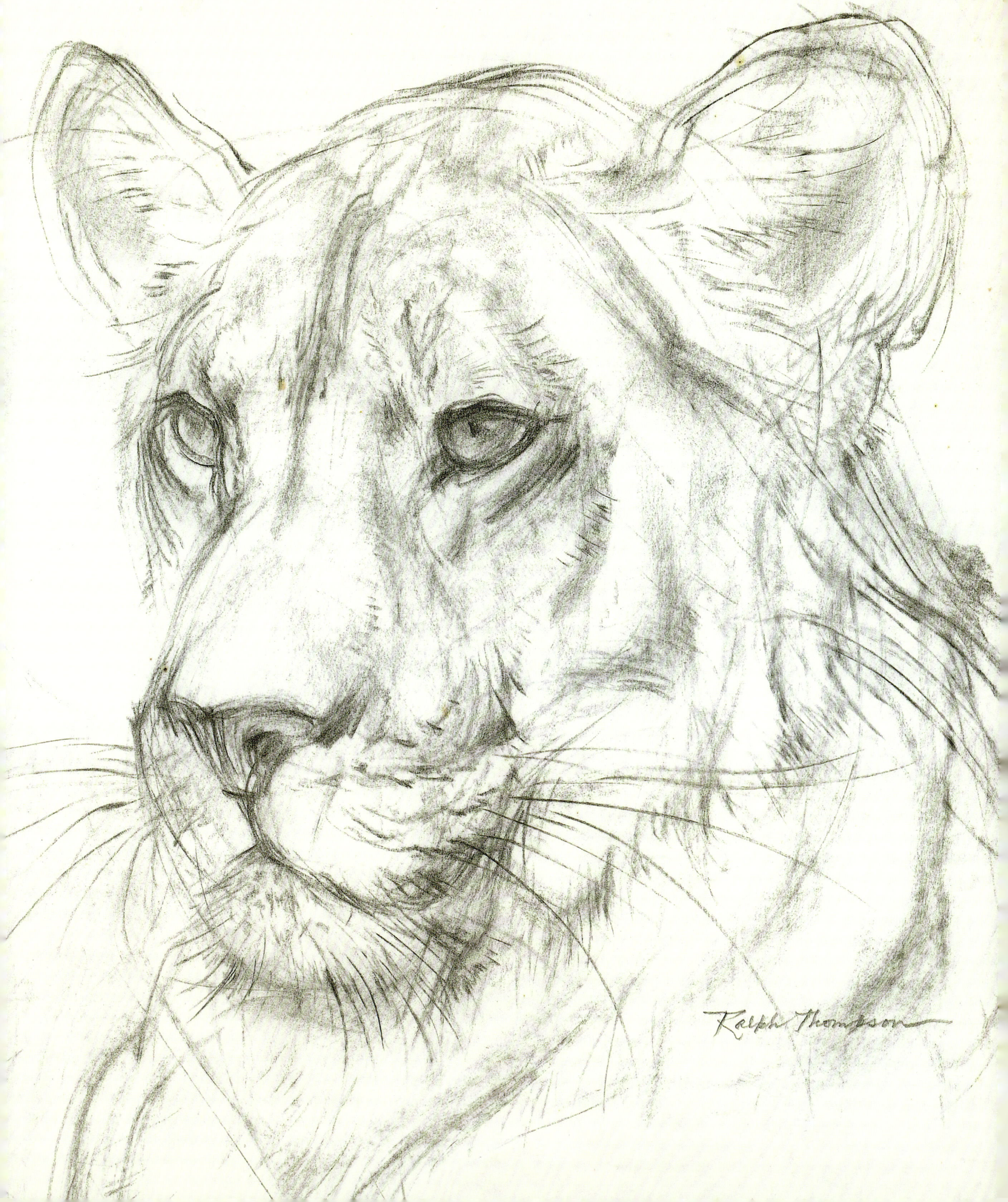
Ralph Thompson

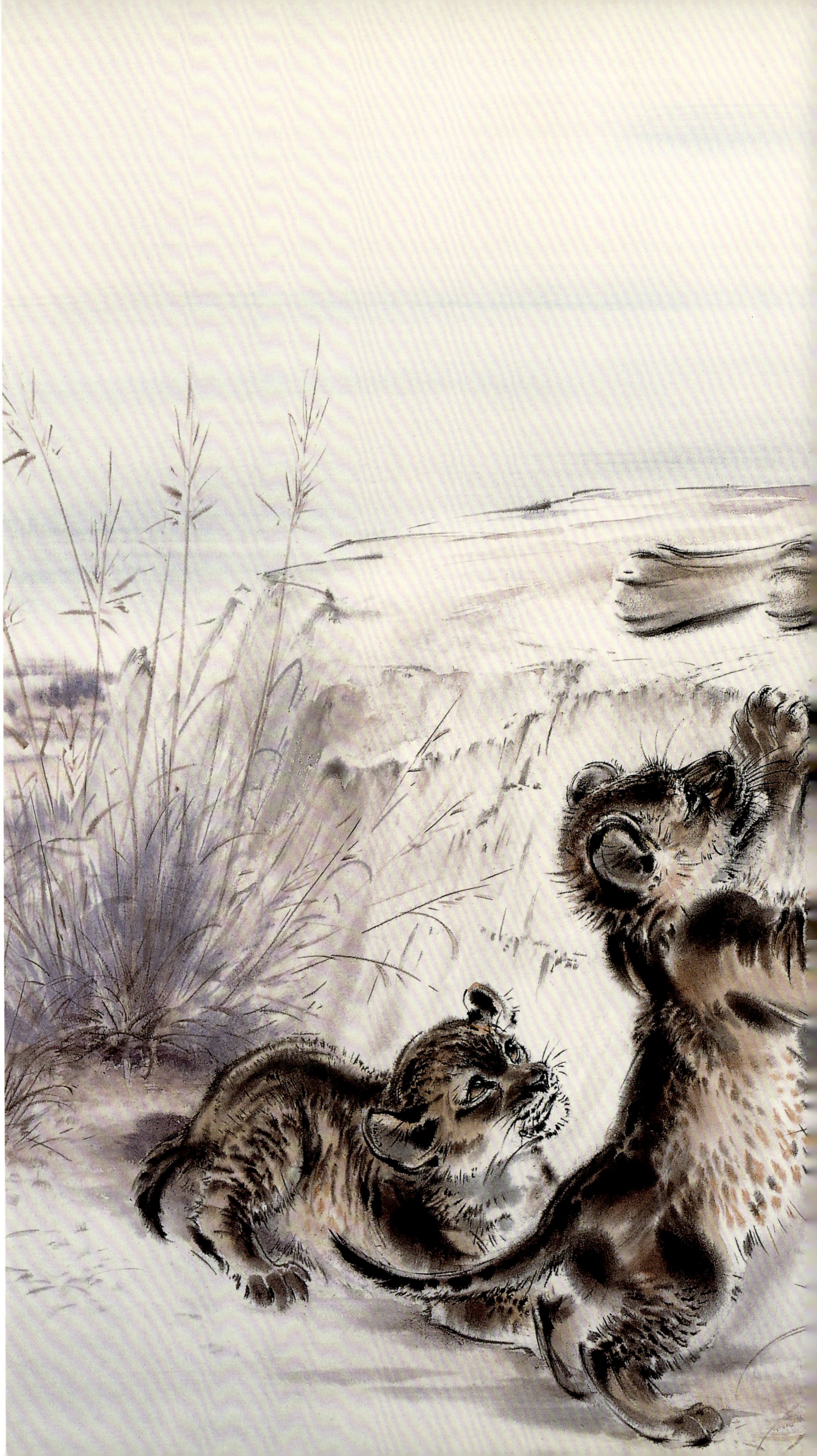

The coveted place
watercolour
800 × 1170mm

previous page right
Lioness portrait
charcoal drawing
400 × 400mm

following page left
Lion cubs
ink
actual size

following page right
Lion cub
charcoal drawing
380 × 560mm

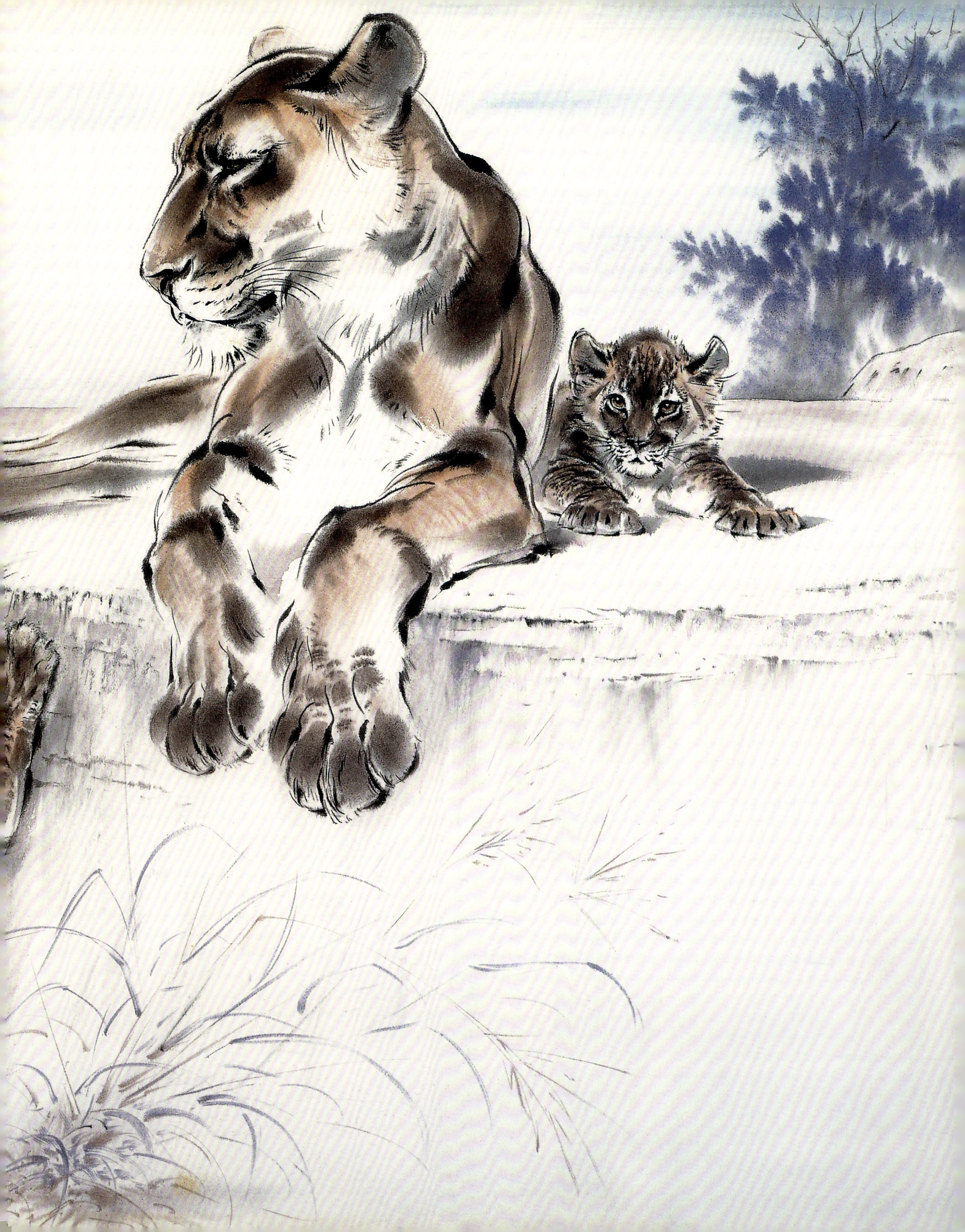

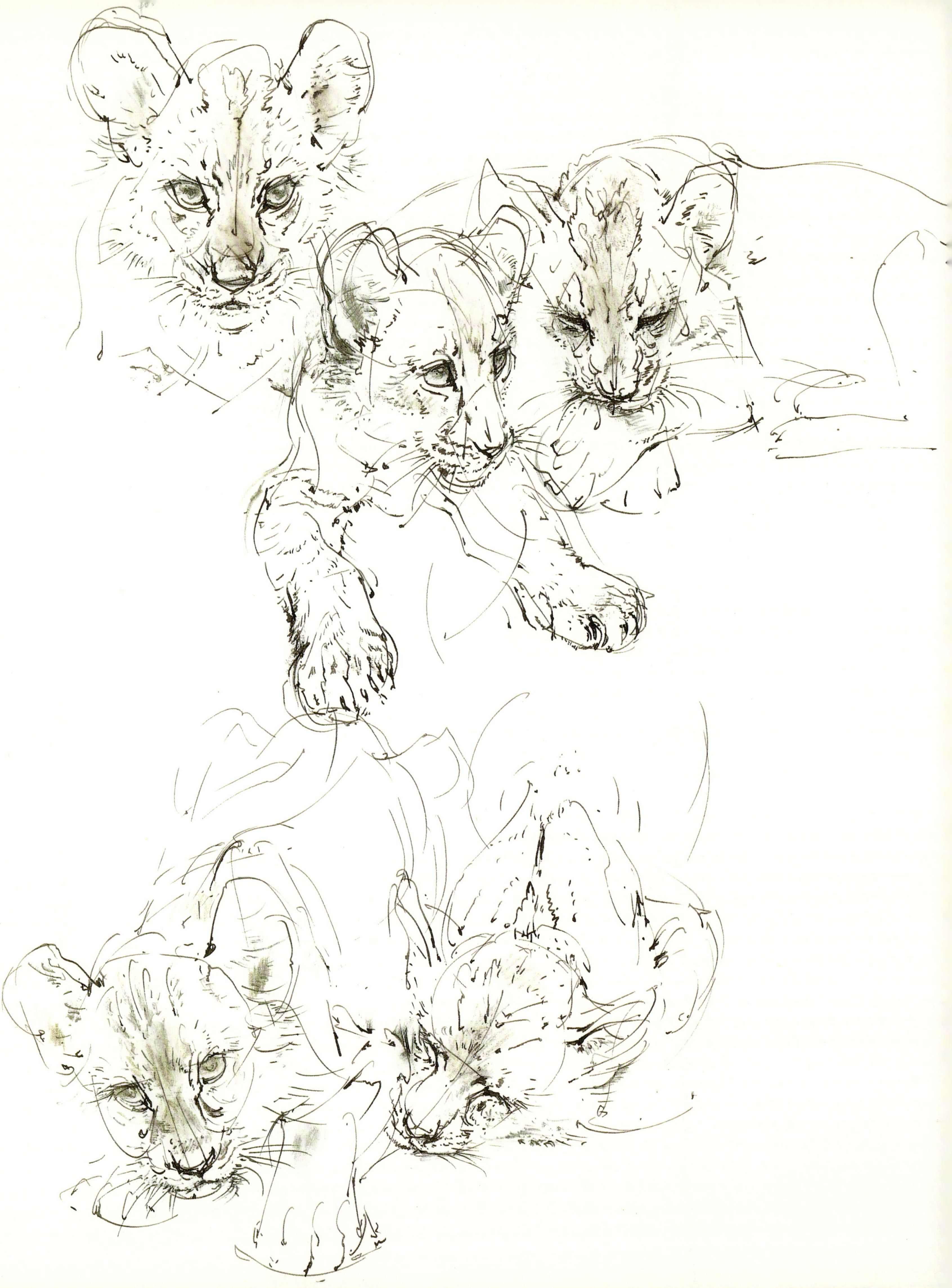

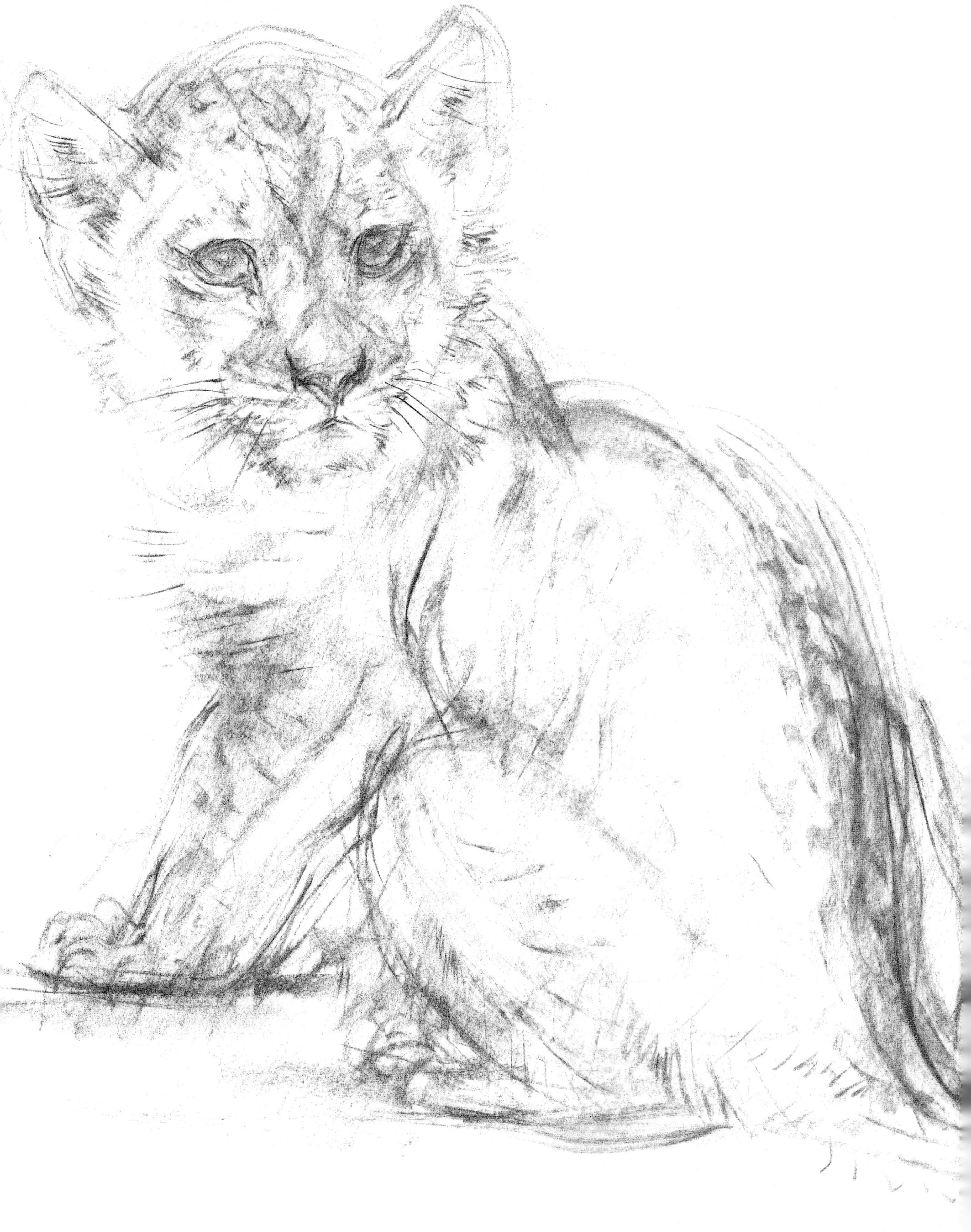

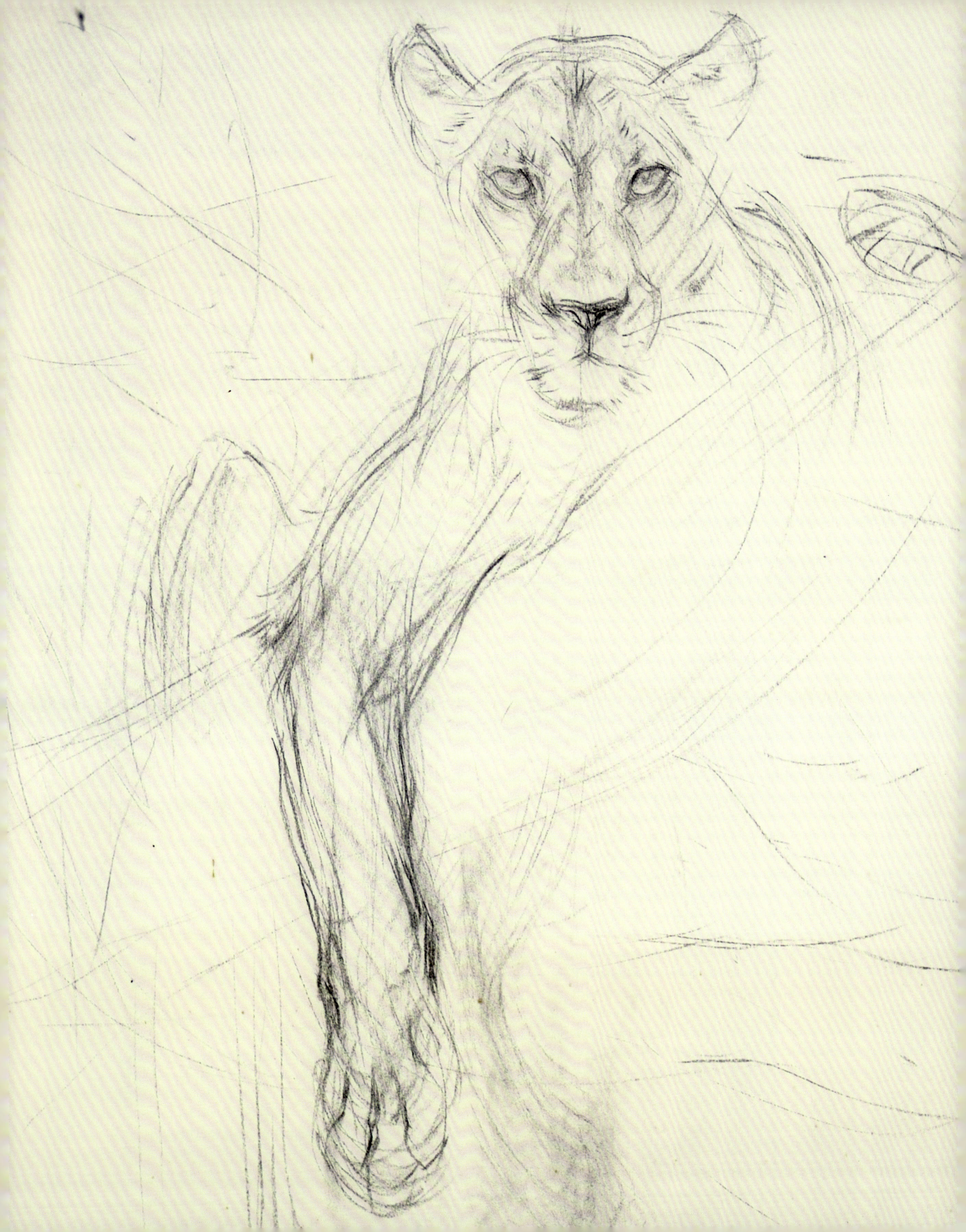

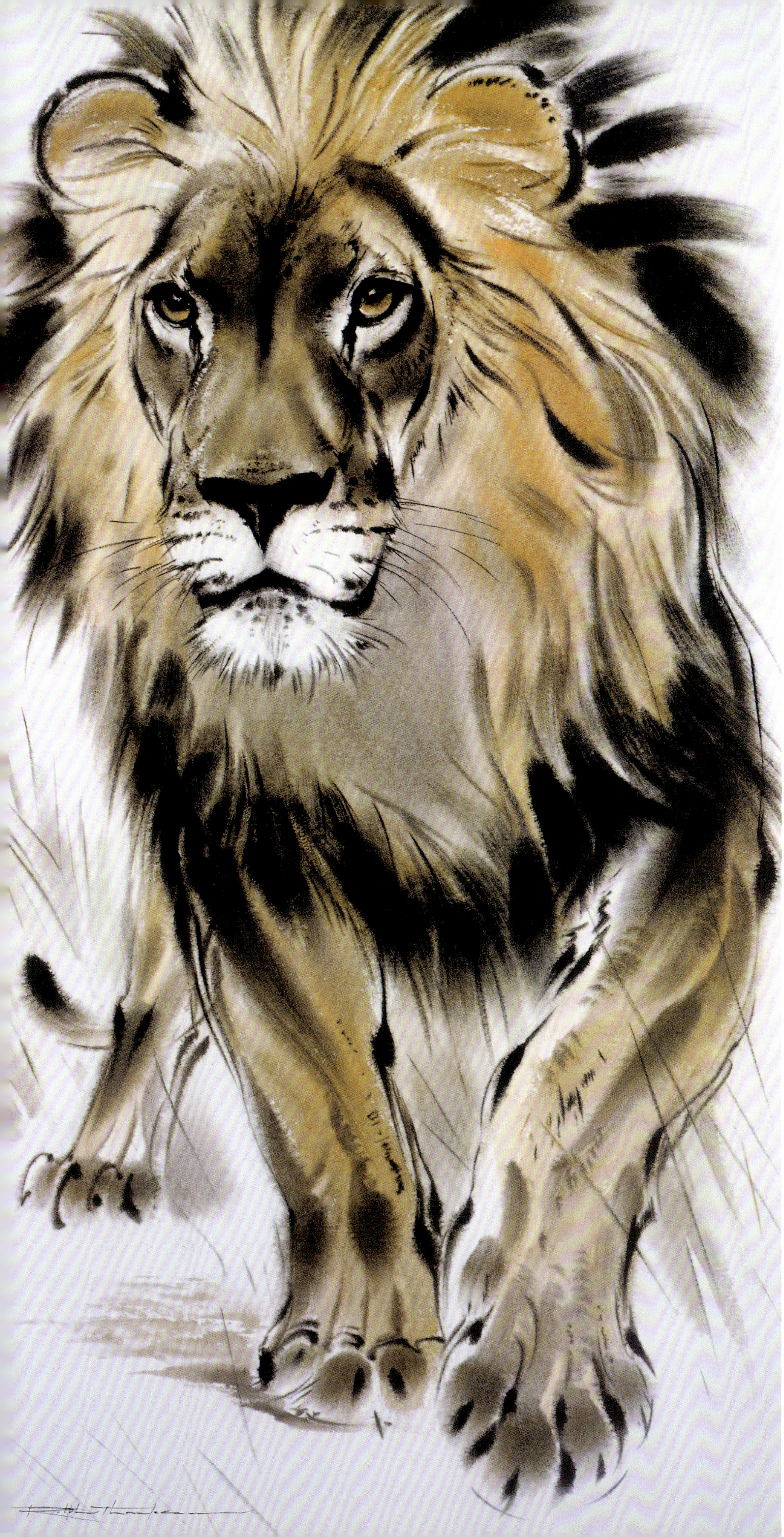

Lion
watercolour

opposite
Lioness in a tree
charcoal drawing
750 × 550mm

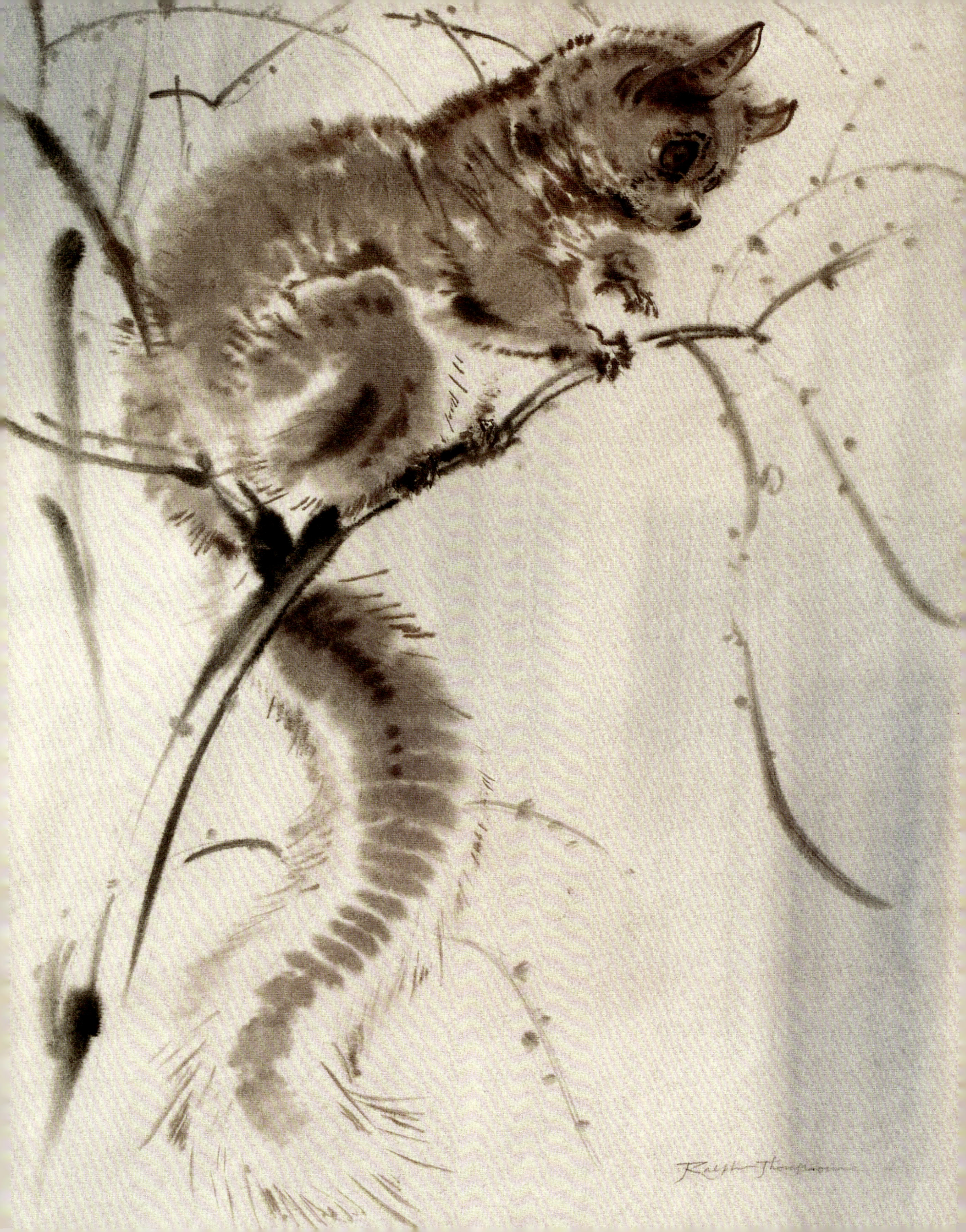
Ralph Thompson

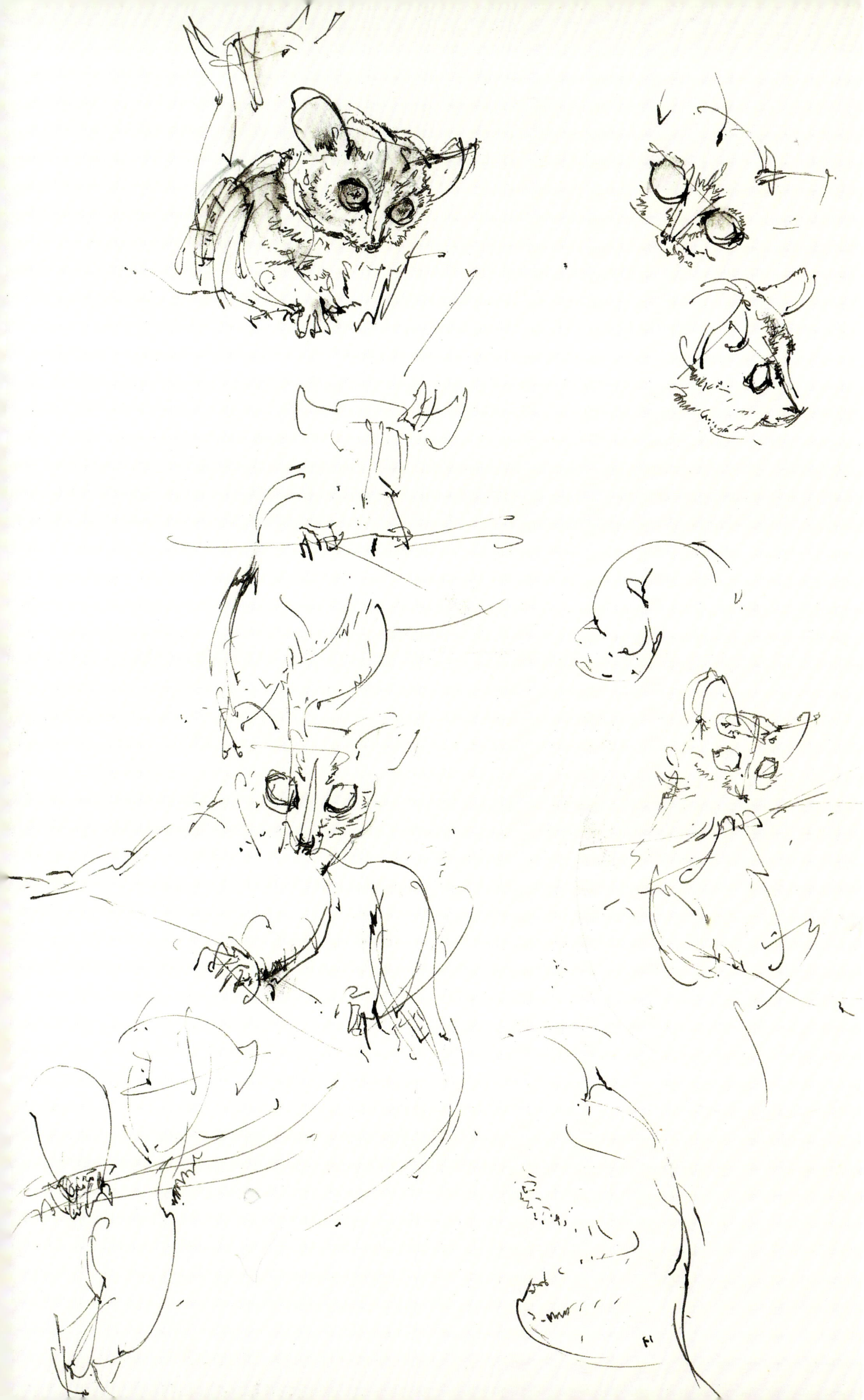

opposite
Bush baby
watercolour
620 × 480mm

following page
Ostrich chicks
watercolour
420 × 800mm

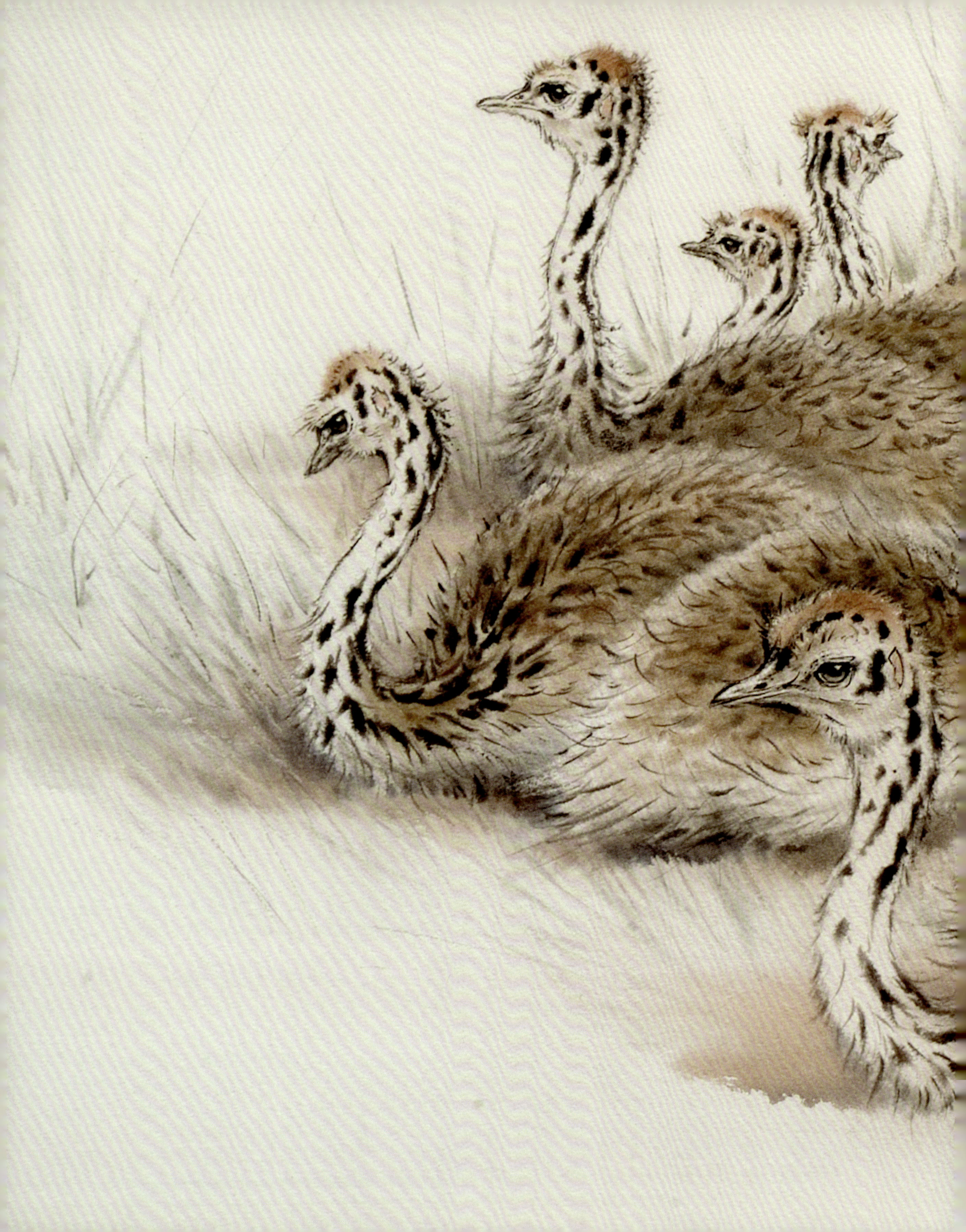

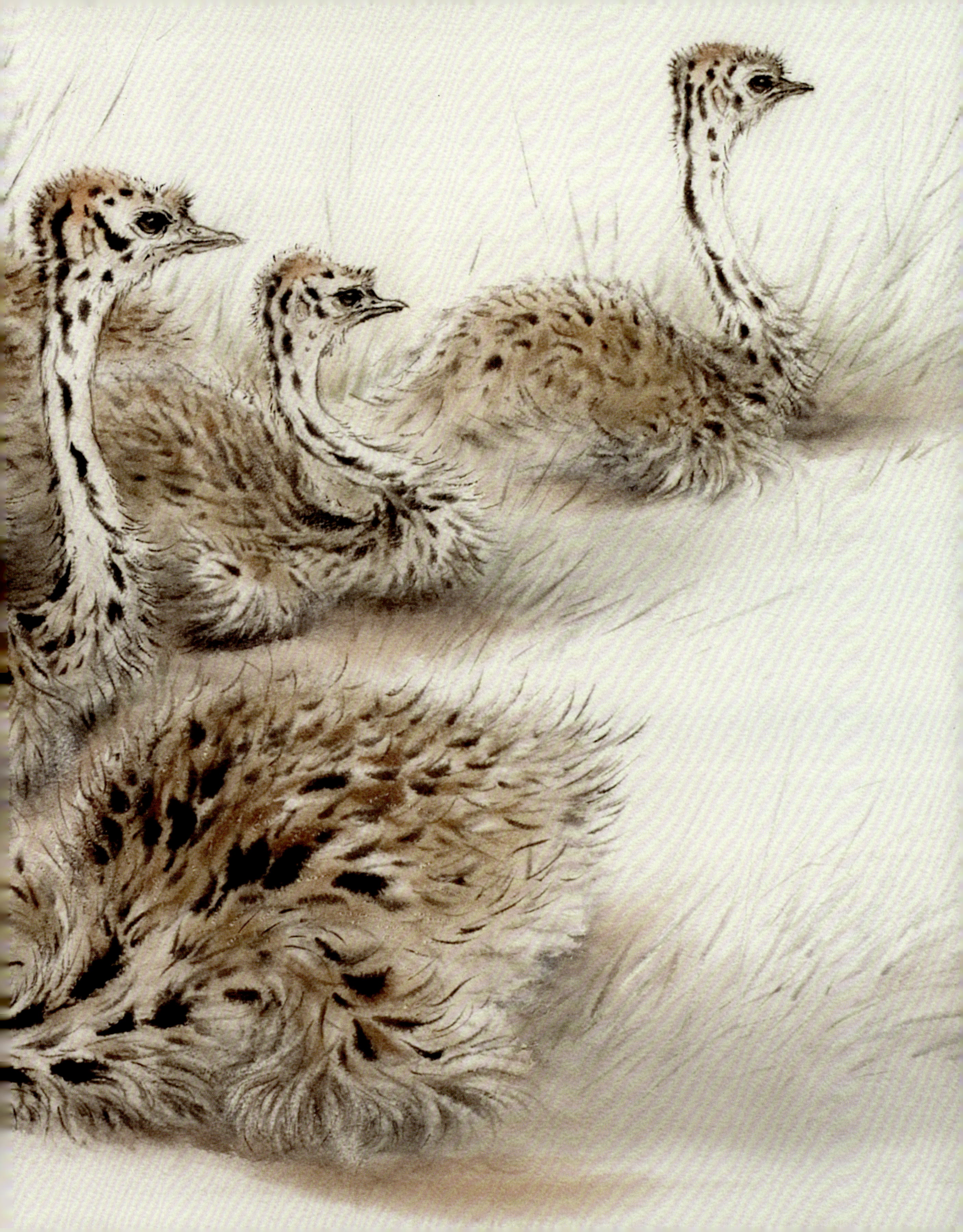

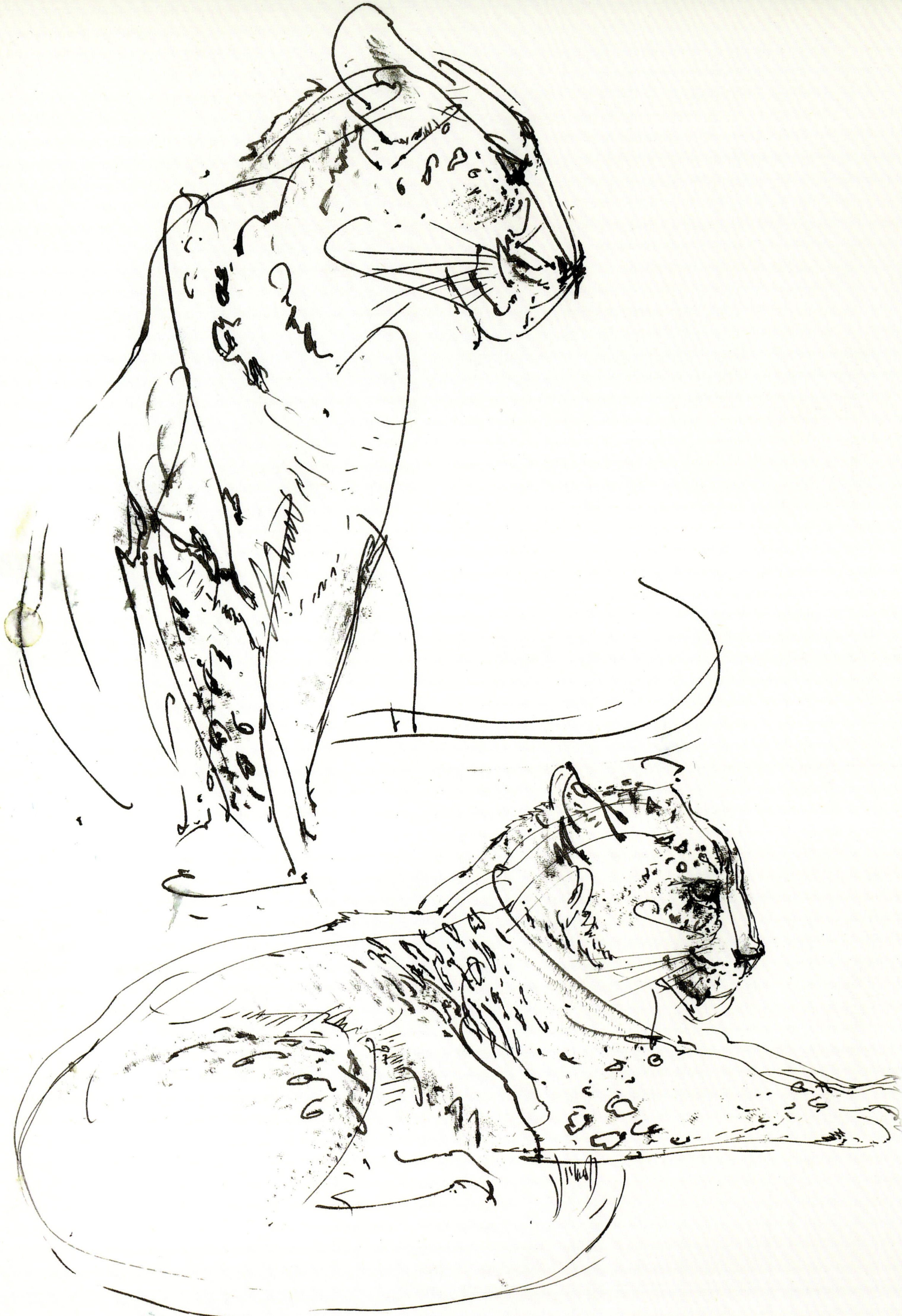

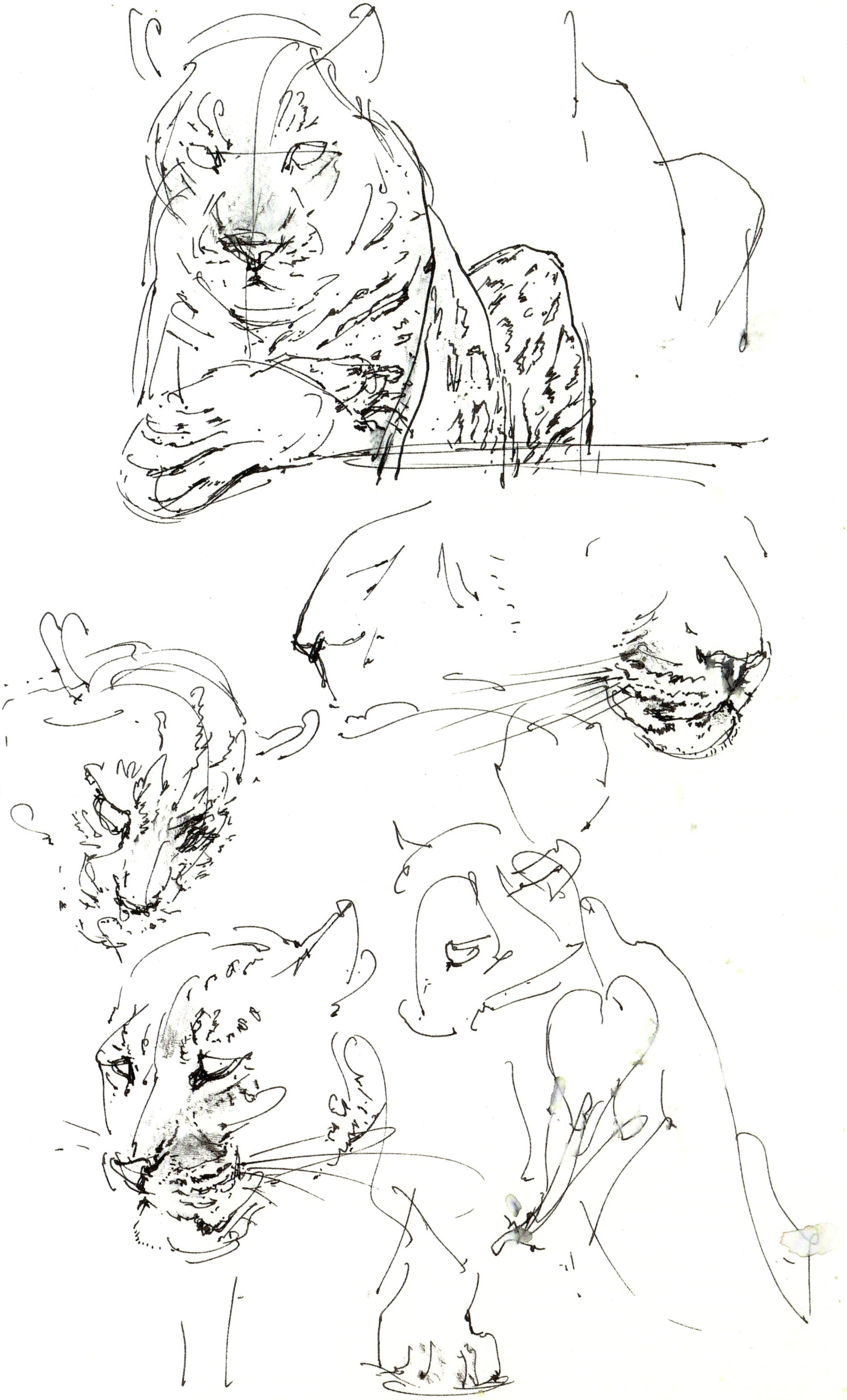

Leopard studies
ink
actual size

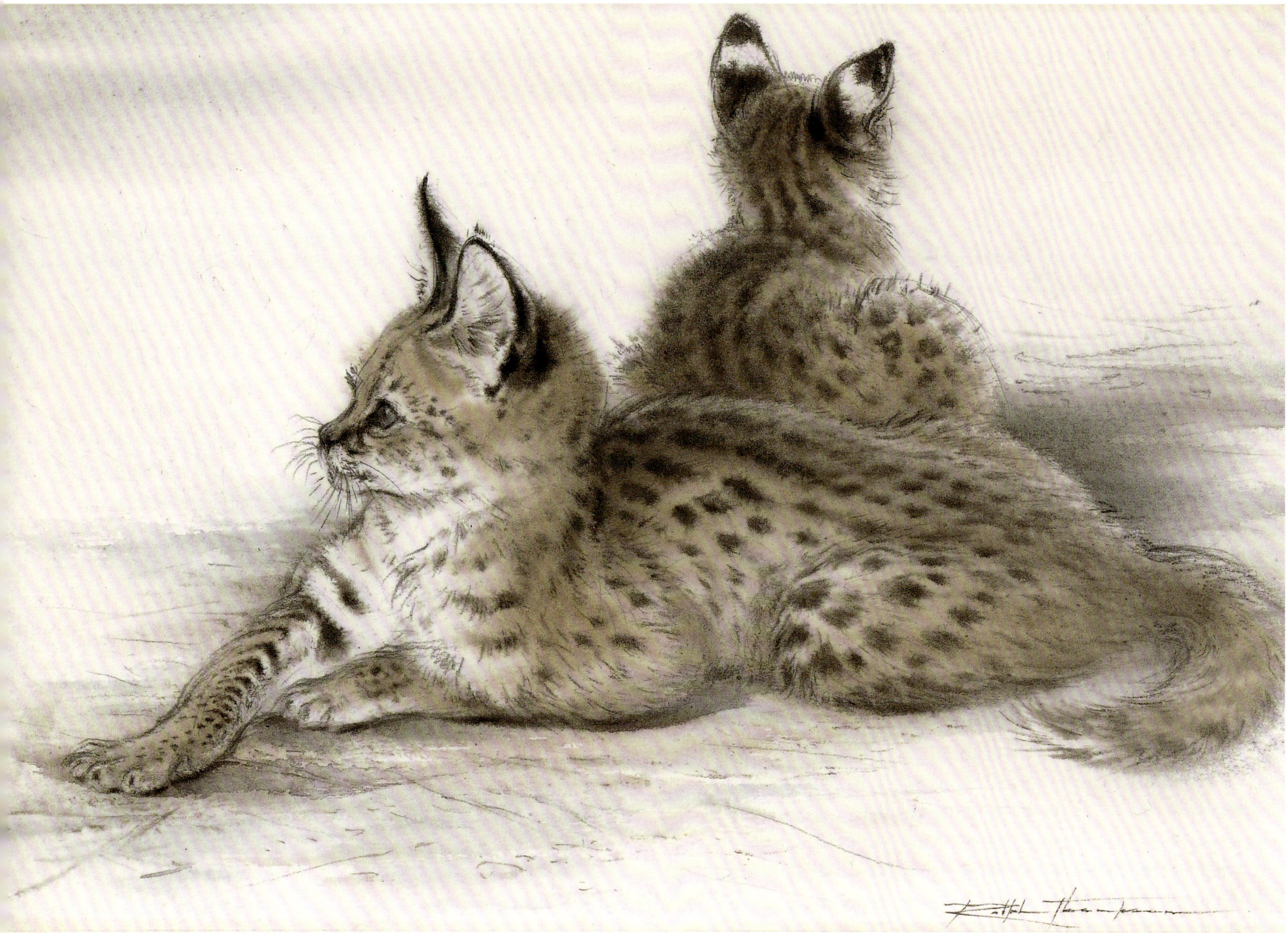

Serval kittens
watercolour
250 × 370mm

opposite
Serval cat in a tree
watercolour
680 × 510mm

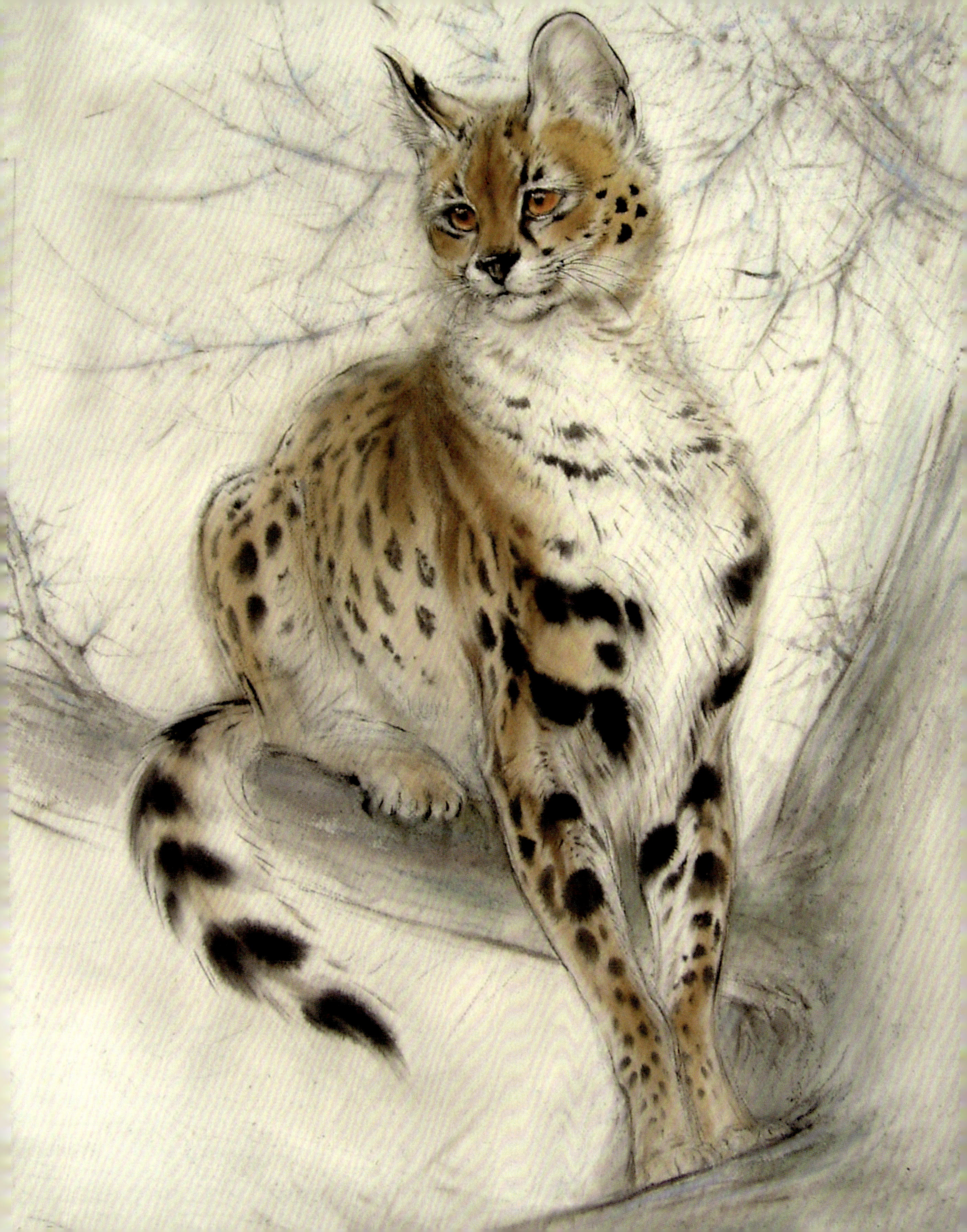

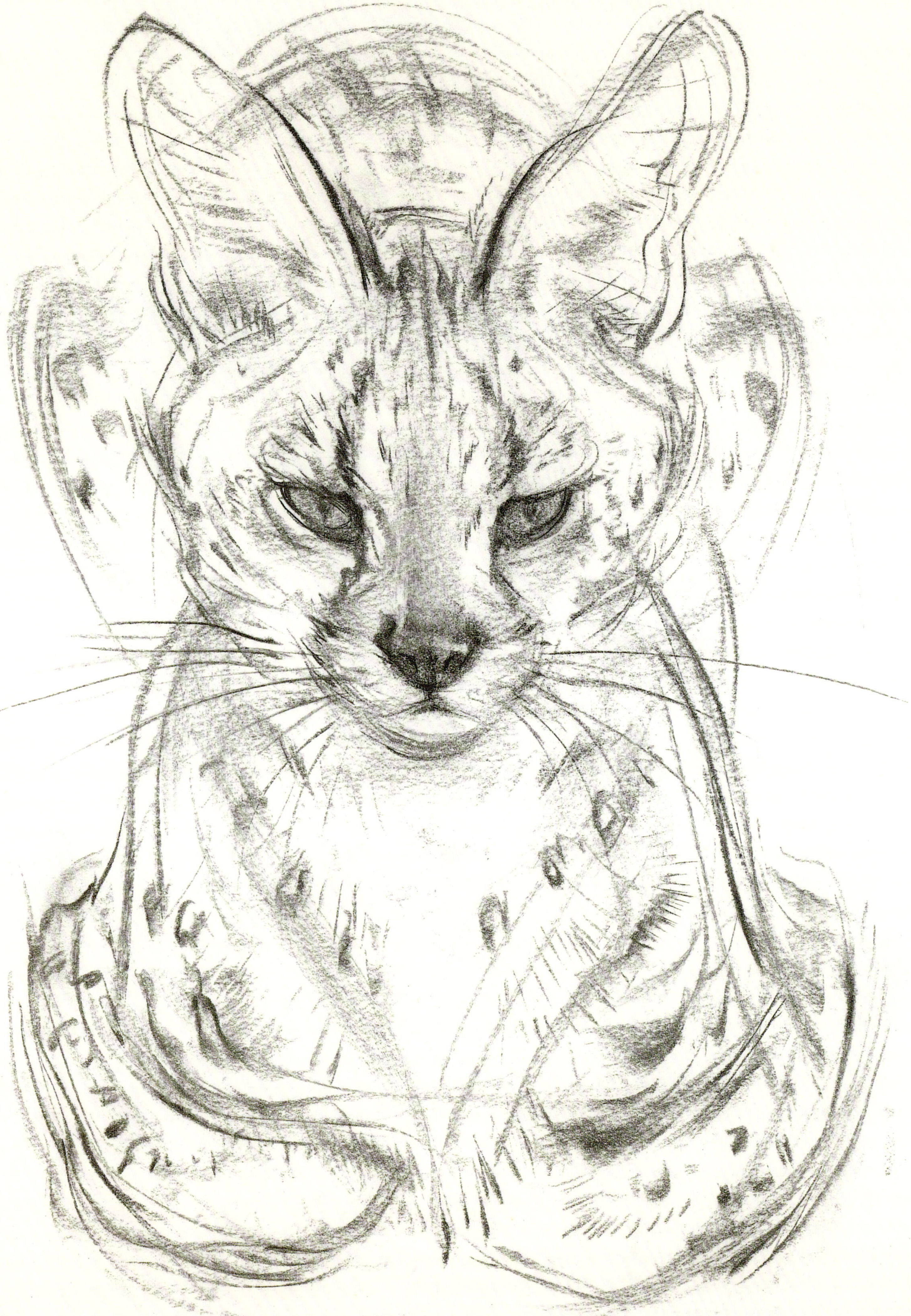

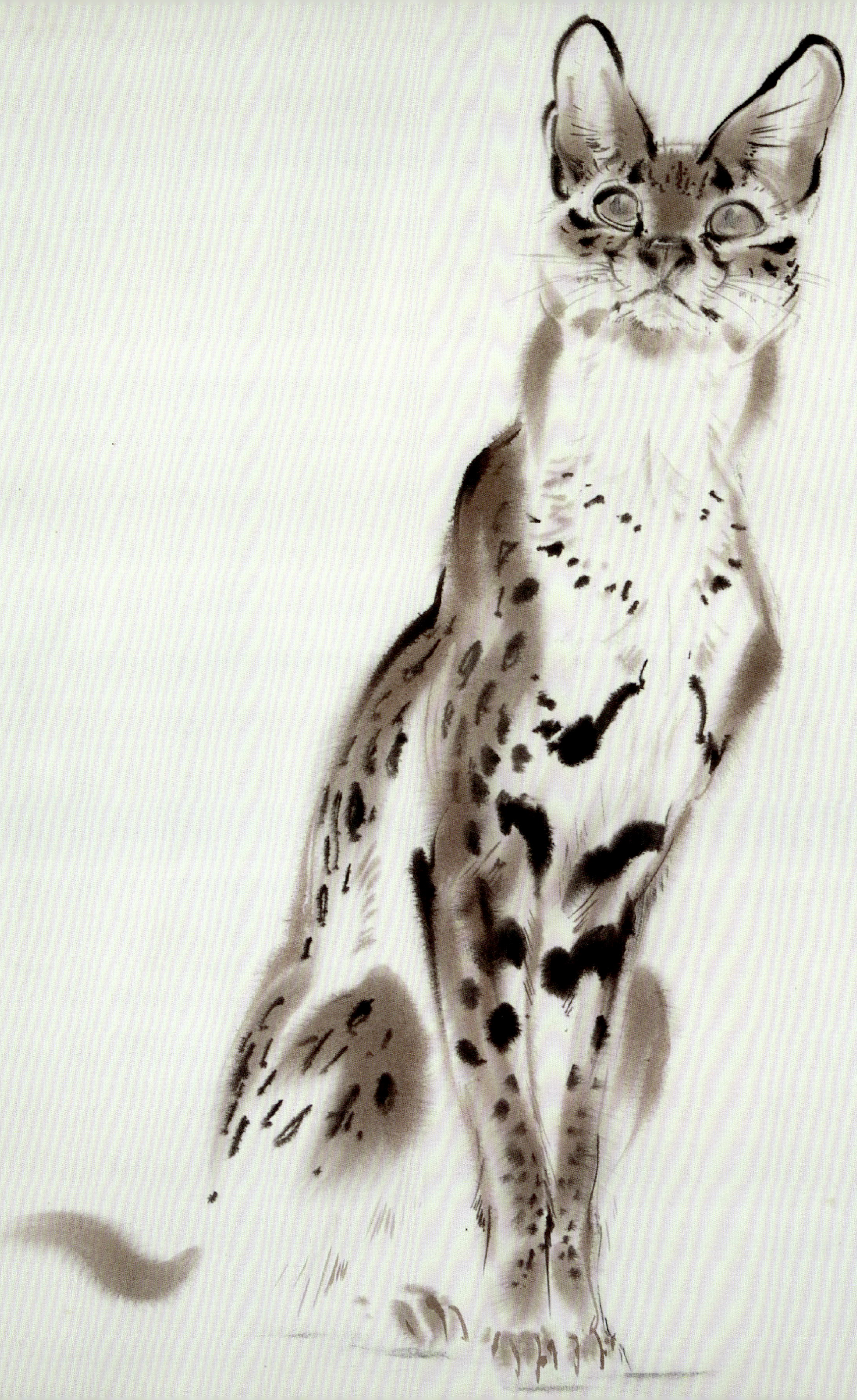

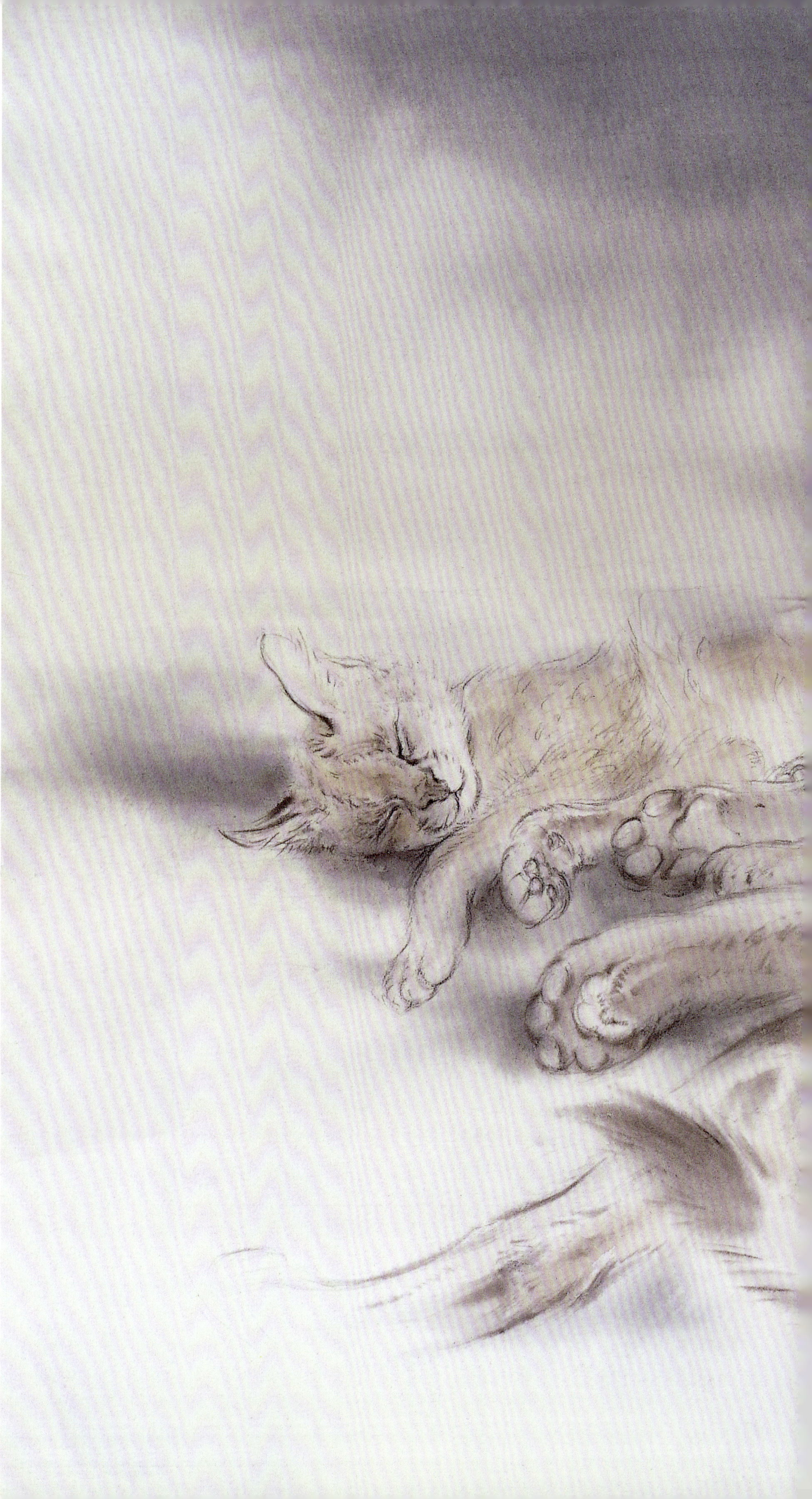

Serval cat and kittens
watercolour
660 × 915mm

previous page left
Serval cat resting
charcoal
510 × 380mm

previous page right
Serval cat
watercolour
680 × 510mm

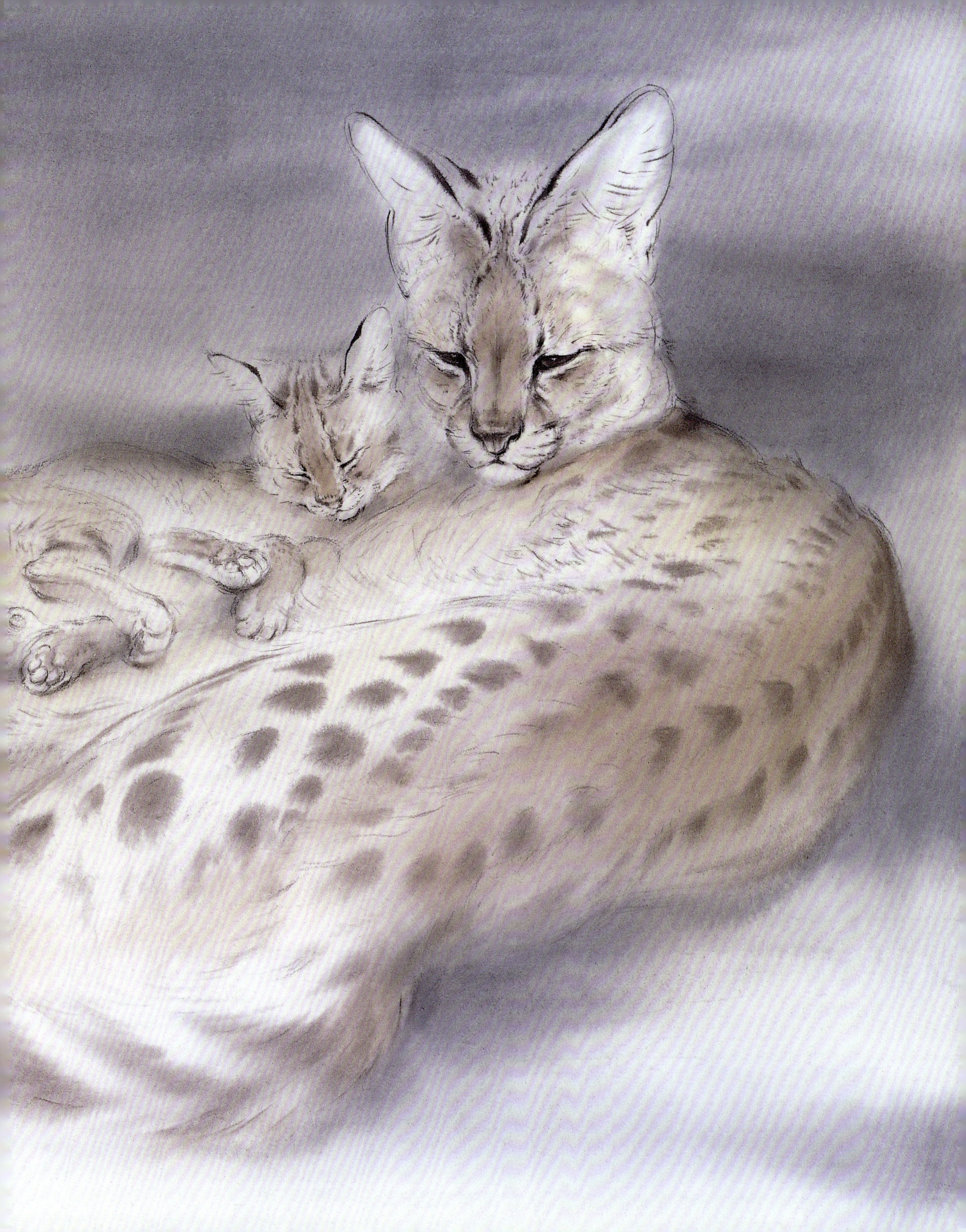

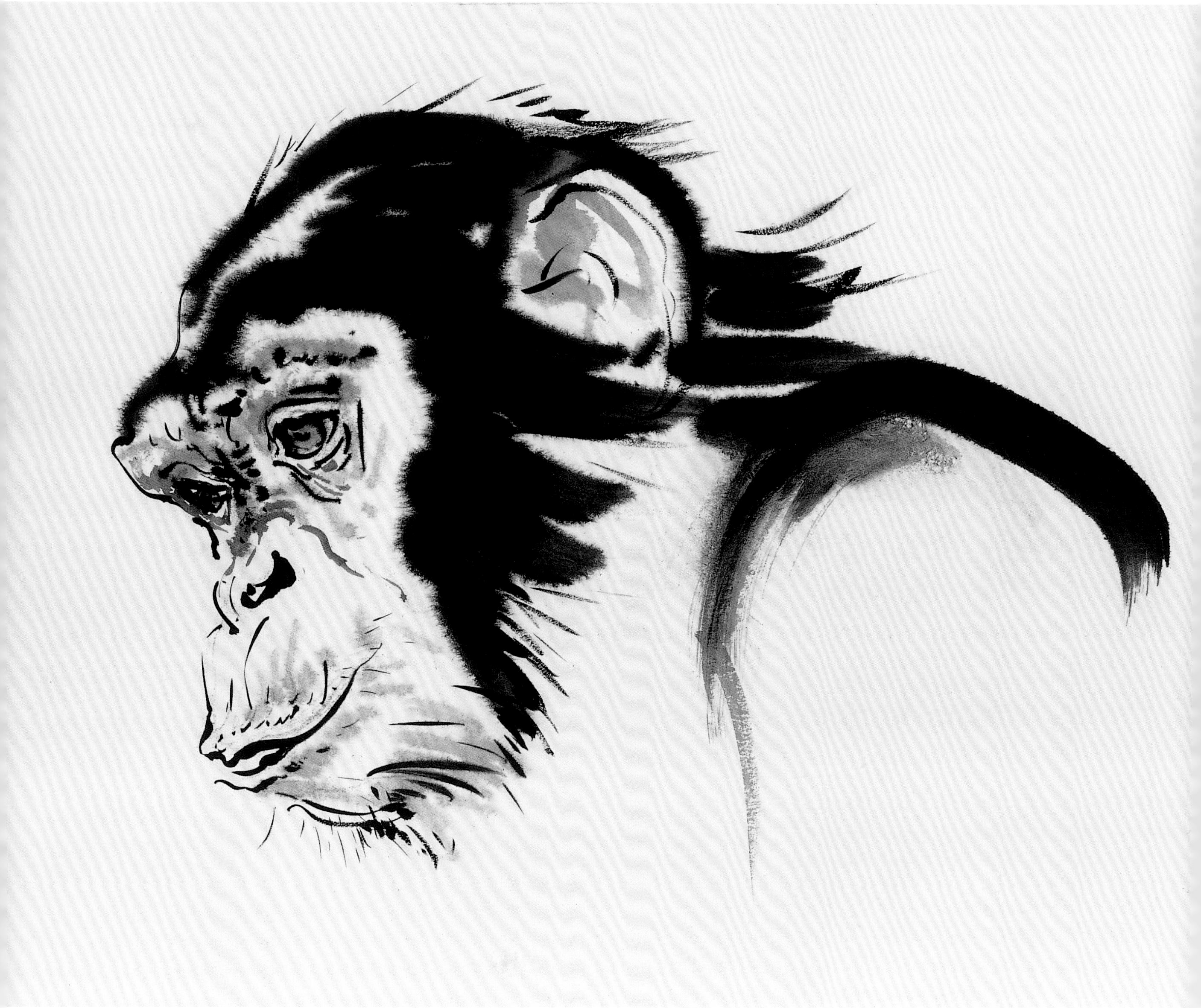

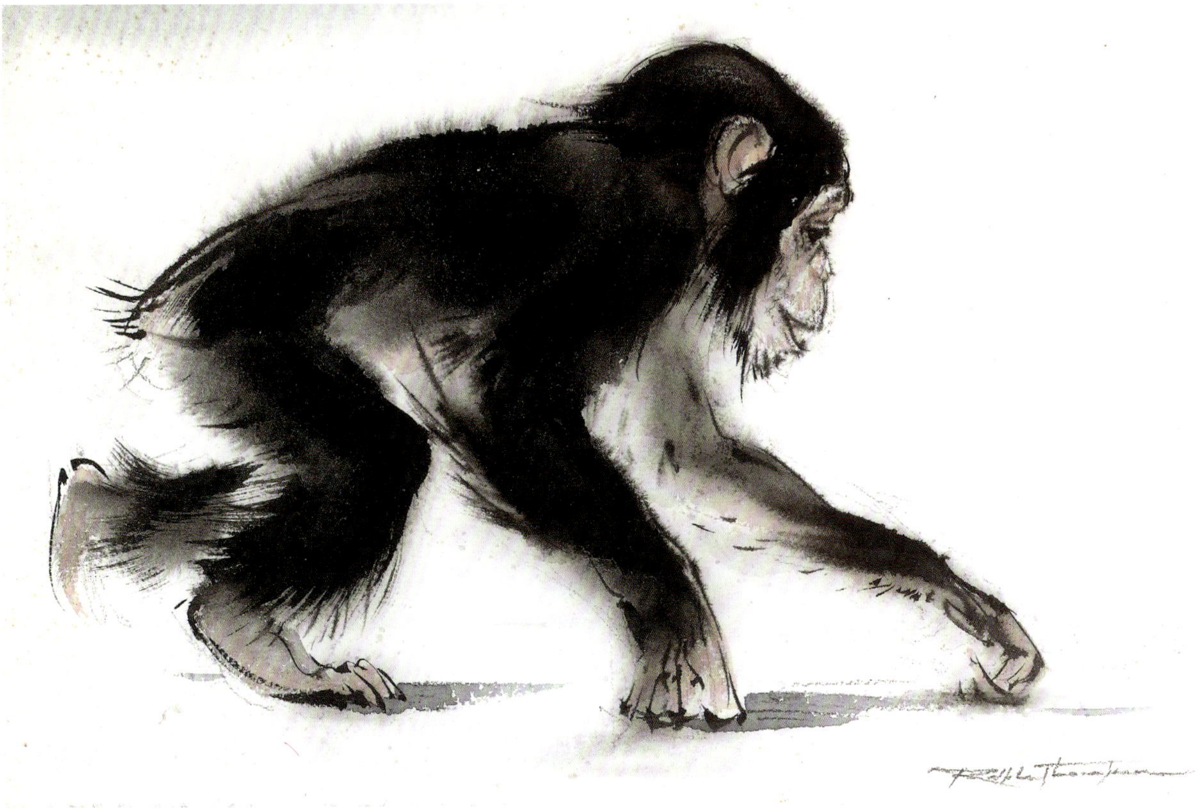

Budongo Forest

One of my reasons for planning a 'safari' in Western Uganda was to visit the Budongo Forest because I was told that there I could see chimpanzees living in their own natural world. We were to be guests in a house with easy access to the forest. A local African would act as my guide. So off we went.

There were some beautiful gloriana lilies and wild pepper plants growing nearby as we entered the forest. I saw a Black mamba, twenty paces away, which thankfully slid off into the distance. Huge trees, made a canopy so dark that the forest floor was almost clear.

It was not long before we could hear chimpanzees, gradually coming closer all the time, making a most alarming commotion, howling and screaming and hammering on the buttress roots as they came. I told myself they sounded like 'fiends from hell.' If they came close, we had been told to crouch down between the buttress roots in a position of complete submission. A party of fifteen or so appeared and made towards us as if to attack. They must have been aware of our intrusion into their world and made this terrifying assertion of their territorial rights for, having done so, their noisy demonstration suddenly ceased and they took to the trees.

Young chimpanzee walking
watercolour
180 × 280mm

opposite
Chimpanzee portrait
ink and wash
310 × 400mm

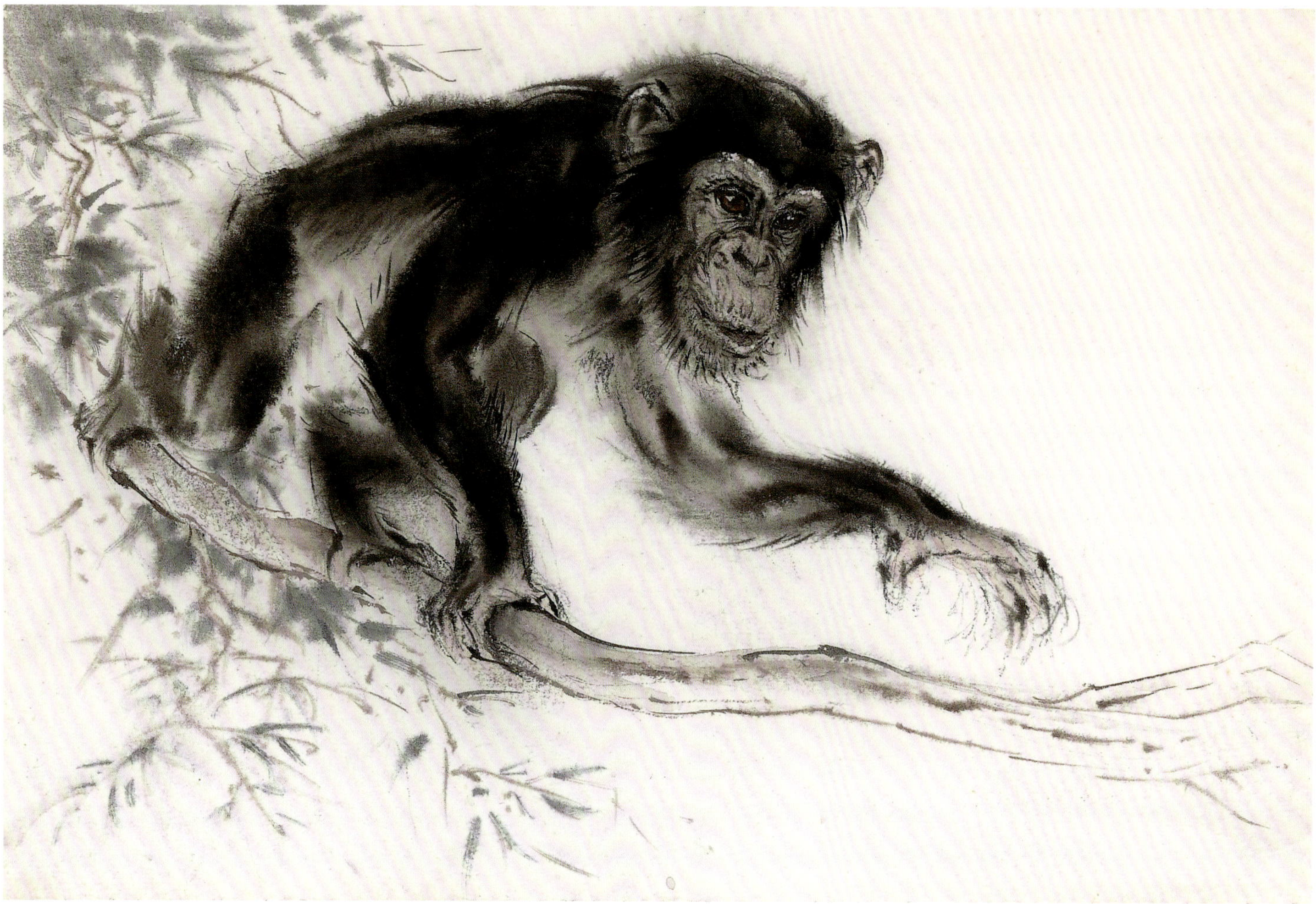

Chimpanzee in a tree
watercolour
190 × 280mm

Up there, they made a totally different impression. They were up those very tall trees in no time and I watched fascinated as chimpanzees of all sizes made breathtaking leaps from one branch to another. Having seen them in captivity only, I had found it difficult to understand their natural colouration. Seen up there in the sunlit branches, 'black' looked so perfectly, triumphantly, right. It was indeed another revelation.

On my route beyond the Budongo Forest I was driving up through tea plantations, where we were told to look for chimpanzee 'nests'. We only found one or two abandoned ones. They evidently build themselves nests in low trees, bending branches together until they have made a platform several feet across. Alas, I had no time to go back to the forest to see more and learn more about them and their 'nests'.

Driving through tea plantations on my planned route, I passed tall trees growing in a dip in the hills by a stream and spotted a party of about fifteen Colobos monkeys. I could not miss them – they are so striking. They are virtually black monkeys with thick black coats and large white capes, which make them very conspicuous – this and a black tail with an enormous long thick white tip. They were busy and happy grooming each other and were

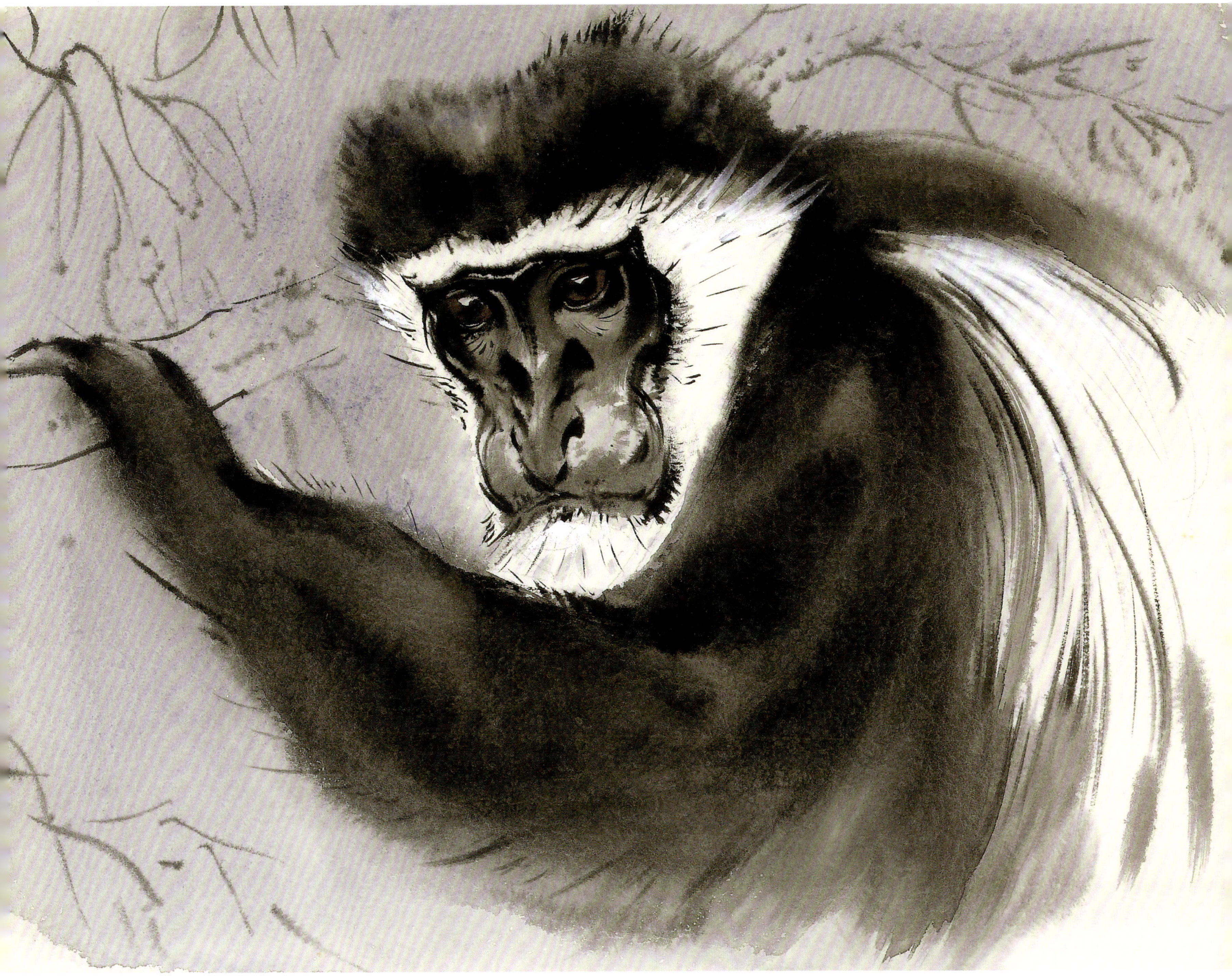

quite oblivious of my presence. I was partly hidden in the car and so able to draw for an hour or so, trying to understand their strange appearance. Surely it was their special adaptation to living together on high ground with such conspicuous colouration keeping them in touch on misty mornings, and their thick coats and large white capes giving extra warmth during cold nights.

I learnt that chimpanzees could work themselves up into a mood for a kill and make a raid on Colobos monkeys. I like to think it is a rare happening, soon over and soon forgotten.

Colobus monkey
watercolour
260 × 350mm

The Murchisson Falls

These are not very high waterfalls, but powerful enough to knock out the Nile perch which are carried over them and become food for the largest crocodiles in Africa.

I had booked to stay a few days at the Baraa Safari Lodge Hotel, a little way downstream from the falls. When I expressed a wish to learn more about the crocodiles, I was introduced to a character in very smart safari gear. This was Hugh Cott. I had heard a little about him; such that he knew a lot about crocodiles, was an artist specialising in black and white illustrations and could take me out in his own launch. Suspicious of his smart safari gear, I felt a little dismissive. I couldn't have been more mistaken. I thought that he must be in his seventies but when, a little later, he leapt on to the bank like a thirty year old, I wasn't so sure.

He promised to show me some crocodile eggs. He dug into the sandy bank with his bare hands, uncovering several eggs the size of a large hen's egg but darker. He then put them back and quickly covered them over. Back in the little launch once more he pointed back to the bank. A large Monitor lizard was now there. They evidently grow fat on crocodile eggs.

I had expected to be taken up to the falls to see the giant crocodiles but perhaps he had found this too dangerous for, instead, he steered the boat to a little backwater out of the main flow of the river. If disappointed at not seeing the giant crocodiles, I was delighted with what Hugh was to show me next. Grasses and reeds washed down by the stream had collected to make what he called a 'crocodile nest'. I was entranced to find tiny little crocodiles 6 to 8 inches long, perfect in every detail in the prettiest iridescent shades of golden greens and browns. I could have watched them for hours. The sight was yet another revelation.

opposite
Genet
watercolour
470 × 370mm

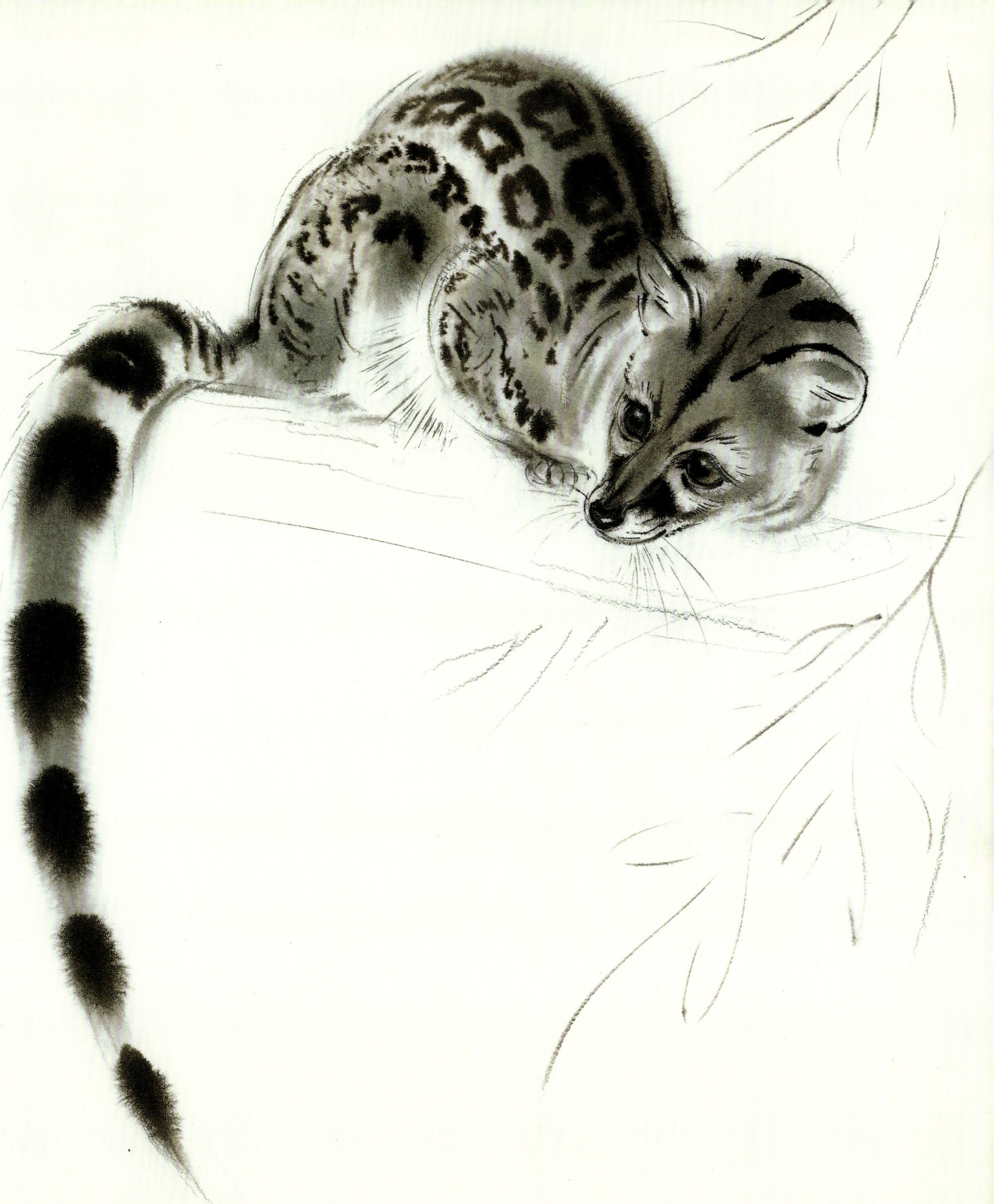

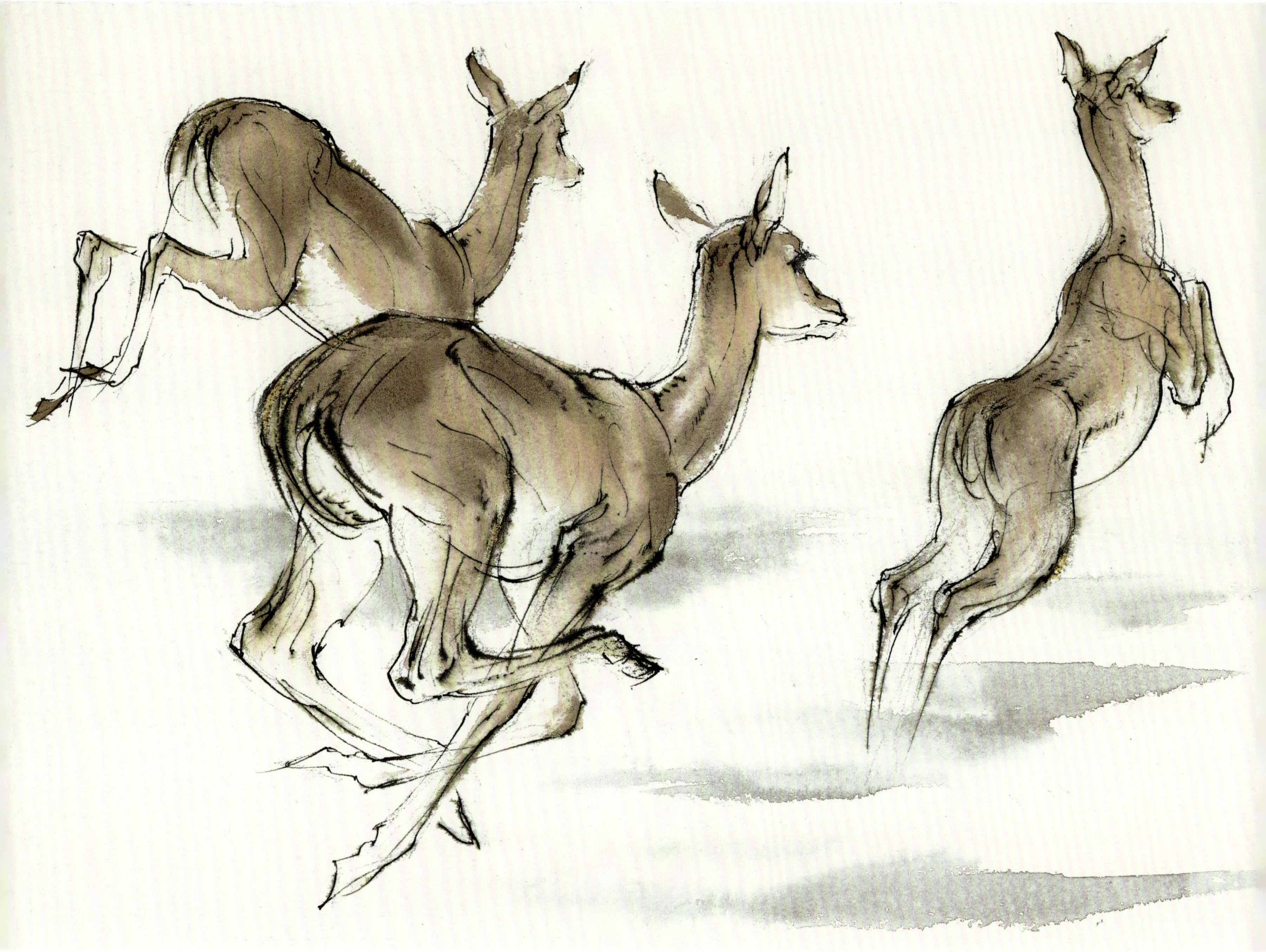

Impala
ink and watercolour
210 × 320mm

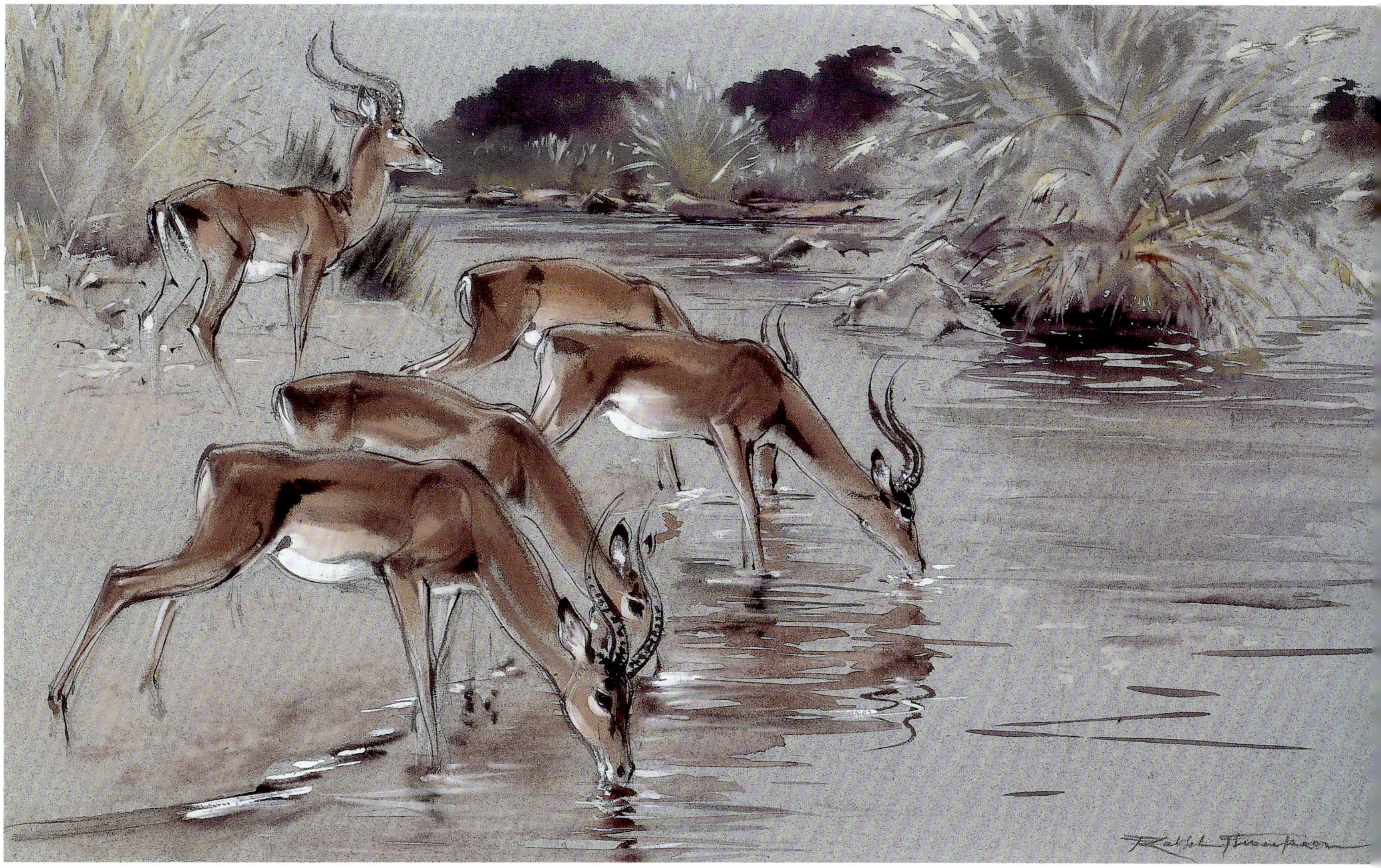

We watched a huge flock of birds with very prominent orange and red beaks and long pointed wings, all taking off from the river at the same moment and landing close together as one. It made a very striking spectacle. Hugh said they were 'skimmers'. They fish together in close formation at dusk or even at night, making shrill whistling sounds. Their lower mandibles are actually in the water. Using a high wing stroke, which keeps their wings dry, they find their prey by touch, not by sight, unlike all other birds. They eat what ever touches their beaks, flipping small fish out of the water and swallowing them. Ploughing the water with their beaks can disturb minute aquatic insects, which again attracts small fish. Skimmers will then turn abruptly and fly back over the same stretch of river and collect a small feast. Their specialised beaks make skimmers unique in the bird world. It was a morning to remember.

Hugh proved to be an eminent zoologist and illustrator of wildlife. He wrote an important book, 'Looking at Animals: A Zoologist in Africa', answering the ancient riddle of why crocodiles deliberately swallow stones. Not, as had always been thought, an aid to digestion, but rather a form of ballast to help them remain submerged more easily. He wrote what became the standard work on crocodile ecology.

Impala drinking
watercolour
450 × 580mm

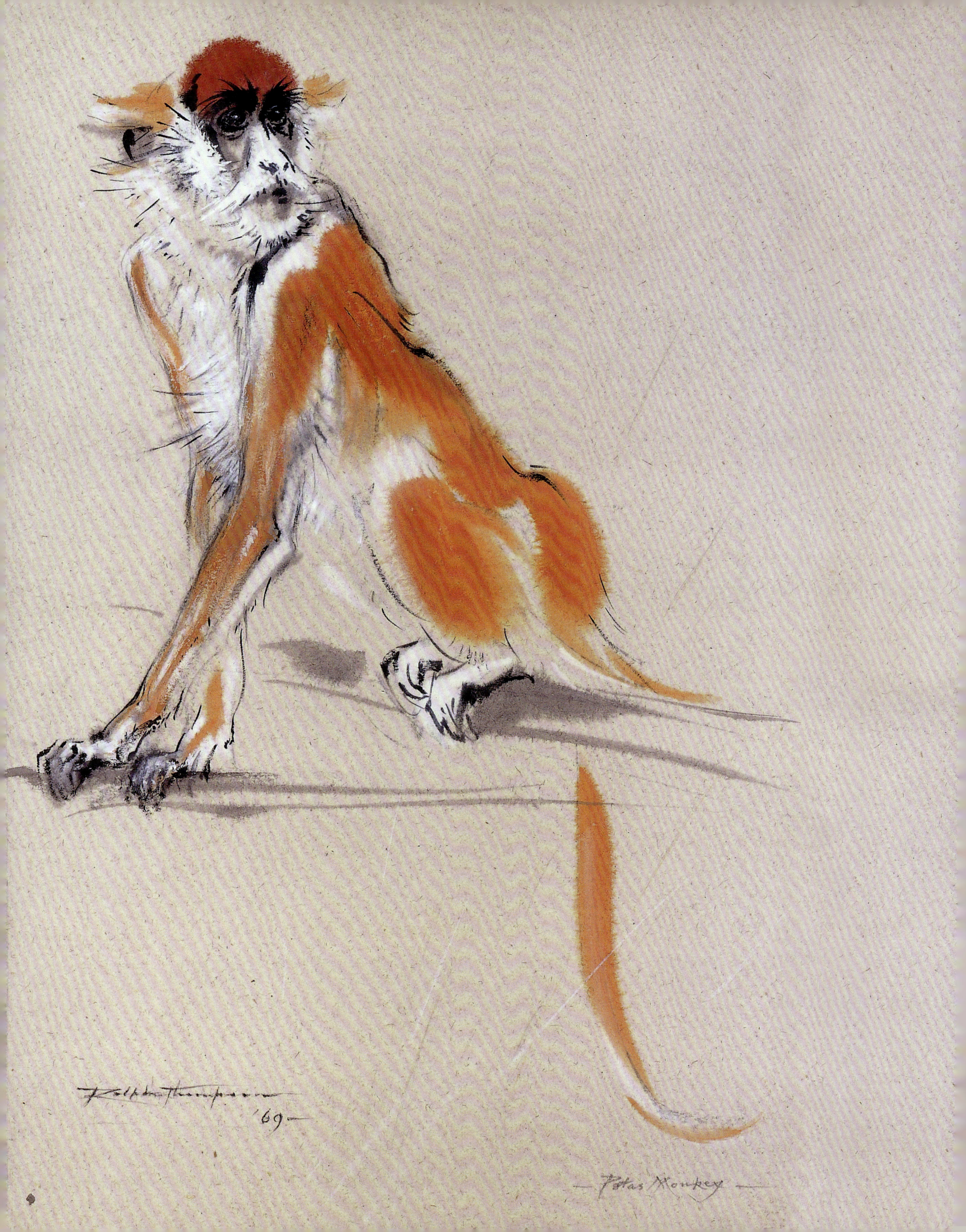
Ralph Thompson
'69
Patas Monkey

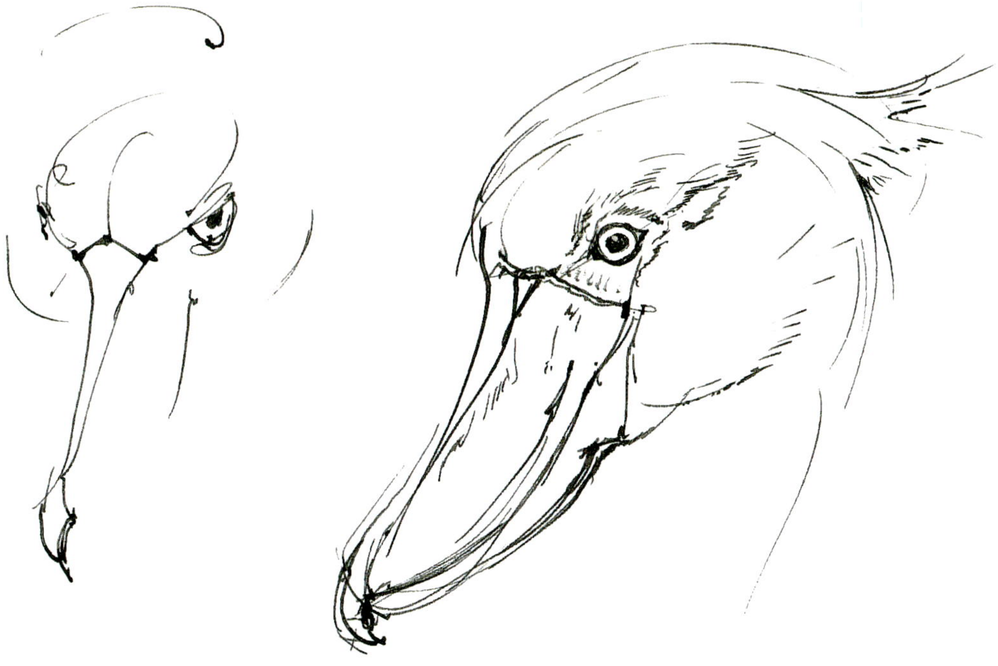

On the Equator

I knew that geographically I was actually on the equator but I found this very difficult to believe. Feelings kept returning from my schooldays, of looking at maps with that straight line cutting across everything, whether mountain, desert, sea or jungle.

I was actually standing on quite high ground, an altitude sufficient to prevent it from being overbearingly hot, and on grassland with a few trees stretching far away into the distance. I was told that the Patas monkey could be found hereabouts. Having seen them only in zoos, I thought of the elegant Patas as the 'intellectual' of the monkey world and nicknamed it after a well-known thinker, writer and television personality. Now, alas, I cannot remember his name. A pity, as it seemed to suit them with their lean faces and little moustaches. They seemed to be about to come out with some wise and surprising comment! Their distinctive red colouring made them even more conspicuous.

Another unusual creature from around here, which I was keen to find, was a very large bird, which I understood, rarely takes to the air. It has a large and shapely, if at first sight clumsy, looking beak. It is only found in swampy areas and is called a shoebill. I hopefully searched a large swamp full of tallish reeds. Perhaps there was just too much cover for I never found any sign of one. So, for me, it became the 'shy shoebill'. I did eventually find one but it was in captivity only, imprisoned for visitors to see in a small pen made of stakes covered with netting. It was certainly a pleasure to see and to sketch but, alas, it was not amongst those tall reeds in the world in which it belonged. The shoebill's beak makes me think of a very old fashioned shoe, with a pointed toe that curves down slightly to give the bird a useful little hook. This odd looking bird, standing about four feet high (if my memory is correct) became quite a favourite subject for my brush drawings. I loved trying to create its remarkable image in just a few brush strokes.

opposite
Patas monkey
watercolour
560 × 380mm

following page
Shoebill
watercolour
480 × 270mm

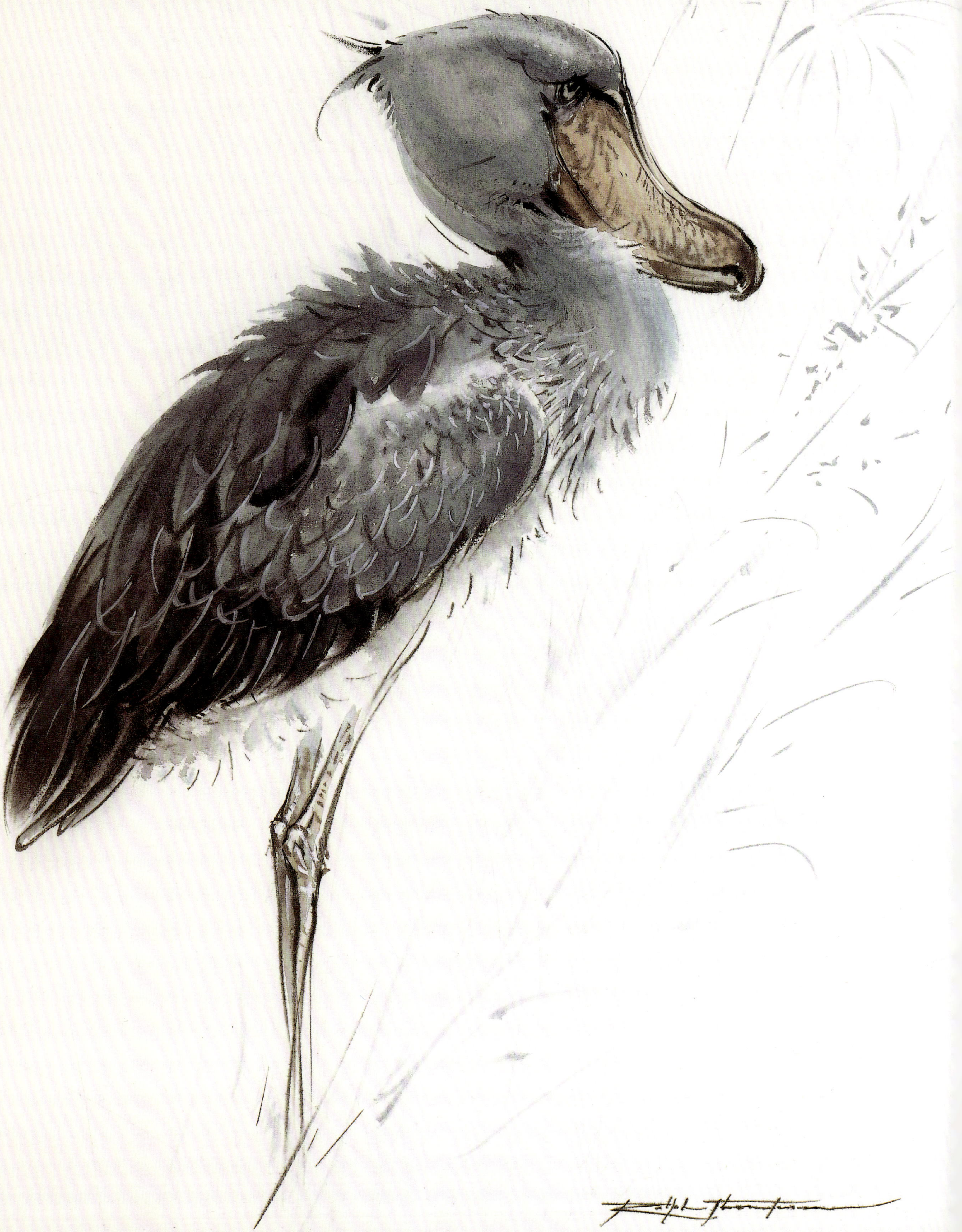

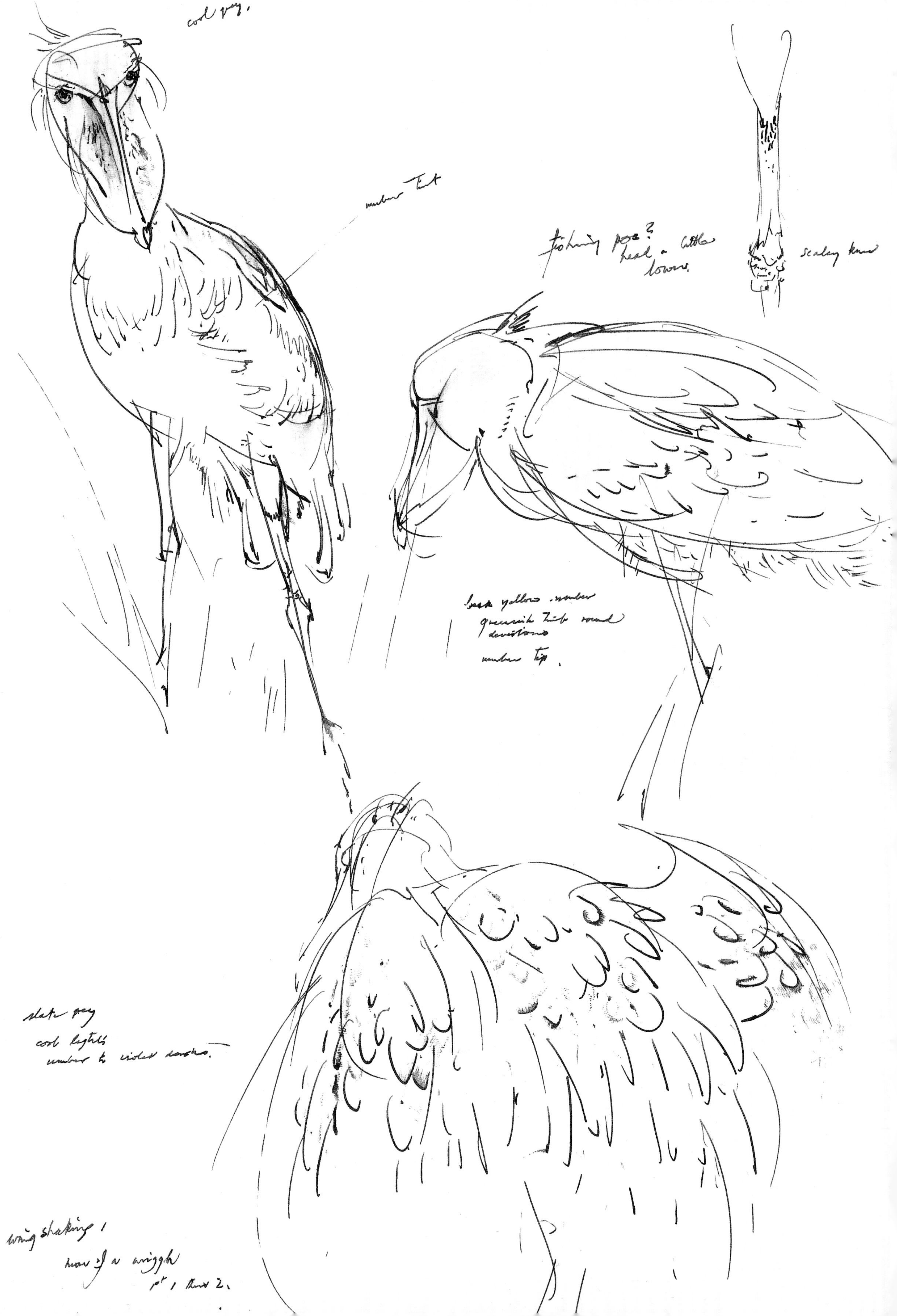
cool grey.
umber tint
fishing pose? head a little lower.
scaley knee
beak yellow umber
umber tip.
slate grey
cool lights
umber to violet darks.
wing shaking,
more of a wriggle

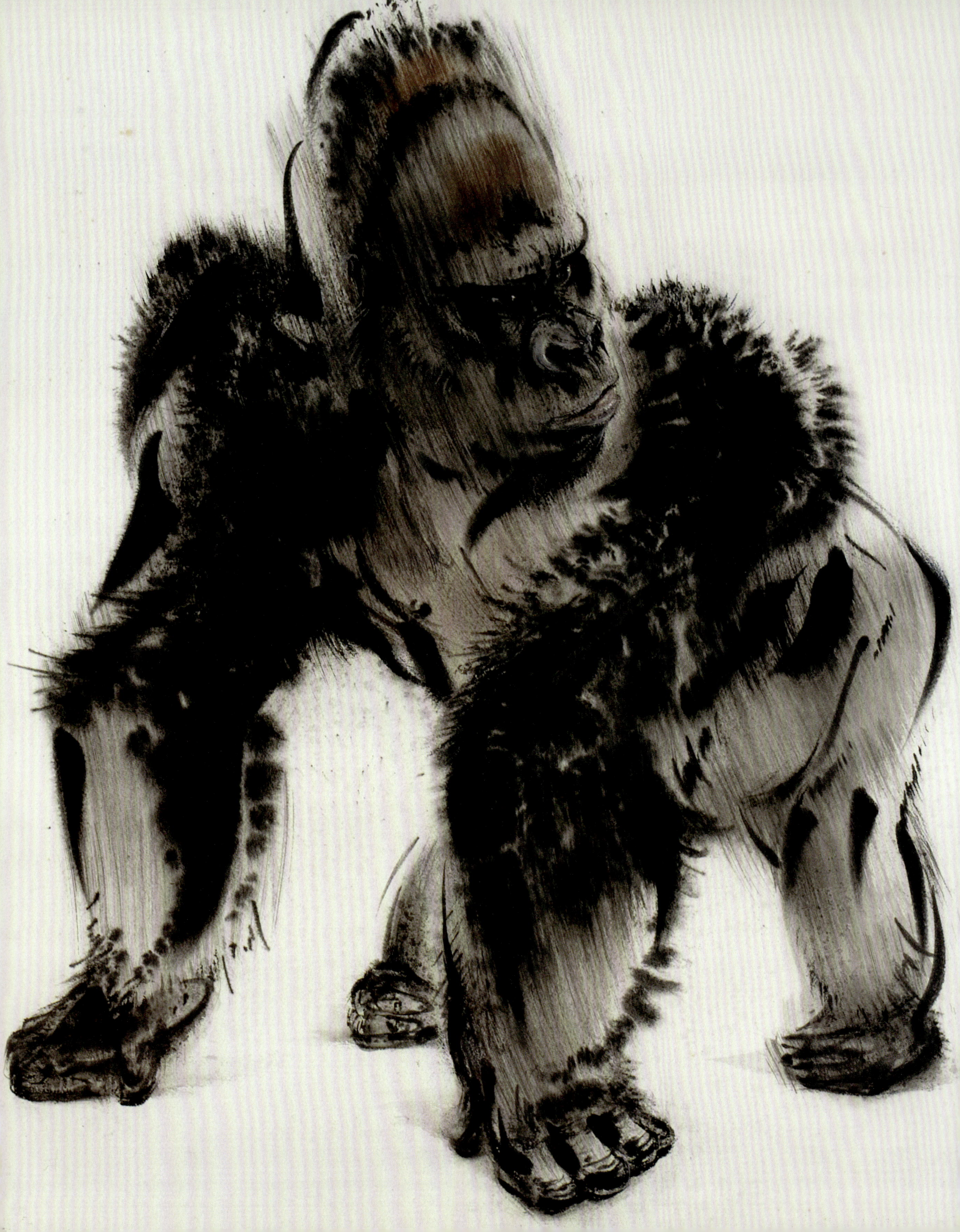

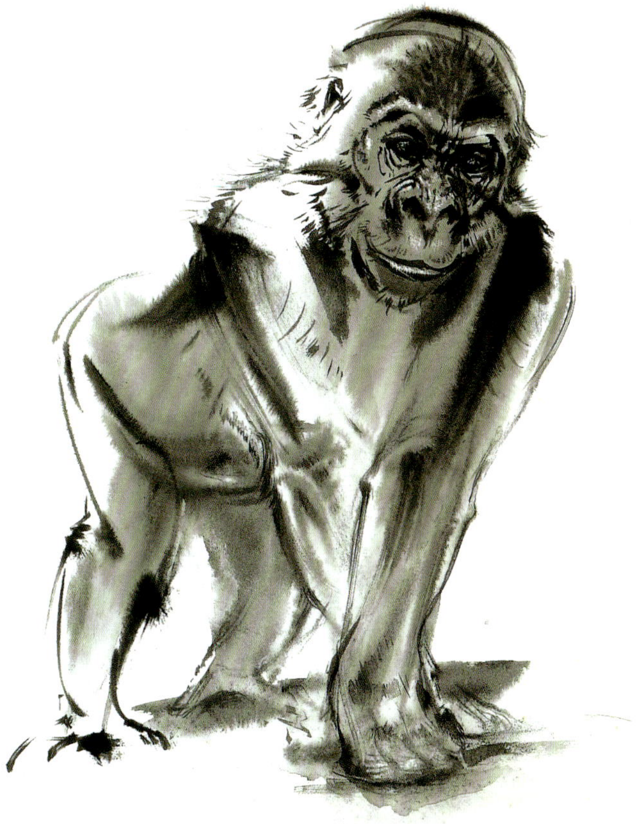

Mountains of the Moon

Seeing the silhouette of the mountains in the distance, I was haunted by their name and the knowledge that somewhere up there were the mountain gorillas.

Bamboo has a special significance for the Chinese and Japanese, related to its flexibility before a storm. It is a favourite subject for painting. When a pupil asked a master for advice, he replied, 'go and live with bamboo, watch it in all its moods. Become bamboo then your every touch will be full of life'. Intoxicated by the name 'The Mountains of the Moon' I became 'bamboo' far too literally.

I asked my guide to drive up a new road in the foothills, made for some mining purposes and to a considerable height. When we reached a safe place to park, at the beginning of a possible climb, I set off hopefully on foot. It was indeed a bamboo forest, wet and slithery with mud underfoot and with the ground rising steeply. I do not know what the Chinese master would have made of it, but I soon found it impossible. It took barely half an hour of 'becoming bamboo' for me to call the climb off. Having very awkwardly slid and slithered down the remarkably few feet of the climb, the last thing I wanted to do was to get out my sketch book and draw. I had to make a humiliating retreat down the same series of breathtaking hairpin bends without ever seeing the gorillas.

Young male gorilla
watercolour
330 × 260mm

opposite
Silverback
watercolour
750 × 560mm

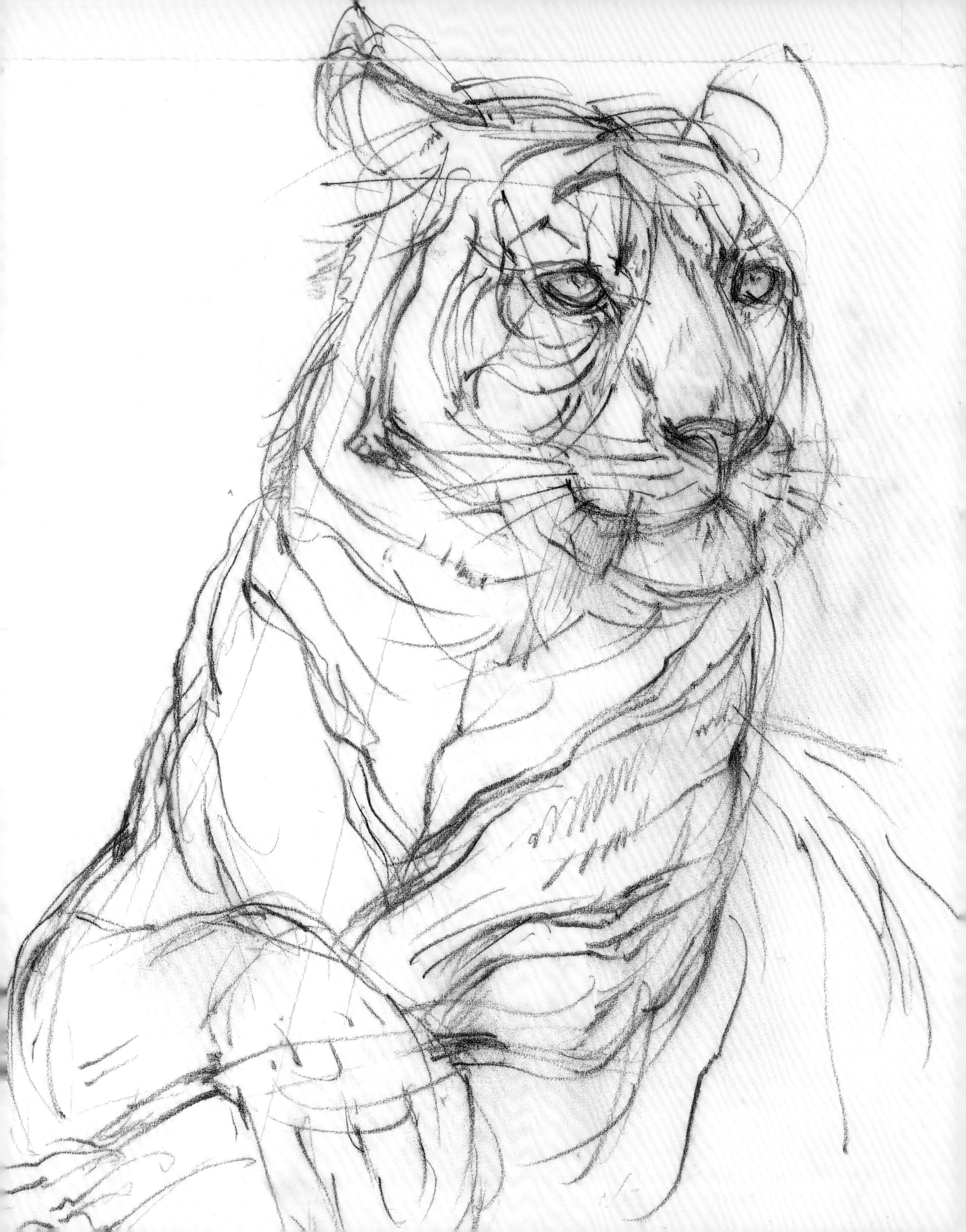

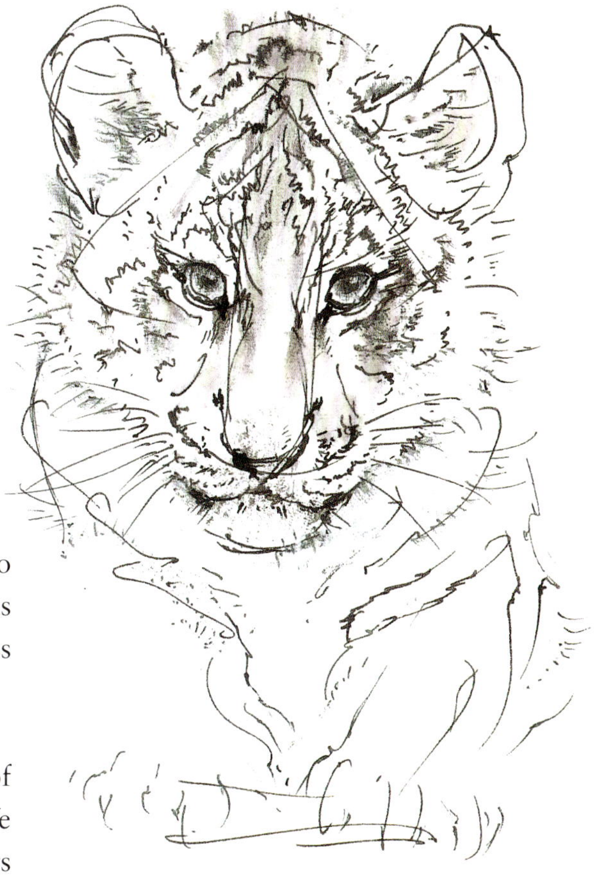

Nepal and India – Tiger Tops

My guide and companion in India was Oliver Brooke, who had proved so valuable with my travels in East Africa lending me his driver Martin, who was also with us at Tiger Tops. Oliver's daughter, Janet, was acting as a hostess there.

A flight from Kathmandu took us to a lonely airstrip in the southern border of Nepal, where the plane was met by a group of elephants and their drivers. We soon found ourselves being helped onto a howdah and the elephants transporting us through the surrounding jungle. Later we transferred to Land Rovers and drove off onto a track with spectacular giant lianas and occasional glimpses of monkeys and spotted deer until we found ourselves at a lodge built up in the treetops. We were at Tiger Tops.

Oliver and I had the use of an empty staff house. I was thus privileged to go out early in the mornings to explore the elephant camp. I would wake to the sound of heavy rain, only to discover that it was merely condensation from the trees. So trees must be avoided when sketching in the camp.

Elephants were being released and harnessed for work with a thick mattress and a howdah. During the night, they were chained by one foot to a thick stake, whilst chickens pecked all around, and so they made good models. I learnt that one elephant took exception to them and would crush one under foot if he got the chance, but the chickens soon learnt their lesson.

There was an area nearby which was declared safe for me to explore in the daytime. Tiger tracks were everywhere. There was a delightful stream, which, in flood, had sculptured the rocks into beautiful shapes, which, in places, opened out to suggest bigger landscape settings for me to use.

Tiger Tops was virtually on an island surrounded by marshland with shallow water and very tall reeds, making an ideal habitat for small deer and the Asian rhino. There was one rhino which seemed to have become a sort of 'pet' to be greeted with astonished wonder by new guests, who fled with laughter and terrified shouts if it made towards them.

opposite
Resting tiger
charcoal drawing
380 × 280mm

following pages
Asian rhino studies
ink
actual size

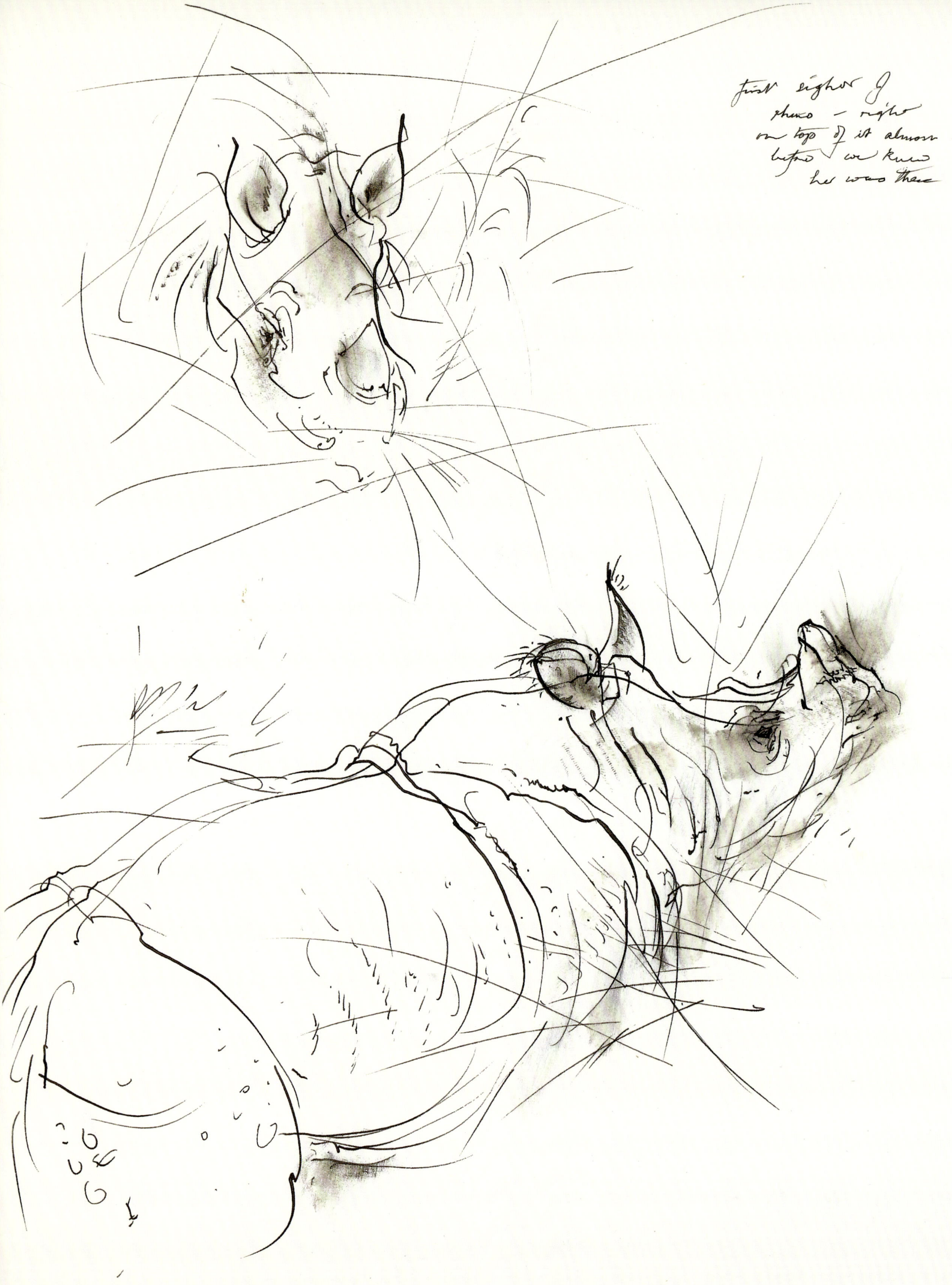

rhino sizes up the situation

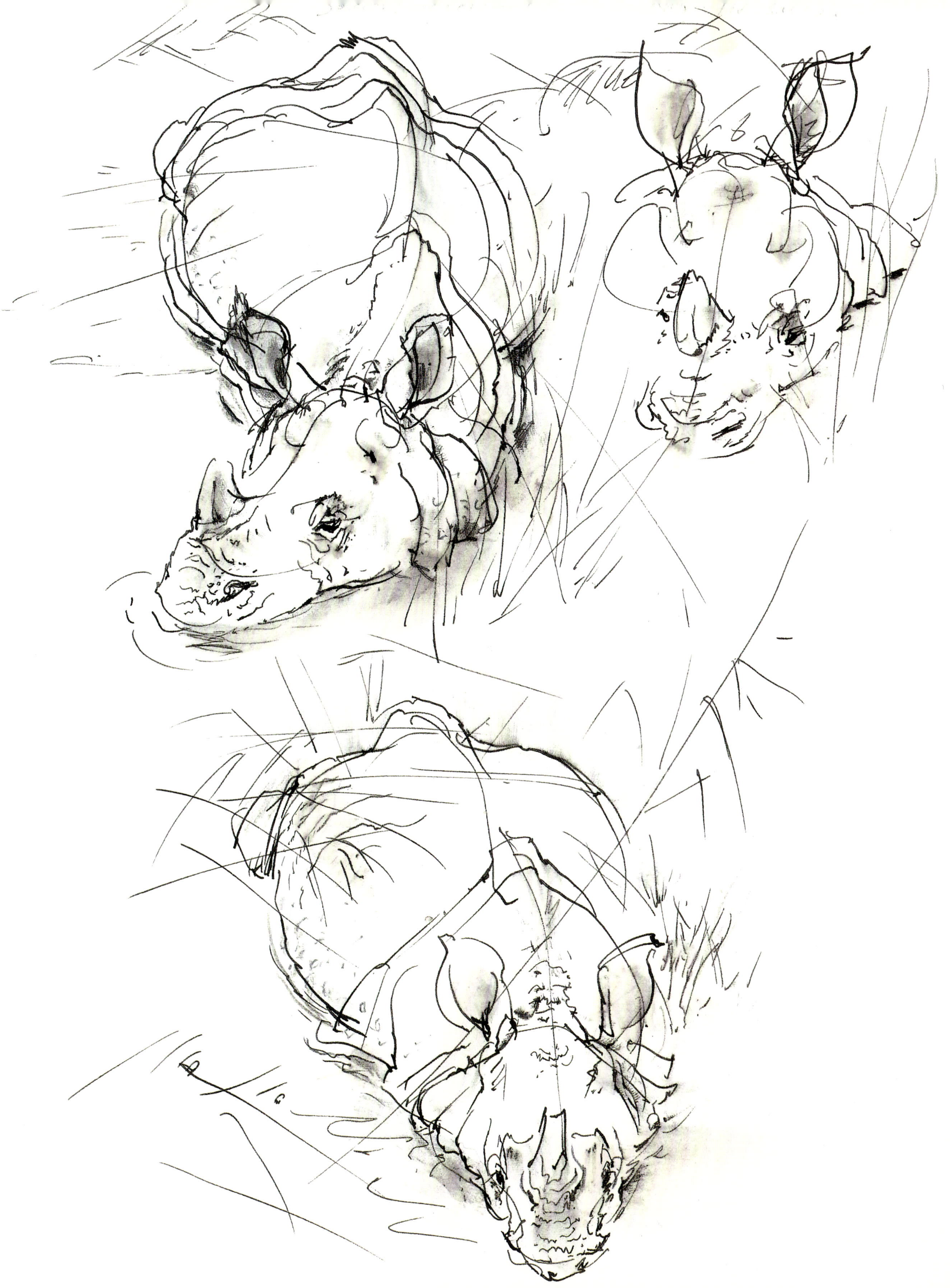

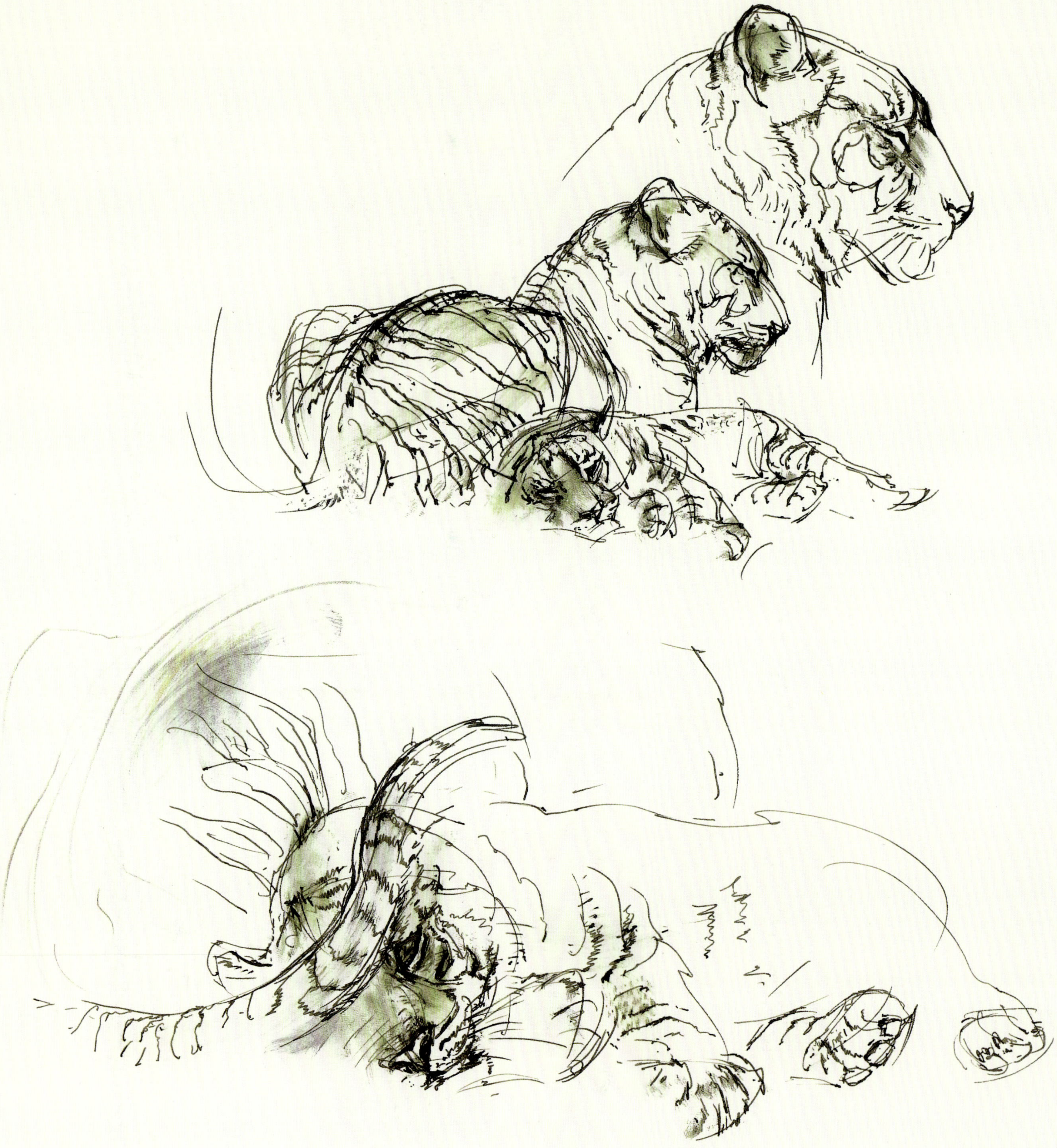

Tiger with cub

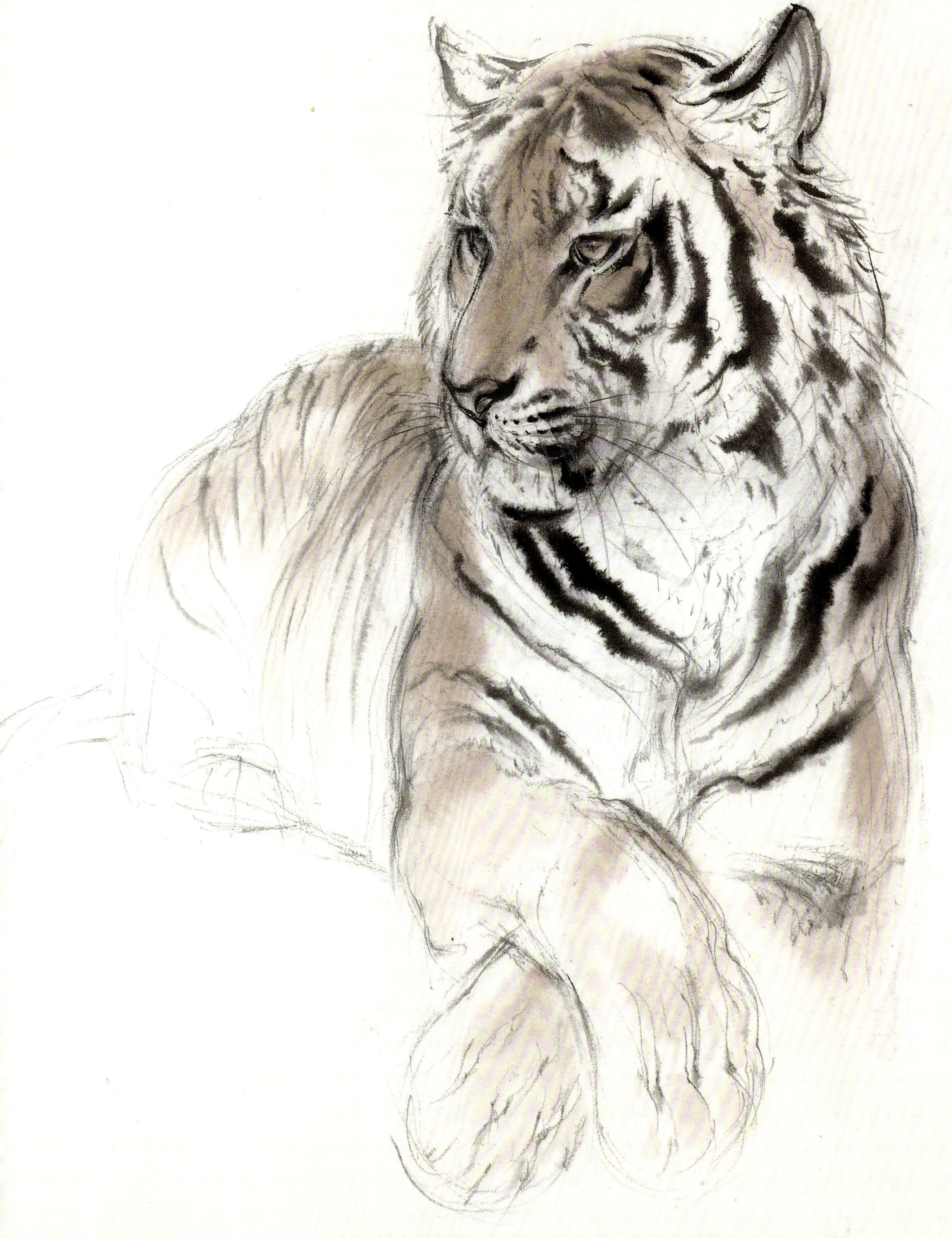

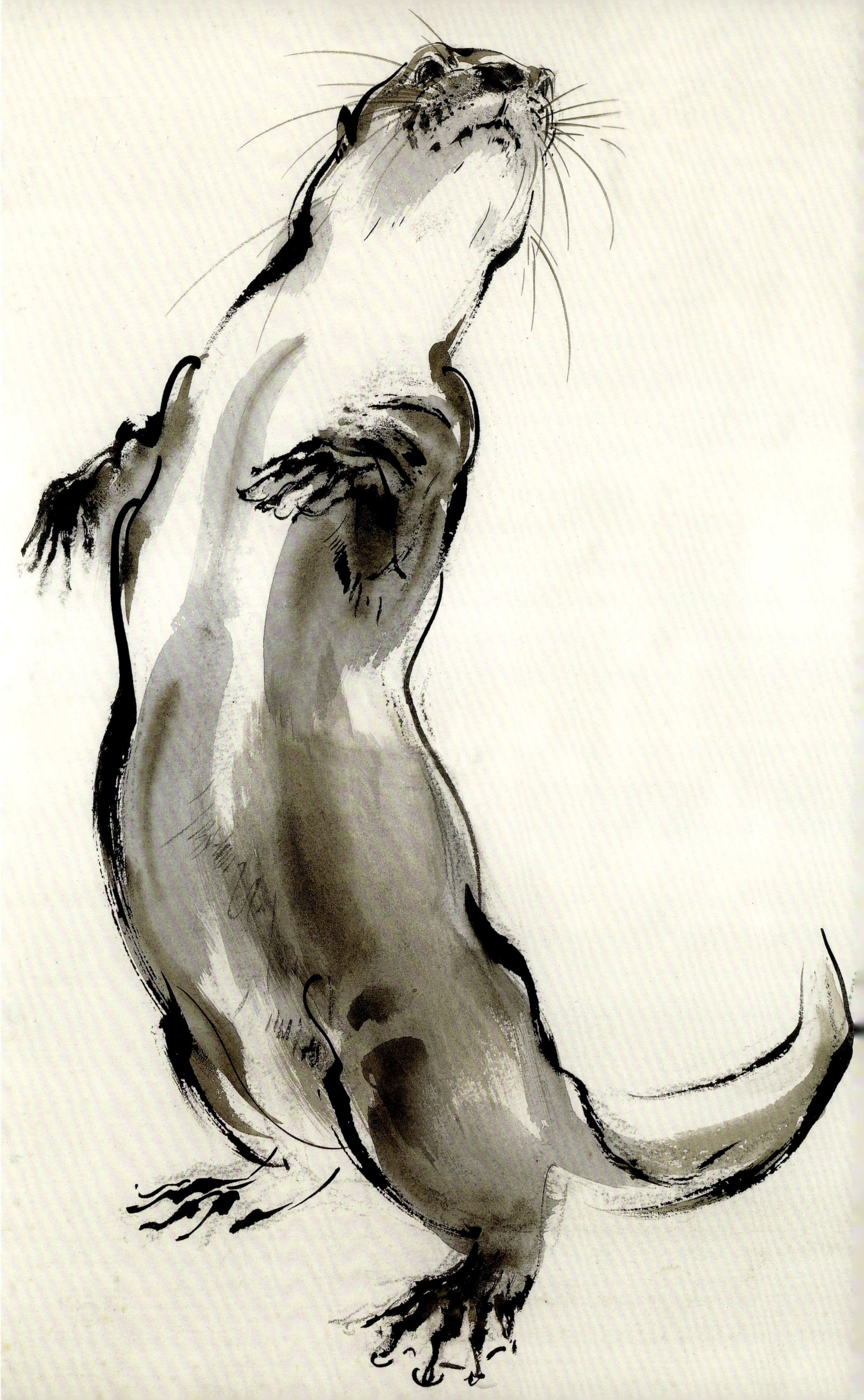

Asian otter
watercolour
570 × 380mm

previous page
Resting tiger
watercolour
480 × 380mm

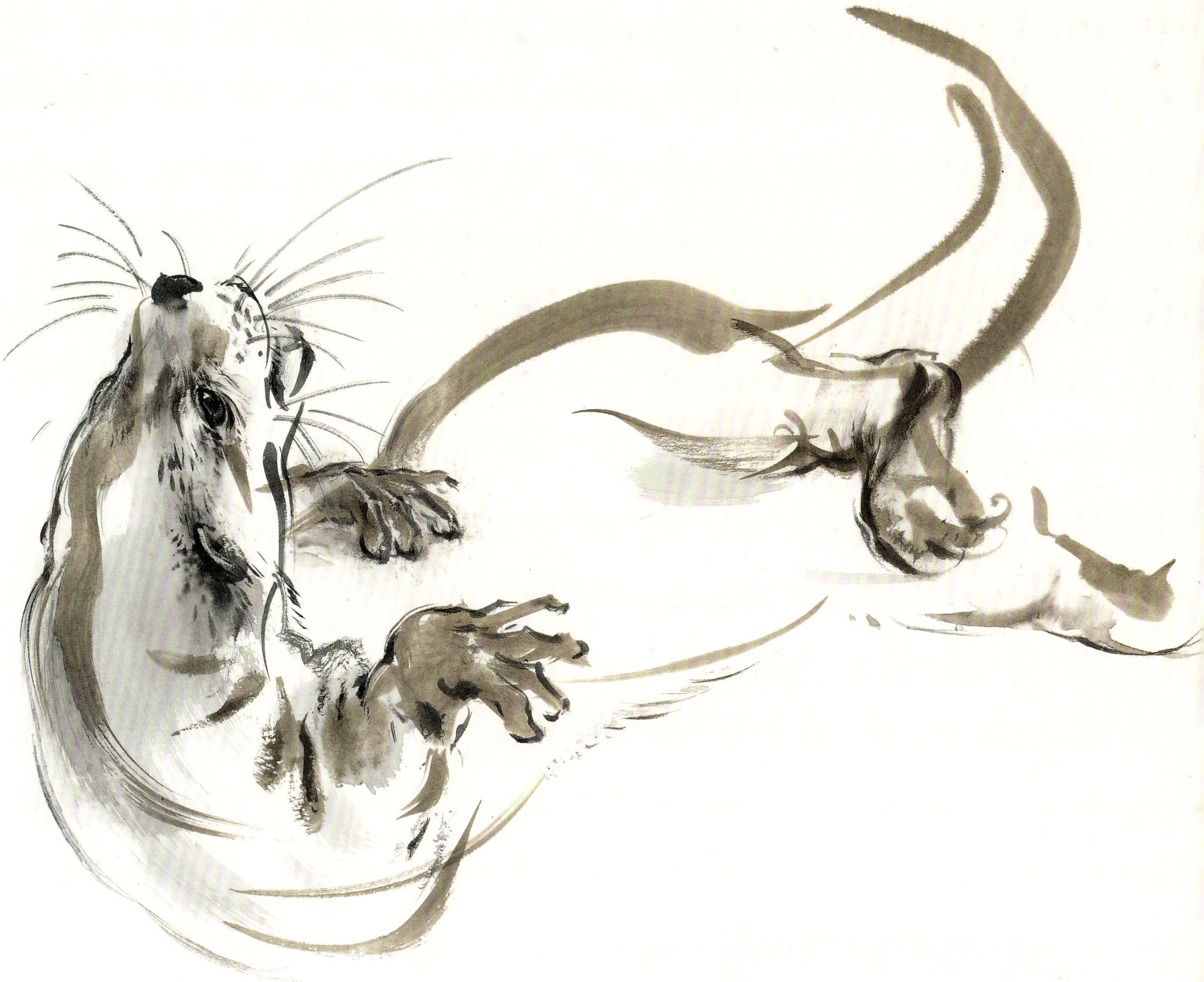

One day Oliver and I hired an elephant to explore our surroundings and sighted a little Hog deer in among the reeds, and then came upon a pair of Asian otters playing by a stream. Possibly it was because we were on elephant back, but they ignored our presence completely and I could work with my sketchbook until eventually they swam right away to become tiny ripples in the distance.

Asian otter rolling
ink and wash
300 × 370mm

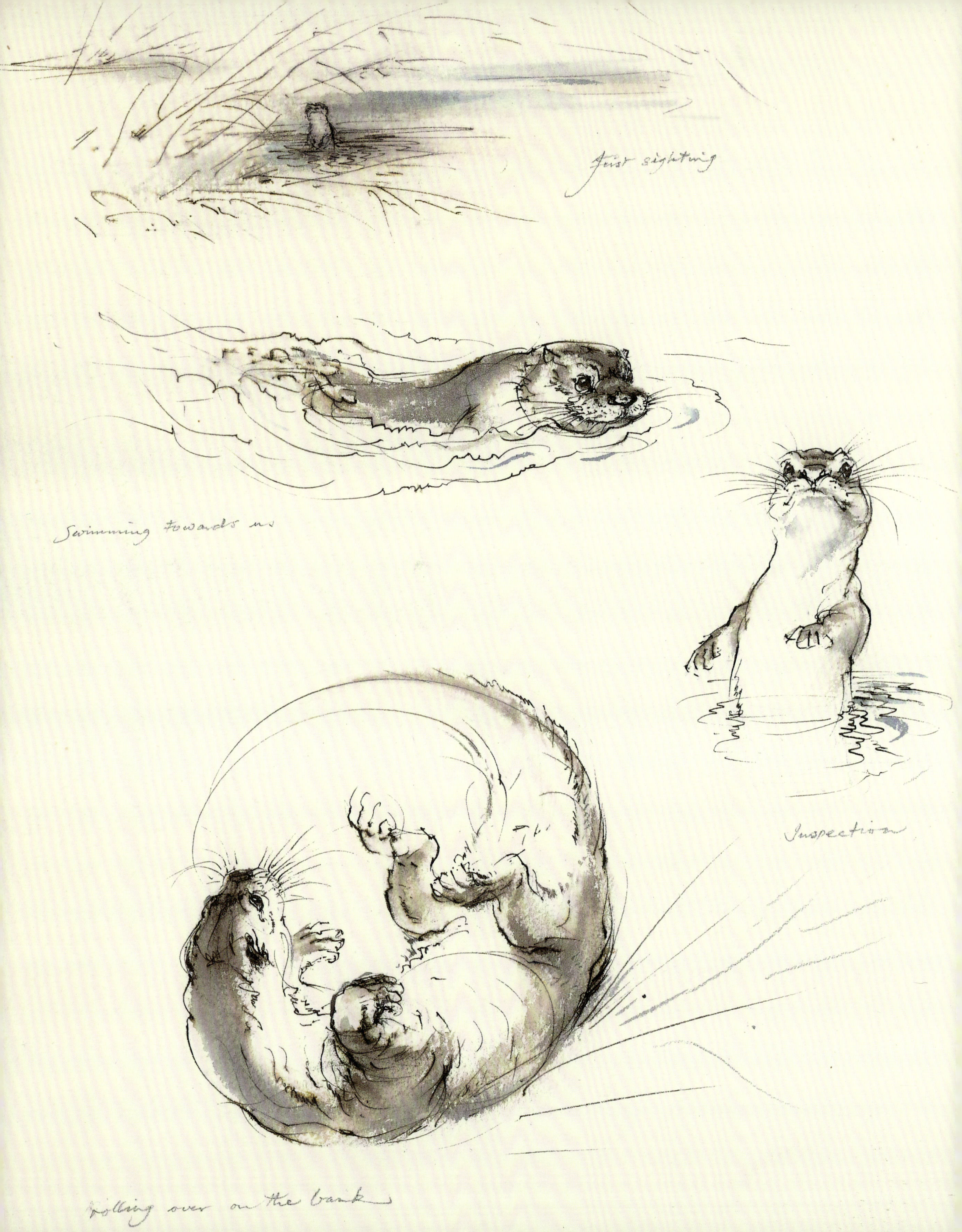
First sighting
Swimming towards us
Inspection
Rolling over on the bank

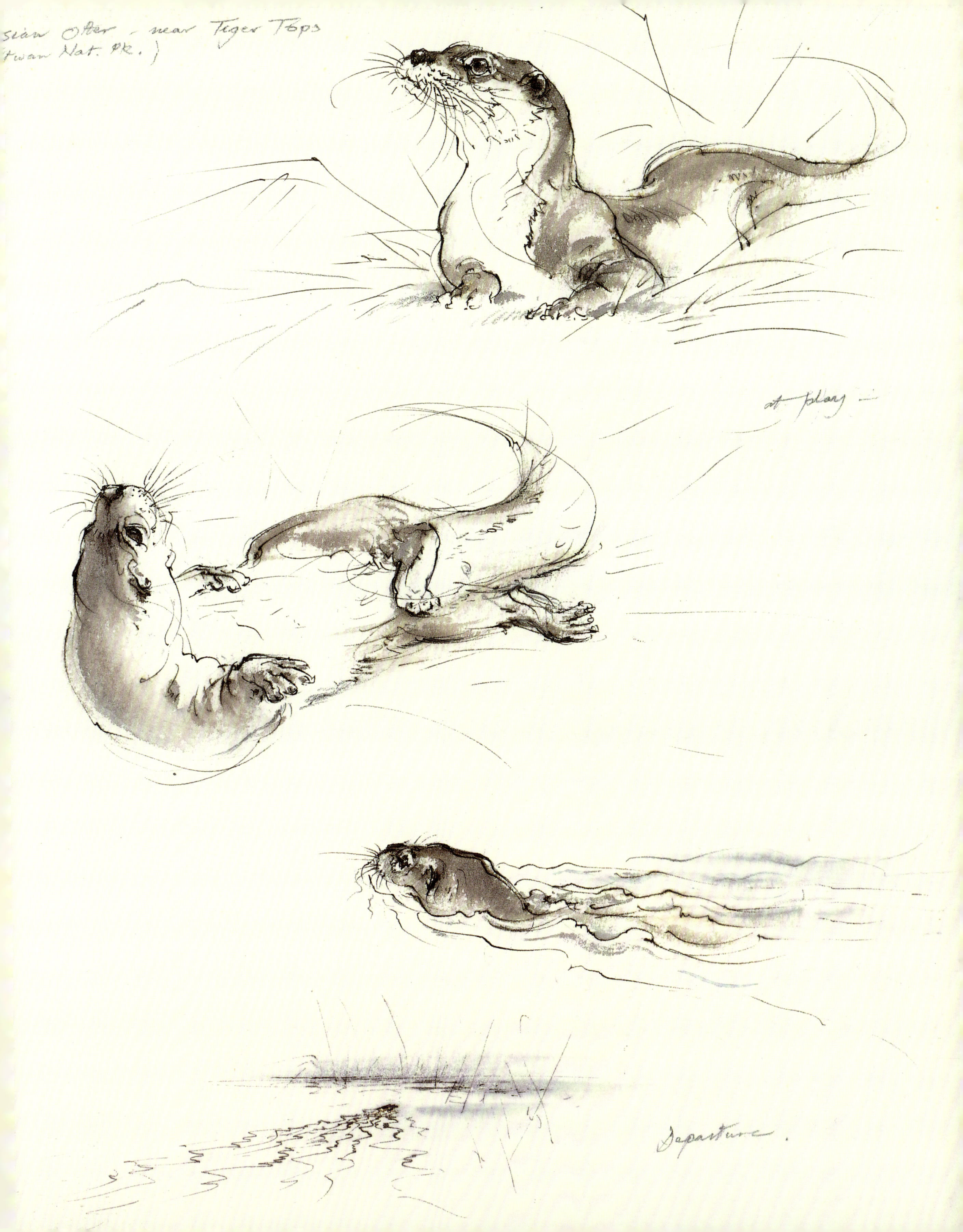
sian Otter - near Tiger Tops
twan Nat. Pk.)
at play -
Departure.

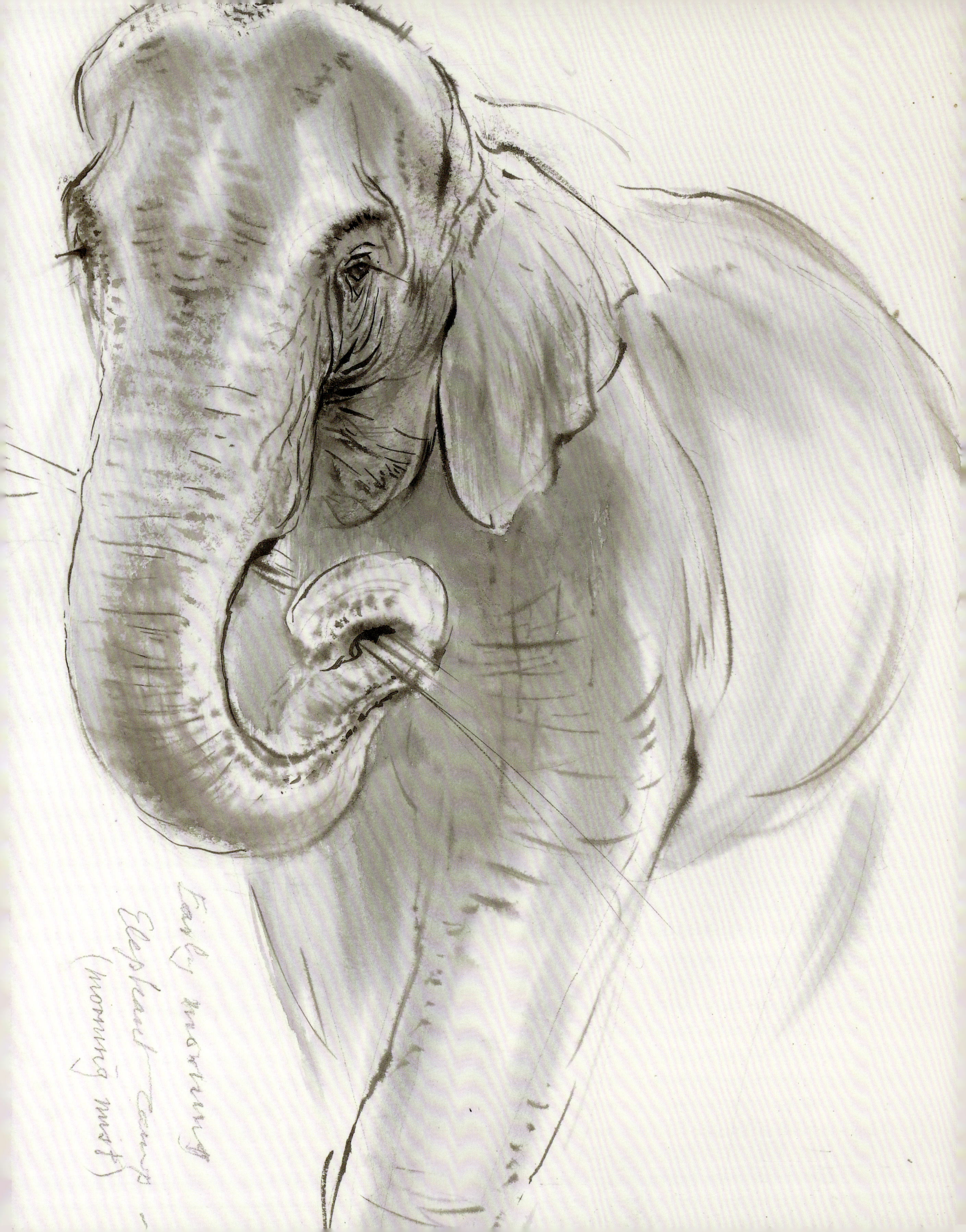
Early morning
Elephant camp
(morning mist)

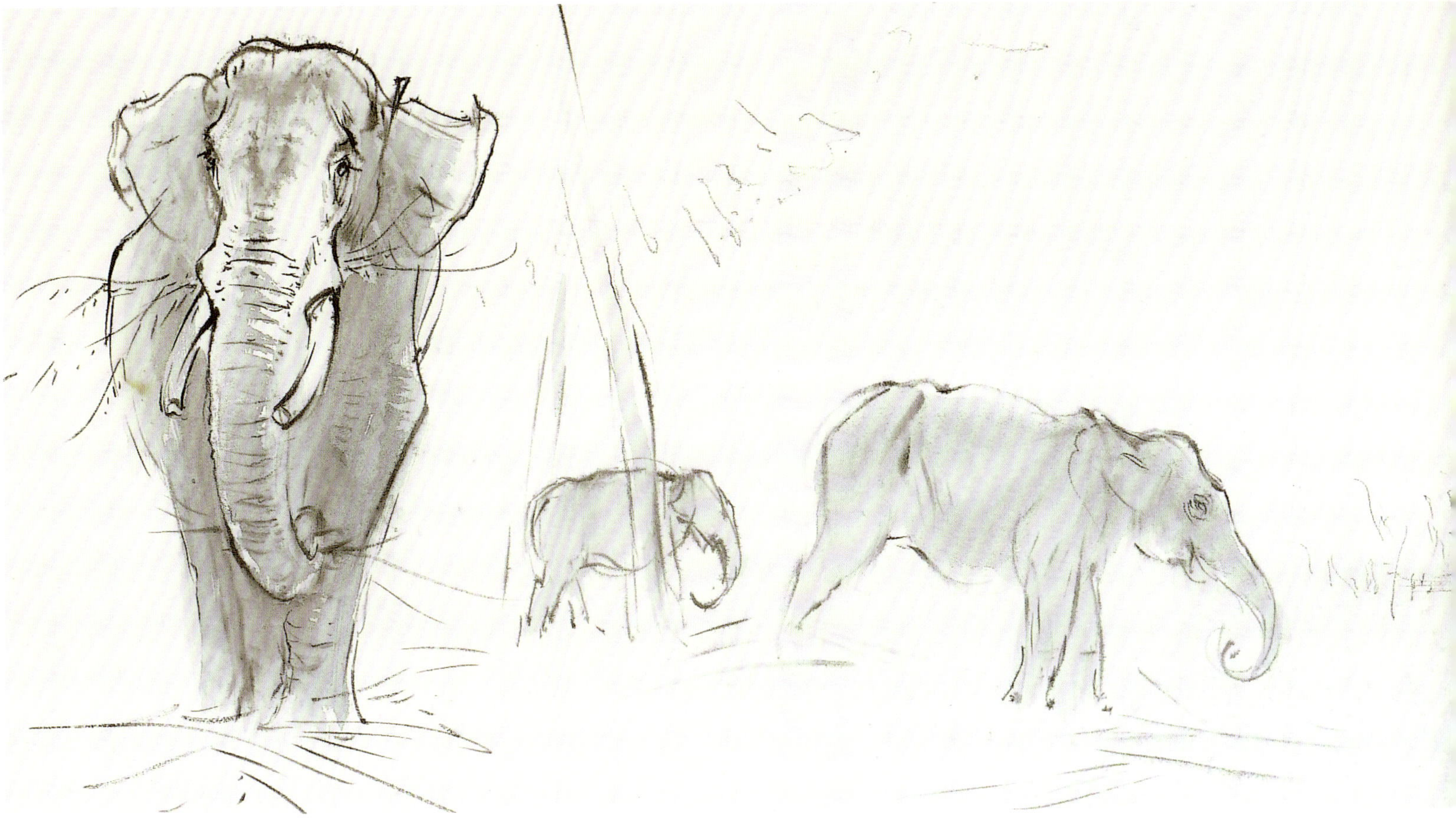

Another day we were told that an elephant was going to collect grass, so we took a second elephant to see for ourselves what happened, following on the typical narrow elephant trails by which elephants can place their feet in almost the same place as the one in front, creating what seems like an impossibly narrow trail through tall reeds and grasses. We presently reached an area of rich tall grass. The men ahead slipped off their elephant, sickles in hand. They wasted no time and were soon loading their elephant with a huge amount of grass. I never learned how they managed to keep it there, but they returned to camp with a giant load.

I was then to watch several men making special tit-bits for the elephants. They took one big handful of grass, deftly folded it over and, reaching out with the other for a handful of cooked rice from a basket already to hand, skilfully produced a packet of rice to toss into a tall wooden container nearby. If a harnessed elephant being led away for the day's work passed near one of these tubs, out would go the trunk to seize one - a game apparently accepted by the Nepalese staff.

At Tiger Tops one could take a small boat and visit the tented camp to look for more tigers. I had hoped to find the fishing cat there, but I think a hide and more time would have been needed. It is the world of the strongly flowing river itself, which, for some reason, haunts my memory – full of birds and coming from the Himalayas two hundred miles away.

opposite, above and following pages
Studies from the elephant camp
ink and wash
actual size

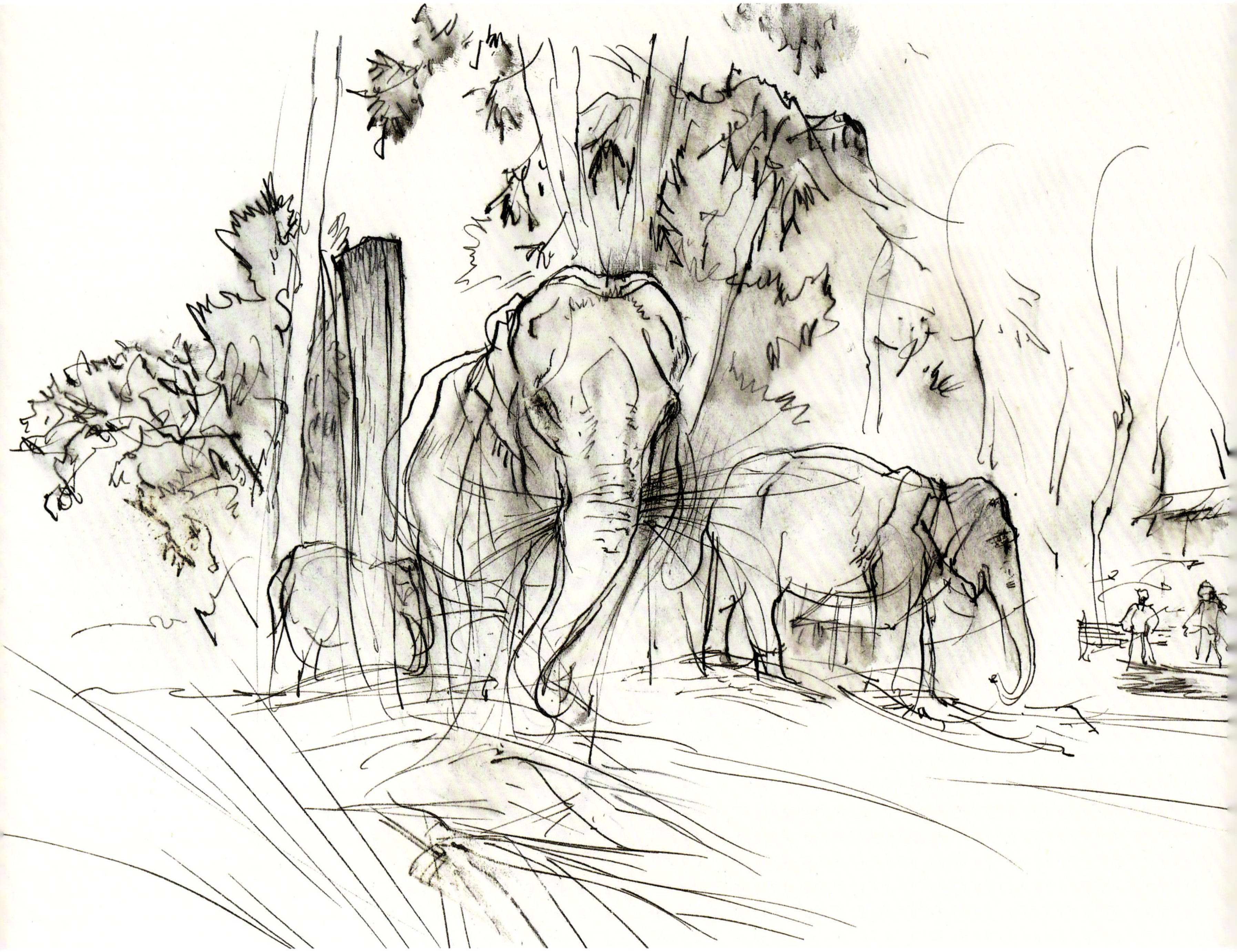

Oliver having left with Janet for a few days in the foothills of the Himalayas, I had opted to stay with the ample material at Tiger Tops. One day I took an elephant and its driver, said to be 'the best tracker in India' to look for the sloth bear and axis deer. We found their droppings only but no memorable sightings, though my tracker did find a nest of a grass owl with half grown chicks. We inched slowly forward but the owl flew away. I made a quick sketch of both the chicks and withdrew.

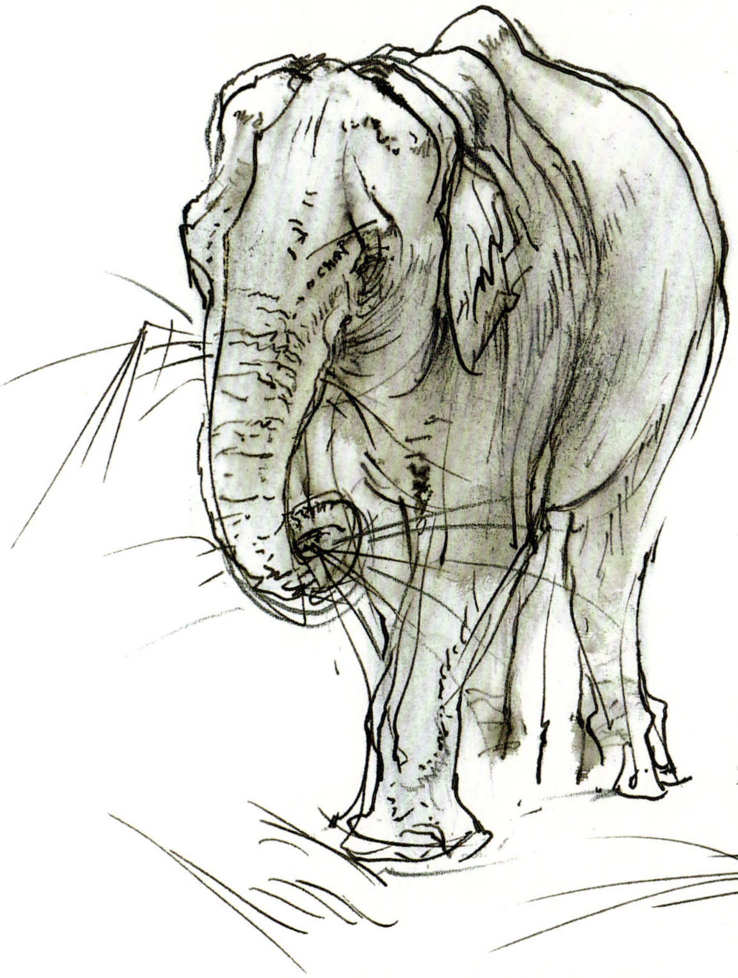

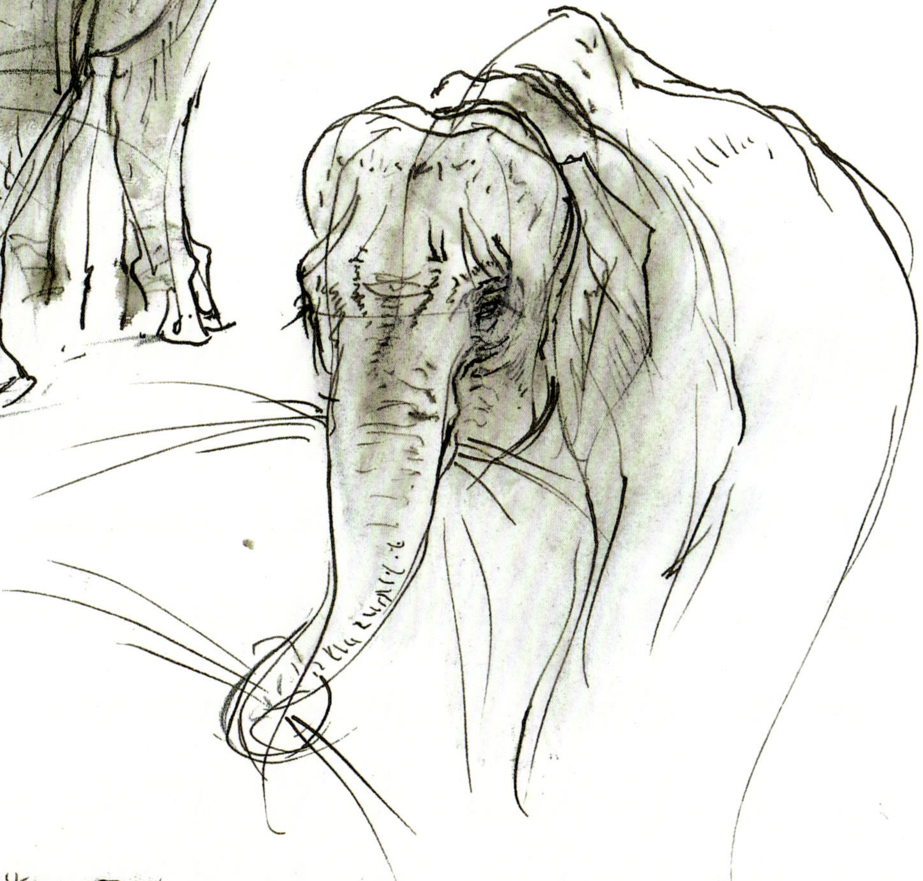

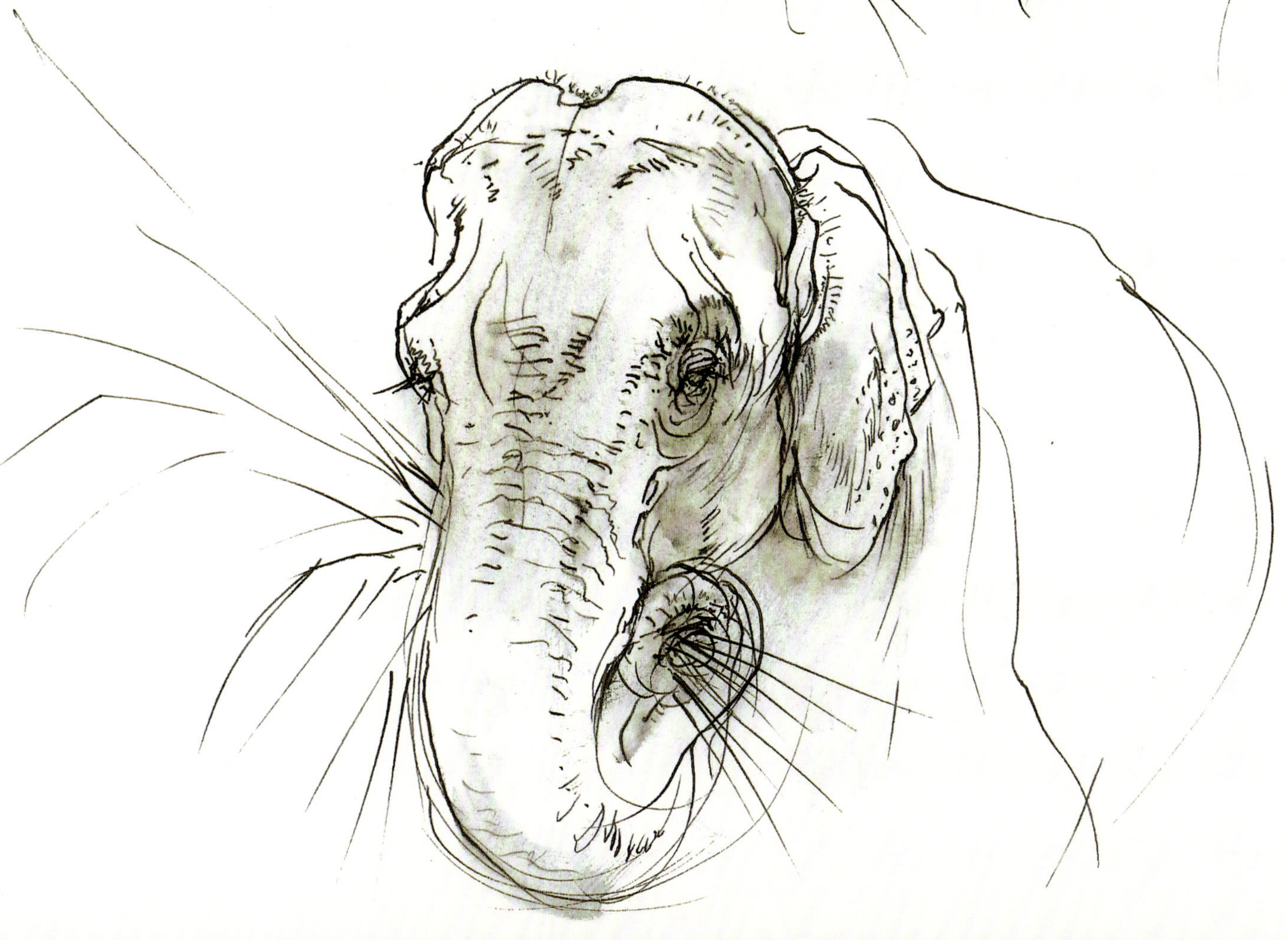

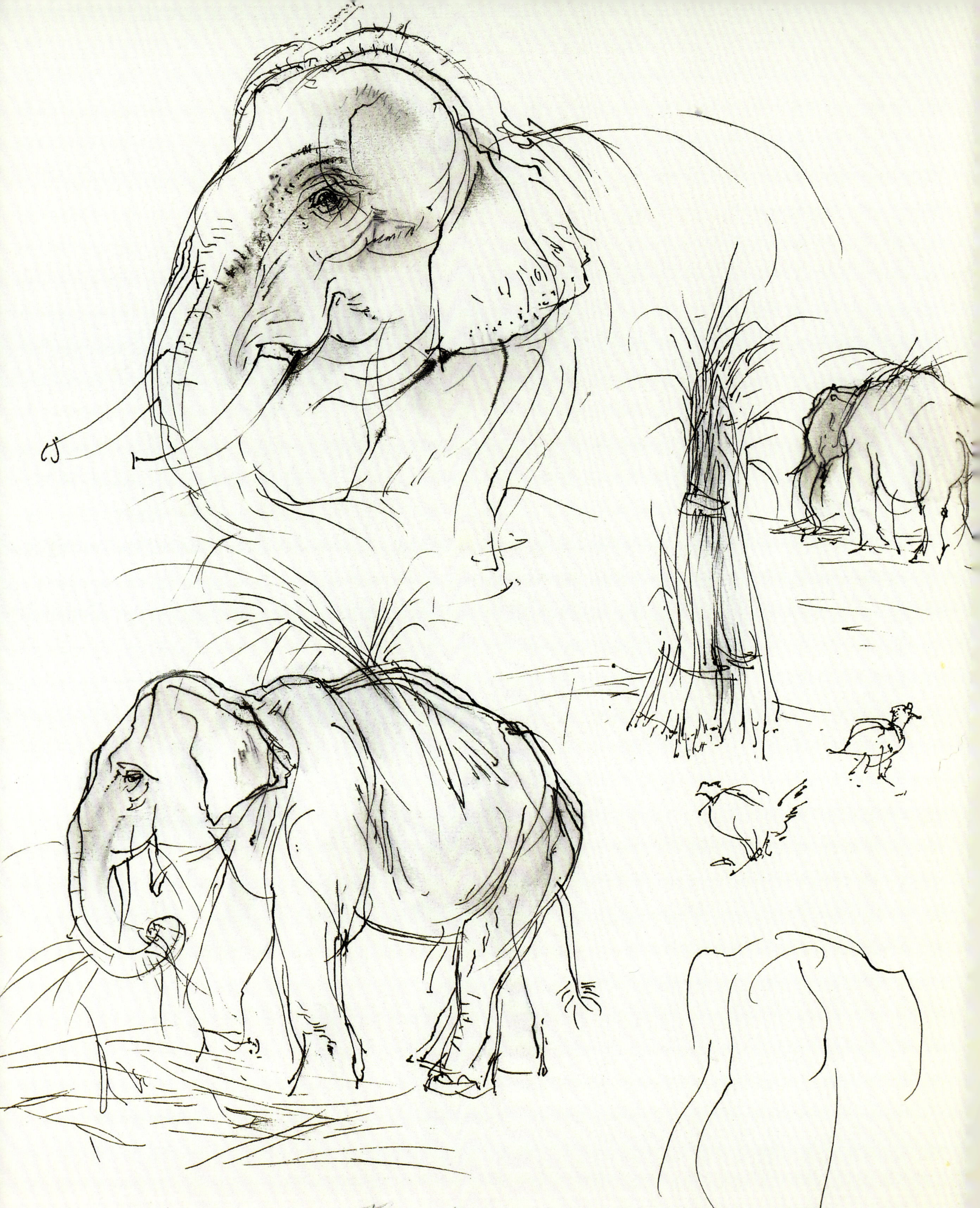

The elephant camp – Tiger tops.

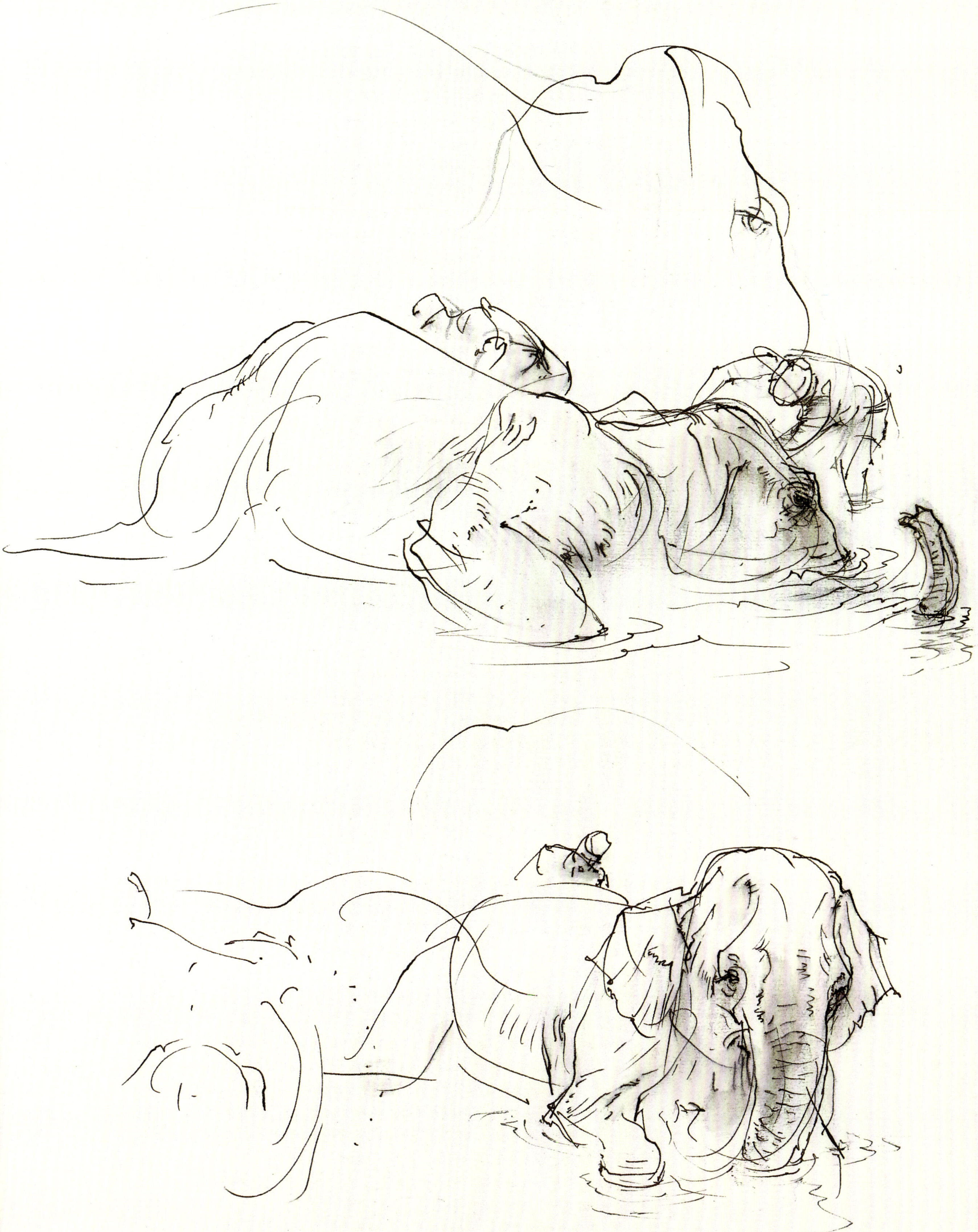

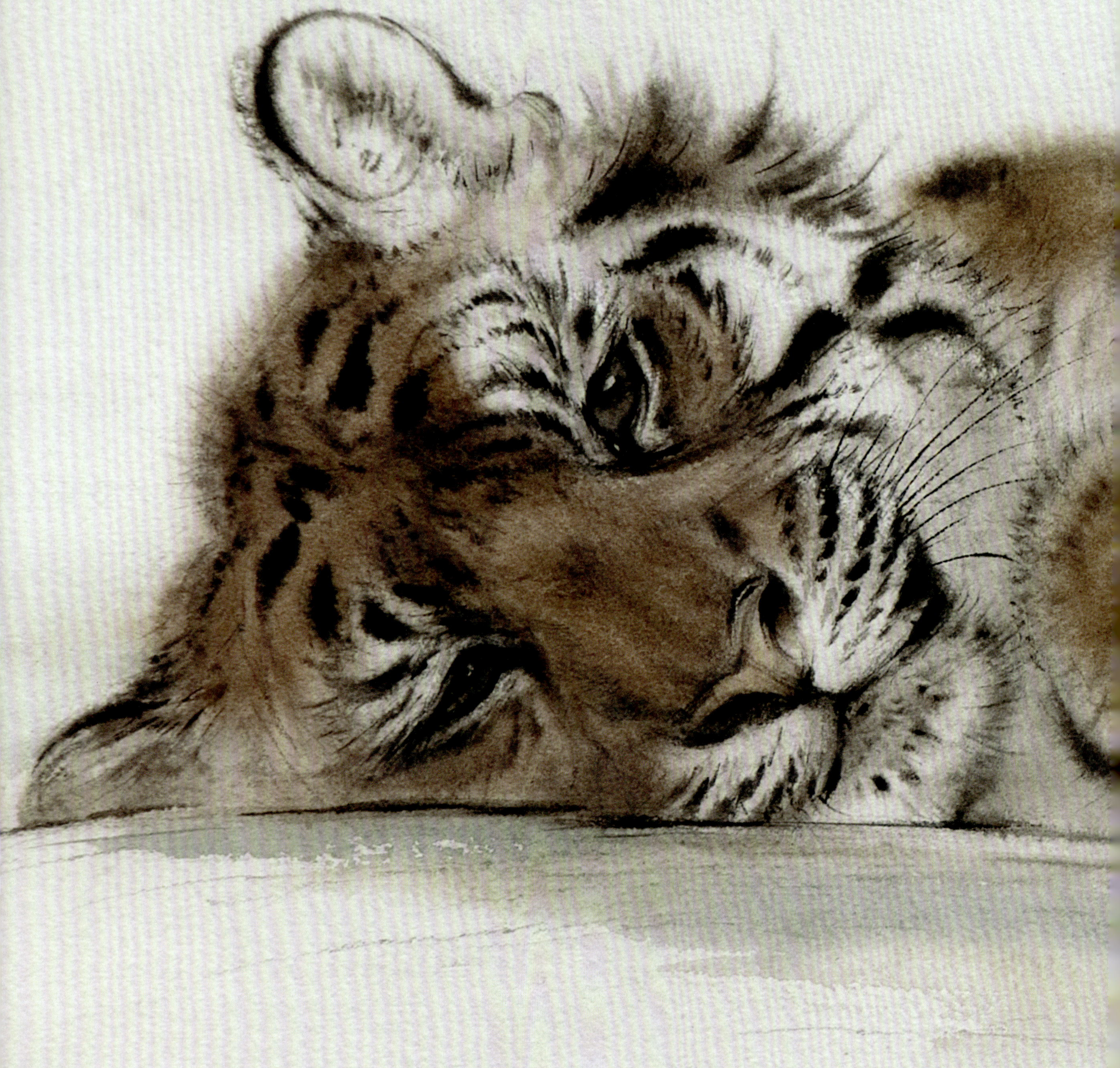

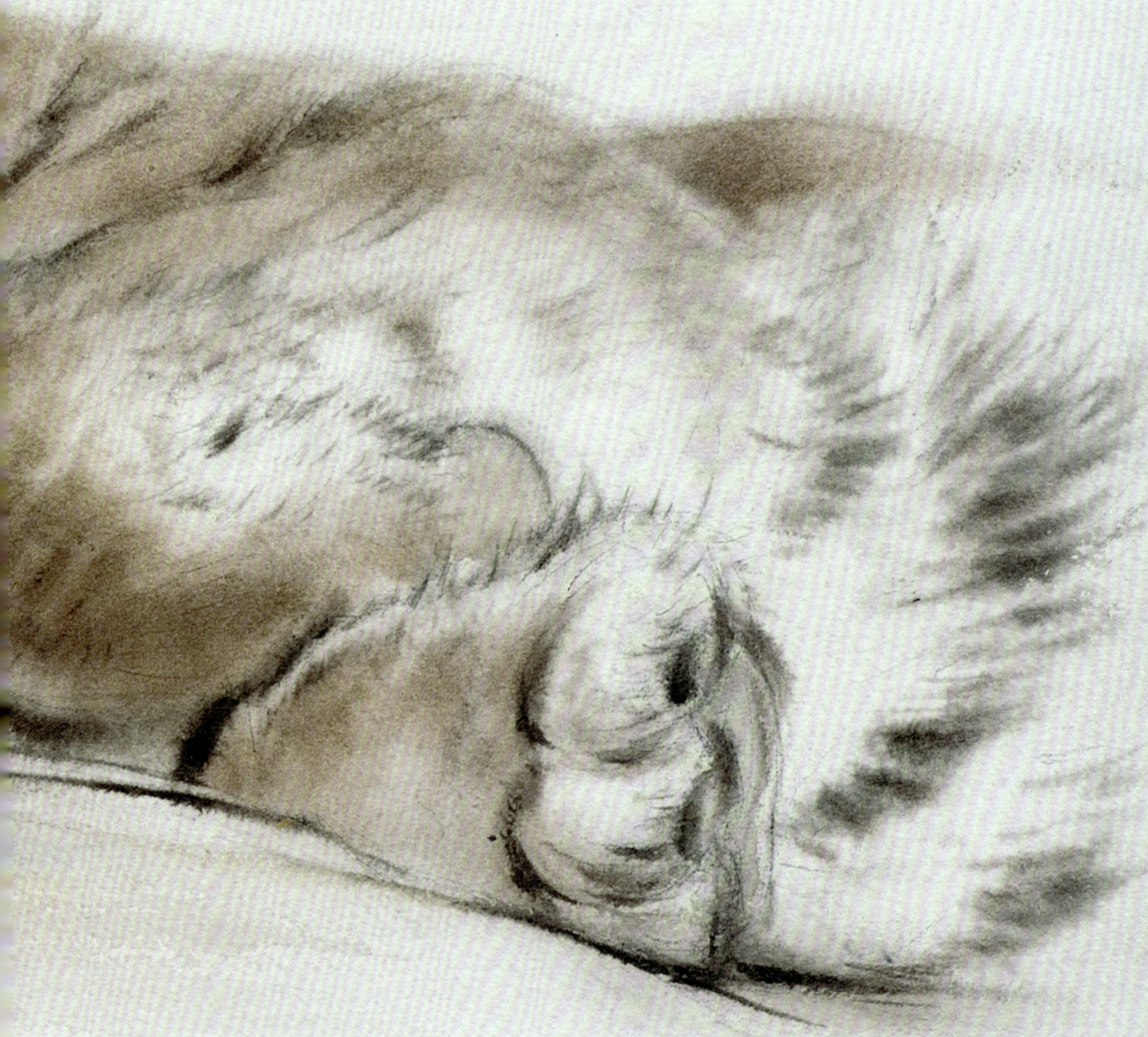

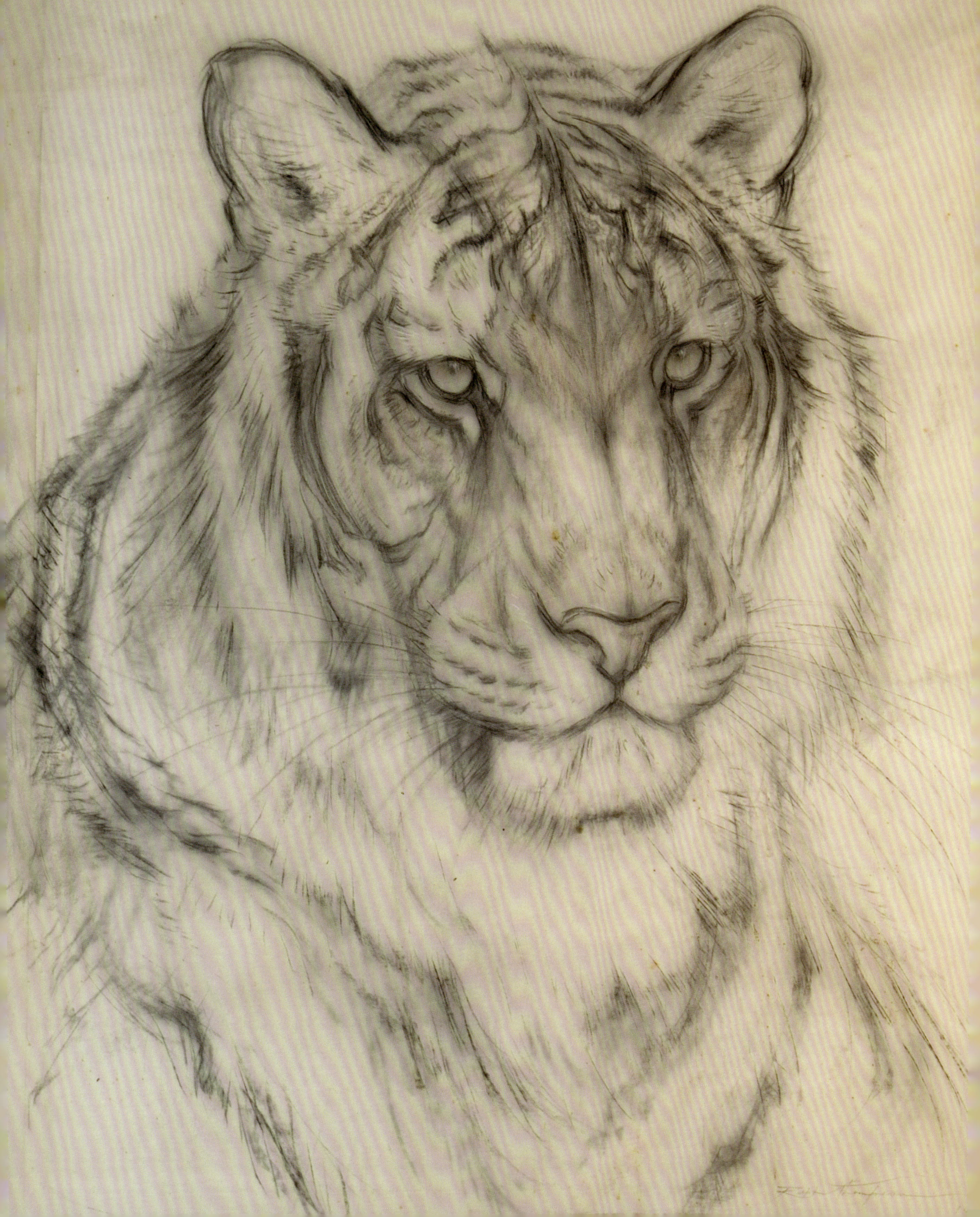

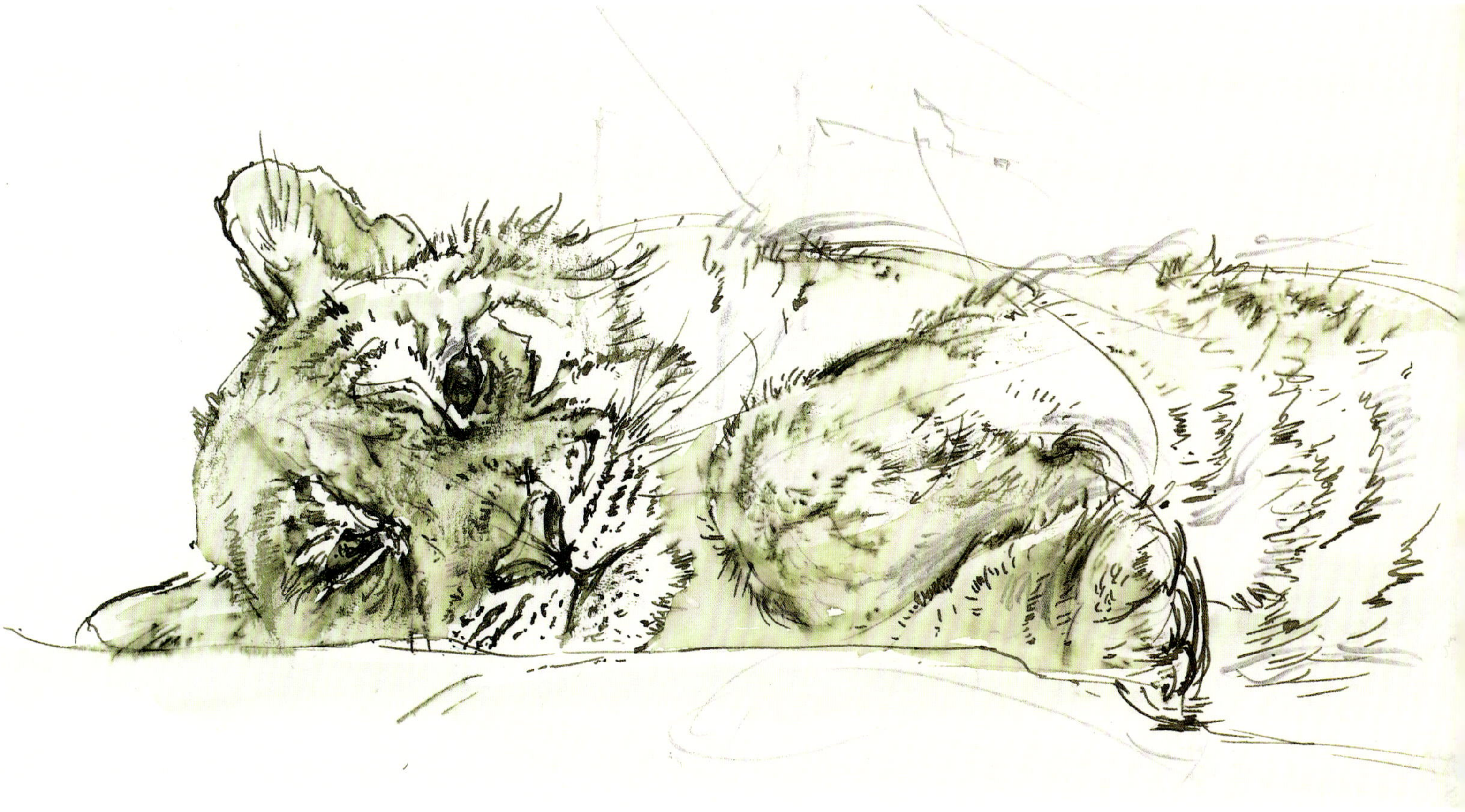

On the map, the game reserve named Kanha looks to be exactly in the middle of India. My driver and I were on our way back from the Taj Mahal and Agra to look for tigers at Kanha and to call en route at the age-old ruins of a famous palace. All I remember now of the ruins are some well-preserved mural paintings of elephants. Driving to Kanha was a bone shattering experience, but interesting because the villages through which we passed had their own particular beauty, a timeless, natural beauty. It was as if they had just happened quite naturally and individually to make interesting shapes. The oxen ploughing the fields looked so serene and beautiful. I was foolishly too excited by the thought of the tigers at Kanha to stop long enough to take photographs and make sketches, something I shall always regret.

So, on we bumped to the forest reserve of Kanha. It had a well-built centre for study and was able to house a limited number of guests. We were to stay for several days searching for tigers in particular. On the following day, several elephants appeared with howdahs on their backs and drivers apparently sitting on their heads. Actually, the drivers were astride their necks. I was placed, with my sketchbook, at the back of the howdah while a group of Americans, bristling with impressive cameras, were poised at the front.

above and following page
Sleepy tiger cub
ink and wash
actual size

opposite
Tiger portrait
charcoal
740 × 600mm

previous page
Sleepy tiger cub
watercolour
370 × 570mm

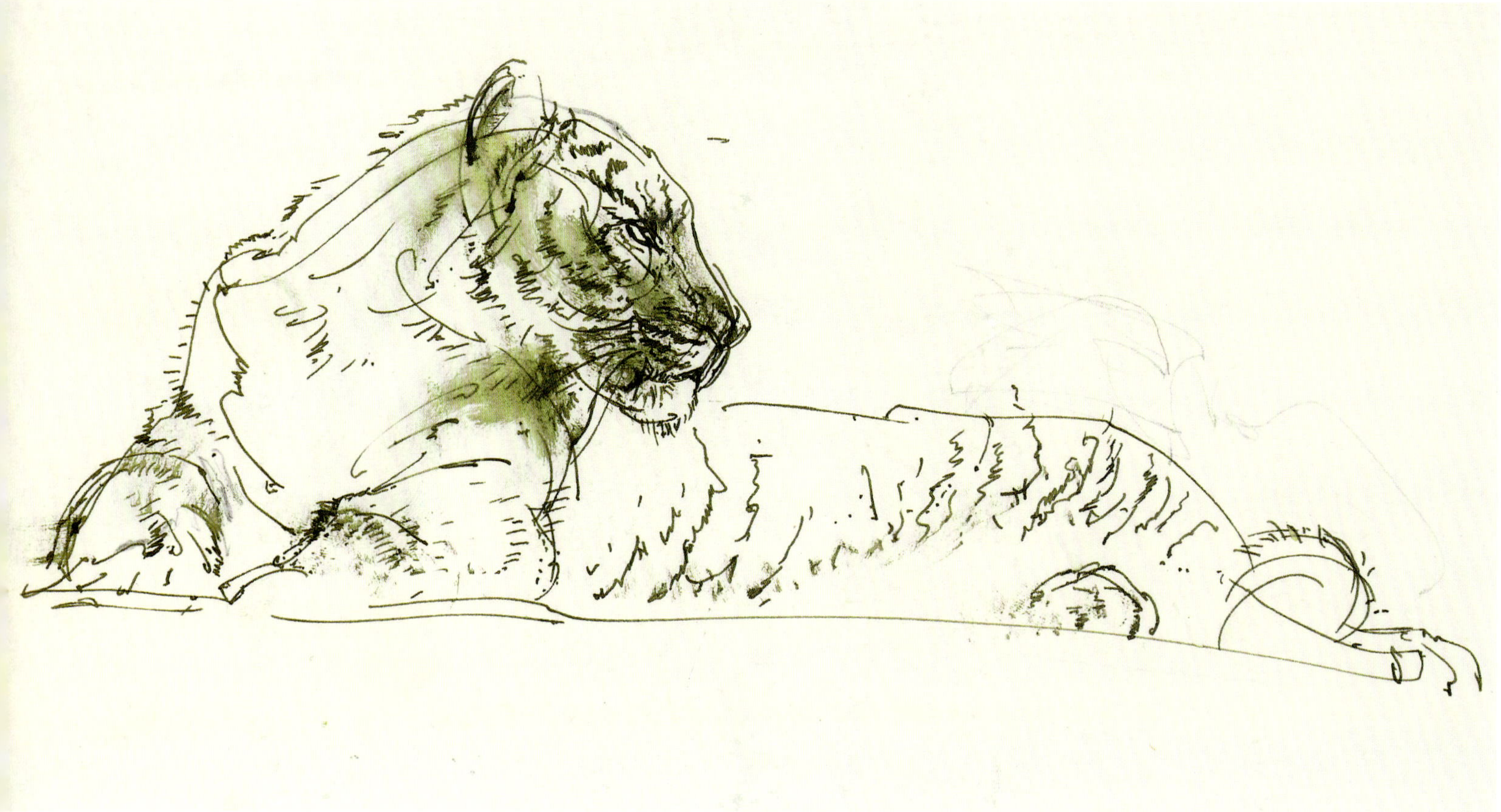

The forest trails along which we were making our way were festooned with huge spider-webs, complete with outsized spiders. It soon became clear that there were drivers of several other elephants combing the area, calling to each other. The forest was dense and the ground rather hilly. I was alarmed at first when our elephant began to traverse a steep slope, but I soon gained confidence in her ability to move up, down or across quite steep slopes at will. The sound signals gradually became frequent and more elephants appeared. After about an hour, we came to a stand still. Our driver pointed to some dense cover directly ahead of us. At first I could not see anything, but gradually I made out the tawny colour visible within the cover. It was my first tiger.

As all the cameras clicked, I managed to draw what I could of the tiger, adding more sketches as it changed position. The tiger seemed from experience to know that this was only a 'camera hunt'. Eventually, it made off into the jungle. We tried to follow it but soon lost sight.

Two more tiger hunts followed with one more sighting. Meanwhile, I was invited to go for a walk with two young leopards. The two young Indians with us were completely unarmed, each carrying no more than a bamboo cane. The leopards must have done this often before. They took no notice of me whatsoever and made no attempt to escape up the forest trees. They obviously enjoyed romping with each other through the forest before returning to their enclosure. For me, this proved to be an extremely valuable experience.

opposite
Tiger in bamboo
charcoal and coloured pencil
585 × 460mm

following page left
Sleeping tiger cubs
ink
actual size

following page right
Tiger cub
watercolour
320 × 255mm

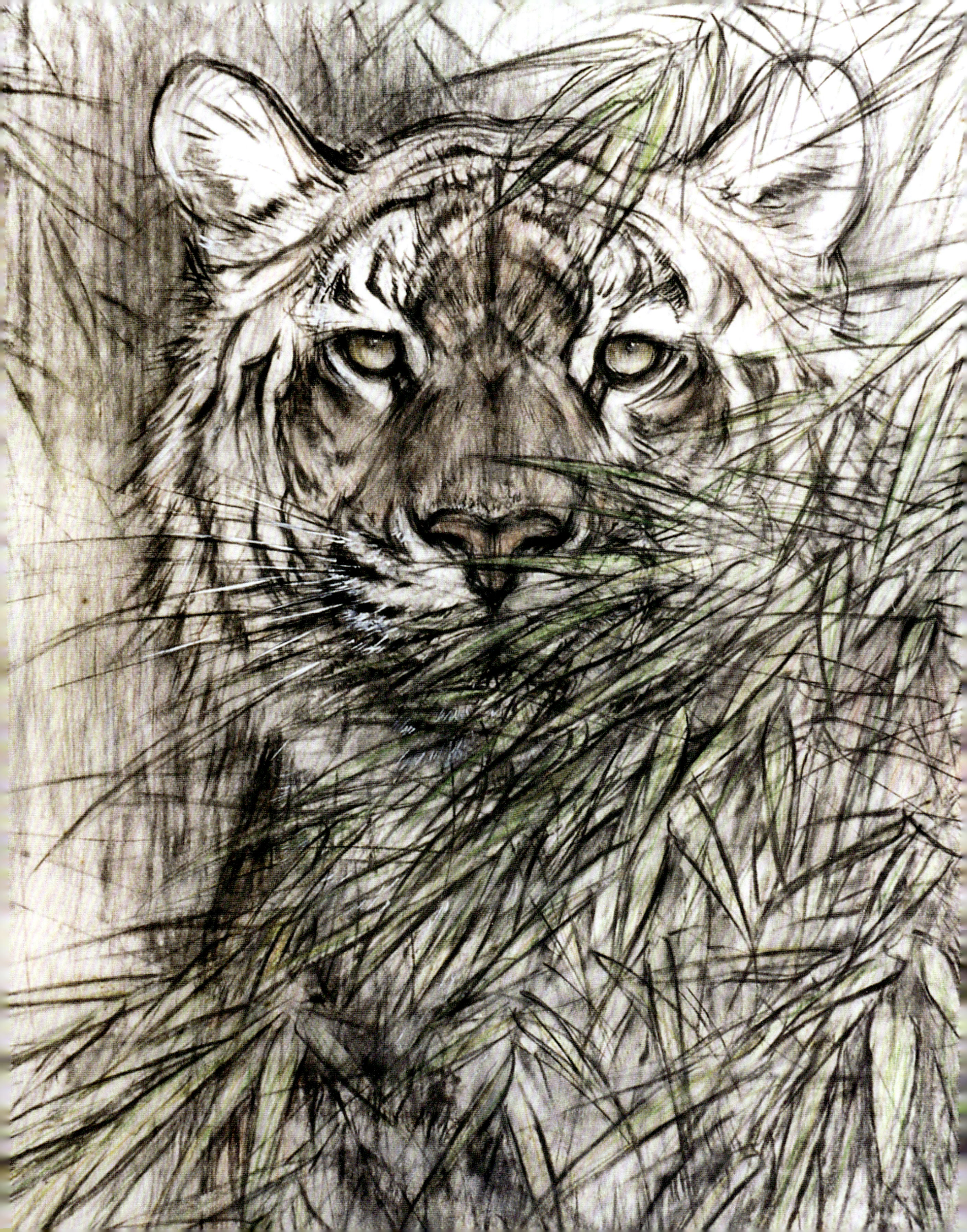

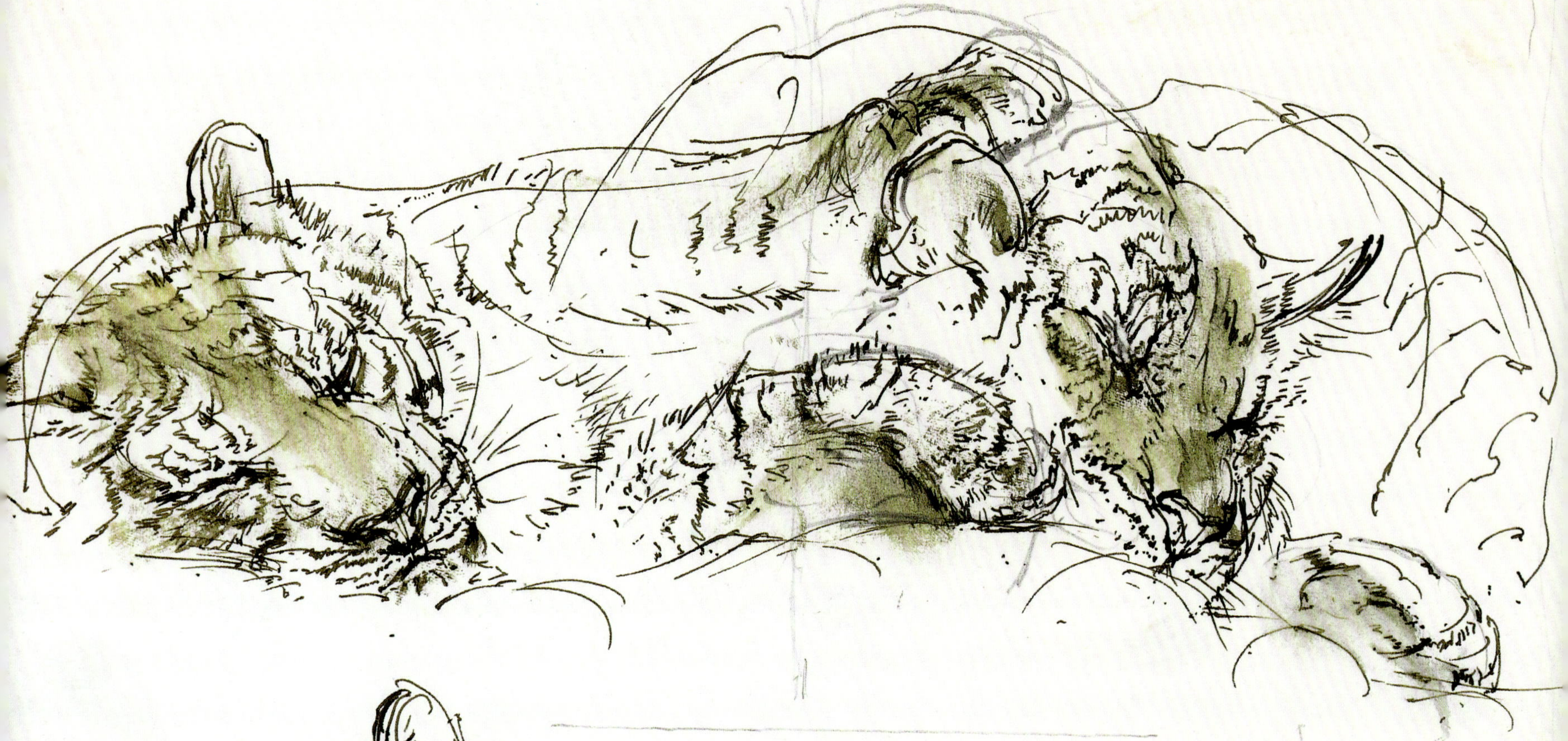

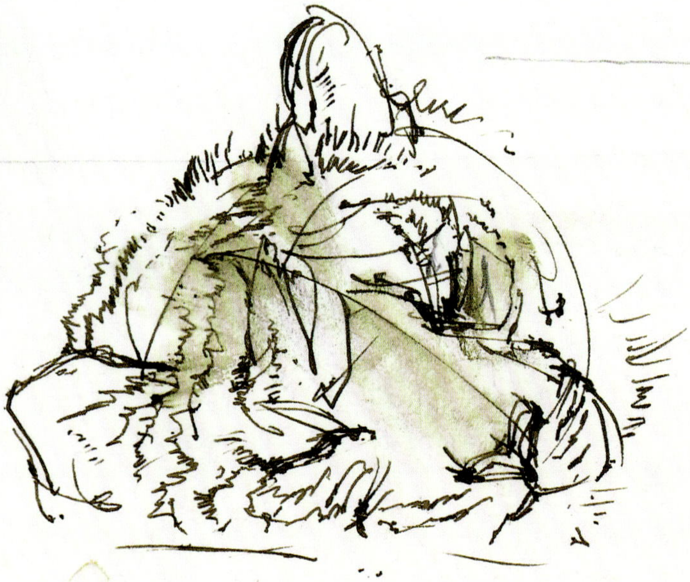

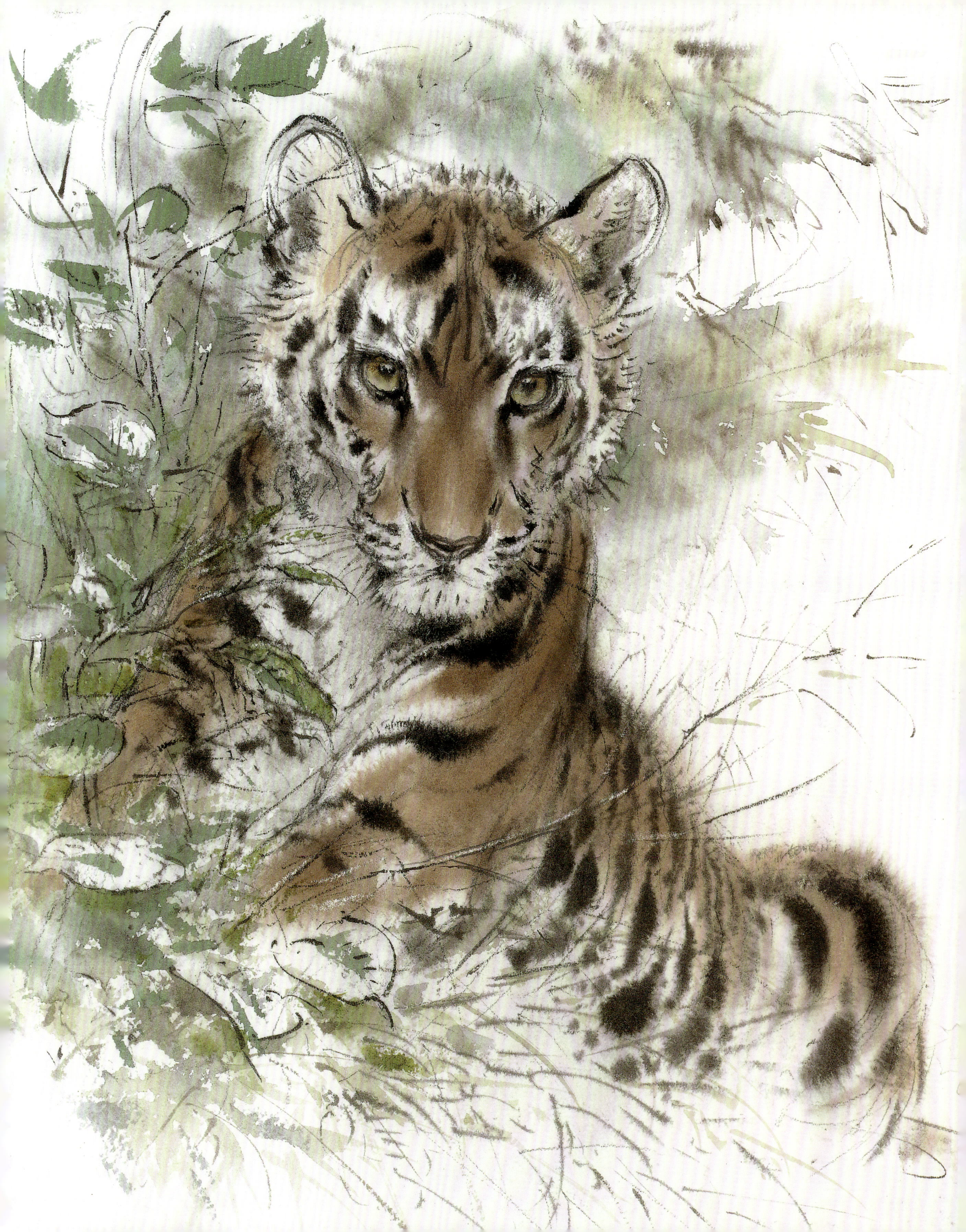

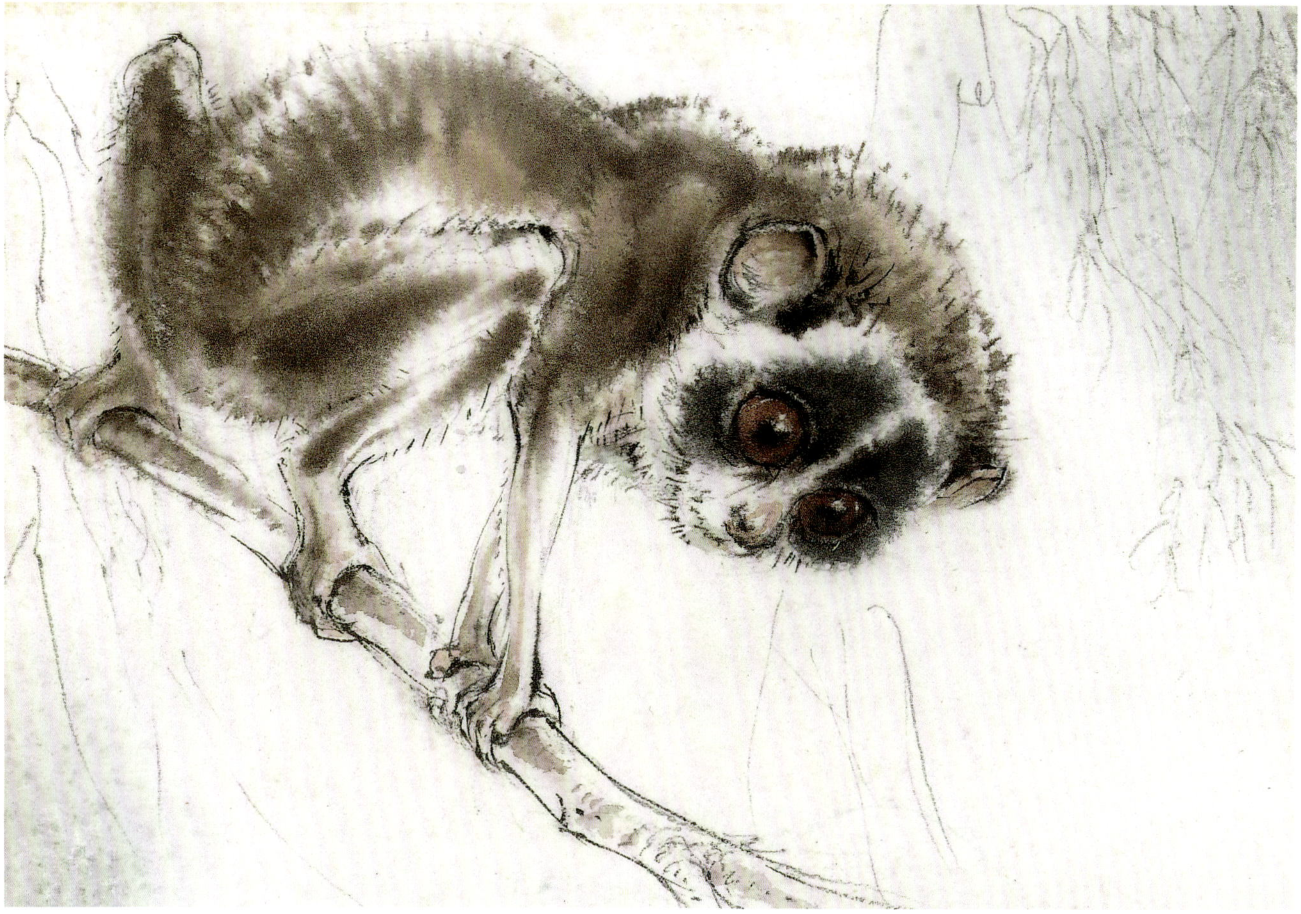

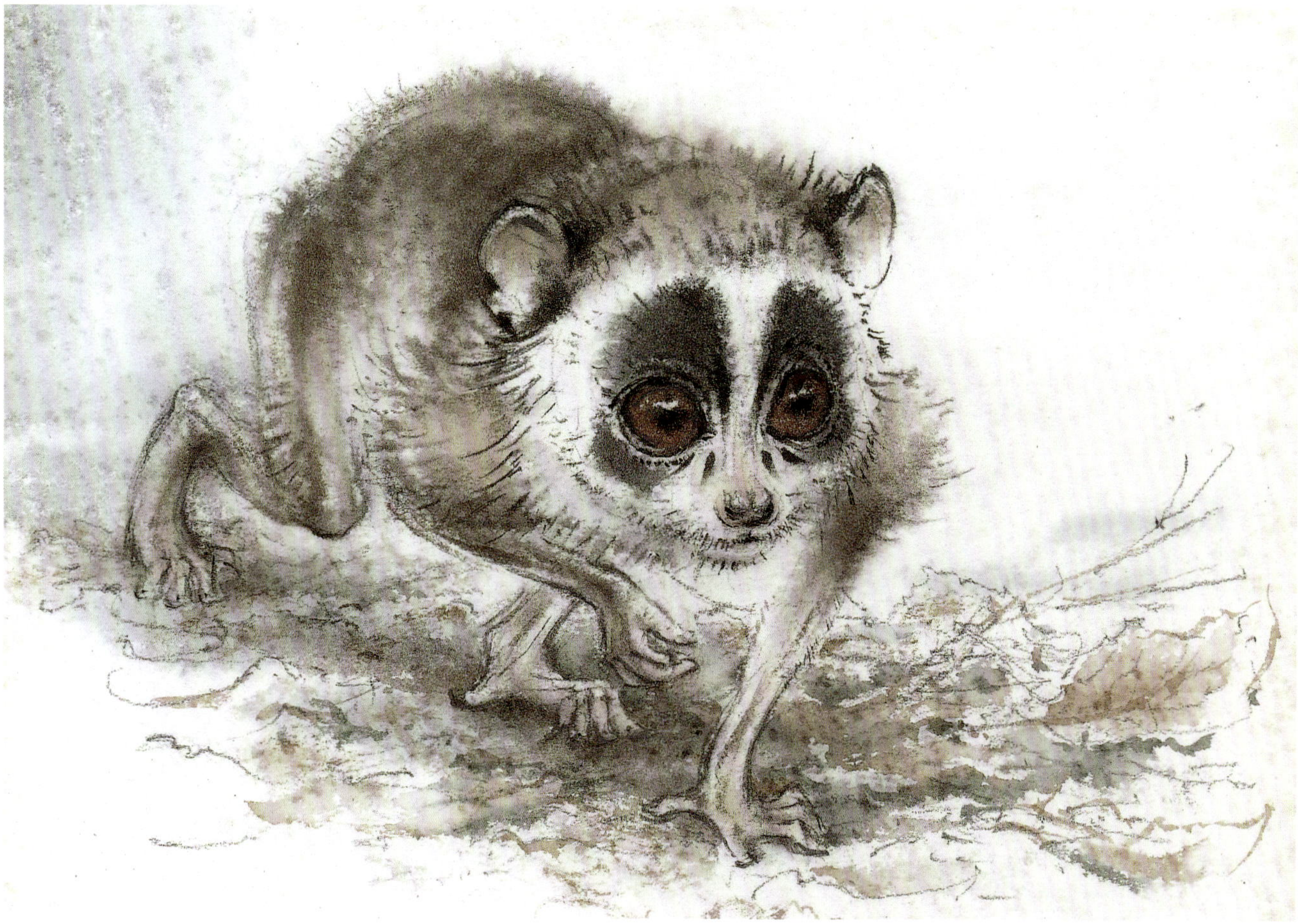

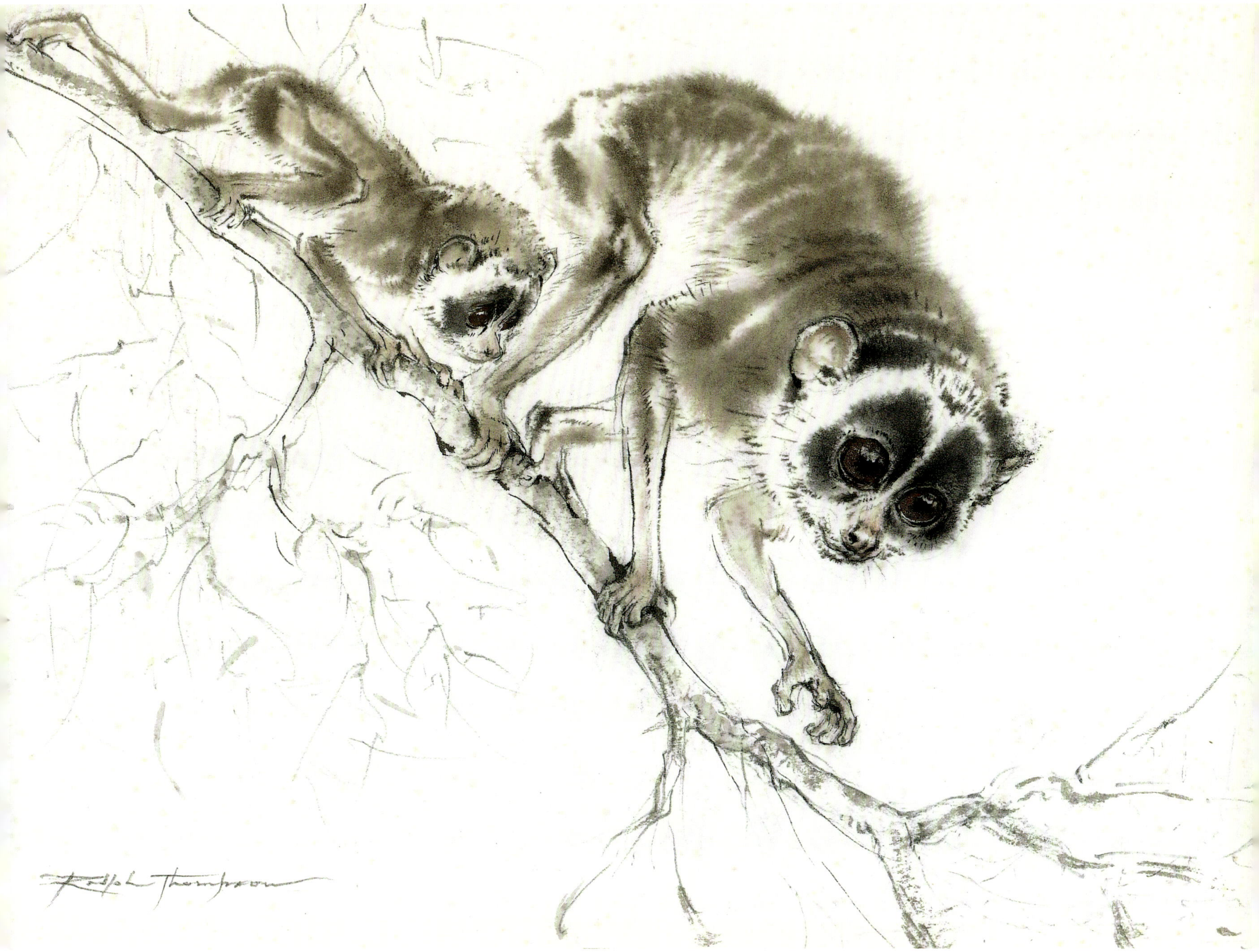

opposite
Young slender loris studies
watercolour
each 135 × 180mm

Slender loris mother and baby
watercolour
230 × 300mm

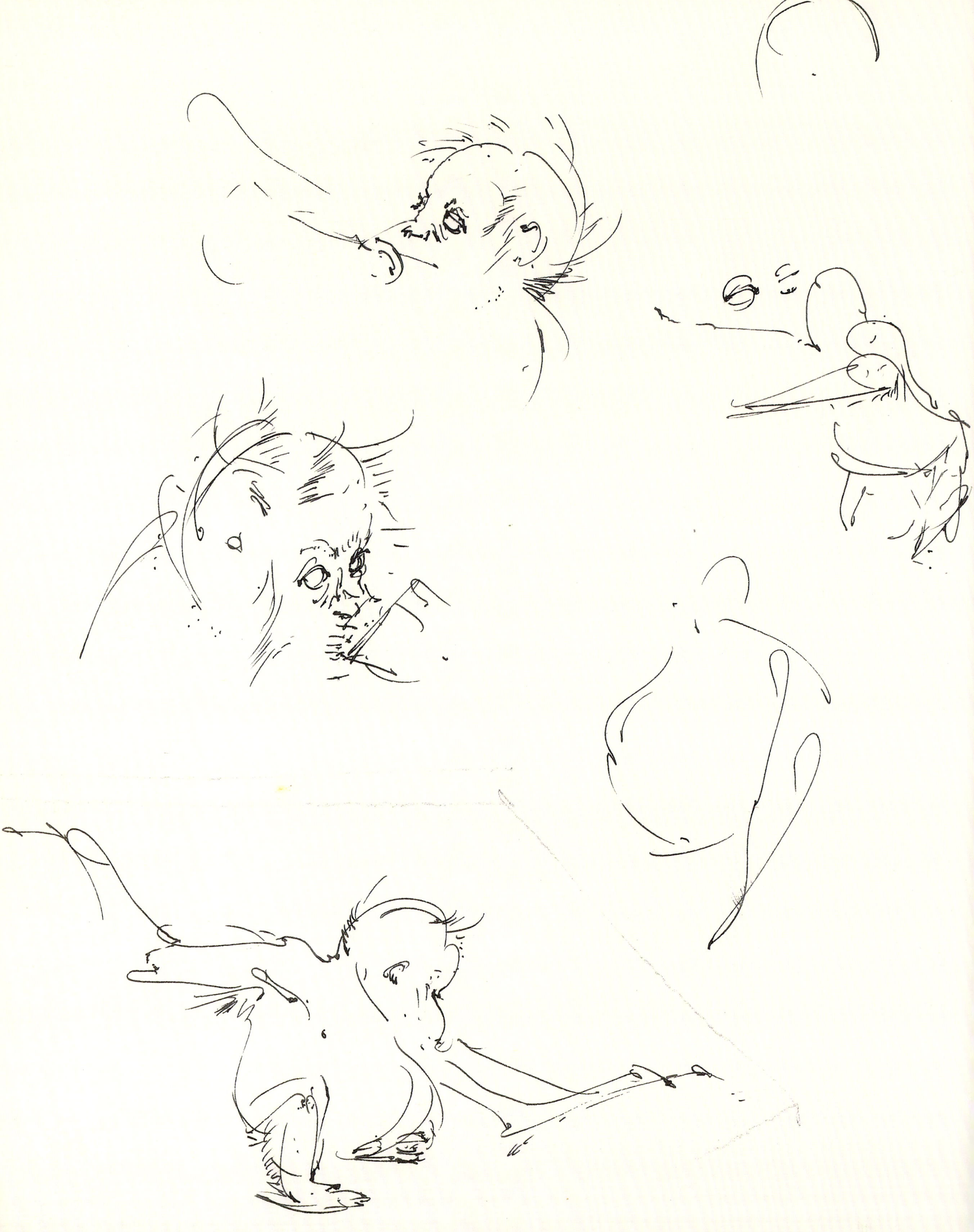

Young Orang-Utan —

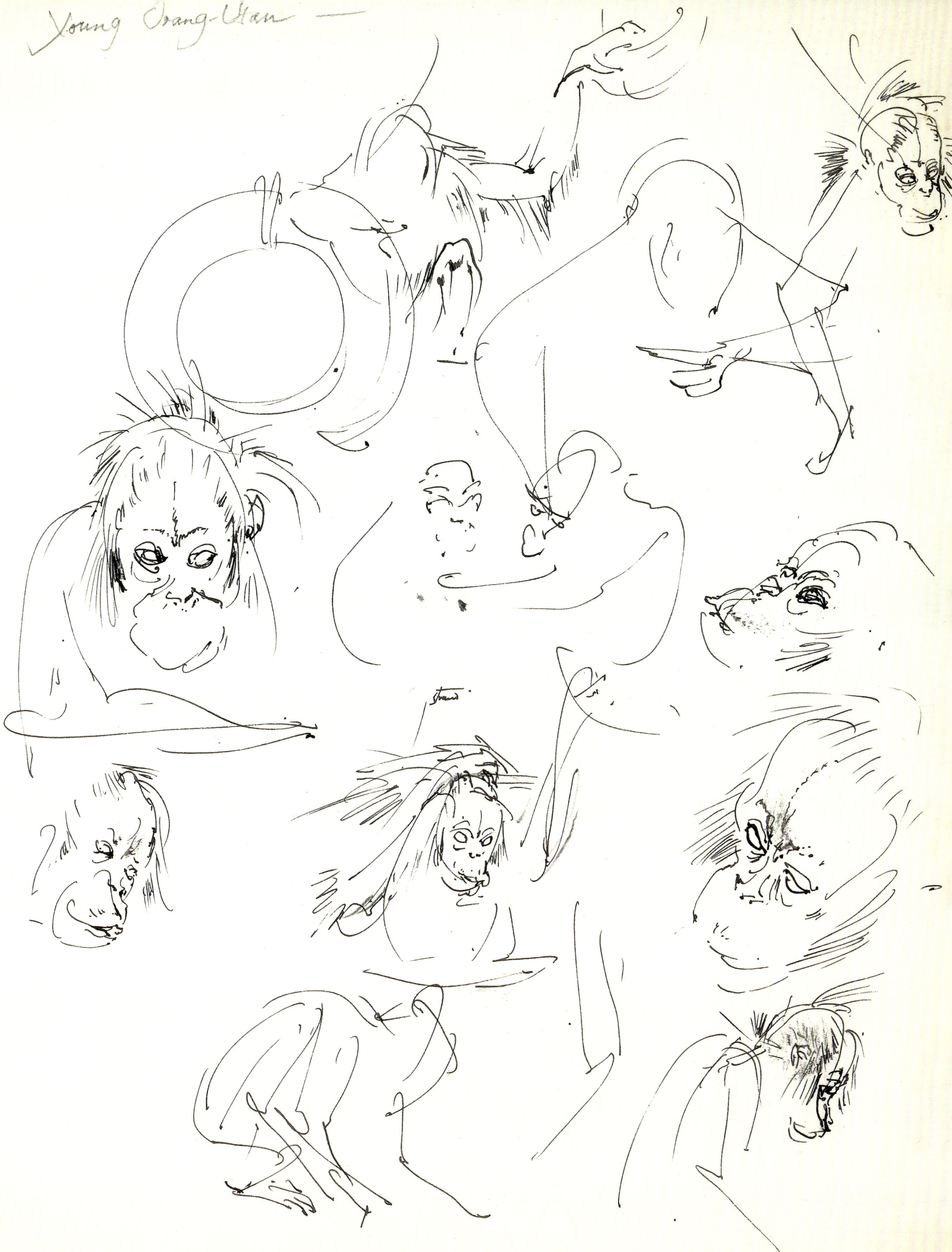

The Leaf Umbrella

It seems a very long time ago, when two extremely dark, little transparencies arrived from the professional photographer, Mike Price, who was then in America. There was no comment other than he hoped I would find them 'interesting'. Their darkness was no surprise, as they had been taken without the aid of a flash and in the middle of a storm. He must have had a very special camera and a fast film to manage them at all. The subject was beautifully realised in both transparencies, one just slightly larger and clearer than the other. Both were of a young Orang-utan sheltering under what looked like a large rhubarb leaf. It could not possibly have been a rhubarb leaf in such a different climate and the stem did not look thick and juicy enough. Nevertheless, his leaf umbrella kept him dry as the rain streamed off its surface.

I did not like the way the stem of this huge leaf led out of my picture. As there was no answer to its identity it left many questions unanswered and so I managed in my own imagination to tear off the stem. I do not think that the young Orang-utan could have done so, nor would it have wanted to, though as adults they are remarkably strong. Satisfied with my solution to the stem problem, I set to work on 'The Leaf Umbrella' – and, here it is.

watercolour 350 × 480mm

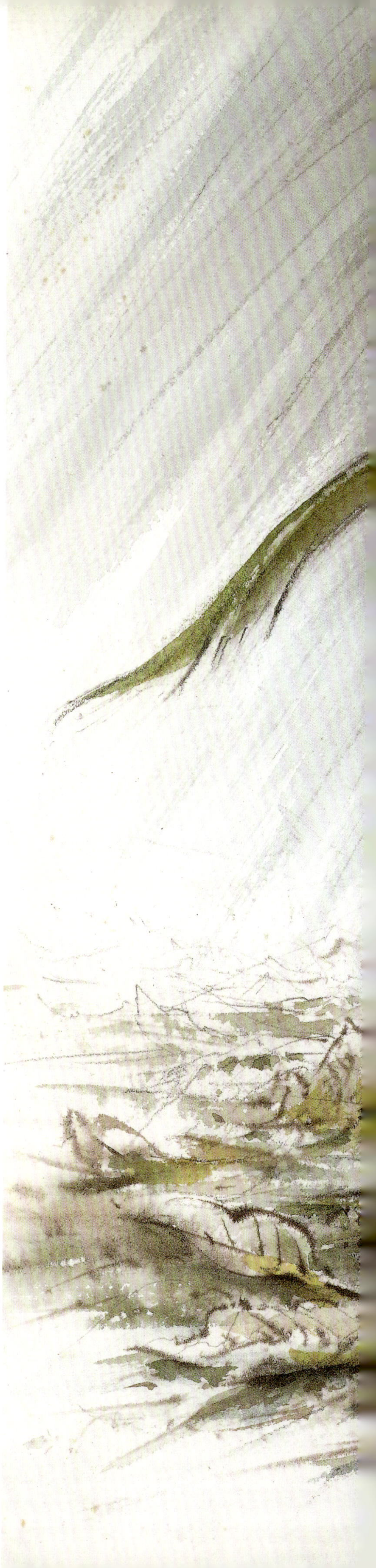

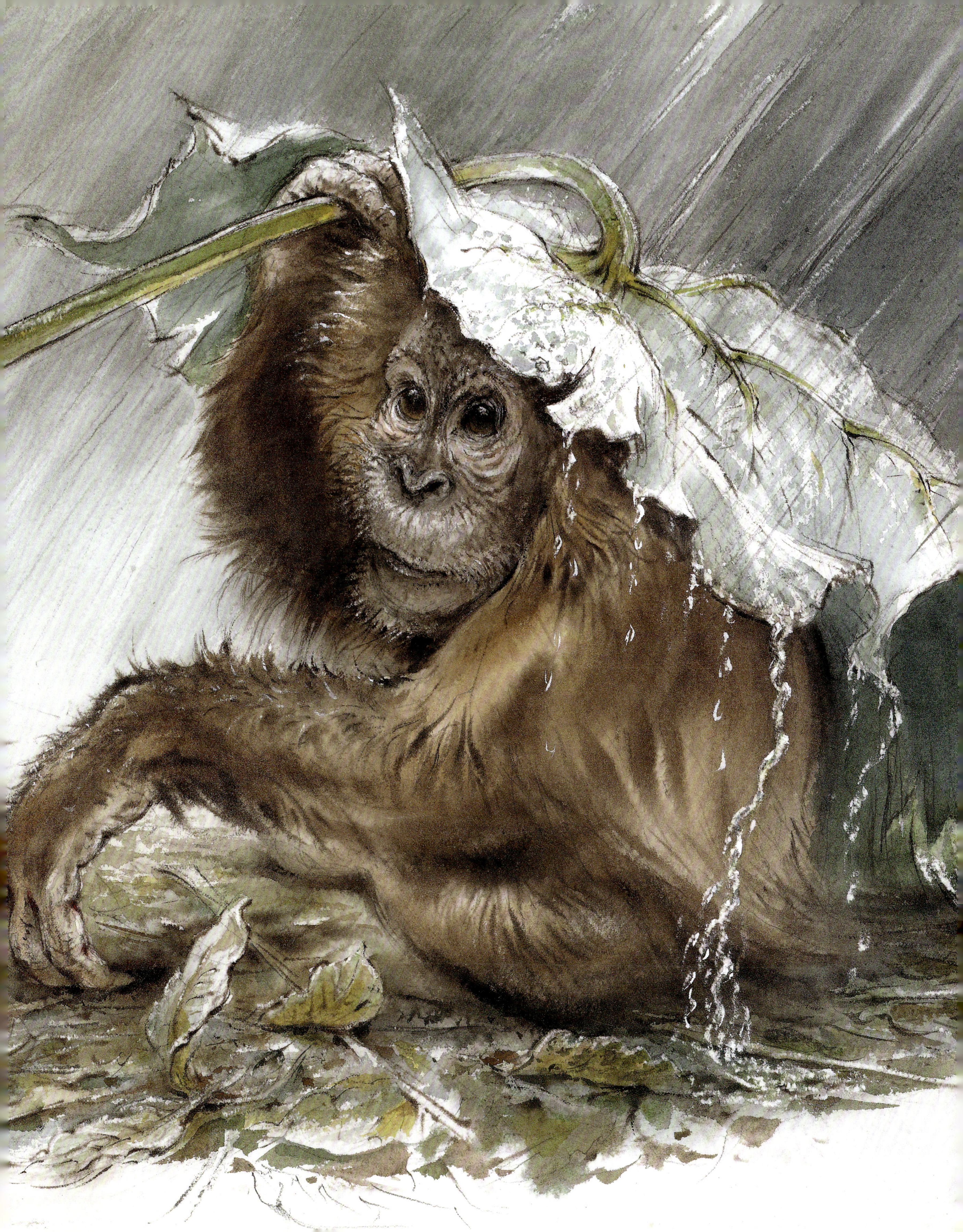

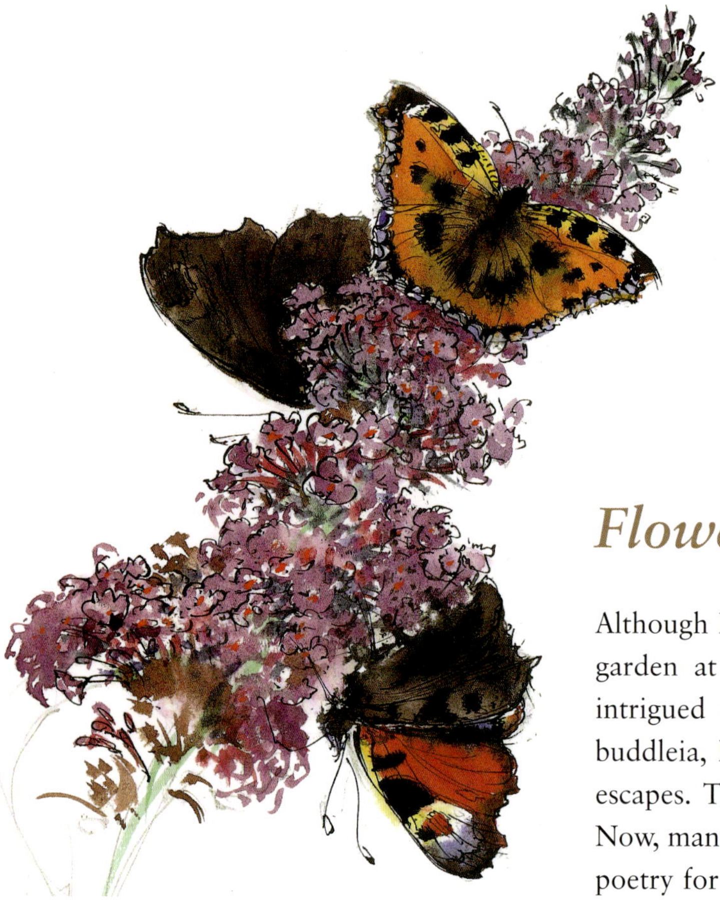

Flowers

Although I am not primarily a flower painter, I found myself living in a large garden at Bigfrith End, much of which had been an old orchard. I was intrigued by the nature of the wild part of the garden with butterflies, buddleia, large golden daisies, dainty macropetala clematis and many garden escapes. Thus, I filled sketchbook after sketchbook in a restless exploration. Now, many years later, it feels as if it were a battle to clarify some sort of visual poetry for myself.

I generally find that one of the greatest problems in drawing plants is seeing the wealth of detail in the right relationship to the main shapes whether it be passion flower, macropetala clematis or water lilies.

When drawing an animal, its movements can help me see the main forms clearly. Plant forms can present worlds within worlds of fascinating details and I can easily lose sight of the whole form which controls them and on which they depend. One flower can also condition a neighbouring one. They become one subject to draw rather than two.

In Summer it was a pleasure, but also a challenge, to sit on a low stool by the lily pond. In spite of periodic thinning of the lily roots, the pond was always overcrowded. The lilies seemed to be trying to climb out to seek a new pond. From my point of view, this was an advantage, in that there were lots making interesting groupings which were always changing round the iris in the centre.

Water lilies have become a favourite subject. When I have been drawing for a while, my eye begins to flow over a number of lilies at a time and my hand makes a spontaneous response.

Looking back I see that these drawings are a very important feature in my work. As I look into these plant forms, my pleasure and delight grows as my eye moved over them, until a moment when a line appears to express it. The decisiveness of a pen line I find more challenging and more satisfying, if more difficult, and I may need to make drawing after drawing to meet it.

opposite
Butterflies on buddleia
ink and watercolour
360 × 260mm

following pages
Studies from the lily pond
ink, pencil and watercolour
actual size

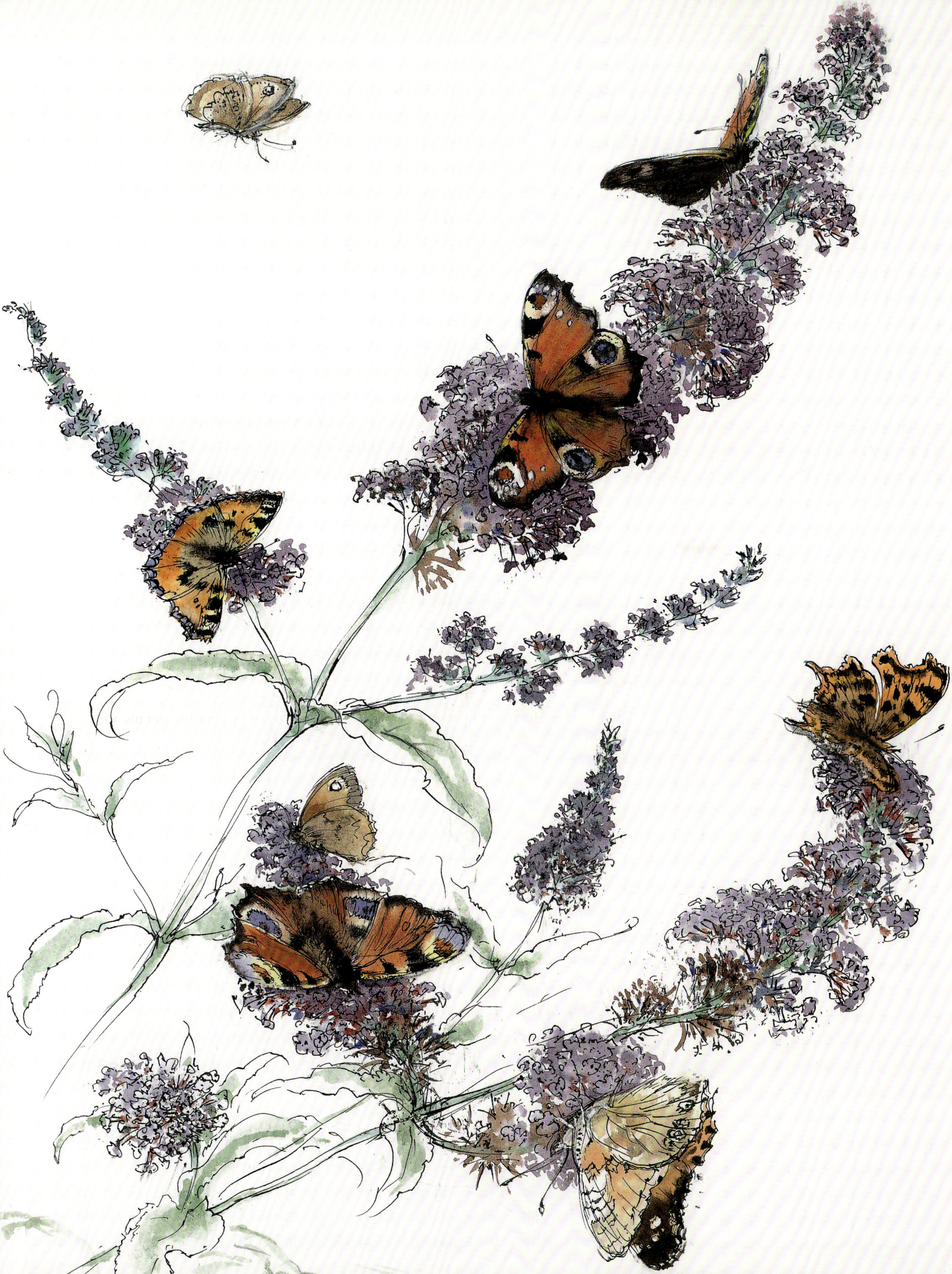

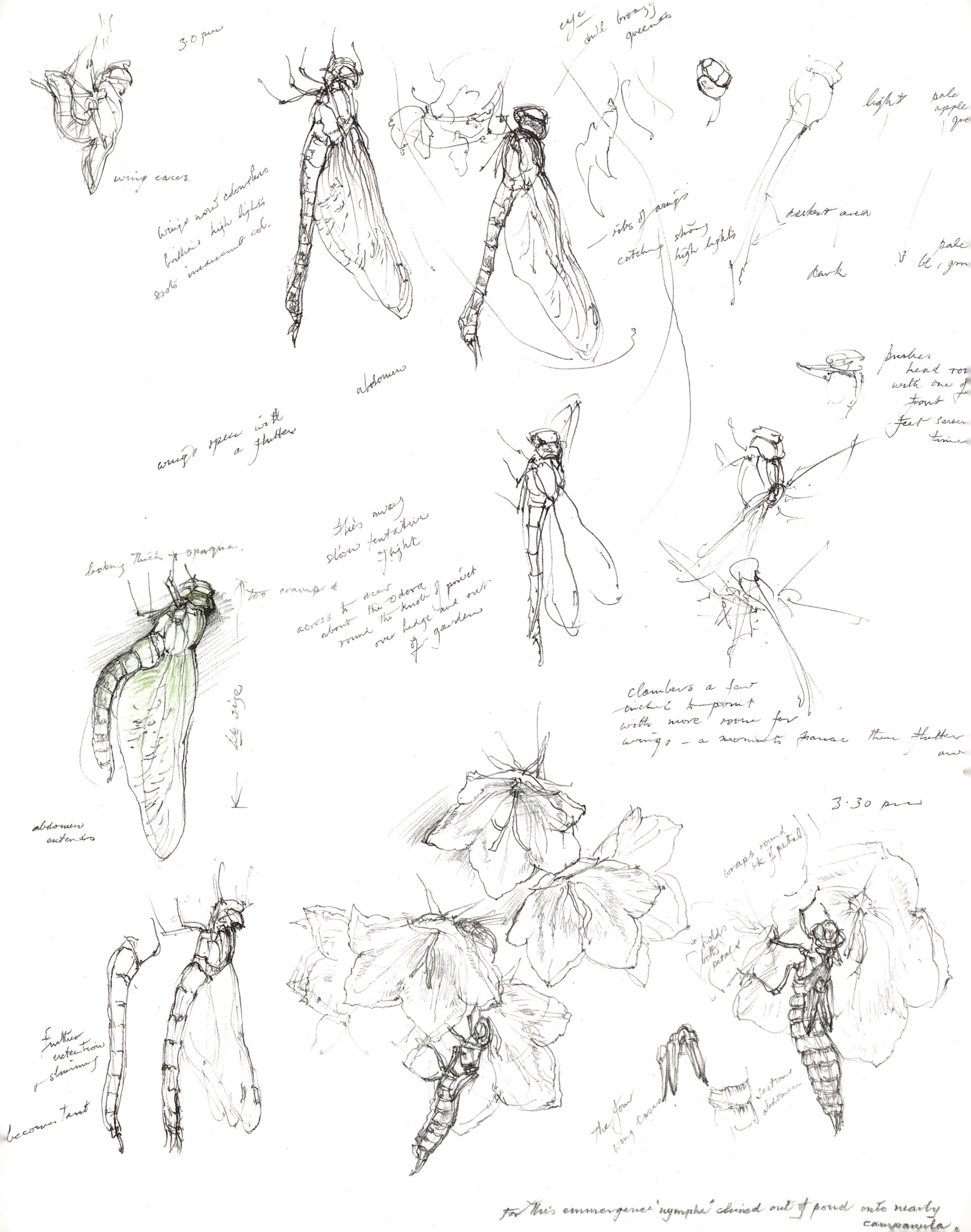
3.0 pm
wing cases
eye dull bronzy greens
light
pale apple green
wings now colourless brilliant highlights spots iridescent col.
ribs of wings catching strong highlights
darker area
dark
pale lt. green
abdomen
wings open with a flutter
pushes head round with one of front feet several times
flies away slow tentative flight
looking thick & opaque.
too cramped
clambers a few inches to point with more room for wings – a moments pause then flutter
3.30 pm
abdomen extends
wraps round bk of petal
holds both petals
further extension & slimming
becomes taut
the four wing cases
sections of abdomen
for this emmergence 'nymphe' climed out of pond onto nearby campanula

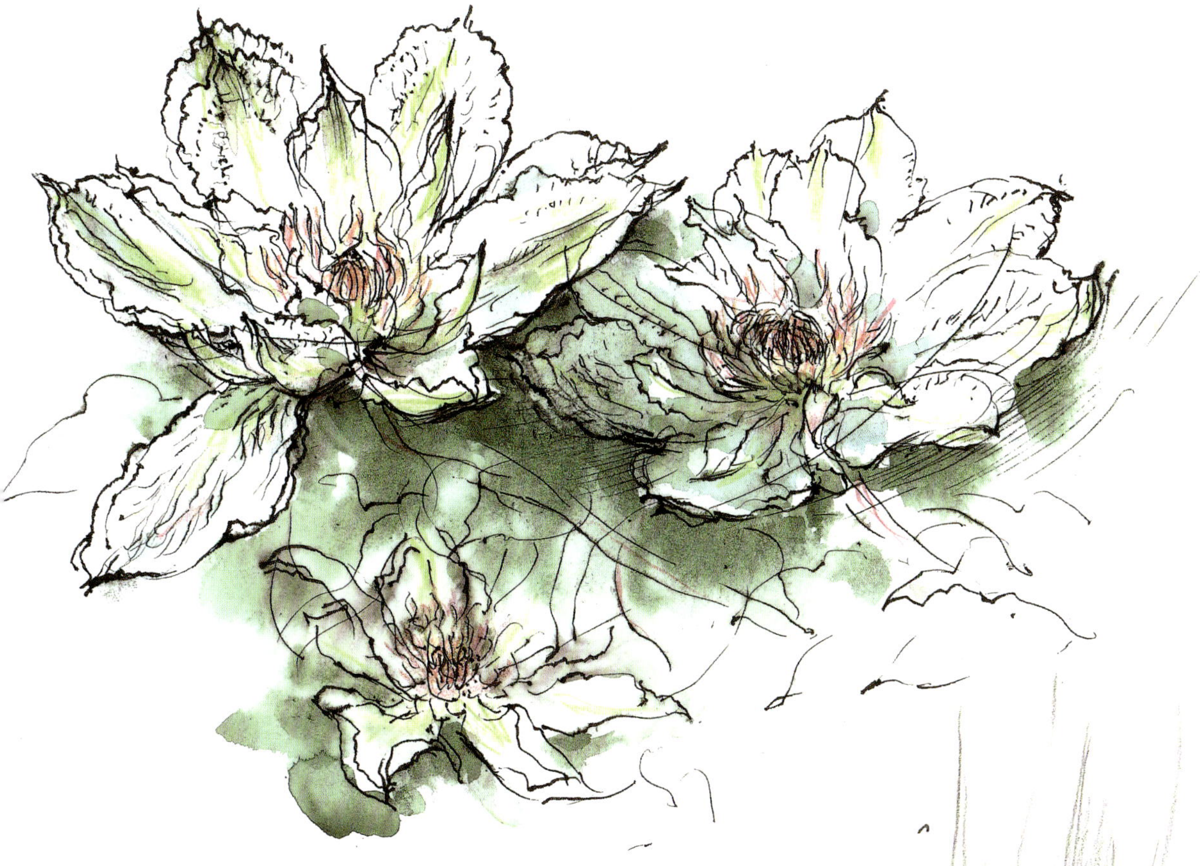

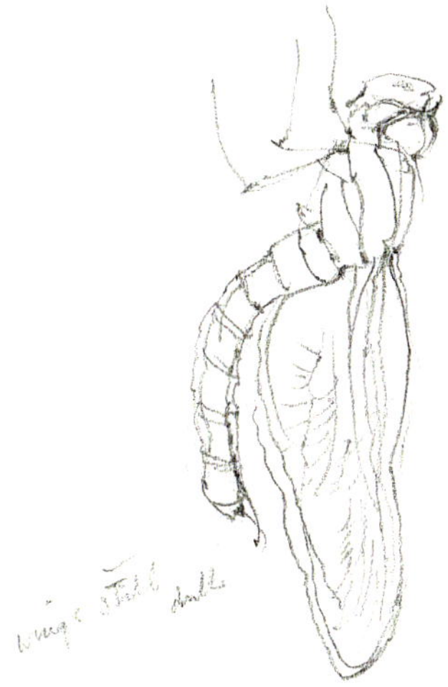
wings still dull

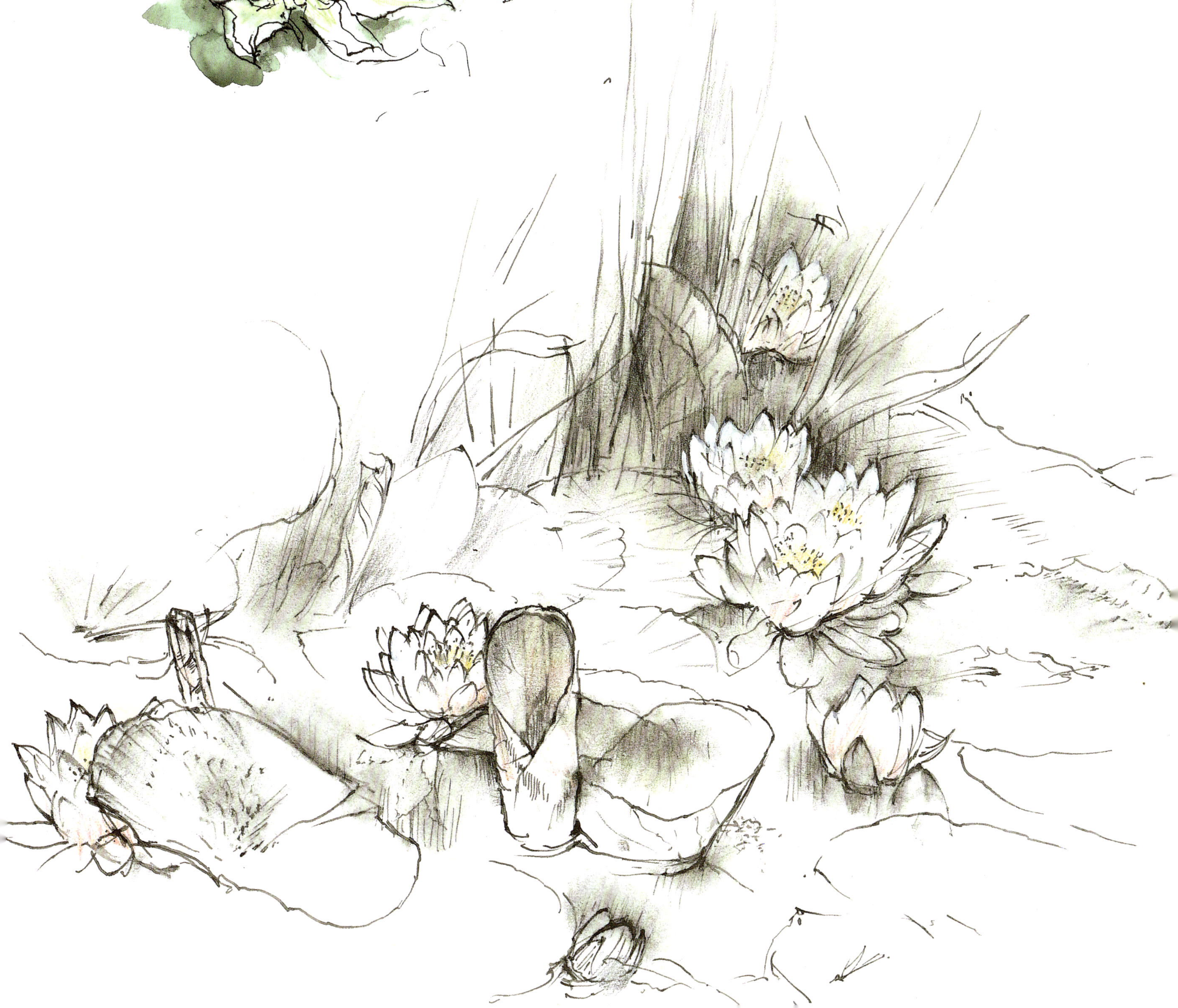

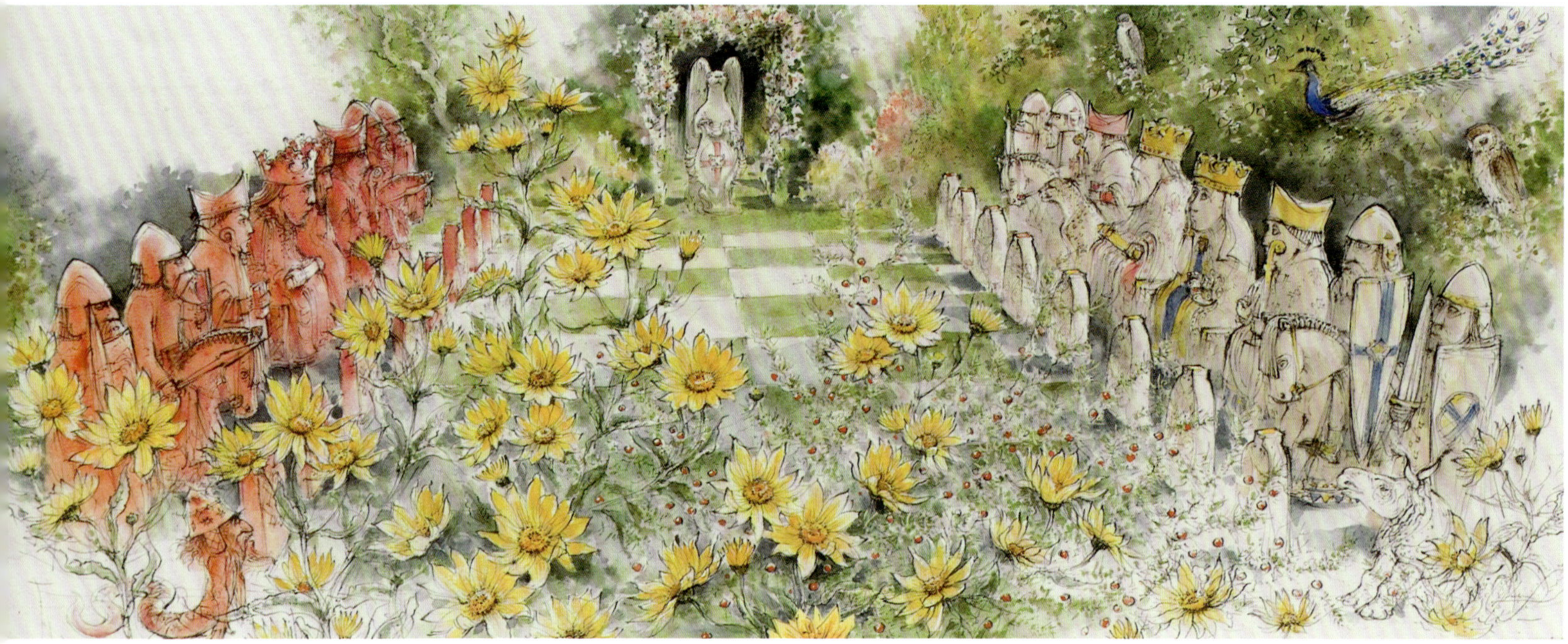

Chess Dream in a Garden

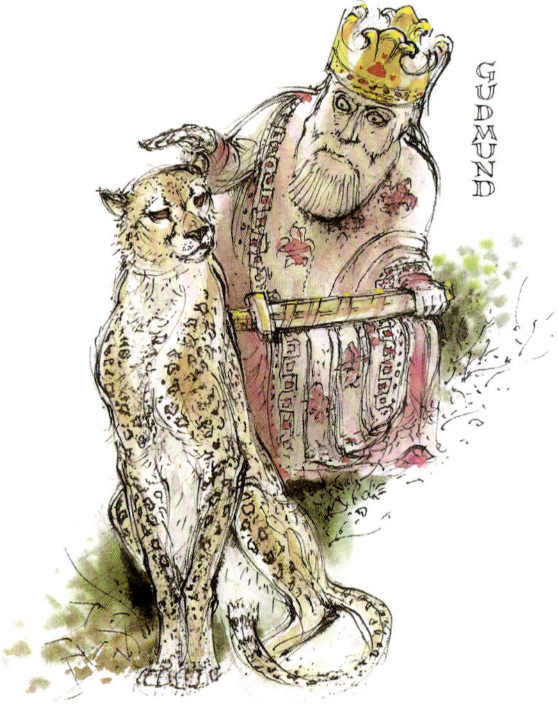

As a student of the Royal College, I was given the privilege, under strict supervision, of studying drawings and paintings of the great masters in the Print Room at the top of the British Museum.

On my way up there I passed through a long gallery of cases full of the museum's treasures. At the very end stood a case with tiny figures carved in ivory. Drawn to look at them each time I passed, I became more and more intrigued. They turned out to be 12th century chessmen from Scandinavia, carved in walrus ivory, discovered in a crate washed up many years ago on the Isle of Lewis.

They had the vitality I had learned to expect from the 12th century, so I bought four resin reproductions – a King and Queen, a Knight and a Bishop – and put them on the high mantelpiece in my living room.

I suppose their strong little characters seen at eye level every day, must have fired my mind and imagination. When, on a visit to the Savill Gardens, I came upon the curious carving of an otter bearing a heraldic shield, to which I could add a pair of wings, the story of these Chessmen began to appear in my mind. So I asked the well known children's author Rosemary Sutcliff to write text to accompany my paintings, the outcome of which was the book 'Chess Dream in a Garden'.

Then the Winged Beast knew that he need wait no longer. He spread his great wings, and the silence deepened behind the singing of the birds; and a brightness sprang out of nowhere and spread and spread, filling all the garden with a power that was like a thousand thunderstorms and a thousand sunbursts and a thousand rainbows.

King Gudmund found his nose lengthening into a strong trunk with a pair of mighty tusks set on either side of it, and he flung it up and trumpeted war.

The Queen, rising from the ground with the dove and the peacock circling about her, felt a silvery horn springing from her forehead and her hands and feet changing into hooves.

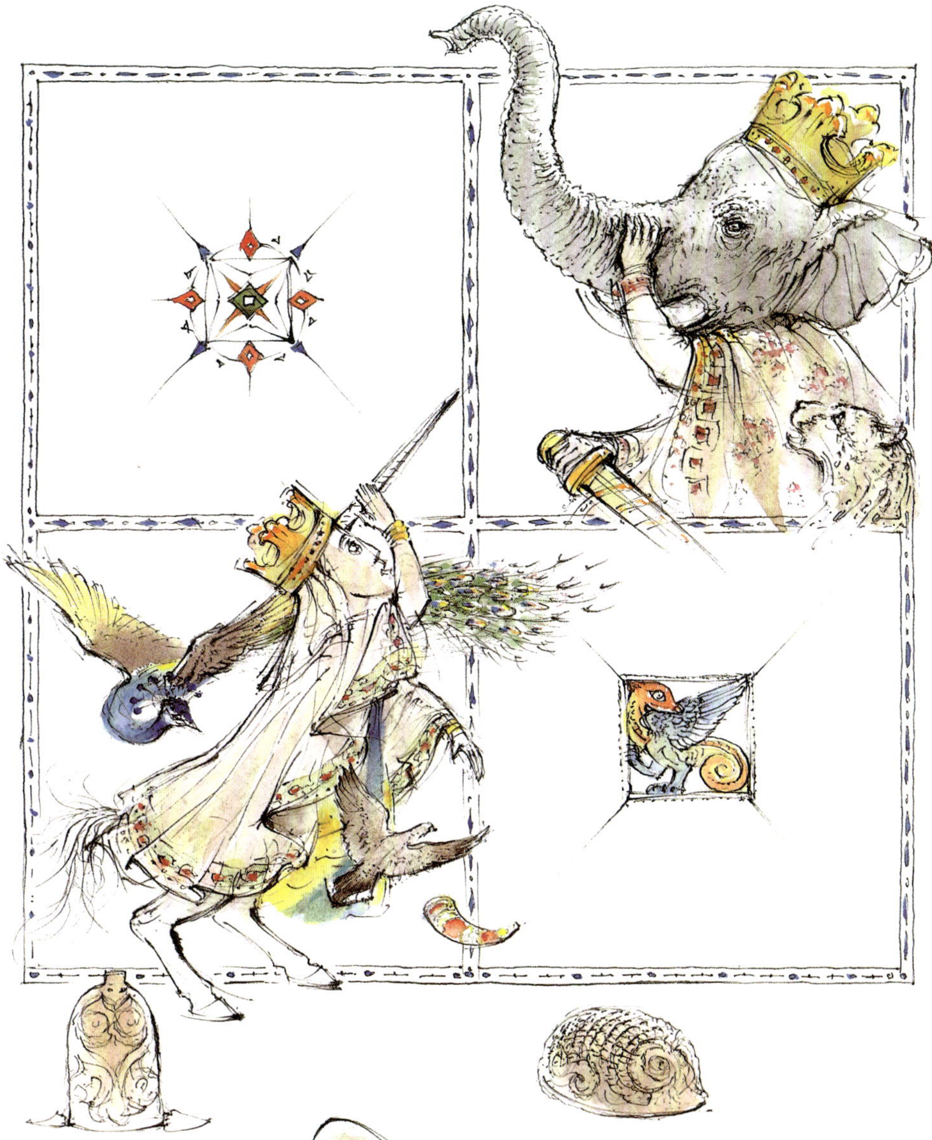

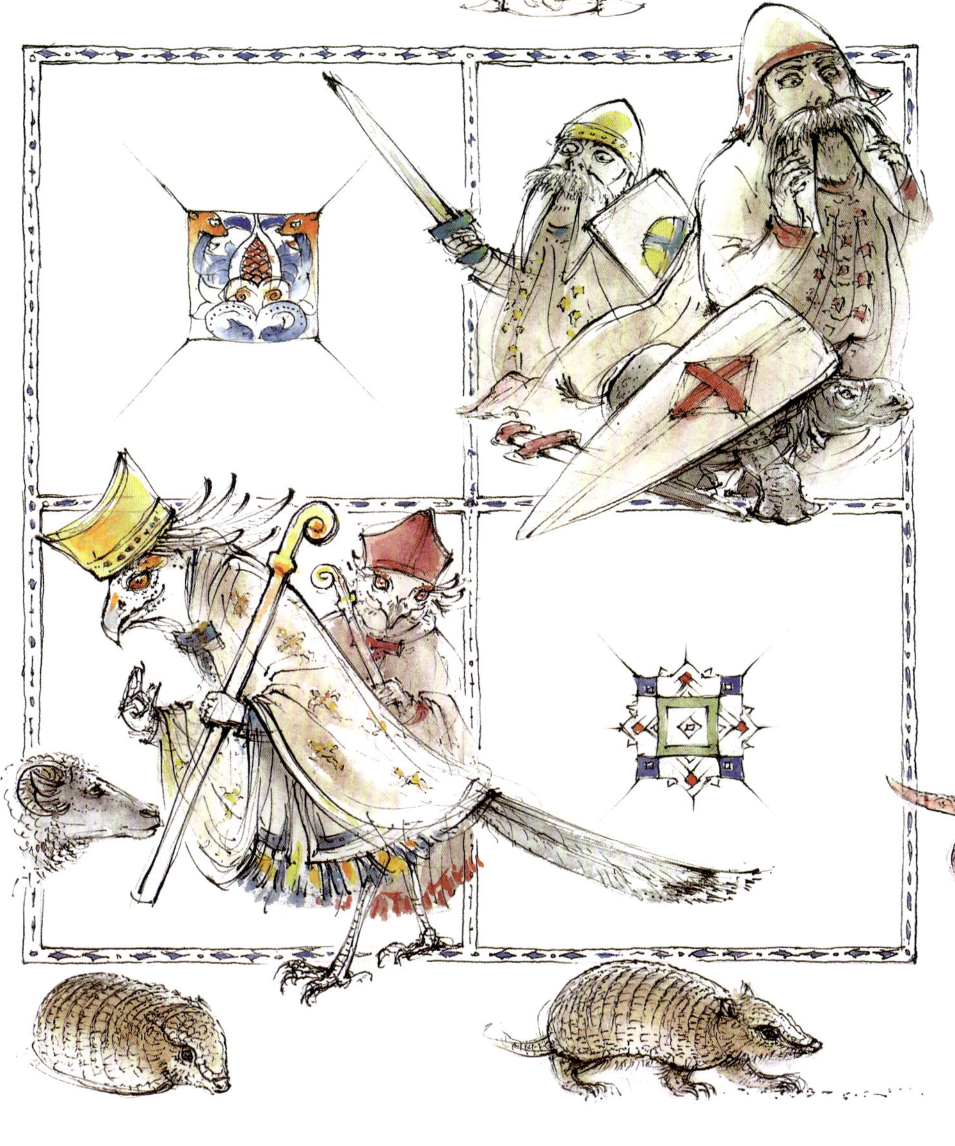

Even those of the White Company who had fallen to the Enemy were changing, each into their dream creature; the wardens finding savage tusks piercing through under their moustaches, and the Bishops growing long, sharp beaks and clutching their croziers in bird-claws while their sheep huddled, stamping and snorting, behind them. Even the pawns turned into their dream armadillos.

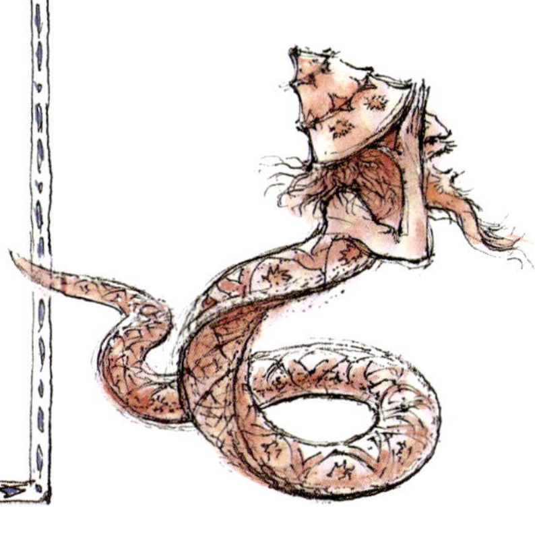

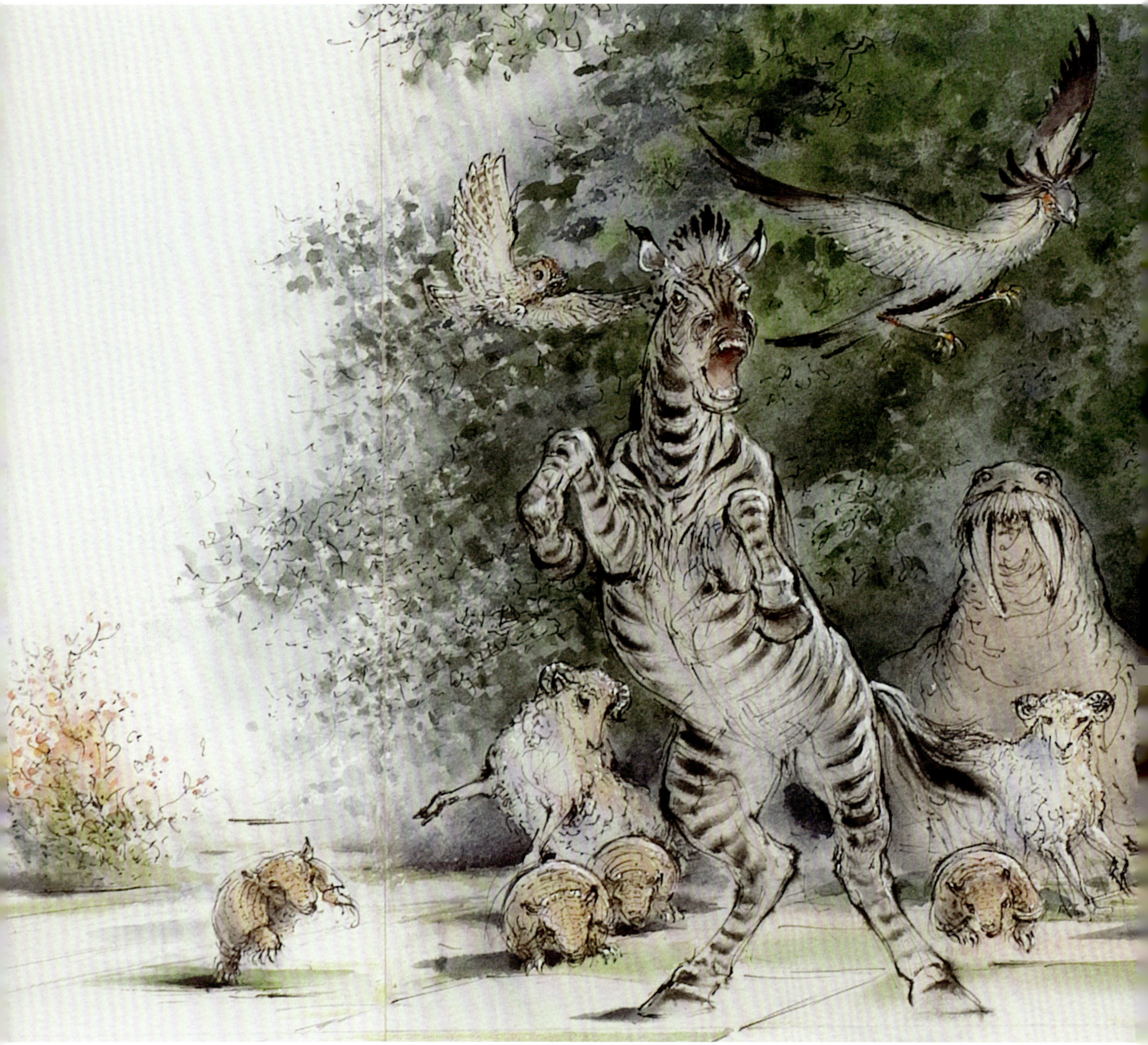

And away in the bushes where he had been banished, Sir Alrek felt his strength grow great; felt his arched neck and rising crest and trampling war-hooves; and with his heart on fire within him, he came rearing and plunging back to lead the charge.

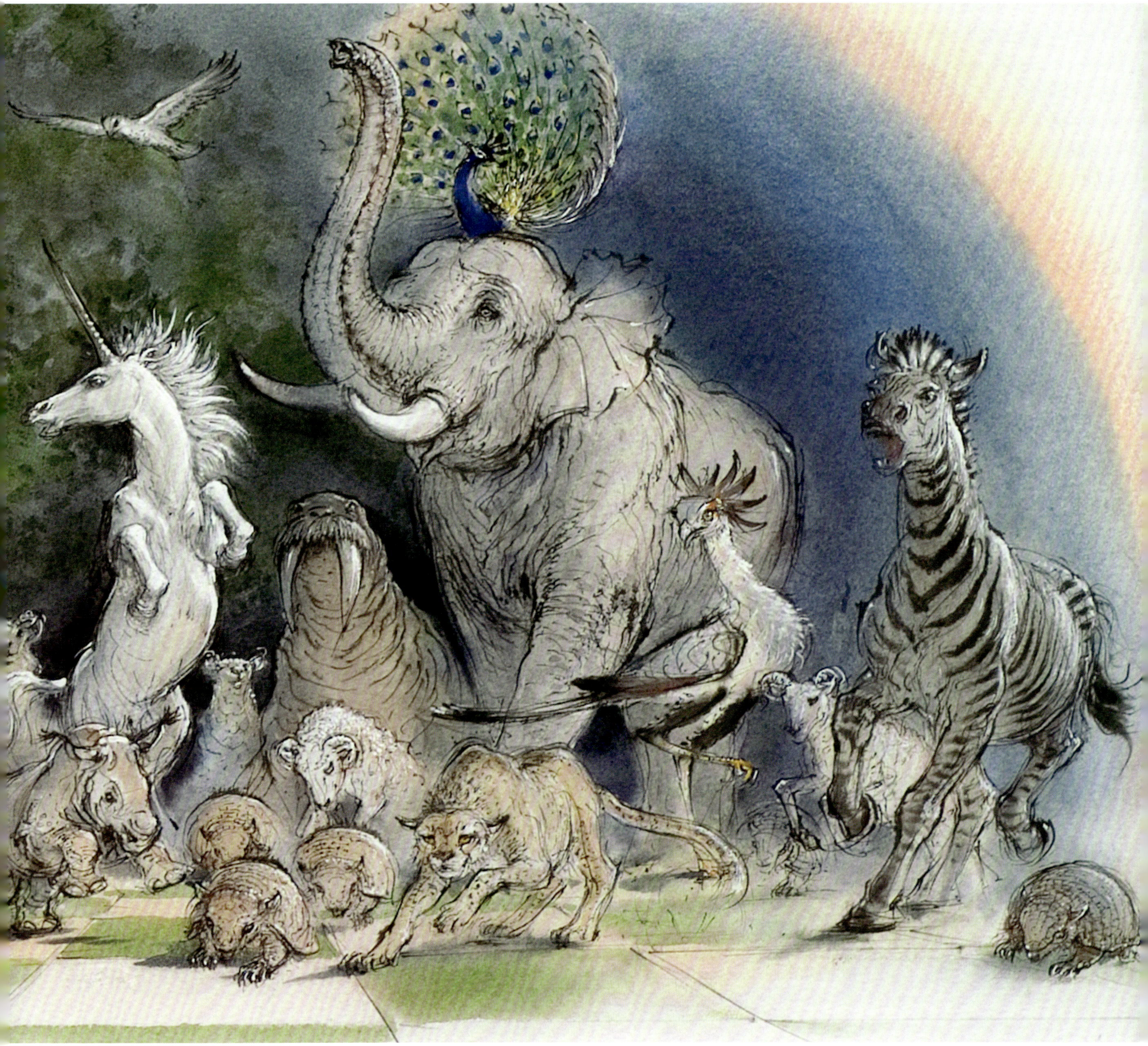

The chess court was full of animals. Roaring and neighing, snarling and trumpeting, they swept down upon the Red Horde, and behind them came Power, arching over them like a breaking wave.

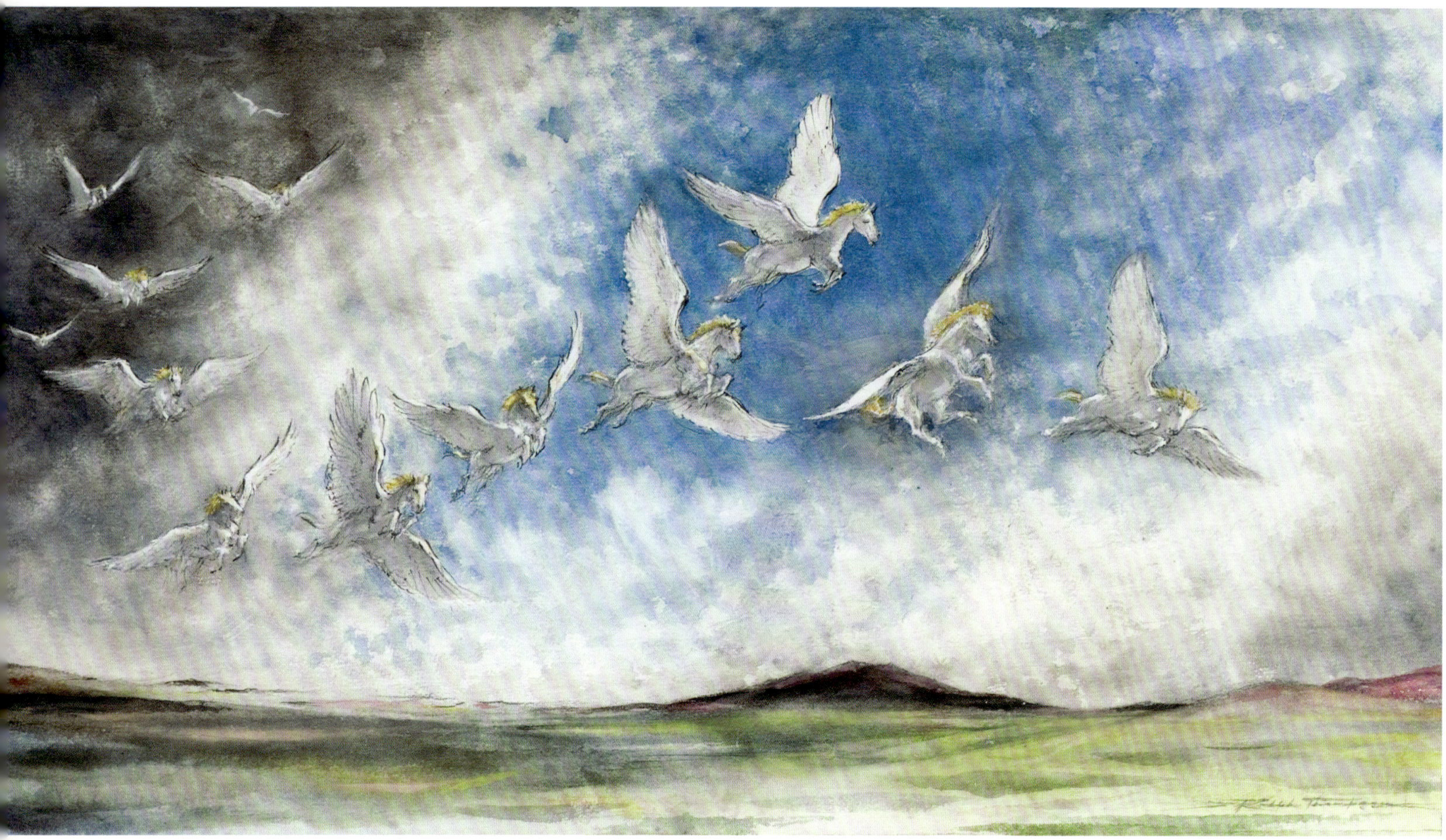

Flying Horses

Horses have a long history of portrayal in art going back to cave paintings. When 'flying' horses first appeared in my work, the clouds came before the horses. They seemed a natural part of them. There came a time in the garden when the drama in the sky seemed to take over. My eyes were always being drawn up there. I thought of the myth of the flying Pegasus and started drawing flying clouds and flying horses.

Pegasus and flying horses often appeared in the wilder parts of Derbyshire, with which I was familiar. I found their forms, shapes and anatomy fascinated me and I valued the link with their age old portrayal in the history of art from cave paintings onwards.

My preoccupation with the horse took over for a while and I tried to ask myself about the imaginative streak appearing in my work. Could an imaginative statement carry as much truth, or possibly more, than a literal statement but of a different kind?

Between heaven and earth
watercolour
370 × 680mm

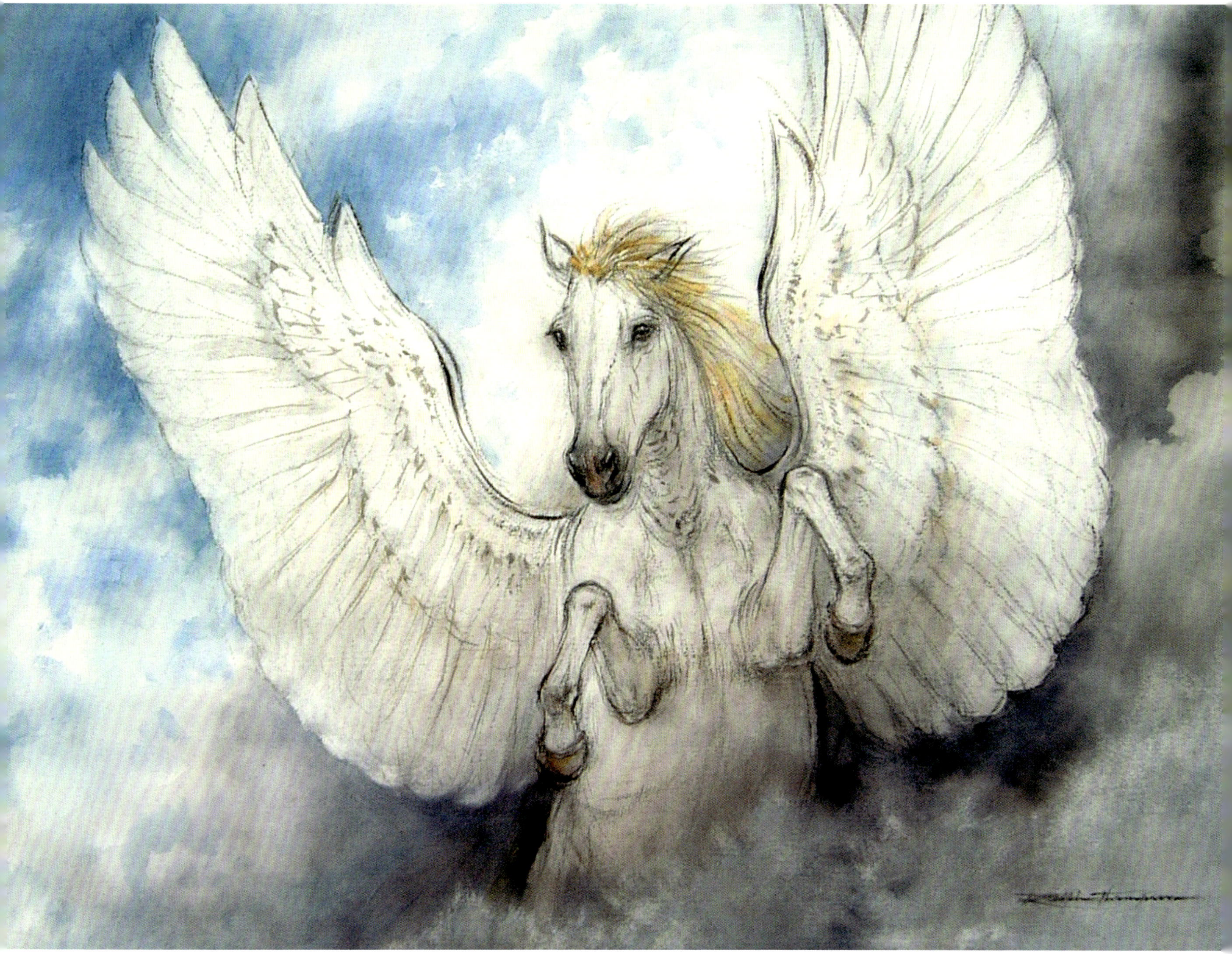

Pegasus
watercolour
520 × 710mm

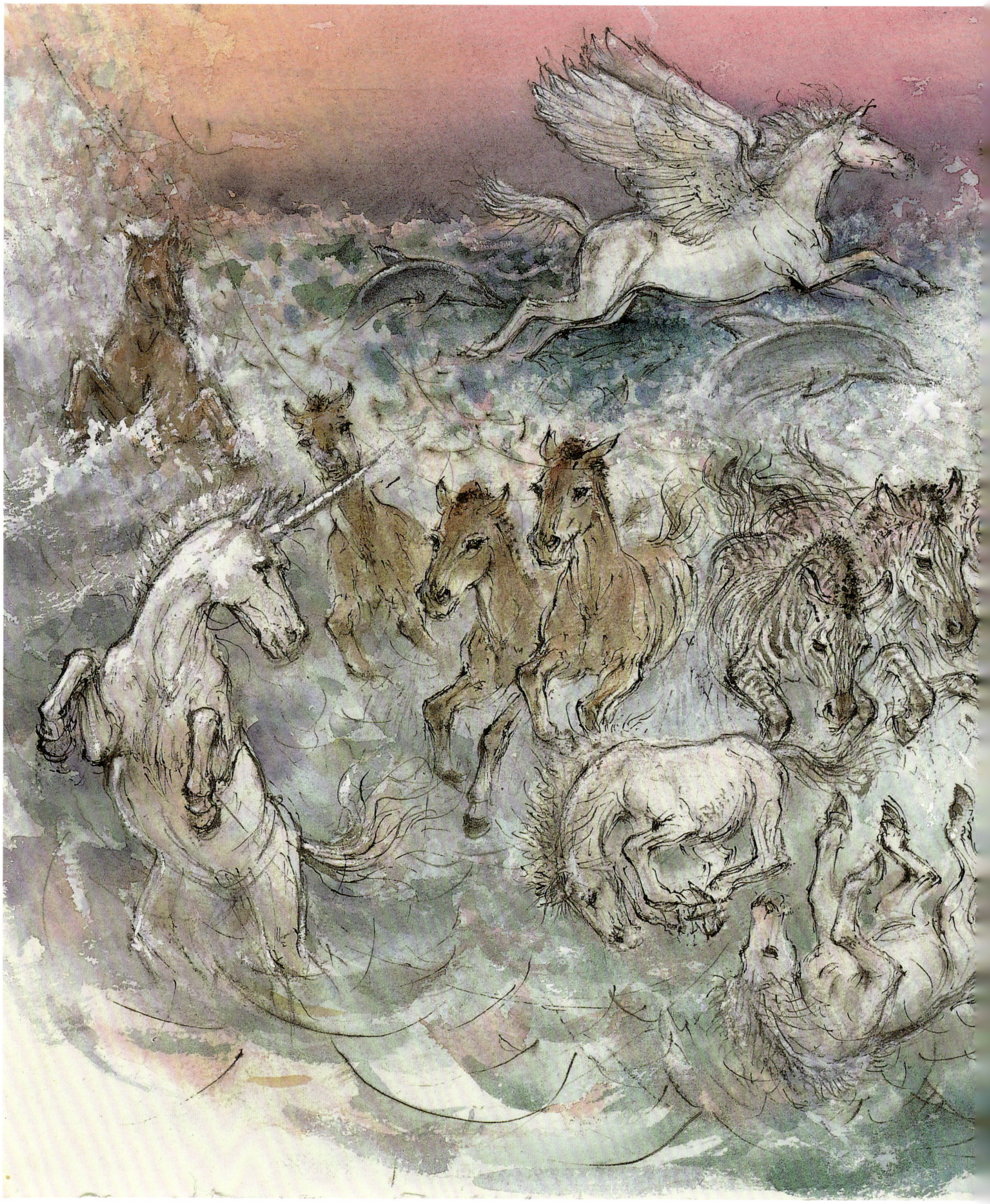

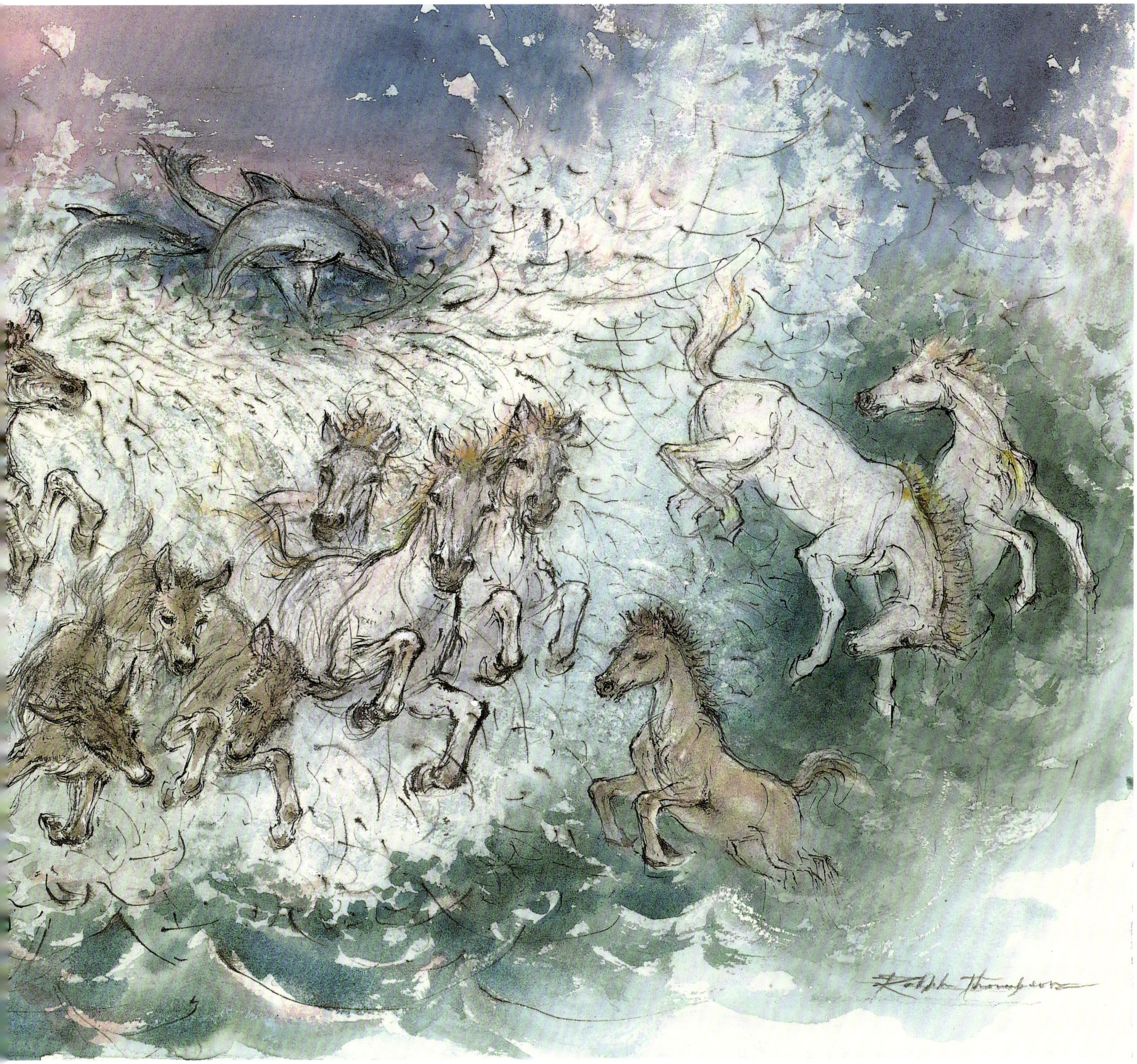

In selecting paintings for this book I have included 'The Wave – A Fantasia' in which I have allowed my imagination to run riot. Pegasus appears against a sunset sky above a great breaking wave with dolphins and every type of horse I could think of. On the extreme left is the mythical unicorn, then some Przewalski, wild horses from Eastern Europe, a small herd of zebras, donkeys representing the wild ass and the wild horses of the Camargue. Two white horses are playing in the wave to the right of the picture and a couple of ponies are foreground left.

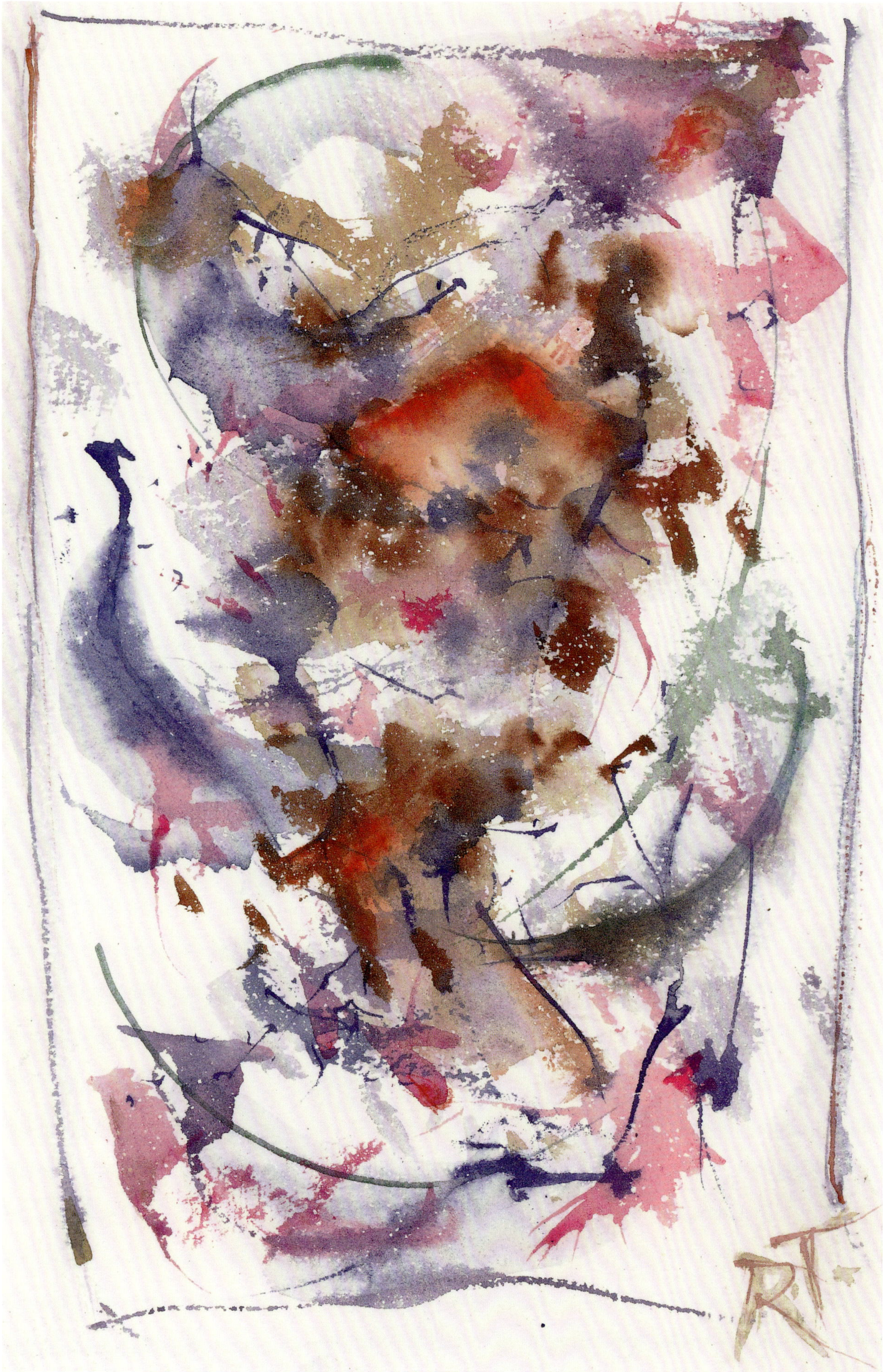

Abstracts

Abstract paintings of many kinds appear in galleries now. I felt the need to explore this way of looking at nature for myself. Could it be possible to relate it to the delight experienced of the zebra head long ago?

In a corner of the garden I came upon a log covered with white fungi, which suggested a tinted drawing. Looking at both my drawing and the log, it then seemed possible to go beyond the actual appearance, so I did a second drawing searching for forms, which lay beneath. I then found that the log covered with interesting fungi had become unrecognisable but the new shapes commanded interest in their own right. It seemed like a beginning of 'abstraction'.

Other experiments followed and a new kind of work evolved. Then (following some blind impulse) a 'doodle' appeared quite free of any reference to nature or natural subjects.

Abstract doodles
watercolour
actual size

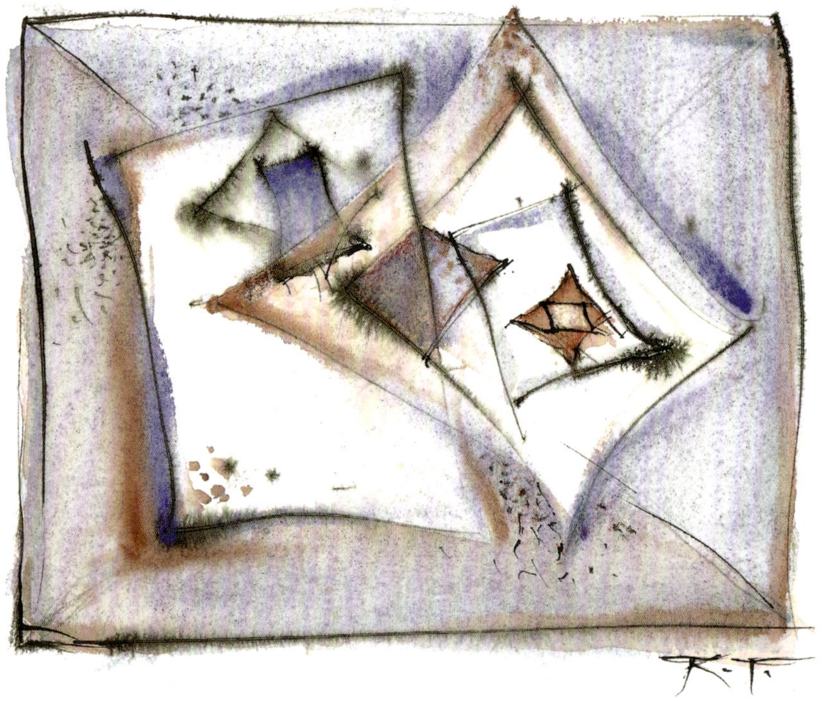

I felt the scope of my work enlarged by the experiment but felt no urge to take it further at that time. Other subjects were on my mind.

Then, much later, when I found I was growing too old to make the responses needed to capture either plants or animals in drawing, I turned once more to abstracts as a means of expression.

These were an attempt to explore the creative possibilities of the intuitive mind. I would take a piece of watercolour paper. In the beginning of the experiment, using the back of a dud drawing or painting, I would deliberately avoid using conscious naturalistic images, but make a line or splodge of colour with no particular objective in mind. I wanted to discover what would happen if I followed this instinctively with new colours and lines. Although I was familiar with drawing on damp paper, this produced the unknown factor of the spread of the line, or brush stroke. I often made use of this technique. The results were a surprise and often a delight. Sometimes it did not work out at first, especially with pen lines using Indian ink. I would persist, producing a mix of drawn lines until they did achieve an instinctive sense of meaning. Introducing areas of colour would then totally change the character of the doodle. One move followed another until I felt the doodle had run its course and was complete, for the moment at least.

I lacked a sparring partner or critic on whom I could rely. So, the doodles multiplied without properly informed criticism, but I did enjoy making them. And, because they often took me by surprise, they brought a feeling of achievement in my old age.

By my 93rd birthday, not surprisingly, they seem to have passed their best.

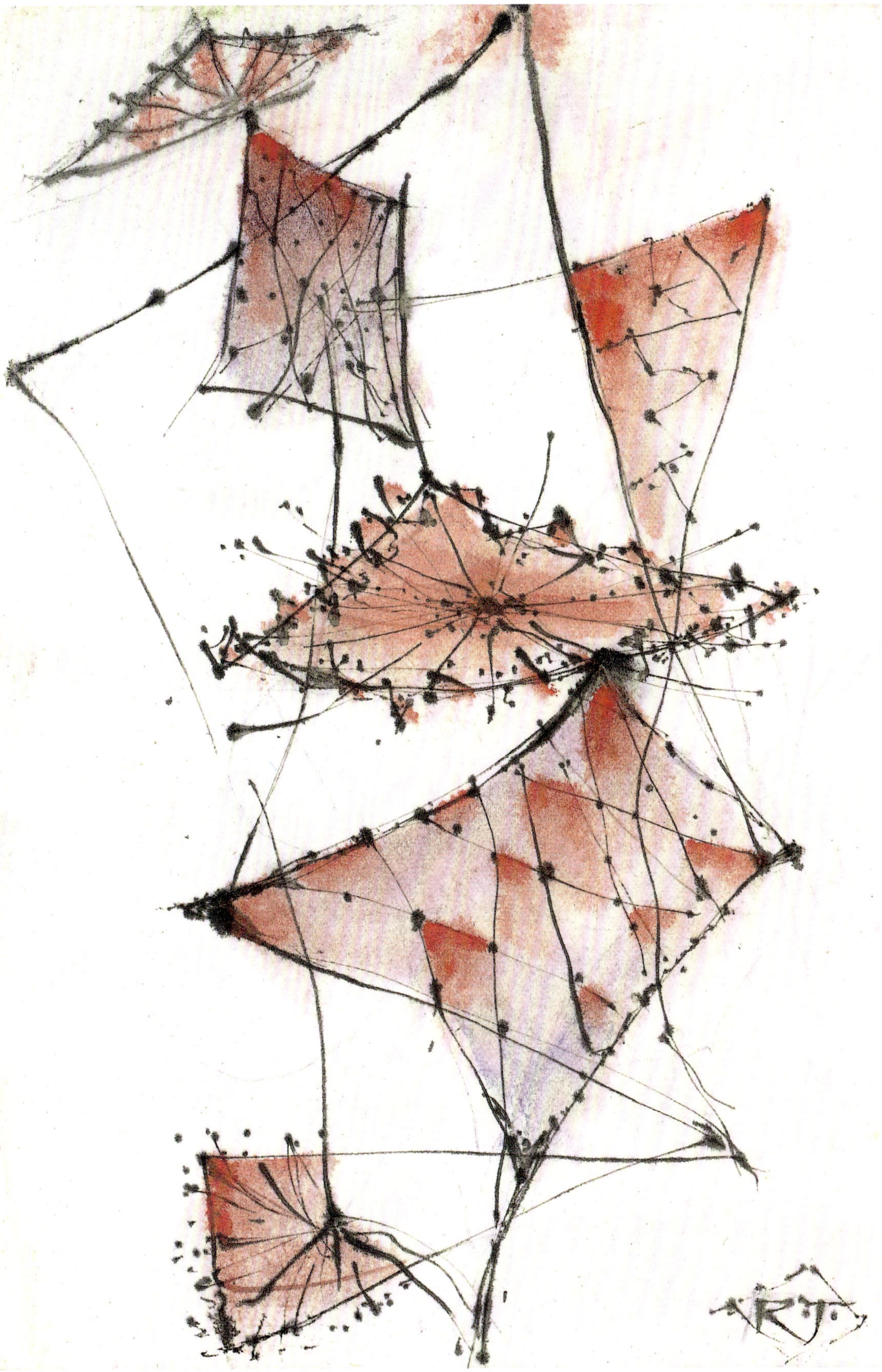

Bibliography

Written & Illustrated

A Brush with Animals	Ralph Thompson	Rupert Hart-Davis 1963
Animals through the eyes of an artist.	Ralph Thompson	Readers Digest 1970
An Artist's Safari	Ralph Thompson	Collins 1970
		New Edition: Collins 1979

Illustrated

Rom-Bom-Bom & other Stories	Antonia Ridge	1946 Faber & Faber
Leopards in the Night	Guy Muldoon	1953 Rupert Hart-Davis
Winkie the Grey Squirrel	Albra Pratten	1954 Oxford Univ. Press
The Bafut Beagles	Gerald Durell	1954 Rupert Hart-Davis
		1958 Penguin
The Drunken Forest	Gerald Durrell	1956 Rupert Hart-Davis
Beyond the High Savannahs	James Wickenden	1956 Longmans
A Weasel in my Meatsafe	Phil Drabble	1957 Collins
		1961 Penguin
The Silver Brumby	Elyne Mitchell	1958 Hutchinson
Encounter with Animals	Gerald Durrell	1958 Rupert Hart-Davis
		1963 Penguin
A Seal flies by	R H Pearson	1959 Rupert Hart-Davis
A Zoo in my Luggage	Gerald Durrell	1960 Rupert Hart-Davis
		1964 Puffin
The Overloaded Ark	Gerald Durrell	1961 Penguin
The Whispering Land	Gerald Durrell	1961 Rupert Hart-Davis
		1964 Penguin
Three Singles to Adventure	Gerald Durrell	1962 Rupert Hart-Davis
		1964 Penguin
The New Noah	Gerald Durrell	1962 Penguin
Watchers at the Pond	Franklin Russell	1962 Hodder & Stoughton
Menagerie Manor	Gerald Durrell	1964 Rupert Hart-Davis
		1967 Penguin
Chess Dream in a Garden	Rosemary Sutcliff	1993 Walker Books

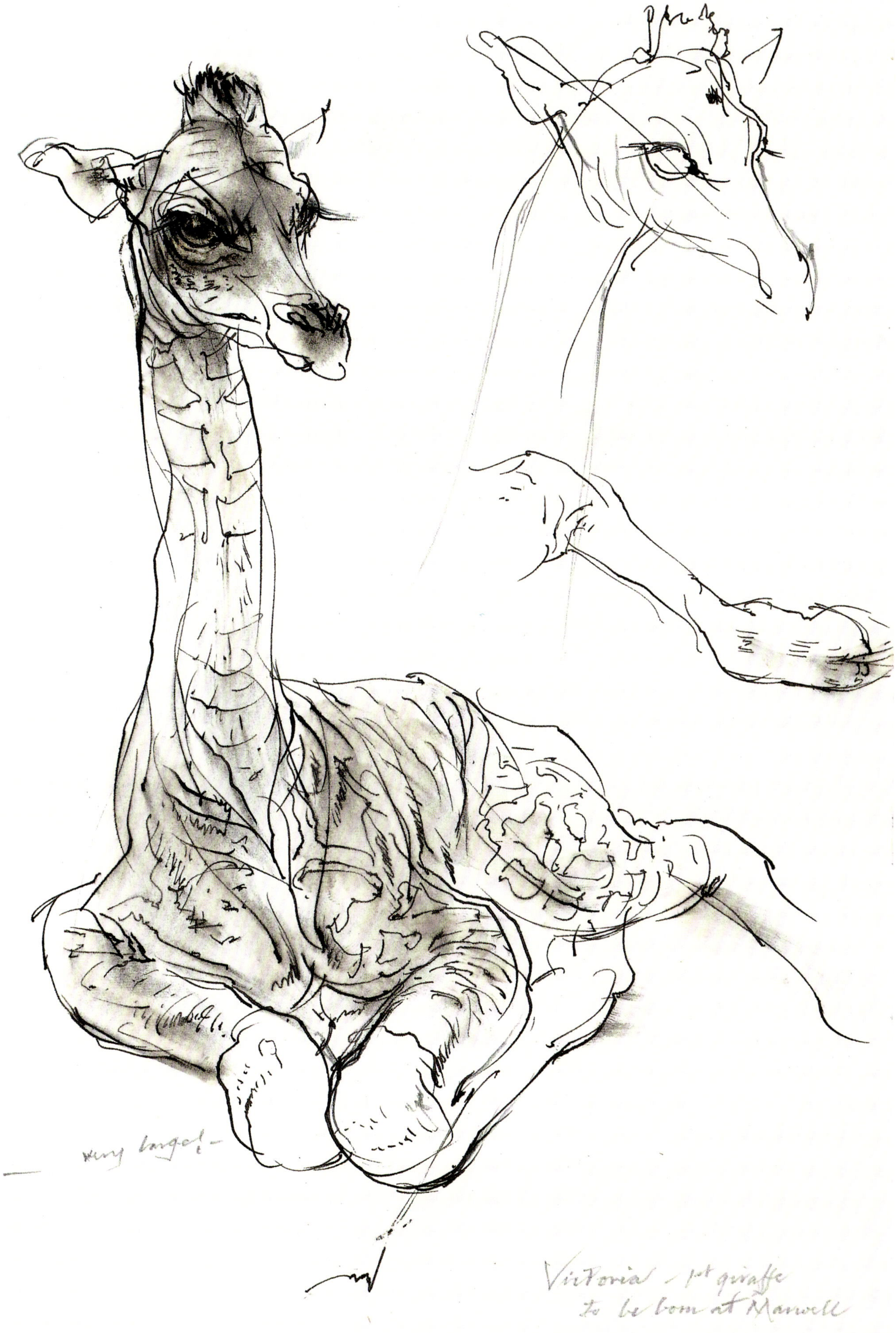
very large! –
Victoria – 1st giraffe
to be born at Marwell

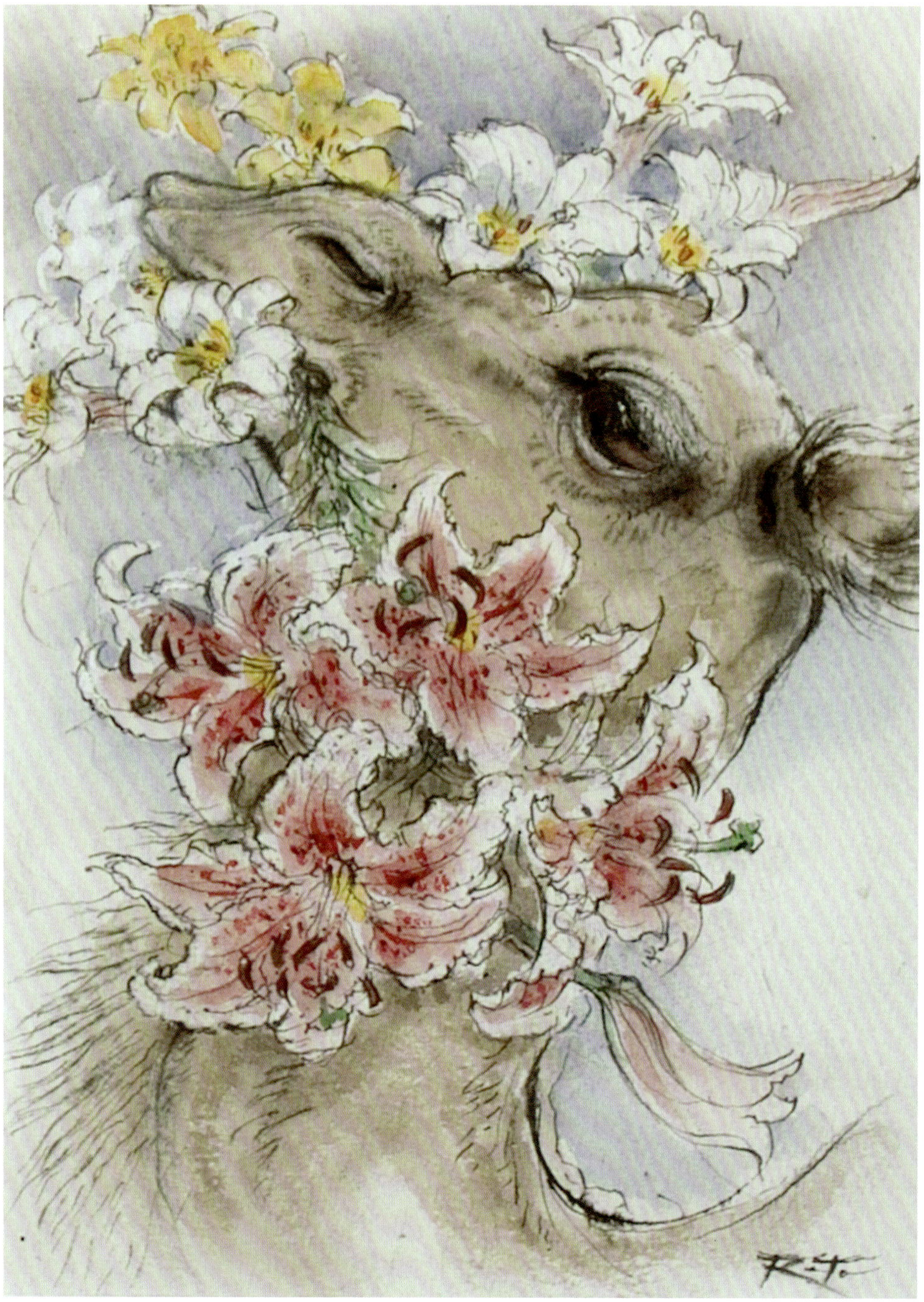

Final Word

As an artist I have attempted to let the fascination experienced in my contact with the natural world penetrate my work with the same shock and delight that I felt when I first came face to face with the zebra so long ago.

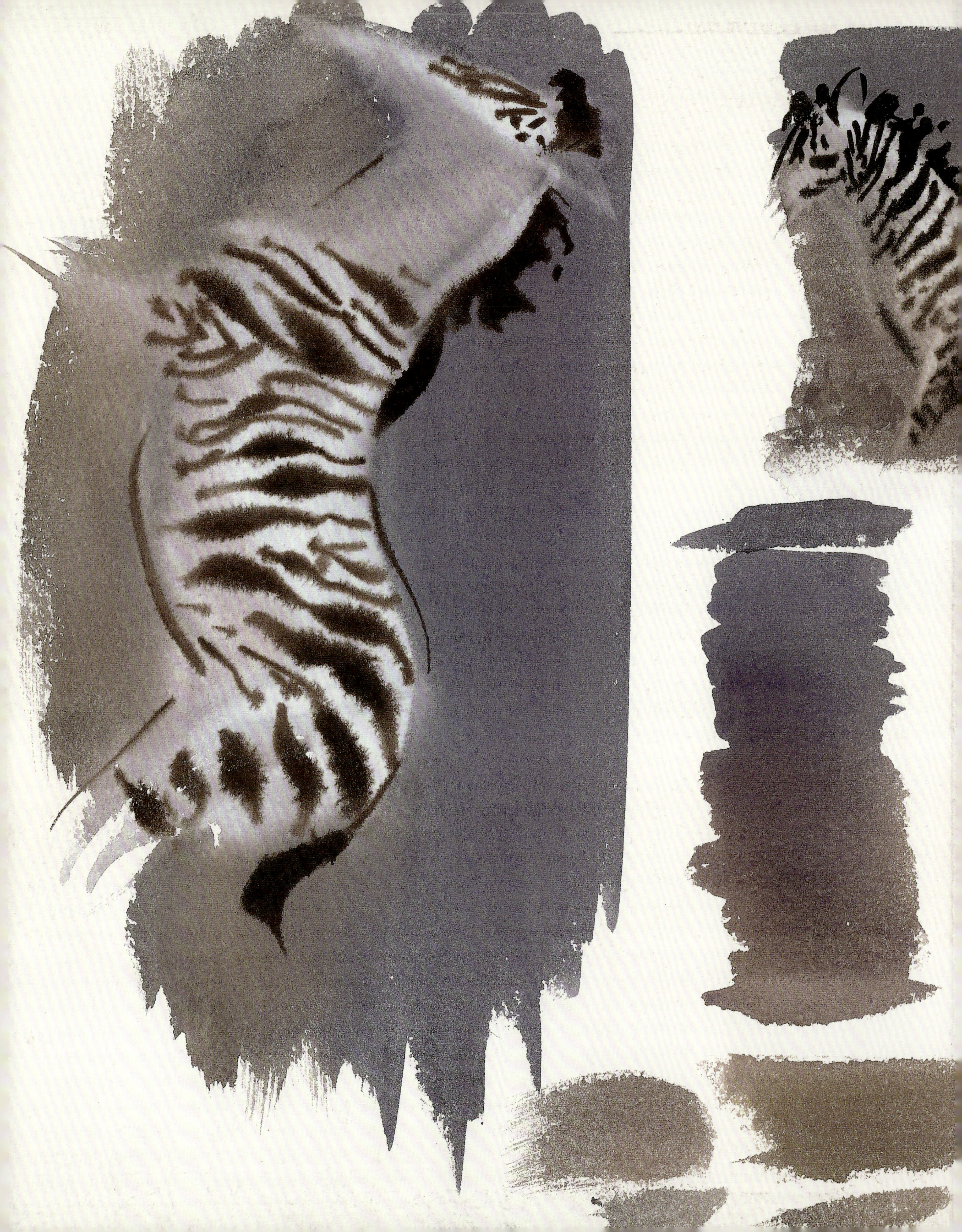